SINGLE LIFE
Unmarried Adults in Social Context

SINGLE LIFE

Unmarried Adults
in
Social Context

edited by

PETER J. STEIN

William Paterson College

ST. MARTIN'S PRESS
NEW YORK

Acknowledgments

Acknowledgments and copyrights continue at the back of the book on page 360 and following pages, which constitute an extension of the copyright page.

Christine Doudna with Fern McBride, "Where Are the Men for the Women at the Top?" Reprinted with permission from *Savvy*, February, 1980, vol. 1, no. 2.

Jon Darling, "Late-Marrying Bachelors." Reprinted with permission.

Robert Staples, "Black Singles in America." Reprinted with permission from *The World of Black Singles: Changing Patterns of Male/Female Relations*, Westport, Conn., Greenwood Press, 1981.

Arthur J. Norton and Paul C. Glick, "Marital Instability in America: Past, Present, and Future," and Robert S. Weiss, "The Emotional Impact of Marital Separation." Reprinted with permission from *Divorce and Separation: Causes, Contexts, and Consequences*, ed. by George Levinger and Oliver C. Moles, © 1979 by The Society for the Psychological Study of Social Issues, Basic Books, Inc., Publishers, New York.

Starr Roxanne Hiltz, "Widowhood: A Roleless Role." Reprinted with permission from *Marriage and Family Review*, © The Haworth Press, Inc.

Beth B. Hess, "Friendship and Gender Roles over the Life Course." Reprinted by permission.

Natalie Allon and Diane Fishel, "Single Bars as Examples of Urban Courting Patterns." Reprinted by permission.

Martha Cleveland, "Sexuality in the Middle Years." Reprinted with permission from the *Journal of Divorce*, © The Haworth Press, Inc.

John Alan Lee, "Forbidden Colors of Love: Patterns of Gay Love." Reprinted with permission from the *Journal of Homosexuality*, ©The Haworth Press.

J. Lee Lehman, "What It Means to Love Another Woman." Reprinted with permission from *Our Right to Love*, by Virginia Vida and the National Gay Task Force, © 1978 by Virginia Vida. Published by Prentice-Hall, Inc., Englewood Cliffs, N.J. 07632.

Robert S. Weiss, "The Study of Loneliness." Reprinted from *Loneliness: The Experience of Emotional and Social Isolation* by Robert S. Weiss by permission of The MIT Press, Cambridge, Massachusetts.

for Michele Murdock

PREFACE

Single people are an important, and growing, part of the adult population. More than 55 million American adults over the age of 18 are unmarried. Many different kinds of people are single: the never-married, the divorced, the widowed, homosexuals, single parents, cohabiting people. Although these people have in common their singlehood—the fact that they are not, or choose not to be, legally married—they vary enormously in their personalities, physical characteristics, ages, and occupations; and it is time to dispel the stereotyped views that others have of them and that they often have of themselves.

Recognition of the increasing importance of the singles population has sparked considerable activity in sociological research and teaching. Scholarly studies have increased both in number and in quality. Courses dealing with family life now regularly treat singlehood as a subject essential to our understanding of courtship, marriage, parenthood, and divorce. Many colleges now offer separate courses on the sociology of singles.

Through some fourteen years of teaching undergraduate, graduate, and continuing-education courses on various aspects of marriage and the family, I have increasingly felt the need for an anthology that would reveal and explain the nature and diversity of single adults. The articles collected in the present volume—some of them being published here for the first time—are the most interesting and pertinent discussions available. They are organized into eight sections focusing on aspects of singlehood in which the diversity among singles is most apparent and significant. The sections deal with the never-married; the separated, divorced, and widowed; friendship, courting, and sexuality; emotional and physical health; living arrangements; work; parenting; and aging. The general introduction presents an overview of contemporary single life, and an introduction to each section provides background information that will help readers interpret and relate the individual articles. Tables showing the latest available statistics on the marital status of Americans are contained in the appendix.

Many people have helped in the preparation of this book. I am indebted to my colleagues Natalie Hannon, Natalie Sokoloff, Lucile Duberman, and especially Starr Roxanne Hiltz, in whose session at an American Sociological Association meeting I delivered my first paper on the single life. Special thanks are due Robyn Sandberg and Margaret Rodkin, who helped me research and select these articles; Karen Theroux, whose editorial suggestions were invaluable; and Susan Kirby, typist *extraordinaire*. Finally, I am grateful to Bob

Woodbury, my editor at St. Martin's Press, who encouraged me to pursue the project, and to Emily Berleth and Charles Thurlow, also of St. Martin's, for their cooperation and support.

—Peter J. Stein

CONTENTS

SINGLE LIFE
Unmarried Adults in Social Context

GENERAL INTRODUCTION

Carol is a forty-year-old mother of two. She lives in the suburbs and works as a clerk in a local insurance office. She is divorced.

Gary is a twenty-year-old college junior. He and his girlfriend live together in a suite in a dorm on the campus of a large midwestern university.

Frank is a widower. He is sixty-three years old and lives in a two-room apartment in a decaying building. Though his neighborhood is changing, several of his friends still live nearby.

Ellen is a lawyer who lives in a large city. She is thirty-four, has never been married, and enjoys her life the way it is: dating, living in a comfortable apartment, working, playing tennis.

What these four have in common is that they are all single. What makes them different is their ages, their resources, their families, their work, their friends, their health—the characteristics that distinguish any one individual from another. Though singles are often subject to stereotyping, their lives are rich in diversity.

Singles are an important segment of the adult population. Their interests, their activities, and their life styles are often in the forefront of social trends. Singles take risks; they experiment; they consume; they set trends. In exploring the life styles of singles, the reader may learn more about his or her own life now, or about what his or her life may be in the future. For any one of us may some day belong to the singles population, if we are not single now. Statistics show that about one-third of young adults currently marrying will divorce; three out of four married women will become widows; many people will live together without marriage. There are many styles of adulthood in our society. Different people may choose different styles, or one person may adopt various styles in the course of a lifetime.

Although personal statements provide us with insight into single experiences, little has been done to provide a more objective examination of singlehood. Singles have often been regarded as a somewhat deviant group, different from "normal" married adults, and until very recently they have been avoided as a subject of serious research. Recognition of the variations that exist within the singles population, and of the goals and concerns they hold in common with other people—meaningful work, friendships, financial security, health care, a home, self-esteem—is a result of new research, much of which appears in *Single Life*.

Who are the singles in this book? They are college couples, mid-life divorcees; black college graduates; homosexual executives; single

1

fathers; and many others. The categories in which these singles belong often overlap—mid-life divorcees may also be single parents, for example—and there are transitions from one category into another. For single as for married people, life involves various stages of adulthood and is always subject to change, some planned and some unanticipated.

Some 1980 singles statistics help to point out why this group is important and how it is growing:

•Almost 50 percent of all women between twenty and twenty-four years of age have never been married (compared to about 30 percent in 1960);

•There are 1.1 million unmarried couples living together—more than twice as many as in 1970;

•The divorce rate has more than doubled in the past fifteen years, from 2.5 per 1,000 in the population in 1965 to 5.2;

•The number of persons living alone increased by nearly 60 percent in the 1970s—to one out of five households.

Statistics also indicate an increase in the number of women attending college, a related rise in the age of first marriage, and an increase in the number of women and men choosing the single life.

The term single continues to mean the legal absence of marriage; the term therefore has meaning only when compared with marriage. Other terms, such as bachelor, spinster, or old maid, bring specific, often negative, images to mind. At its best, the term single is more useful for those who study or write about them than for the singles themselves. Like any other label—male/female, young/old—it does little to clarify the many categories of singles, or the variety within each category. In fact, among singles there is such a wide range of age, social class, parental status, previous marital status, sexual practice, and other characteristics, that they are just as diverse a group as the married population. Why then do others so often treat singles as a homogeneous group? The purpose of this book is to move beyond stereotyped ideas through data that refute these stereotypes, to a more accurate portrait of single individuals. Single people are discussed in terms of loneliness, intimacy, and the search for support, in terms of continuity and of changes throughout life. Their adjustments, their economic and personal resources, their households, and their careers are all explored here.

Many social factors—changes in gender-role definitions; an increase in numbers of women attending college and developing careers; a reexamination by men and women of their needs for self-expression; a questioning of the validity of traditional marriage; and the entire women's movement—have led to a need for a book that provides a new interpretation of singles life. Changes have also occurred in life expectancies. Women outlive men by many years—

years which are often spent as singles. Changing sexual norms and standards, reflecting greater openness in couple relationships and greater attention to gay sexuality, also affect the singles picture.

Understanding the relationship between single adults and the larger society is clarified by an understanding of the concept of life chances and life styles. Life chances are the opportunities individuals have to meet their goals through use of their resources—chiefly money. Life styles are the ways individuals live their lives—by being a partner in an unmarried couple; as a single parent; in a retirement community; as part of the gay scene—based on the individual's life chances. For example, most widows exist on social security payments and meager savings. Their life styles are constrained by the amount of money available to them. In contrast, two single professionals living together in an urban area, who have good educations and employment opportunities, have a very real choice about how to live, to spend free time, to interact with others. The better a person's life chances, the more choice one has of a satisfying life style.

Our examination of life chances, life styles, and many other singles topics begins with a look at the never-married. Though most never-marrieds are younger people whose likelihood of marrying is fairly great, there are others—woman executives, middle-aged bachelors, middle-class blacks—whose less typical experiences add to our understanding of single life. Part Two explores the lives of the once-married—people who are separated, divorced, or widowed—emphasizing their problems and adjustments. Part Three explores the many paths toward adult intimacy—through sexual and nonsexual relationships, for homosexuals and heterosexuals, in traditional gender-role patterned friendships, and in new styles of interaction. Part Four discusses emotional and physical health in terms of depression, feelings of happiness, ability to cope with problems, and overall physical health; we shall find that marital status affects the health of men and women quite differently. Part Five is concerned with the growing trend toward cohabitation and the importance of friends for singles living alone. Part Six explores various aspects of work as it affects people of different races, socioeconomic status, and sexual orientation. Part Seven compares the single-parent experience to traditional family life and explores custody alternatives. Part Eight examines the unique experiences of older singles.

Certainly no article or group of articles in this volume can provide all the data needed to draw definite conclusions about the lives of all single people. Many of the articles in *Single Life* point out the need for further research, or for changes in public policy. These readings are best used as the basis for discussion and to stimulate further thought and study. The reader will realize that researchers study their live subjects at a particular time in the subjects' lives and at a specific time in history. Therefore much research is essentially static—snapshotlike—while social life is a process. The continual change of people and social arrangements lead the reader not only to read but to question.

PART ONE

THE NEVER-MARRIEDS

Heading the list of the singles population is the group we may call the never-married. The career woman, the college student, the gay activist, and the priest are only a few of the diverse people who make up this group. The U.S. Bureau of the Census reports that in 1979 never-marrieds made up 23 percent of the male and 17 percent of the female population of this country. And yet, as the articles in this section point out, the never-married person has been consistently treated as a member of an insignificant and deviant group, worthy of study only for its departure from the normal married state.

Stereotypes die hard, and it has taken years of shifts in population and a new wave of sociologists to bring an awareness of the positive side of singleness to the professional world and to the population at large. It is true that not everyone who wants to be married will be. But it is also true that many people—more every year—are freely choosing to be part of the never-married group.

These figures help tell the story: Between 1970 and 1979 the number of twenty-to-twenty-four-year-old women who had never married grew from 35 percent to 49 percent; for men in the same age groups the increase was from 54 percent to 67 percent. The percentage of never-marrieds for the age group twenty-five to twenty-nine also increased during this period. Most never-married people are younger singles who are delaying their first marriage. The median age at first marriage by 1979 increased to 22.1 years of age for women and 24.4 years of age for men. (See Tables 1, 2, and 3 in the Appendix for a full enumeration of the data.)

How can we account for the increase in numbers of young adults postponing marriage, and for the dramatic shift in the age of first marriage? By noting the following important social developments:

1. The increase in the number of women enrolled in colleges and in graduate and professional schools;

2. Expanding employment and career opportunities for women;

3. The impact of the women's movement;

4. The excess of young women at the currently "most marriageable" age, resulting in a marriage squeeze;

5. A shift in attitudes about the desirability of marriage among both college and noncollege youth;

5

6. The increasing divorce rate, which has led many people to question the traditional appeal of marriage and family life;

7. The increasing availability and acceptability of birth-control methods.

In addition, some researchers suggest that people today are moving away from marriage and family norms as these norms conflict with the potentials for individual development and personal growth (Duberman, 1977; Gagnon and Greenblat, 1978; Glick, 1979; Melville, 1980; Stein, Richman and Hannon, 1977).

There are many causes behind the growing singles trend, and there are many individuals living out very different lives under the heading of Never-Married. In addition to the young singles waiting for later marriage, there are those for whom marriage is not desirable or possible. These include older singles who will never marry, either because they have not found an eligible partner or because they are satisfied with singlehood and/or opposed to marriage. There are priests and nuns whose career choices preclude marriage. Some men and women prefer homosexual relationships to traditional marriage. And other individuals may have physical or psychological impairments that keep them from finding a mate.

Clearly the many types of singleness deserve many approaches in research. The readings in this section concentrate on some interesting never-married groups, including late-marrying bachelors, middle-class blacks, and successful career women. The reader will not only absorb the facts and findings presented in each article but will get to know the people behind the numbers and raise further questions about the life styles presented here. The four articles in this chapter cannot fully examine the never-married population in all its variety, but together they do explain many of the reasons for singleness, many of the situations that cause people to move away from singleness, and the factors that sometimes prevent this move.

"Understanding Single Adulthood" introduces important concepts and new vocabulary for understanding the single experience. The stages of singlehood are described as voluntary or involuntary and stable or temporary; these terms help the reader to grasp the continuum of singleness and provide categories for future discussion or research. The ideas of life cycle and life spiral—a new term to describe the course of one's life through many alternative roles and situations—are compared and explored. There is also a description of the factors—the pushes and pulls—which influence people to marry or not, to live alone or with a lover or in some other arrangement. After reading this survey of the variety of adult single experiences, the reader may want to ask such questions as: How has my view of the never-married person changed? What insight have I gained into not only the lives of others but my own life as well?

"Where Are the Men for the Women at the Top?" ask the authors of the next article. The answers are varied and illuminating. Christine Doudna and Fern McBride interviewed many successful women about their dissatisfactions with their available choices in men. Demography, society, money, and education all operate against these women when it comes to finding men they can connect with. Some find ways of working out their problems—with older or younger men, with men less successful than they are, or through a series of short affairs—while the others channel their sexual energies into further career achievements. How do the private problems of these women reflect complex public issues? Where will we find these women five or ten years from today; will other women face this trend in the future? Finally, how do these women channel their personal and social resources into successful adaptation to remaining single as they grow old?

Many men also adapt successfully to the single state—only to turn around and marry later in life. John Darling studied a group of these late-marrying bachelors, searching for the forces that kept them single for so long. The people and situations with which these men interacted seemed to work against society's strong pressure to marry. When situations changed and these men did decide to marry, they entered their new state with all the enthusiasm of religious converts. Darling's work topples another popular stereotype: that of the bachelor as a peculiar psychological type. His observations on turning points also give the reader food for thought. How do changing situations influence these men's decisions? To what degree is our marital state within our own control and to what degree under the influence of family or others?

In his article on black singles Robert Staples notes that many blacks do not see their singleness as a viable choice, but as a condition forced upon them by certain vicissitudes of life in America: being single and black is problematic. Census figures indicate that the proportion of never-married black men and women is higher than that of never-married whites for every age group to sixty-five. In the twenty-five to twenty-nine age group, 39 percent of black men are single compared to about 28 percent of white men. Among women, about 34 percent of blacks compared to about 17 percent of whites have not married.

Staples' study, based on questionnaires and interviews with about 500 black middle-class single men and women, indicates both similarities and differences in the life styles and life chances of black and white singles. Staples examines the influence of racism and sexism and structural discrimination on marriage and singlehood among blacks. What are the similarities and differences in the single experience for whites and blacks? What are the conditions of singlehood for black men and women?

REFERENCES

Duberman, Lucile. *Marriage and Other Alternatives.* New York: Praeger, 1977.

Gagnon, John, and Cathy Greenblat. *Life Designs.* Glenview, Ill.: Scott, Foresman & Co., 1978.

Glick, Paul C. "Future American Families," *COFO Newsletter,* summer/fall, 1979, pp. 2–5.

Melville, Keith. *Marriage and Family Today.* New York: Random House, 1980.

Stein, Peter J., Judith Richman, and Natalie Hannon. *The Family: Functions, Conflicts, and Symbols.* Reading, Mass.: Addison-Wesley, 1977.

1/ UNDERSTANDING SINGLE ADULTHOOD

Peter J. Stein

The word single describes a number of life styles and life chances. There is a rich variety of unmarried adult men and women in American society.

More than 55 million American adults over the age of eighteen are unmarried. As Table 1 illustrates, this is 33 percent of American men and almost 40 percent of American women over eighteen. The unmarried population varies with respect to age; previous marital status; and if formerly married, marital termination as a consequence of desertion, divorce, or death; living arrangements; sexual preferences; educational, occupational, and income levels; class background and identification; ethnic and racial identification; religion; and parental status.

It is a testament to the imperialism of marriage that singles are regarded as a residual category. People are either married or they are not married, i.e., they are single. The legal distinction tells us little about the kind of interaction that occurs within single or married relationships.

The lives of the unmarried are as complex and heterogeneous as those of the married. This is not always apparent, because singles are

TABLE 1
THE MARITAL STATUS OF THE U.S. POPULATION, AGE 18 AND OVER, 1979 (IN THOUSANDS OF PERSONS)

	Total	Married	Never Married	Divorced	Widowed	Separated
Men	72,715	48,816	16,970	3,471	1,945	1,513
Women	80,628	48,771	13,644	5,355	10,449	2,409
Percent Distribution						
Men	100	67.1	23.3	4.8	2.7	2.1
Women	100	60.5	16.9	6.6	13.0	3.0

Note: For a complete enumeration, see Appendix Table 1.

Source: U.S. Bureau of the Census. Marital Status and Living Arrangements: March 1979. *Current Population Reports,* Series P-20, No. 349. Washington, D.C.: U.S. Government Printing Office, 1980.

subject to stereotyping, which partly determines the way other groups and social institutions respond to them, and partly determines the reactions of the singles to themselves.

A TYPOLOGY OF SINGLEHOOD

The following typology (Table 2) attempts to group the heterogeneous population of singles according to whether singlehood is voluntary or involuntary and stable or temporary. These categories assume that we can determine the extent to which single people want or do not want to be single at a particular time and the extent to which they define their single state as a temporary one or a relatively stable one. The typology is a way of identifying different groups of single adults and determining the extent of their probable commitment to a single life. Of course, membership in these categories changes over time.

VOLUNTARY TEMPORARY SINGLES
Among those who have chosen to be single on a temporary basis are the younger never-marrieds and the divorced who are postponing marriage or remarriage for some finite period of time. They are open to the possibility of marriage, but the search for a mate has a lower priority than other activities such as education, work, career, politics, self-development, and so forth (Schwartz, 1976). It also includes men and women who have lived together in order to try out marriagelike arrangements (Macklin, 1978; Lewis, 1975; Yllo, 1978). However, not all of the voluntary temporary singles will marry "on time," since some will not find appropriate mates and others will marry at a later date than desired (Glick, 1975).

VOLUNTARY STABLE SINGLES
Among those who have chosen to be single as a stable condition are those who have never married and are satisfied with that choice (Stein, 1976; Adams, 1976); those who have been married but do not want to remarry (Stein, 1976); cohabitators who do not intend to marry (Cole, 1977); and those whose life styles preclude the possibility of marriage (e.g., priests and nuns). Also included are single parents, both never married and formerly married, who are not seeking mates and who are raising their children alone or with the help of relatives or friends (Bernard, 1975).

INVOLUNTARY TEMPORARY SINGLES
This category consists of singles who would like to be married and expect to do so within some finite period of time. It also includes

TABLE 2
TYPOLOGY OF SINGLEHOOD

	Voluntary	Involuntary
Temporary	Never-married and formerly married who are postponing marriage by not currently seeking mates, but who are not opposed to the idea of marriage	Those who have been actively seeking mates for shorter or longer periods of time, but have not yet found mates Those who were not interested in marriage or remarriage for some period of time but are now actively seeking mates
Stable	Those choosing to be single (never-marrieds and formerly marrieds) Those who for various reasons oppose the idea of marriage Religionaries	Never-marrieds and formerly marrieds who wanted to marry or remarry, have not found a mate and have more or less accepted being single as a probable life state

younger never-marrieds who do not want to be single and are actively seeking mates, as well as somewhat older men and women who
had not been interested in marriage but are now actively seeking
mates. It includes the widowed (Lopata, 1973) and divorced (Duberman, 1975) seeking remarriage; and single parents seeking mates
(Weiss, 1979; Monahan, 1978). These are men and women who
believe in marriage and would like to be married.

INVOLUNTARY STABLE SINGLES

This category consists primarily of older divorced, widowed, and
never-married people who wanted to marry or to remarry, have not
found a mate, and have come to accept being single as a probable
life situation. It also includes those singles who suffer from physical
or psychological impairment which prevents them from being successful in the marriage market (Kuhn, 1955).

It is important to note that classifications in the typology vary
according to the stage of the life span occupied by members of the
group being classified. For example, as younger never-marrieds who
regarded singlehood as a temporary state become older, some
marry. Others, unable to find an appropriate mate, remain single
involuntarily and become increasingly concerned about the possibil-

ity that they will never find a mate. Others may enjoy their single state and begin to see it as a stable rather than a temporary condition. The same person can identify singlehood as a voluntary temporary status before marriage, then marry and divorce and become single again. This person may then be a voluntary stable, involuntary stable, or involuntary temporary single, depending on his or her experiences and preferences.

THE LIFE CYCLE OF SINGLE ADULTS

The concept of the life cycle, initially proposed by Erik Erikson (1959), adds a dynamic aspect to this otherwise static continuum. The stage of the life cycle is also related to issues of life style and life chances and the need and availability of social support systems.

Levinson (1978) has suggested a model for the various stages of adult life. He compares these stages to the seasons of a single year and suggests that development occurs in predictable segments which follow each other in chronological order. His model, developed from studies of married men, is useful when applied to the lives of single people, but it is limited.

The stage model assumes that development is hierarchical, sequenced in time, and cumulative. The implications of life stages are that (1) every "normal" adult must pass through the stages; (2) each stage has distinctive qualities which are tasks that must be accomplished during that stage; (3) an individual is more or less successful in negotiating these crises; (4) successful resolution of a prior stage is necessary for the successful resolution of subsequent stages; and (5) each stage is tied to chronological age (Brim, 1977). According to Levinson, "although important changes go on within it, each season or era has its own distinctive and unifying qualities, which have to do with the character of living" (Levinson et al., 1978, p. 18).

Etzkowitz and Stein (1978) suggest that life has many seasons and that a spiral more accurately represents life's configuration. Development is not necessarily related to chronological age, and themes of development may be resolved at one age only to need reevaluation later on. Developmental stages may overlap; one may never resolve certain issues. Life is an ongoing process with themes and patterns which repeat. It is less like the seasons of a single year than like a panorama of seasons.

These two contrasting models may be seen as representing a continuum. For adults whose lives follow fairly traditional patterns of development, the cycle, with its stages, may accurately represent their lives. Less traditional lives may be more accurately described by the spiral model. There may be changes over the span of one's life: the spiral may be more accurate at one period, the cycle more accurate at another. This paper will consider first the cycle and then the spiral models of single adulthood.

THE YOUNG NEVER-MARRIEDS

We can identify various stages of the adult life cycle. The years from the early twenties to about twenty-eight are the period of "getting into the adult world," when the focus of one's life shifts from the "family of origin to a new home base in an effort to form an adult life of one's own" (Levinson et al., 1974, p. 246). It is a time of exploratory searching and provisional choices" (p. 247). It is also a time of assessing the correctness of such initial choices and increasing the commitment to choices.

The twenty-year period from 1960 through 1979 witnessed an increase in the percentage of both men and women between the ages of twenty and twenty-nine who have remained single (Table 3). In 1960 the median age at first marriage for women was 20.3; in 1979 it increased to 22.1. The corresponding median age for men at first marriage increased from 22.8 in 1960 to 24.4 in 1979. With the increase of young adults who remain single has come the tendency for people in this group to maintain their own households. The number of persons under age thirty-five who were living alone almost trebled between 1970 and 1978, increasing from 1.5 million to 4.3 million. A somewhat larger proportion of single men than of single women in the twenty-five to thirty-four age group maintained their own households. Census data indicate that a majority of the singles population is concentrated in large cities and in specific areas of such cities. Over 60 percent of all single persons, compared to under 40 percent of the adult population ever married, live in large cities (Carter and Glick, 1976). Major

TABLE 3
WOMEN AND MEN REMAINING SINGLE (1960–1979)

	1960	1970	1979	Change from 1970 to 1979
Women remaining single:				
Ages 20–24	28.4%	35.8%	49.4%	+13.6%
Ages 25–29	10.5	10.5	19.6	+ 9.1
Men remaining single:				
Ages 20–24	53.1	54.7	67.4	+12.7
Ages 25–29	20.8	19.1	30.2	+11.1

Source: U.S. Bureau of the Census. Marital Status and Living Arrangements: March 1979. *Current Population Reports*, Series P-20, No. 349. Washington, D.C.: U.S. Government Printing Office, 1980.

concerns of singles are with finding meaningful work, satisfying living arrangements, and congenial friends. Large cities have the occupational and social structures to satisfy these concerns. Adjustments to the world of work and patterns of forming friendships provide crucial connections and a positive sense of self (Starr and Carns, 1972).

THE AGE THIRTY TRANSITION

Levinson further suggests that for many the years between twenty-eight and thirty-two involve considerable turmoil, confusion, and struggle with societal pressures, with family, and with oneself. For others these years involve a quieter reevaluation of goals and values and an intensification of efforts to achieve such goals. Many men and women who remain single into their thirties report that the middle to late twenties was a period of great difficulty (Adams, 1976; Kurth, 1975; Schwartz, 1976).

During those late-twenties years the number of singles decreased dramatically. Among thirty-to-thirty-four-year-olds only 15 percent of the men and 10 percent of the women have never married. These men and women experienced intense societal and parental pressures to marry, and at that time of their lives some of them worked hard at finding prospective spouses. Yet many derived little intrinsic satisfaction from the search for a mate and some reported negative experiences and decline in self-esteem.

A major source of difficulty during these years was work-related. This transitional period marked a deeper commitment to an occupation for some, but for others it involved a rejection of earlier occupational choices as too constricting and not meeting initial expectations of satisfaction (Starr and Carns, 1972). More women than men had no clear occupational goals upon graduation from college, and a substantial number of women viewed their occupations as temporary, unsatisfactory, and noninvolving. Similarly, living arrangements were seen as temporary, often with a same-sex roommate, to be changed with marriage. "As these singles approached 30, many became critical of those patterns and began to reevaluate their lives . . . [recognizing] the possibility that they might never marry and that they themselves had the responsibility for designing meaningful lives" (Schwartz, 1976). They reexamined earlier occupational decisions, weighed possibilities of starting or returning to graduate or professional schools, reevaluated living situations and improved living places, developed new interests, started new activities, and expanded and reinforced circles of friends.

This group of never-married adults is joined by the increasing number of those who married earlier but are now divorcing, their marriage having lasted, on the average, 6.5 years. The median age at divorce after first marriage is currently 30.3 for men and 28.2 for women (Current Population Report, 1977, 323).

THE MIDDLE YEARS: HIS AND HERS SINGLEHOOD

By 1979, in the thirty-five to forty-four age group only 8.3 percent of men and 5.9 percent of women had never married. (These percentages of never-married decrease to 6.9 percent and 4.4 percent respectively in the forty-five to fifty-four age group.)

In a summary of studies of the state of marriage, Bernard concluded that while "his" marriage is physically, socially, and psychologically good, "her" marriage is filled with frustration, dissatisfaction, negative feelings, unhappiness, and other problems. The situation with respect to singlehood is quite the opposite—long-term singlehood tends to be experienced as a more positive state for women and a more negative state for men. This is particularly true of the older never-married singles.

Bernard reports that women who remain single are superior to single men in terms of education, occupation, and income. These women are often more upwardly mobile than married women, educationally and professionally. By 1970 one in every five women around the age of forty with some graduate school education, or with an income of $20,000 or more, had not married—compared to only one in every twenty women with no college education.

In contrast, a number of studies have reported that older never-married men are likely to show mental health problems, including depression, severe neurotic symptoms, phobic tendencies, and passivity. In summarizing more than a dozen mental health studies, Gove (1972) reports that among the unmarried, including the never-marrieds, the divorced, and the widowed, men have mental health problems more frequently than women.

How can these findings be explained? Is the experience of singlehood more stressful and more contradictory for men than for women? Or do the men who remain single have more psychological and interpersonal problems to begin with?

CONTEMPORARY ADULTHOOD: LIFE CYCLE OR LIFE SPIRAL?

The nature and extent of social changes that affect the lives of adult men and women, as well as the emergence of new adult roles, call into question the validity of the life cycle model composed of stages. The *life spiral* model may reflect varying patterns of adulthood more accurately by accommodating a pluralistic universe of adult life styles and structures, incorporating both traditional and alternative roles in the life course (Stein and Etzkowitz, 1977).

The life spiral is a nonlinear definition of the life span. It enables us to view individuals, such as the never-married, who choose alternate paths of adult life not as deviants (their definition under stage theory) but as conscious actors who occupy new roles in one or more areas of life. The focus is on identifying the presence or absence of traditional patterns, on the emergence of new roles, and on alternative sequences of new and old roles.

This model incorporates a theory of human needs and an analysis of the different ways that individuals and groups meet these needs. While needs are universal, many particular roles may equally well fulfill a particular need. Once survival needs for food, shelter, and clothing are satisfied, a second level of human needs becomes of central personal importance. These include work, intimacy, avocational activities, and social communality. Such needs appear as issues to be dealt with throughout the adult years.

THE LIFE SPIRAL STUDY OF ADULT SINGLES

In 1976 I conducted interviews with a sample of sixty middle-class unmarried men and women aged twenty-five to forty-five. At the time of the interviews, most had completed their formal education and were pursuing professional careers. With respect to both intimacy and work roles, the lives of these men and women followed a mixed pattern. About 30 percent of the men and women had initially followed the traditional pattern of early marriage (between the ages of eighteen and twenty-two). The average duration of these marriages was three and a half years. Another 20 percent of the sample had cohabitated for an average of two years. For the remaining 50 percent, singlehood included several important intimate relationships, sexual or nonsexual. Some of these relationships were relatively short-term; others lasted several years. Virtually every one of the thirty singles was or had been in at least one stable intimate relationship lasting more than two years.

For all these adults a major source of intimacy was opposite and same-sex friendships (Stein, 1981). In the absence of marriage these single adults noted the importance of substitute networks of human relationships that met their needs for intimacy, sharing, and continuity. While pressures from external sources to leave singlehood continued, their membership in various support networks and in validating reference groups enabled them to discount negative evaluations. Such support networks included women's and men's groups, political groups, therapy and encounter groups, and organizations formed around specialized interests. Although not restricted to singles, they were particularly well adapted to meet the needs of single people. These groups were cited as helpful in legitimizing alternative roles and supportive in critical life events.

With respect to work, the adult life course of these men and women involved experimenting with job and career possibilities, exploring vocational and avocational activities between the completion of school and full-time entry into the labor force, and a return, for some, to schooling in the middle and late twenties.

For some of the women and men in our sample the rejection of earlier, more tentative occupational choices did not crystallize until their late twenties and early or middle thirties. About 40 percent postponed "entry into the adult world" (for Levinson ages twenty to twenty-eight) because they were in graduate school or professional school. About 20 percent were unable to break economic and psychological ties with their family of origin until their early thirties; their lives fit a pattern typified by experimenting with different life styles, searching for career orientations, and wanting to keep options open.

For these men and women issues of intimacy and work do not surface "on time" but appear earlier or later than suggested by Levinson's cycle model. Moreover, even when issues are resolved during the expected age period, they may reappear at later times and in different settings.

While Levinson's model of adulthood indicates that specific issues are dealt with in stages and transitions through the life course, our data suggest that issues of adulthood are not symbiotically linked to age stages.

ELEMENTS OF CHOICE: PUSHES AND PULLS

My study of voluntary singles reveals the complex factors that enter into the decision to remain single, to live with a lover, to marry, or to separate (Stein, 1976). These factors can be seen as a series of pushes and pulls and are so presented in Table 4.

Pushes represent negative factors in a situation; pulls represent attractions to a potential situation. The strength of these pushes and pulls varies according to a number of other variables, including stage of the life cycle, sexual identification, extent of involvement with parents and family, availability of friends and peers, and perception of choice. For some, dating patterns, pressures from parents, and acceptance of the cultural script led to early marriage. At a later time in their lives, these same people found greater pulls toward satisfying careers, work colleagues, and developing friendships, all of which seemed more possible outside of marriage.

Others never married and found the single state satisfying. These men and women offered many positive reasons, or pulls, for remaining single. They spoke of freedom, enjoyment, career opportunities, developing friendships, economic self-sufficiency, enjoyable sexual

TABLE 4
PUSHES AND PULLS TOWARD MARRIAGE AND SINGLEHOOD

Marriage

Pushes (negatives in present situations)	Pulls (attractions in potential situations)
Pressure from parents	Approval of parents
Desire to leave home	Desire for children and own family
Fear of independence	Example of peers
Loneliness and isolation	Romanticization of marriage
No knowledge or perception of alternatives	Physical attraction
	Love, emotional attachment
Cultural and social discrimination	Security, social status, social prestige
Against singles	Legitimation of sexual experiences
	Socialization
	Job availability, wage structure, and promotions
	Social policies favoring the married and the responses of social institutions

Singlehood

Pushes (to leave permanent relationships)	Pulls (to remain single or return to singlehood)
Lack of friends, isolation, loneliness	Career opportunities and development
Restricted availability of new experiences	Availability of sexual experiences
Suffocating one-to-one relationship, feeling trapped	Exciting life style, variety of experiences, freedom to change
Obstacles to self-development	Psychological and social autonomy, self-sufficiency
Boredom, unhappiness, and anger	
Poor communication with mate	Support structures: sustaining friendships, women's and men's groups, political groups, therapeutic groups, collegial groups
Sexual frustration	

Source: Stein, *Single,* Englewood, Cliffs, N.J.: Prentice-Hall, 1976.

experiences, and personal development. They experienced the factors Adams (1976) cites as making singleness a viable life style: economic independence, social and psychological autonomy, and a clear intent to remain single by preference.

The interview data suggest that singlehood contributes to a developed personality. Singles are highly adaptive. Without the clarity of role models or the support of society as a whole, they shape their lives by taking risks and forging into uncharted territory. Without the support of a partner and with varying social and cultural support, adults who choose singlehood can be understood as pioneers of an emergent cultural life style.

NOTE

1. This paper was originally presented at the National Council on Family Relations annual meeting, August 14–18, 1979, Boston, Massachusetts. The author gratefully acknowledges the assistance of Robyn Sandberg in the preparation of the manuscript.

REFERENCES

Adams, M. "The Single Woman in Today's Society," in A. Skolnick and J. Skolnick (eds.), *Intimacy, Family and Society*. Boston: Little, Brown & Co., 1974.

*Adams, M. *Single Blessedness*. New York: Basic Books, 1976.

Bernard, J. *The Future of Marriage*. New York: World Publishing Co., 1972.

Bernard, J. "Note on Changing Life Styles, 1970–1974." *Journal of Marriage and the Family*, 1975, *37*, 3.

Brim, Orville Jr. "Remarks on Life Span Development," presented to the American Institute on Research, 1977. Mimeographed.

Carter, H., and P. C. Glick. *Marriage and Divorce: A Social and Economic Study*. Cambridge, Mass.: Harvard University Press, 1976.

Cole, C. L. "Cohabitation in Social Context," in R. Libby and R. Whitehurst (eds.), *Marriage and Alternatives*. Glenview, Ill.: Scott, Foresman & Co., 1977, pp. 62–79.

Duberman, L. *The Reconstituted Family*. Chicago: Nelson-Hall, 1975.

Duberman, L. *Marriage and Other Alternatives*. New York: Praeger, 1977.

Durkheim, E. *Suicide: A Study in Sociology* (J. A. Spaulding and G. Simpson, trans.). New York: The Free Press, 1975. (Originally published, 1897.)

Erikson, E. H. *Identity and the Life Cycle*. New York: International Universities Press, 1959.

Etzkowitz, H., and P. Stein. "The Life Spiral: Human Needs and Adult Roles." *Alternative Lifestyles*, 1978, *1*,4, 434–446.

Gagnon, J. H., and C. S. Greenblat. *Life Designs: Individuals, Marriages, and Families*. Glenview, Ill.: Scott, Foresman & Co., 1978.

Glick, P. C. "Some Recent Changes in American Families," in U.S. Bureau of the Census, *Current Population Reports: Population Characteristics*, Series P-23, No. 52. Washington, D.C.: Author, 1975.

Gould, R. "The Phases of Adult Life: A Study in Developmental Psychology." *American Journal of Psychiatry*, 1972, *129*, 521–531.

Gove, W. R. "The Relationship Between Sex Roles, Marital Status and Mental Illness." *Social Forces*, 1972, *51*, 34–44.

*Indicates selections included in this volume.

*Higginbotham, E. "Social Mobility and the Single Black Woman." Paper presented at the annual meetings of the Society for the Study of Social Problems, September 1978, San Francisco.

Knupfer, G., Clark, W., and R. Room. "The Mental Health of the Unmarried." *American Journal of Psychiatry*, 1966, *122*, 841–851.

Kuhn, M. "How Mates are Sorted," in H. Becker and R. Hill (eds.), *Family, Marriage and Parenthood*. Boston: D. C. Heath, 1955.

Kurth, S. "A Process of Identity Transformation for Non-Marrieds." Paper presented at the annual meeting of the Society for the Study of Social Problems, 1975, San Francisco.

Levinson, D. J., C. M. Darrow, E. B. Klein, M. H. Levinson, and B. McKee. "The Psychosocial Development of Men in Early Adulthood and the Mid-Life Transition," in D. F. Ricks, A. Thomas, and M. Roff (eds.), *Life History Research in Psychopathology* (Vol. 3). Minneapolis: University of Minnesota Press, 1974.

Levinson, D., et al. *Seasons of a Man's Life*. New York: Knopf, 1978.

Lewis, R. A., C. F. LeHecka, G. B. Spanier, and V. L. Storm. "Commitment in Married and Unmarried Cohabitation." Paper presented in the Family Section at the annual meeting of the American Sociological Association, August 1975, San Francisco.

Lopata, H. Z. *Widowhood in an American City*. Cambridge: Schenkman, 1973.

*Macklin, E. D. "Heterosexual Cohabitation Among Unmarried College Students." *The Family Coordinator*, 1972, *21*, 463–472.

Macklin, E. D. "Nonmarital Heterosexual Cohabitation." *Marriage and Family Review*, 1978.

Melville, K. *Marriage and Family Today*. New York: Random House, 1980.

Micossi, A. L. "Rethinking the Urban Commune." Unpublished ms., University of California at Berkeley, 1977.

Monahan, K. "Single Parenthood." Unpublished ms., 1978.

Schwartz, M. A. "Career Strategies of the Never Married." Paper presented at the annual meeting of the American Sociological Association, August 1976, New York City.

Starr, J., and D. Carns. "Singles in the City." *Society*, 1972, *9*, 43–48.

Stein, P. J. "Changing Attitudes of College Women." Unpublished ms., Rutgers University, 1973.

Stein, P. J. "Singlehood: An Alternative to Marriage." *The Family Coordinator*, 1975, *24*, 489–503.

Stein, P. J. *Single*. Englewood Cliffs, N.J.: Prentice-Hall, 1976.

Stein, P. J. "Men and Their Friendships," in Robert Lewis (ed.), *Men in Troubled Times*. Englewood Cliffs, N.J.: Prentice-Hall, 1981.

Stein, P. J., and H. Etzkowitz. "Life Spiral or Life Cycle: A New Conceptualization of Life Stages. Paper presented at the annual meeting of the Society for the Study of Social Problems, September 1977, Chicago.

U.S. Bureau of the Census. "Marital Status and Living Arrangements: March 1979," in *Current Population Reports*, Series P-20, No. 349. Washington, D.C.: U.S. Government Printing Office, 1980.

Weiss, R. *Marital Separation.* New York: Basic Books, 1975.

Weiss, R. *Going It Alone.* New York: Basic Books, 1979.

Yllo, Kersti Alice. "Nonmarital Cohabitation: Beyond the College Campus." *Alternative Life Styles,* February 1978.

2/ WHERE ARE THE MEN FOR THE WOMEN AT THE TOP?

Christine Doudna with Fern McBride

When Diane Keaton blurts out in *Manhattan,* "I'm smart, I'm beautiful, I deserve something better," we laugh off her complaint as the raving of a charming neurotic. She's the archetype of the new woman, with a successful career and glamorous New York life, but she has a man problem. Her only choices appear to be a married man or the witty, intelligent but ultimately unprepossessing Isaac Davis (besides, he's in love with a seventeen-year-old).

Keaton, of course, is dismissed as a flake—whose own neuroses, whose woundedness, add up to her being unmarriageable. But like all of Woody Allen's characters, she's playing in a very familiar reality. And whatever the cinematic fictions, her lament is one which more and more women are expressing. Though most of them might still prefer to share that concern with their psychiatrists rather than a reporter, the issue is starting to come aboveground.

Says Julie, a thirty-year-old Hollywood producer: "I can't figure it out. I'm just not meeting men my age. I tell my friends, 'I think we have to look at it as if there were a war and all the men went to battle and never came back.' "

Harriet, a forty-seven-year-old Manhattan bank vice president: "I've had many discussions with women about this. We're attractive, bright career women. We've all made it. But we're all without men."

Joanna, a thirty-four-year-old magazine writer in Los Angeles: "Where are the attractive men? Many are married, many are living with people. Younger guys think I'm too old. Who am I supposed to be with?"

Patricia, a thirty-six-year-old real-estate agent in San Francisco: "Men in this town are either gay or among the walking wounded."

Elaine, a fifty-six-year-old widow who runs a manufacturing company in the Midwest: "By the time you get to my age I don't think there's a man left alive."

A journalist summed it up: "A few years ago, everyone was saying, 'Why do I meet so many more interesting women than men?' Now it's just, 'Where are the men?' "

The question may have a rhetorical ring, but it can be answered with some striking evidence. The fact is, there is a real shortage of men. The fault lies not in our stars *or* ourselves but in a grim set of demographic data. We are in a state of single shock, a crisis of numbers. It is not that there are, literally, *no* men at the top, but there are precious few.

For starters, there are 1,321,000 more single women than men between the ages of thirty and fifty-four. That's about 128 women for every 100 men. If you break down the figures by age, there are 135 women for every 100 men in the thirty-five-to-thirty-nine age group; 132 women for every 100 men in the forty-to-forty-four group; and 147 women for every 100 men in the forty-five-to-fifty-four group. If you further examine the forty-to-forty-four group, for instance, and filter out the never-married men, presumably confirmed bachelors, you end up with 290 unattached women for every 100 men—or less than half a man for every woman.

The situation is worse for women at the top. The men they want are those who are least available—statistically. Ten years ago writer Caroline Bird characterized a new aristocracy of single women—those who had postponed, or ended, marriages in order to pursue other lives—as the "leftover elite." Men in the same circumstances rarely seem to get "left over." They are, to use sociologists' language, on an opposite marriage gradient: Educated, professional men marry earlier and stay married longer than other men, while their female peers marry later and have a higher probability of divorce than other women. These contradictory patterns create a crunch which has been exacerbated by the rapid emergence of the new class of single professional women. There's been a sudden growth on the demand side of the market and very little movement in the supply lines. The female elite have become demographic losers; they've priced themselves out of the market. The problem that used to concern only heiresses—where to find a suitable mate among the sparsely stocked and heavily fished pool of men at the top—now afflicts an entire class.

The plight of the female elite begins with the "marrying up/marrying down" syndrome—the traditional tendency of women to want men who are older, more successful and better educated than they, while men want just the reverse. Therefore, a direct comparison of the men and women in each bracket underestimates the problem. Thirty-year-olds don't neatly pair off together; even less do forty-year-olds. In first marriages, men tend to choose women who are two and a half years younger. When they remarry, they look for someone close to four years their junior. That's in the remarriages of youth. When a man is older, say a Woody Allenish forty, he's likely to choose someone ten years younger, according to political scientist Andrew Hacker.

So, therefore, the real questions for a thirty-year-old woman may be, How many forty-year-old men are there to go around? and, How many women aged nineteen to forty is she competing with?

Education and income further worsen the situation. There is nothing unaccustomed about a male Ph.D. marrying a woman who has only a B.A., or a doctor marrying a nurse, but the reverse is viewed, and felt, as socially deviant. As John Gagnon, a sociologist, says, "What's a woman who's made it in the medical profession going to do—find a senator or a college president? Those guys are all married." According to Hacker, of the women between thirty-five and forty-four years of age with some graduate education or earnings over $20,000, about 20 percent have never married—as compared to 5.4 percent of other women their age. As for income, only 11.8 percent of married women currently earn as much or more than their husbands. "It is hard not to conclude," Hacker notes in *The New York Review of Books*, "that as women enter positions once held by men they become either less attracted to marriage or less attractive as marriage partners. Nor is it clear that even openminded husbands want wives with attainments approaching their own."

Meanwhile, those very attainments are being acquired by ever-increasing numbers of women, and things can only get worse as they grow older, richer and more successful. The ironic twist to this story is that the class of men who are statistically most available are the least educated. So we have a puzzle with completely mismatched pieces. As sociologist Jessie Bernard puts it, in the pool of eligibles, the men are the "bottom of the barrel" and the women are the "cream of the crop."

Special groups have special problems. Single women in their twenties and early thirties are caught in a "marriage squeeze" created by the steady and dramatic rise in birth rates at the end of World War II. In the words of Arthur Norton and Paul Glick, "During their lives members of the baby-boom generation have faced and will continue to face greater competition for fewer opportunities than their predecessors did or their successors will." When that competition is played out in the marriage market, it's women who get the squeeze because they look to an older, and therefore smaller, group of potential mates. Though single men still somewhat outnumber single women in their twenties (women get married earlier), the percentage of single men in that age group has been declining since 1970.

Professional women at the tail end of that squeeze group may be in for further problems. Not only are they in the most crowded age brackets, they also have a greater tendency to postpone marriage for their careers. The light at the end of the tunnel is that the post-baby-boom generation will see a slight reversal in the early 1980s. With a declining birth rate, it's men who will eventually get the squeeze.

For single women in their late thirties, divorce causes a special crunch. Single divorced women outnumber single divorced men in the thirty-five-to-thirty-nine age group by almost two to one (659,000 to 380,000). If it takes two to divorce, why does divorce leave more women than men alone in its wake? Part of the answer is that men remarry more frequently—and more quickly—than women: Five out of six divorced men remarry as compared to three out of four women. Another part of the answer is, again, the marrying up/marrying down syndrome: A thirty-eight-year-old man who divorces his thirty-six-year-old wife, for example, is likely to leave her in an already crowded pool while he dips into less troubled waters.

For women over forty, death begins to be a factor, as women outlive men by an average of 7.7 years. The widow from the Midwest wasn't so far off when she complained that all the men her age were dead: In the forty-five-to-fifty-four age group there are 854,000 unmarried widows and 176,000 unmarried widowers, a ratio of nearly five to one.

So the news is bad all around for single women in the marriage market. And that's not taking into account the growing number of gay men in our society, who by all estimates far outnumber gay women: 13 percent of the male population is reportedly gay.

Single black women have even more dramatic problems. Sociologist Robert Staples estimates that there are five eligible black women for every black man. In addition to the Vietnam War, which brought 7,224 black fatalities, he factors in the high mortality rate of black males aged twenty to thirty-five due to homicide and suicide. It's roughly three times the rate for white males of that age and four to five times that of black females. One black woman interviewed points to an additional aggravation of the statistics—the "snowbird" problem. Now that cries of Black-is-Beautiful have quieted down somewhat, interracial marriage is climbing back up, and black men are crossing over at about three times the rate of black women.

Where does all this demographic gloom lead? What does it mean for our society if the best and the brightest women don't marry or have children? Will women settle for less? What is life like in No Man's Land?

To find out, we interviewed twenty-five women in the new professional class. They range in age from twenty-nine to fifty-six. Their professions include television executive, college professor, copywriter, graphic designer and bank vice president. Their incomes range from $10,000 to over $100,000. Eleven are divorced, twelve never married, two are widows, eight have children. They live in

New York, Chicago, Washington, San Francisco and Los Angeles, and one is from a small town in the Midwest (though she keeps a *pied-à-terre* in Chicago). All are bright, articulate, successful in their careers and attractive—in some cases, beautiful. They talked about their relationships with men, what their options and aspirations are and how, if at all, they may be changing. All requested anonymity as a condition of being interviewed.

The emotional landscape of these women's lives ranges from desperation to resignation—but mostly there's a sense of confusion. The battle of the sexes may be a cliché, but these stories sound as though there's been no cessation of hostilities. Carol, a thirty-three-year-old New York television executive who earns $45,000 a year, describes a recent encounter: "We went out to dinner, spent seven hours talking. He is bright and sensitive and I was having a wonderful time for the first time in ages. I usually don't go to bed with a man on the first date, but this time it seemed almost wrong not to. He asked me to stay over and kept telling me how wonderful it was, how beautiful I am. Then in the morning he took a shower, came out and said, 'I want to thank you very much for last night.' I never heard from him again. I said to myself, 'Goddamn it, here we go again.' I mean I *know* it was a good night. It's not as if I expected him to marry me, but why couldn't he want another special evening?"

Sally, a thirty-one-year-old copywriter, described a relationship with a man who was at first very attentive: "For the first few weeks he called every day. He told me, once, 'I think I'm falling in love with you.' When I began to really care for him, he turned off almost immediately and his calls dropped to once a week. I wanted to believe he was scared so I kept quiet. Then we spent a lovely night together. The next morning, he made pancakes for breakfast and said he'd call later that day. I never heard from him again."

Almost all the women we interviewed are veterans of long-term relationships of one sort or another, and in most cases the accounts of these relationships build to a crescendo of unfulfilled expectations and a great deal of pain. The inability of men to make commitments and to tolerate women's success were oft-repeated themes. Julie told of a four-year relationship which ended when she took a high-paying executive position. "He would never come to my office. When I expressed an opinion a derisive tone would come into his voice and he would say, 'Oh, the *executive.*'" Rebecca, a beautiful fifty-year-old divorcee who runs her own video production company and earns over $100,000 a year, describes an eight-year relationship: "He gets scared when he gets really close. I think almost every woman who has known a head and a heart and body connection with a man, a really loving connection, has had that happen. Men will flirt with the connection for a while, move in with it, and then run away."

Whether the complaint is not finding men who can take "yes" for an answer or not finding men, period, women are experimenting with the available options. One solution, if you can call it that, is celibacy. "A lot of women I know haven't had sex for a year and a half," says Julie. Ever since Dyan Cannon broke the taboo by admitting there had been no man in her life for four years, abstinence has achieved a certain respectability, and several of the women interviewed mentioned it. At the other extreme, one thirty-nine-year-old professor placed an ad in the *New York Review of Books* and dutifully checked out each of the fifty responses. Peggy, a beautiful twenty-nine-year-old architect, has tried younger men, older men, bisexual men and married men. ("The only thing I haven't found is *appropriate* men.") One woman considered lesbianism but refrained from trying it, because the gay women she knows say problems with women are no different from those with men. ("All the gaming, it's win and lose.") A black woman noted that lesbianism was unheard of ten years ago in her community, but is now considered a real option.

Some women are stepping up their efforts to attract men—from the graphic designer who attends every New York art opening, to the bank vice president, who's taken to wearing "things that are a bit more frivolous, dresses that are more open." Carol said that she leaves matchbooks from fancy restaurants around, so a man might assume she's been there with other men. A friend of hers suggested she might try wearing a Band-Aid—"so men can feel that I need them."

Although stereotypes about women's sexual relationships are giving way in the face of their unprecedented freedom to experiment, the traditional relationship with the older man endures. The era of the emerging woman executive may in fact give new luster to the vogue of "old man's darling," for it may be the older man who can deal most comfortably with a woman's professional success. Julie, age thirty, is currently involved with a very successful fifty-three-year-old. At her level—she earns $100,000 a year—the traditional ideal of the more successful man is in direct collision with the scarcity of such men. But, she says, "No matter how much I try to tell myself differently, I still respond to the power, the money, the success, the three-piece suits, the cigar after dinner." Will it last? "He thinks so, but I don't. . . . I'm bothered by it. He talked about something he did in 1953, and I said, 'I was five then.' "

Another woman reports that "from twenty-three until twenty-eight I was never with a man who didn't have gray hair." And a third: "My whole thing for the last seven years has been older men."

The married man is another traditional—if traditionally unsatisfactory—solution. Peggy has been having a relationship with one who fulfills "maybe 80 percent of my needs." When she started another affair she stopped sleeping with the married man, but continues to see him on a regular basis. Harriet recently ended a five-year relationship with a married man, and says she and her friends could see married men every night of the week. "It's very disappointing that these seem to be the only relationships open to us. Each of us has vowed we won't have one again because these relationship are all losers."

Clearly, the numbers crisis is hardest on women over forty-five. Polly, a fifty-three-year-old professional musician, says: "Most of the women I know are depressed because the men they date are married. They are all professional women, all trapped in situations in which there is no solution. Obviously, if men haven't gotten divorces in all these years, they're not about to now. I think a lot of it is property; they keep talking about 'my house.' "

Perhaps in response to the scarcity in their own backyards, women are ranging farther and farther afield in search of partners. A San Francisco woman reports that all her recent boyfriends have lived either in New York or Los Angeles. A New York woman fantasizes about giving up her life as a television producer and joining her boyfriend in northern California. Another New York woman is in love with a man in Ceylon whom she's known for over a year. They've seen each other several times, and she's convinced they'll spend a great part of their lives together. Whether these stories say more about the risks women will take in an age of diminished opportunities or the desire they have to keep romance at a safe distance varies from case to case. But the long-distance romance is clearly an option born of a new aristocracy.

Another less traditional solution is one which Polly, Peggy, Julie and a growing number of other women have tested: a relationship with a younger man. Julie says hers was nourishing in a way curiously similar to one with an older man—he wasn't intimidated by her success. "I met him at a party last year and he was just full of life. It was wonderful and very strange. I paid for everything because I made much more money. It lasted about five months. But finally, I didn't feel comfortable bringing him to some of the places I had to go. Intellectually he was my equal but I had eight years on him. When he's thirty he'll be wonderful."

Peggy was amazed at her own story: "He's twenty-six, and a young twenty-six. He's a very successful Paris model, he's absolutely gorgeous, he didn't finish high school, and I fell head over heels for him! We had shaving cream fights! It was such a revelation to me. I don't need someone intelligent to have a relationship with; I spend my days with intelligent people. What I want is someone to have fun with."

Mary is a forty-one-year-old magazine editor who likes younger men because "they're so flattered by having your attention. It makes you feel good. I'm going down socially and in age, but it's much more fun that way."

If it's fun, must it be frivolous? Consider the story of Joanna, who has had a string of glamorous short-lived affairs—a rock star, an astronaut, a couple of radical lawyers, a fading movie star—"very fading." She's thirty-four, never married, and is very anxious to have a good relationship and a baby. Her current lover? A twenty-four-year-old factory worker from Detroit who never went to college. ("He says 'them' for 'those.' ") "Much as I'm drawn to men who wear silk shirts and have power, I'm very ambivalent about that world," she says. "I'd like to be able to talk to someone about whether Joan Didion is getting better or worse—I don't have that with this man—but if I had to make a choice right now, I'd choose him.

"That I made myself available just amazes me," she continues. "He's smart, very attractive—it's very sexual—and I like him." They met in Atlanta. "I was there on assignment, he had gone there with some idea of starting his life over. When I had to leave for Los Angeles, he drove me to the airport. We had never even kissed, and he said to me, 'I'm coming out to Los Angeles.' I just looked at him. And he said, 'You're supposed to say, 'I believe you.' I caught my breath. I haven't been so moved by anyone in a long, long time. And I've missed that more than I miss talking about Joan Didion."

There are other frustrations. "There's no point in bringing home croissants, because he likes Wonder Bread. I like everything under-cooked, he likes everything overcooked, so that is the way I do it. Now and then I sneak in a quiche—I say it's a cheese pie. About three weeks ago I got very irritated and thought, all this man likes to eat is pork chops. And then I thought, well, if all he wanted to eat was pâté, that would irritate me, too."

Joanna's story is a particularly dramatic reflection of some of the profound changes that have occurred in male/female relationships in the long decade since Mick Jagger sarcastically rhapsodized about waiting for a factory girl. Challenging traditional notions of class as well as age may bring great social pressure. "Age is less important than status," says Elizabeth Roberts, director of the Project on Human Sexual Development at Cambridge, Mass. "If you're involved with a younger man who's a top-flight attorney and you're a mid-level executive, it may not be so bad. But choosing a man who is lower in status than you professionally means you're doing it because you're having fun: you're making choices that women were not taught to make. You're flaunting your sexuality."

She also believes that these new choices have far-ranging impact: "There are very exciting opportunities in status reversal. Women don't usually get the chance to be mentors, much less mentors to men. Women in higher management positions find themselves as mentors to both younger men and women. This can fulfill their needs to feel important and offer what they know. These are basically nice human needs—we fulfill them with our children, with our

friends, and now there's an opportunity to fulfill them professionally
and sexually as well."

The mentor can, of course, turn into the tired teacher. Rebecca
complains, "If you're their teacher, they go on to have a good relationship with someone else." Roberts reports one woman saying:
"I'm not going to give Course 100 on Older Women or How to Deal
With a Feminist to one more younger man." But she points out that
men in their forties and fifties may need as much "tutoring" as men
in their twenties, if not more—they may have spent twenty-five years
in relationships where the rules were entirely different.

Sociologist Cynthia Epstein tends to dismiss the younger-man phenomenon as representing a "fling mentality." "People in New York
are trying it but precious few are marrying. The norms of society are
not comfortable for either partner." But fling or no fling, these
kinds of relationships are clearly on the rise, and they may signal a
shift in attitudes in the society as a whole.

If the testing of new alternatives is in some sense a response to a
numbers crisis, the alternatives themselves reflect other levels of social change. It may seem like yesterday's news to say it all began in
the sixties, but there is some interesting evidence to consider. The
mid-sixties saw the maturing of the first members of the baby-boom
generation and a simultaneous trend toward postponement of marriage. Divorce rates began to soar. A new generation of women
began pursuing higher education and professional careers. Women's
enrollment in colleges more than doubled between 1960 and 1978,
bringing the ratio of men to women close to 50-50. During the same
time, women nearly doubled their numbers in the labor force (from
23,240,000 to 41,878,000), going from one out of three to two out of
five of all workers in this country. Professional women made particularly striking employment gains in the seventies: From 1972 to 1975
they increased by 24 percent while men increased by only 1 percent.
Postponement of marriage likewise increased in the seventies for
both men and women.

The sixties brought it all—college career, copulation, contraception, and abortion on demand. (Although the Supreme Court didn't
legalize abortion until 1973, there were landmark changes in individual states in the late sixties which foreshadowed the ruling.) And, of
course, there was the women's movement.

With a nod toward both the chicken and the egg, one can argue
that the numbers crisis contributed to these changes. The thesis that
male-female ratios are responsible for a wide variety of social phenomena was developed by sociologist Marcia Guttentag. A book based on
her work, *Too Many Women: Demography, Sex and Family* by Paul Secord, will soon be published. Among other things, Secord argues that
feminism flourishes whenever women outnumber men.

Since the late sixties, single women in the thirty-to-fifty-four age bracket have increasingly outnumbered men. Although the particular social and economic conditions in this country during this time have no real precedent, other historical periods offer some interesting parallels in terms of what sheer numbers can mean to the status of women.*

In classical antiquity, for instance, though men apparently outnumbered women most of the time, some interesting changes coincided with periods when men were off at war. Aristotle noted that Spartan women enjoyed a certain freedom during the long absences of Spartan men, and indeed their lives offer a sharp contrast to Athenian women of the time. Spartan women managed and controlled property, indulged in extramarital relations when their husbands were away and dressed in short, slit skirts which gave them great freedom of movement; while Athenian women enjoyed almost no legal rights, were kept cloistered from social interaction and wore long, voluminous gowns.

In the late Middle Ages, a surfeit of upper-class women (the result, primarily, of the Crusades) coincided with an upsurge of feminism. Women began running feudal estates for the first time. They entered convents in increasing numbers, and their power in the Catholic Church increased, giving rise to the cult of the Virgin Mary. The convents were, in fact, so crowded that female communes called "Beguines" evolved outside the church and produced radical literature that argued that women might commune directly with God without going through male priests. The spinning wheel, invented in twelfth-century France, made it possible for the first time for a woman to have some economic independence (hence the derivation of the word "spinster").

In seventeenth- and eighteenth-century Europe, the excess of women led to a strong upsurge of feminine mysticism. When religious leaders from Europe tried to transplant that tradition to America—which in those days offered the much rarer phenomenon of a sex imbalance favoring females rather than males—the reception was very different: Religion flourished in the new world, but mysticism did not. Historian Herbert Moller notes that "the vast majority of women had no reason to withdraw to solitary lives and to indulge in fantasy gratification, since their chances of marriage were excellent and their economic utility high." Societal attitudes seem to follow the numbers. Moller also notes that "American men penned affectionate letters to their wives and sweethearts when in contemporary Europe . . . expressions of tenderness between husband and wife were ridiculed and therefore dissembled when felt."

*We are indebted to Paul Secord for his suggestions in this section.

While Don Juan was the model lover in both literature and real life in Europe in the seventeenth and eighteenth centuries, men in America were complaining about the fickleness and inconsistency of women.

Nicholas Cresswell, a British traveler in America in the eighteenth century, called America "a paradise on Earth for women. . . . That great curiosity, an Old Maid, the most calamitous Creature in Nature, is seldom seen in this country."

Though it would be simplistic to suggest a direct causal link between the numerical imbalance arising in the sixties and the beginning of contemporary feminism, the plurality of women, coupled with post–World War II economic growth, created a more fertile ground for feminism than had existed ever before in history. "You get feminist movements only in particular times," says social psychologist Carol Tavris, "but not when women are a scarcity. Consciousness is the result of social and economic conditions, and not the other way around."

Professional women may be on the cutting edge of that contemporary consciousness. John Gagnon says, "What we have here is a big change—and it's taken place almost exclusively on the part of women. They've moved into male domains and have acquired all the desirable attributes—assertiveness, confidence, competence—while men have not moved."

Along with these new attributes, women have acquired unprecedented expectations—they want terrific careers, egalitarian relationships and, usually, families. And they don't want to compromise. "I'm a believer that we can do it all," says Julie. "We can have the children, we can have the career, we can do it."

Marriage is a high priority (and 94 percent of all Americans marry at some point in their lives), but children are clearly the most pressing issue. Almost without exception, the women we interviewed in their thirties who hadn't had children expressed a very great desire for them. Many of them are obsessed with the looming biological deadline. A thirty-six-year-old said she believes her "statute of limitations has about run out." A thirty-eight-year-old said she felt confident she could wait as late as her early forties. A thirty-year-old told of a conversation with her gynecologist: "I asked, 'Well, doctor, how long do I have?' as if I had a terminal disease, and he screamed, 'Why are you doing this to yourself? You have ten good years.' " Many said they were considering becoming single parents. One has already set aside money for a child ("I'll have one with or without a man"); a highly placed White House official was thinking of doing the same, but thought if she went ahead, "Jimmy Carter would probably have a heart attack."

Though neither marriage nor children were imminent prospects for the women we talked to, most were confident that they could indeed "have it all." Sociologist Mirra Komarovsky believes that there is a "utopian element" to what people want now—"a disjunction between very much heightened aspirations, on the part of both men and women, and the social means to achieve them." She thinks that the tradition of American individualism, the belief that "I can make it on my own," is preventing the logical next step—which is to obtain the social means to fulfill these aspirations. "Enough people break through to keep the ideology alive, but there are limits to what can be done by individual ingenuity. There has to be concerted action."

Elizabeth Roberts agrees: "A lot of us went into the workplace, following Betty Friedan with streaming banners, determined to have the kind of productive careers we wanted, only to find out it was goddammed exhausting, a big juggling act. Institutions haven't caught up with us. We haven't been able to break through the myth that if a woman can afford to stay home she will, statistics notwithstanding."

John Gagnon thinks that men are caught even more in the institutional bind: "Take a look at how weak the men's movement is; there are no social incentives for men to change. Look at the guy who wants to be president of I.T.T.—do you think he wants to share child rearing and household chores? One of the props of masculinity is to take deference for granted. With women on a par with you, you've got to earn the deference. And though it may be attractive that she pays half the bills, it's less attractive that she's making decisions too."

Raised expectations on a personal level are still fraught with ambivalence for many. One woman complained that her ex-husband has a relationship now "that he should have had with me. He takes out the garbage, cooks half the time and participates in that stuff because she is radical and I never was. He was perfectly willing to do it. I never asked him to." Roberts believes that women are still afraid to put an apron on their sons and make them unmanly, and "no husband of theirs is going to be caught with a dust mop in his hand."

And confusion reigns in the sexual sphere. Diane, a thirty-one-year-old college professor, fluctuates from feeling very depressed—"When I was sixteen I had to protect it and now I can't give it away"—to longing for a relationship of real intimacy: "I'm no longer fascinated by the abruptness of many relationships. There's a lack of formality, no courting. You meet somebody, go home to bed with him, and many times you don't even talk to each other. The contacts are more contests of skill than real intimacy."

Many women indicated that they were changing their attitudes about casual sex. Elaine, the fifty-six-year-old businesswoman, says, "There were several times when I hopped into bed very quickly. Once it was very embarrassing because the next day there was this man and, my god, what do you say to him? I think going to bed with people immediately leads to hurt feelings because you give people the idea that it means something more than it does. I'll never do that again."

Patricia, the thirty-six-year-old real-estate agent from San Francisco, believes that "sexual liberation was a nice thing to happen because it broke down some barriers, but boy, I don't think there's anything more elegant and erotic than a good monogamous relationship. Screwing around is empty, bad, exactly nowhere; so it's back to the old chastity."

The tale is not one of uninterrupted backlash. One woman told of a recent affair that was "really casual, and I knew that's just what it was, but really nice. By the end of the weekend I knew very intimate things about him—I knew that his father was a suicide, his uncle was a suicide, his grandfather was a suicide, that he was a terrific cook— but I literally didn't know his last name. That to me is very casual."

She may be the exception that proves the rule. Most of the women expressed little interest in casual sex. And if they resort occasionally to promiscuity without guilt, it is also without much satisfaction. Rebecca articulated it most simply: "I think monogamy is something you choose eventually. If you really love someone, it's not worth going back to zero with someone else."

Many women wondered if they may be preventing themselves from achieving their new expectations. Harriet suspects that she and her single female friends are "deliberately creating barriers somewhere—because we don't want to make an emotional commitment, for whatever reason. Intellectually, all of us will tell you that we want to be loved, want to get married. Our goals are set very high—it's not Prince Charming, but it's what we think we're entitled to."

Whether or not they get what they are entitled to, these women are thrashing out the contradictions of a changed society. Women, like men a hundred years before them, have now pretty much left the home as their place of business. While historians, sociologists, psychologists and feminists argue over what that change means for the future of the family, the exodus is now clearly an irreversible tide. We have reached a watershed of sorts, where a biological and economic formula that has applied at least since the industrial revolution, and arguably since the beginning of history, has been jettisoned—that of man as breadwinner and woman as homemaker.

This change presents a serious challenge to the long-ingrained tradition of marrying up. There are a few historical precedents to a reversal in the age pattern (in England in 1599, 21 percent of wives were older than their husbands; in France in 1778, 27 percent were older). And as Ali McGraw, Jane Fonda and Dyan Cannon hit their forties, more people may be questioning traditional criteria linking beauty and sexuality to youth.

But the change cannot be easy. "It's going to take a massive poking into the worlds of fashion and cosmetics; we have to say the lines are beautiful, the extra pounds are beautiful," says Julie. "We have such intense connections between sex and power in this society," adds Elizabeth Roberts. "With the shift in power I'm not sure what's going to happen in terms of what's perceived as attractive and sexy. It's all so new. We're still feeling our way around." But Roberts, like Norton and Glick and many others, believes that the growing exposure of men and women to one another in the workplace may ultimately relieve a lot of emotional trauma. "The little research we have indicates that the best way to break up sexual stereotypes is to put people together—which is contrary to a lot of the research on racism. I think what will really make a difference is breaking through a lot of myths about what's attractive and what's unattractive."

In the meantime, singlehood is probably here to stay. The single professional woman is caught in an age of particular uncertainty, but she may also be in the vanguard of a revolution. Marrying up may give way to marrying across, if not down. The I-want-it-all syndrome may lead to the realization that social change is necessary to get it all. Equality may still turn out to be the most revolutionary notion of all.

If women are the "emotional specialists of our society," in the words of sociologist Philip Slater, the dramas of the single professional woman may be a kind of dress rehearsal for the rest of society. As an economic group, such women can afford to experiment with their raised expectations. As singles, they present the most visible dramas of what happens when those expectations collide with reality.

3/ LATE-MARRYING BACHELORS

Jon Darling

MEN WHO DON'T "FIT THE MOLD"

One of the traditional curiosities about human behavior has been why some people never develop a close, intimate, sociosexual relationship with another and the parallel question why some persons develop such a relationship for the first time rather late in life. Most studies of marriage and marrying have been studies (1) of those who *do* marry and (2) of those who marry "on schedule"—the young. The implication has been that normative statistical patterns reflect "normal" personality development and unusual statistical patterns reflect "abnormal" personality development. Consequently, researchers have neglected important questions about the marrying process, biased their studies to reflect the social situations of the relatively young, and reinforced common stereotypes (Stein, 1978).

This paper reports on an interactionist investigation[1] of the life histories of heterosexual men of varied social classes who entered into bachelor careers[2] and who married for the first time when they were over thirty-five. The sample used in this study consisted of twenty never-married men over thirty-five and twenty men who first married after the age of thirty-five. The study was designed around the idea that marriage or living together in a marriagelike relationship, like all other human relationships, develops as the end point of a series of situations, turning points, and commitments. The purpose was to discover the ways in which the subjects interacted with others and the places and situations in which this occurred and led to extended states of nonmarriage, and also to discover how those patterns subsequently changed direction to encourage marriage at a relatively late age (Darling, 1976).

THE CAREER OF BACHELORHOOD

Late marriage is, of course, a career development of bachelorhood and can be understood only in that context. Through involvement in one's significant society, such as family and friends, one comes to structure views of the world and views of oneself. These bachelors were not basically different types of people but were men whose socialization histories were somewhat unusual compared to the experiences of most men their age.

In adolescence, the bachelors were typically involved with family or "significant others" who served to insulate them from the usual peer group pressure to date. (However, such involvements, by themselves, do not account for a bachelor career.) In postadolescence bachelors remained within social settings where marriage was not defined as important or appropriate for them. These men found themselves deeply committed to their families, to their careers, or to friendships that fulfilled their needs. Any sociosexual relationships that did develop were generally left to drift beyond the point when a commitment to marriage might be expected. As long as the men were "comfortable" with their situations, they were not likely to seriously seek a change such as marriage.

For the men in this study, their careers in nonmarriage were characterized by a lack of the two conditions that seem to be necessary for early marriage: (1) socialization in early marriage expectations and (2) the development of an interactionally successful relationship in which the other person becomes a significant other to the bachelor. Indeed, many of the bachelors were not at all sexually active during major periods of their single lives. Their lives had become so organized around other orientations and concerns that they drifted further and further away from influences that could have aligned them to marriage norms.

Of course none of these orientations is unique to bachelors. Some men, after all, marry *and* care for their aging parents at the same time or marry in the midst of active professional careers. Thus the events in bachelors' lives may not differ significantly from those in the lives of men who marry early, but *the timing, definition, and perception of those events seem to vary considerably between the two groups. This produces and sustains important differences in identities, commitments, and consequent career patterns.*

In general, then, bachelors were buffered from the effect of marital norms because of their integration into personally significant societies. When that society disintegrated, or its buffering effect diminished, bachelors were "ripe" for marriage.

TURNING POINTS AND LATE MARRIAGE

A look at turning points reveals a pattern in which old situations broke down, old patterns of meanings became reworked, and stabilized relationships with significant others began to be interrupted to make way for new ones. Such transformations are rarely a smooth, even-flowing process; they are almost always marked by advances and retreats along available alternative courses of action. In the words of one bachelor:

> There was, after the first glow of the proposal and living together, I'd say a period from December into mid-March that was a very painful time for me . . . I think I was scared . . . I think, subconsciously, I was trying to run away. . . . The last two months, I just calmed down and it was great.

For bachelors with strong ties to their families, a typical turning point was the death of an aged parent. In other cases bachelors married while their parents were alive—at their parents' insistence. Some bachelors were no longer comfortable at home when the situation there changed:

> I think I was rather desperate because in breaking up with _____ and my mother's deteriorating health, I felt many avenues had been cut. . . . home was no longer a place of refuge, and I was under fire from many directions.

Similarly, others married at points when they were about to receive a promotion or make a career change that necessitated moving to a new place, where they feared they would be lonely:

> Before I told [the company] I was leaving, I tried to figure a way to get in a final apartment hunting trip to Delaware [where the new job was]. We [he and a woman he had been dating] went together. I took her to Washington to meet my mother, not knowing where I stood [in the "relationship"]. Apartment hunting was awkward. Who was this woman traveling along behind? Rental agents thought she was my wife. We were both surprised that no one seemed upset that we might not be married and would just be living together. We spent that evening in conversation, she telling me about her unhappy background, her unhappy marriage—the subject matter escapes me beyond that—just a slow building of emotional feelings.

Among the late-marrieds in the study, timing of events was more important than the events themselves. Men married when they felt particularly vulnerable and/or were encouraged by a significant other. Most of the late-marrieds had short courtships; they were ready for marriage and did not want to lose the opportunity when one developed.

Late marriage by bachelors socialized in this manner can perhaps best be understood within the framework of "conversion." Indeed, bachelors themselves often described the experience as one of being "born again," and the similarity between the experience of the bachelors discussed here and the religious converts described in another study (Lofland and Stark, 1965) is striking. Prior to their conversion, the religious converts were in a state of "seekership"; current solutions to their problems were inadequate enough so that they were "shopping for" a new perspective. While in this state of seekership, the religious converts happened to meet a member of the cult who became a significant other for them. This is paralleled in the case of the late-marrieds by meeting and gaining the emotional support of their future wives. Those who finally converted were generally loners or members of a friendship group in which everyone joined the cult at the same time. Similarly, bachelors married when they had no friends, or most of their friends were marrying, and/or their parents or significant others approved of their marriage plans. Final conversion to the cult might be equivalent to finally marrying for the bachelors.

One goal of this study was to clarify the degree to which bachelorhood represented a deviant status in which labeling was a major determinant of a bachelor career. The conclusion was that labeling, as such, did not play as significant a role in the stabilization of bachelorhood as had been expected. Insofar as labeling did play a role, it was more important in inducing them to marry eventually than in confirming them as bachelors. The idea of marriage was sometimes initiated by a series of what might be called labeling episodes, episodes that emphasized the negative aspects of singleness:

> The only time I ever thought about [not being married], at least about it the most, was after [encounter sessions paid for by his employer] four years ago [when he was thirty-six]. A couple of people raised the issue of whether or not I really loved anyone; that is, whether I could love anyone. . . . I thought about it and resolved it by saying yes, I had loved them. And then I periodically thought about it . . . although I didn't discuss it with anyone [over the two years before he married].

Several other findings were of considerable interest. One was that 65 percent of the men in the late-married sample married women who were eight to seventeen years younger than they. There was a double standard operating: these men could understand why men such as themselves had not married, but they were very suspicious of women their age who had never married. Hence they seemed to prefer women who had "proven" themselves through a prior marriage or women who were young enough to just be entering the marriage market—and who often looked up to older, more "sophisticated" men.

The problem that the late-marrieds mentioned most frequently involved having children. Many of the men were not sure they could make an adjustment to children of their own:

> [She] married me knowing that I wasn't totally convinced that I wanted to have children. . . . I guess as I looked at it, the relationship of two people, their own lives for themselves, can be as selfish as my living my own life for myself. . . . we were both working, and weren't sharing

with anyone. We talked about it. [They have since had two children.]

An even greater worry was about the age gap between the spouses:

> How would I react to her when I was retiring and when the kids would be graduating from college? I'd be ready to die when she's just middle age. We talked about that as we began to get romantically inclined. She said she wasn't worried about that, why should I be? We can have several years of happiness together—let's live it up.

Most of the late-married men strongly recommended that others marry late. They pointed out that waiting allowed individuals to grow mature and gain some economic basis for a successful marriage. Overall, they felt that their marriages were and would continue to be much more successful than earlier marriages. Furthermore, they felt that they had had their chance to try all sorts of things that people who marry early often claim their marriages prevent them from doing.

The findings of this study support the contention that nonmarriage and late marriage are primarily situational conditions rather than conditions that develop because of the abnormal traits of individuals. The sociological study of unusual patterns of relating to marital norms offers much potential for correcting stereotypes and for improving our understanding of the relationship between society and the individual.

NOTES

1. Interactionist investigation refers to a study of the social process by which people come to make certain decisions.

2. Career means the movement through a series of social statuses and the changes in the way one perceives oneself through such movement.

REFERENCES

Darling, Jon. 1976. An interactionist interpretation of bachelorhood and late marriage: the process of entering into, remaining in, and leaving careers of singleness." Ph.D. dissertation, University of Connecticut.

Lofland, John and Stark, Rodney. 1965. "Becoming a world saver: a theory of conversion to a deviant perspective." American Sociological Review 30:862–875.

Stein, Peter. 1978. "The life styles and life chances of the never-married." Marriage and Family Review, Vol. 1, No. 4 (Spring).

4/ BLACK SINGLES IN AMERICA

Robert Staples

Most societies, including ours, have always provided some acceptable mode of being single—most often within a religious context. Singlehood during adolescence and early adulthood, and following the death of a spouse, has also been acceptable, at least in modern societies. But few if any provisions were made for singlehood outside of very clearly defined institutional boundaries. Except for those who voluntarily entered religious orders, being single had little or nothing to do with the wishes and desires of the individual; it was a category of status within some well-defined parameters.

Historically, the concept of singlehood that we are attempting to appraise, could not have been considered. There was no socially accepted identity outside the context of the family or some other prescribed and accepted group. Marriage was therefore not merely a union of two individuals but a union of representatives from socially established groups. The transformation of the family from a rural to an urban setting, effects of industrialization in weakening the economic base of the family, and the recent increase in leisure time set the stage for a new view of singlehood.

Even now it is hard to imagine a society in which large numbers of people reject the idea of marriage. America's founders obviously considered singlehood a threat when they imposed a special tax on bachelors. But as we look at contemporary America, we see that the proportion of never-married young adults in the United States is increasing dramatically. It would be easy to assume that Americans are simply delaying marriage until a later age, but the proportion of singles has also increased for the age group twenty-five to twenty-nine. While many will eventually marry, it is conceivable that a large proportion will remain single throughout their entire lives. Moreover, if we consider the number of individuals divorced, separated, or widowed, there are over 50 million adult Americans—a third of all people over the age of 18—who are single.[1]

These changes in marital patterns are historically unprecedented for the population at large, and the alteration of marital patterns among Afro-Americans is even more pronounced. The increase in black singlehood seems consistent with the conventional wisdom that marriage failed to take on an institutional character among blacks— that because of the vicissitudes of slavery, the formal and legal aspects of marriage have never been a strong norm in the Afro-American community. Although slaves were not permitted to consummate legal contracts such as marriage, marriage relationships between male and female slaves were socially, if not legally, recognized. After slavery ended, a legal marriage was a symbol of freedom to a group deprived of such rights for centuries. By the beginning of the twentieth century the majority of blacks were lodged in nuclear families.[2]

Contrary to prevailing stereotypes about black attitudes toward marriage as an institution, the newly freed slaves rapidly entered the conjugal state once the right for freedmen to marry was created by governmental decree. A legal marriage was a status symbol, for a group so long deprived of this right. The black middle class set great store by proper culture and respectability, and marriage was regarded as essential to the proper functioning of this group. Marriage and family respectability were the foundation of high status in black culture.[3] One indication of this view of marriage is the fact that a larger percentage of black women marry than their white counterparts. In the 1970s among black women of sixty-five and over, only 3.5 percent had never married; for white women the figure was 6.9 percent.[4]

CHARACTERISTICS OF BLACK SINGLES

Among the younger generations, however, as among younger whites also, the new trend toward singleness is unmistakable. In a fifteen-year period the proportion of blacks married and living with a spouse has undergone a steady decline. In 1960, 63 percent of all black men fourteen and older were recorded as married. By 1975 this percentage had dropped to 53. Among black women in this age group the proportion declined from 60 to 49 percent. In 1978 the proportion of blacks who were married and living with a spouse was a distinct minority (47 percent). Between the ages of thirty-five and forty-four, during which most people either marry or remain permanently single, 7 percent of black men and 8 percent of black women were still single. A slightly higher proportion of men living in the North and West (12 percent) had never married, in comparison to men residing in the South (10 percent). The reverse was true for black women living in the North and West (7 percent), in contrast to women of the South (9 percent).[5]

OUR SAMPLE

This study of the lives of single black Americans is based on a nationwide sample of blacks classified as single—that is, never married, divorced, separated, and widowed. All subjects were between twenty-five and forty-five, and lived in metropolitan areas of more than 100,000 population. (Most singles live in such areas, and singles who do not generally lead very different lives.) Since the economic variables that impinge on one's marital status were not part of the study, it was decided to concentrate exclusively on blacks who had obtained four or more years of a college education and thus, presumably, had some choice of life style.

Thus our data are derived from some 500 college-educated black men and women studied during 1975–1979. Since they have at least four years of higher education, they can be classified as middle-class in terms of values, if not in terms of occupation or income. The data were obtained through some 400 self-administered questionnaires and personal interviews. The modal educational level of respondents was five years of college and their median income was $13,000 a year. Approximately 80 percent of those who returned the questionnaires were female.

Additionally, over a hundred in-depth interviews were conducted by the writer and two interviewers, one male and one female, in the San Francisco–Oakland metropolitan area. Each interview averaged about three hours and covered a range of topics related to being black, middle-class, and unmarried. Half of these subjects were male and half female. Most of them had been born and reared in other parts of the country. Thus they represented a cross-section of the national black population, what we call a network sample. We found our first interview subjects at meetings of professional associations and asked them for further names. Our method of data analysis was qualitative in that we sought patterns in the data rather than attempting to quantify the responses. The responses were analyzed into categories so that it was possible to read all the excerpts that dealt with a particular subject.

Among the group of blacks that have the greatest interest for this study—middle-class, aged twenty-five to forty-five—a clear picture emerges. As income level rises, so does the number of men who are married and living with their wives. Many are still married to the first wife, and those who divorced have subsequently remarried.[6] On the other hand, black women who have graduated from college are the least likely of all blacks to have married by the age of thirty.[7]

Among those who do marry, especially those who have had five or
more years of college, their divorce rate is higher and their remarriage rate lower than those of black women with less education.
Black men least likely to marry, or remarry, are those with less than
a high-school education.[8] This suggests that marriage rates are a
function of education (or status) for black men and for black women,
but a function that operates in different directions. A basic problem
for middle-class black women is that men who have a similar status
are married and that the largest number of black men in the eligible
pool are those with a lower status.

The history of blacks helps to illuminate the causes of this situation. For a number of years the proportion of black women graduating from college exceeded the proportion of men. When most blacks
were still living in the rural South, many black families preferred to
send their daughters to college. A wider variety of occupations was
open to men, while women's only choices were to be college-
educated schoolteachers or domestic servants. Moreover, in the
agrarian South, the sons were likely to remain on the farms. As
recently as 1956, for example, 62 percent of all the college degrees
awarded to blacks went to women.[9] And as a result, in the year 1975
there were 411,000 black women with four years or more of college
compared to only 342,000 black males.[10] In the years 1965–1975 the
gap between male and female college graduates began to narrow,
but in 1977 there were still some eighty-four thousand more black
women enrolled in college than black men. Among whites there
were 672,000 more college men than women.[11]

The pool of eligible black male cohorts for black women is further
decreased by a number of other factors. Many college-educated
black men marry women with less education. It is also estimated that
the number of black male homosexuals exceeds that of female homosexuals. We know too that black men marry outside their race at a
rate three times higher than black women, and most of those men
are members of the higher socioeconomic group.

Thus, paradoxically, many of the eligible men do not have the
opportunity to marry due to their low level of education and income,
and the women fail to marry because of their high level of education
and income.

TYPES OF SINGLES

Singles are not a monolithic grouping. The categories used by the
United States Census Bureau are the never-married, the widowed,
the separated, and the divorced. Among blacks in general, the largest
number in the twenty-five to forty-five age group are the separated.
Lower income blacks have long used physical separation as a form of

marital dissolution, since the expense has generally deterred many of them from seeking legal divorce. For most middle-class blacks the time between physical separation and divorce proceedings is brief, except when there is ambivalence about terminating the marriage. Among some men extended separation may be a ploy to ward off pressures for future marriage. Those who are separated do not differ greatly from the divorced except for a reduced desire to remarry.

The divorced form the second largest category in the twenty-five to forty-five group, and they may be seen as qualitatively different from the never-married. They are usually older and many have children, although college-educated black women have the lowest fertility rate of all women in the United States. Only 14 percent of black children live in single-parent households that have an annual income of $15,000 and over.[12] Actually, the majority of middle-class black singles are formerly married. Only in the age range below thirty is there a majority of never-marrieds. Divorced people with children often form attenuated families to carry out most functions, as do other nuclear families. For them, the pull of marriage may not be as great as among the childless singles.

Very few of this age and class group are widowed. Although the average married black woman loses her husband at an early age,[13] only a very small number of the middle-class black singles we studied had lost a spouse through death. The never-married group is much larger. Men and women under the age of thirty and women who had five years or more of college were more likely never to be married.[14]

Although all individuals who are not married and living with a spouse are part of the singles category, not all of them are single in the same way. For our study of black singlehood we have used the concept of a singles career. This concept designates objective movements that one may make through the singles world. The most common is the free-floating single. This type of single is unattached to any other person and dates randomly with or without the purpose of seeking a committed relationship. Another type is the individual in an open-coupled relationship. This person has a relatively steady partner but the relationship is open enough to encompass other individuals in a sexual or romantic relationship. Sometimes it is an open-coupled relationship in a unilateral sense, with one of the partners pursuing other people; this may be a matter of deception or merely rest on the failure of the couple to define the relationship explicitly. In the closed-coupled relationship, on the other hand, the partners look exclusively to each other for their sexual and affectional needs. By mutual agreement, fidelity is expected and the partners are emotionally bound to each other.[15]

The next group, which may be called the committed singles, consists of individuals who are cohabiting in the same household and are engaged to be married or have an agreement to maintain a permanent relationship. Those committed to a permanent relationship are usually so emotionally bound to each other, as long as the commitment lasts, that they spend most of their leisure time together and encounter few of the problems of other singles groups.

Another singles stage through which people may pass is accommodation, either temporary or permanent. Among younger singles (under age forty-five) the accommodation to their single status is likely to be temporary. They will lead a solitary existence except for friendships, refusing all dates and heterosexual contacts. Some accommodationists may temporarily adopt an alternative life style or sublimate through work, school, or religion. The permanent accommodationist will generally be in an older age group.

THE PUSH AND PULL TOWARD SINGLEHOOD

People may be temporarily single for a variety of reasons. In his study of white singles, Stein identifies negative pushes and positive pulls toward singlehood and marriage.[16] While any combination of these factors may keep a person in the single status, certain ones seem paramount among black singles. First, and of basic importance, is the imbalance in the sex ratio. There is an estimated excess of one million women in the black population, resulting in a ratio of 90 males per 100 females. The ratio is even lower in the conventionally marriageable years (eighteen to thirty-five) and in the large cities. Though there is a census undercount of black males, a statistical correction for the undercount places the "real" ratio at 95 males per 100 females.[17] Many of the black men not counted are transient and unemployed, and so in any case unacceptable to most of our middle-class black singles.

The imbalance in the sex ratio is due to a number of sociological factors. Young black men have a comparatively high mortality rate and many are confined to prisons or mental hospitals or are in the military. The higher rates of male homosexuality and interracial marriage that deduct a large number from the eligible pool are perhaps even more relevant to the situation of middle-class blacks, and the sex ratio is subordinate to the class parameters drawn around the eligible pool. Most single middle-class black women could choose a mate from the pool of men at a lower socioeconomic level, but they are less and less inclined to "marry down." For many of them only men with a comparable or higher status are acceptable. Thus large numbers of women are pushed into singlehood by the lack of men with the requisite characteristics.

Another push factor linked to the sex ratio is the inability to find a compatible mate. Middle-class black men are able to screen out cer-

tain types of women among the abundant number in the eligible
pool. Most likely to be screened out are assertive, independent
women and the physically unattractive. Women who have some opportunity to screen out, if not always to screen in, may be setting
unrealistic standards in terms of the quantity and quality of the
available pool. Women who want a sensitive, supportive, and affectionate mate find that men are socialized into emphasizing the values
of success, leadership, and sexual performance.

Many forces operate as pulls toward singlehood. For example,
marriage may well mean sacrifices, compromises, and sharing. As
modern-day capitalism has shifted its emphasis from production to
consumption, materialist values have been promoted in pursuit of an
individualistic, distinctly nonsharing life style. Some blacks who have
ascended into the affluent middle class, have acquired these values.
The black liberation movement, based on group unity, has, for
some, turned into a cult of the self. As one sage observer noted:

> A movement whose strength had been its non-material-
> ism, a movement fueled by the Black church and rooted
> in Southern folkways and national Black culture, was
> turned into its opposite by America's concessions. . . . In
> the scramble nearly everyone was dancing to the Isley
> Brothers' tune, "Do your own thing, do what you want to
> do" . . . pursuing his or her own interest to the exclusion
> of all else.

How many black singles have succumbed to the materialist tempta-
tions of middle-class America is not known. The imbalanced sex
ratio makes it difficult to sort out the "voluntary" and involuntary
single women. But it is clear that many black singles have determined that marriage, and the commitment and responsibility it entails, is incompatible with pursuit of the good life. Of course, many
will continue to involve themselves in social movements and civic
activities because they have the resources and time to do so. It is
incumbent upon us to note, however, that only a minority of middle-
class black singles participate in such activities.

THE CASE FOR AND AGAINST MARRIAGE

One of the biggest push factors in singlehood is the fear of an
unhappy marriage. And there is some evidence that marriage is an
unhealthy institution, especially for women. One investigation
found that of all the possible sources of stress, marriage and family
problems rank as the primary stress inducer.[19] At the same time
that other studies show the family to be the greatest source of

satisfaction to Americans, the suicide rates, which were formerly lower for married women, are beginning to be higher than those of single women.[20]

Although partisans of singlehood point to such figures to show the negative impact of marriage on basic health, there is another side to the argument. Data on rates of mental disorder (as measured by admissions to mental institutions and outpatient psychiatric care) show that single people have higher rates of mental illness. This is true for both blacks and whites, men and women.[21] The National Center for Health Statistics found that the overall measures of health status indicate that married persons had fewer health problems than nonmarried persons.[22] In one of the most extensive and thorough investigations of the impact of marital status on health, Dr. James Lynch discovered that people at every age who live alone have death rates two to three times higher than those of married individuals. Among nonwhites, for instance, in the critical ages between twenty-five and fifty, twice as many who are divorced or widowed die from hypertensive heart disease as married people of comparable ages. His conclusion is that individuals who live alone are more susceptible to physical and emotional illnesses because they lack the tranquilizing influence of human companionship during life's stresses.[23]

Nevertheless, marriage is obviously a mixed blessing for many people. Studies of black attitudes indicate that from the onset of adolescence, many black men express a desire to shun marriage. Black women are more likely to express their dislike for marriage after having experienced it; research consistently shows the black housewife to be more dissatisfied with her marriage than her white counterpart.[24] Much of this disenchantment is due to the effects of racism and poverty: as income rises, so does marital happiness. Still, with a divorce rate twice as high as whites, the distaste for marriage among blacks in general is clear.

THE RISE OF FEMINISM

Feminism as an organized social movement has attracted very few black women, but its effect on their attitudes toward women's roles has been noticeable. Women typically bear the brunt of the demands of marriage. They are still expected to subordinate their career mobility to the males, to carry most of the burden of housework and child care, and to have their friendships, movements, and activities constrained by their marital status. Although some single black women express the need for egalitarian marriage, it is a demand that can hardly be placed before black men who operate as buyers in a buyers' market. Therefore some single women refuse to consider joining an institution in which their needs have a low priority.

Other signs of feminism are more visible. A number of black
women's organizations devoted to women's issues have been formed
in recent years. One group of black women issued a manifesto that
declared sexism to be a destructive and crippling force within the
black community.[25] *Black Macho and the Myth of the Superwoman*, by
Michelle Wallace, strongly attacked black male sexism.[26] The play,
"For Colored Girls Who Have Considered Suicide," by Ntozake
Shange, with its negative portrayal of black males, has personal appeal for its largely female audience. Unlike white feminism, black
feminism is not a protest against black male political and economic
domination but reflects both societal and interpersonal tensions. One
black woman writer felt compelled to assert:

> The problem is that the personal pain which forms the
> subtext of many White and now Black feminist pro-
> nouncements, a pain which is being experienced most
> acutely in the area of male/female interaction, has social
> origins that have little or nothing to do with sexual polit-
> ics. People are in pain because their personal lives are
> being ravaged as the warfare of the marketplace increas-
> ingly filters into the social order.[27]

Full political and economic equality will hardly be shared by the
ruling white male elite of this country before the grievances of white
women are redressed, and indeed, few expect black women to
achieve equality independent of the race as a whole. It is to be hoped
that the protests of black women will generate some constructive
dialogue between the sexes. On the other hand, black males, belea-
guered themselves, may continue to be defensive and angry. In the
words of Jean Carey Bond, "To the extent that feminists are pro-
moting the very conflict between men and women that they profess
to abhor by . . . [obscuring] the socioeconomic causes of male/female
antagonism, the movement is functioning more as a part of the
problem than as an instrument of the solution."[28]

Black women are victims of sexist values and practices emanating
from within and without the black community. But it is to some
degree different from the sexism faced by white women. There is
less inequality of income between black women and men. Black
women earn about 80 percent of the income of black men while
white women earn 56 percent of white male income. The college-
educated black women in our study actually have a higher median
income than college-educated white women and earn 90 percent of
the median income of college-educated black males.[29] Still, it is the
complex interplay of racism and sexism that places black women in
the dilemma of professional success and interpersonal failure.

SINGLEHOOD AND THE BLACK COMMUNITY

Those who support singlehood as a viable alternative to a monogamous marriage appear to be misreading the relationship of the individual and the culture. In the black community, the family is the major institution in which the hopes and values of blacks are anchored. To view singlehood as a matter of personal choice is to ignore the family's vital role in the maintenance of a cohesive cultural entity. Singlehood as an ideological preference represents the primacy of individual needs over cultural prerequisites. Hence we should use our study to do a sort of cost-benefit analysis of singlehood as a way of life.

The causes of singlehood may be divided between ideological preference and structural restraints. Much of black singlehood among the lower classes is due to structural restraints. The institutional decimation of lower-class black men is so massive that the women of that class are left with few desirable mate choices. These women, however, marry and bear children which they raise with the support of the absent father or an extended family system.

The disadvantages of the single-parent family are reflected in its impact on class mobility. When lower-class black families were intact, the pooling of resources through the joint efforts of the husband and wife enabled many of them to expand their life chances. Because of the decline in the nuclear family unit, that coping technique is not as available. In 1978 black families accounted for 10 percent of all families and only 7 percent of all married-couple families.[30] This decrease is partly responsible for the increase in the gap between black and white family income. From 1970 to 1973, black family income declined from 61 percent to 58 percent of white family income, primarily because of the reduction in the number of blacks married and living with a spouse. As further evidence of the monetary value of the nuclear family, the U.S. Census Bureau reports that young black husband-wife families (husband under thirty-five) in the Northeast and West recently achieved income parity with their white counterparts.[31]

Changes in black marital patterns may have to await larger changes in the social structure. On the other hand, many middle-class black singles maintain their status via an ideological preference. A troublesome singlehood is preferred rather than a compromise of standards for a mate. This choice has some serious implications for the black community. A crucial function of the family is the bearing and rearing of children. Most middle-class black singles are childless.[32] Although blacks as a whole have a higher fertility rate than whites, college-educated black women have the lowest fertility rate of all groups in the United States. The black middle class seems to have defaulted on the task of educating and socializing children. Whether or not singlehood is a matter of individual choice, its ramifications must be borne collectively.

NOTES

The full study of black singles on which this article is based appears in *Black Singles in America*, to be published by Greenwood Press in 1981.

1. U.S. Bureau of the Census, *Marital Status and Living Arrangements: March 1977*. U.S. Government Printing Office, Washington, D.C., 1978.

2. Herbert Gutman, *The Black Family in Slavery and Freedom, 1750–1925*. New York: Pantheon, 1976.

3. St. Clair Drake and Horace Cayton, *Black Metropolis*. Chicago: University of Chicago Press, 1945.

4. U.S. Bureau of the Census, *Marital Status and Living Arrangements: March 1973*. U.S. Government Printing Office, Washington, D.C., 1974.

5. U.S. Bureau of the Census, *Marital Status and Living Arrangements: March 1977*, op. cit.

6. Paul C. Glick and Karen Mills, *Black Families: Marriage Patterns and Living Arrangements*. Atlanta: Atlanta University, 1974, p. 9.

7. Alan Bayer, College impact on marriage. *Journal of Marriage and the Family* 34 (November 1972) 600–618.

8. Glick and Mills, op. cit.

9. Jean Noble, *The Negro Woman College Graduate*. New York: Columbia University Press, 1956, p. 108.

10. U.S. Bureau of the Census, *Money, Income and Poverty Status in 1975 of Families and Persons in the United States and the West Region, by Divisions and States*. U.S. Government Printing Office, Washington, D.C., 1978, pp. 21–22.

11. Number of Blacks Attending College Triples in Decade. *Washington Post*, June 10, 1978, p. A1.

12. U.S. Bureau of the Census, *The Social and Economic Status of the Black Population in the United States: An Historical View 1790–1978*. U.S. Government Printing Office, Washington, D.C., 1978, p. 108.

13. Ruth Gossett, Black Widows, in *The Sexually Oppressed* (H. and J. Gochros, eds.). New York: Association Press, 1977, pp. 84-95.

14. U.S. Bureau of the Census, *Marital Status and Living Arrangements: March 1977*, op. cit.

15. The terms "open-coupled" and "closed-coupled" are borrowed from Bell and Weinberg's typology of homosexual relationships. See Alan Bell and Martin Weinberg, *Homosexualities*. New York: Simon & Schuster, 1978.

16. Peter Stein, *Single*. Englewood Cliffs, N.J.: Prentice Hall, 1976, p. 65.

17. *The Social and Economic Status of the Black Population 1790-1978*, op. cit., p. 16.

18. William Strickland, The rise and fall of black political culture: or how blacks became a minority. *Monthly Report of the Institute of the Black World*, May/June 1979, p. 3.

19. Norval Glenn, The contribution of marriage to the psychological well-being of males and females. *Journal of Marriage and the Family* 37 (1975) 594–599.

20. Jesus Velanco-Rice and Elizabeth Mynko, Suicide and marital status: A changing relationship. *Journal of Marriage and the Family* 35 (May 1973) 239–244.

21. Roger Bastide, *The Sociology of Mental Disorder*. London: Routledge and Kegan Paul, 1972, pp. 154–155; M. Harvey Brenner, *Mental Illness and the Economy*. Cambridge, Mass.: Harvard University Press, 1973, pp. 11–81.

22. Unwed healthier than married. *The San Francisco Examiner*, June 20, 1976, p. 1.

23. James J. Lynch, *The Broken Heart*. New York: Basic Books, 1977, pp. 42, 52, 53.

24. Robert Blood and Donald Wolfe, *Husbands and Wives*. Glencoe, Ill.: The Free Press, 1960; Karen Renne, Correlates of dissatisfaction with marriage. *Journal of Marriage and the Family* 32 (February 1970) 54–67.

25. Statement of the National Black Feminist Organization, 1973.

26. Michelle Wallace, *Black Macho and the Myth of the Superwoman*. New York: Dial Press, 1978.

27. Jean Carey Bond, Two views of "Black Macho and the Myth of the Superwoman." *Freedomways*, First quarter, 1979, p. 20.

28. Ibid.

29. Cf. Diane K. Lewis, A response to inequality: Black women, racism and sexism. *Signs: A Journal of Women in Culture and Society*, Winter 1977, pp. 339–361.

30. Single-woman American households are increasing, census reports. *The Washington Post*, August 14, 1978, p. A24.

31. *The Social and Economic Status of the Black Population 1790–1978*, op. cit., pp. 26–27.

32. U.S. Bureau of the Census, *The Social and Economic Status of the Black Population*, op. cit. p. 129.

PART TWO

THE SEPARATED, DIVORCED, AND WIDOWED

The number of marriages ending in divorce in the United States continues to increase. This trend began about twenty years ago, and today marriage partners have about a one in three chance of becoming divorced within the first seven years. Children have about a one in two chance of spending part of their lives in a single-parent home. Even a person who avoids divorce first-hand may end up in a marriage with a divorced person. Separation also affects at least 2.6 percent of the population over eighteen (mostly men between forty and forty-four and women between thirty-five and thirty-nine) and most separations do end in divorce.

While the Census Bureau deals with the figures of the public side of separation and divorce, individuals struggle with the private trauma it brings to them, their friends, and their families. Social scientists meanwhile look for the link between these points of view. For example, when a group of psychologists conducted a telephone survey of households in the Boulder, Colorado, area to determine the community's need for marriage and divorce counseling and for community intervention programs, they found that the likelihood of any married couple experiencing a separation was nearly 5 percent in one year (with the higher risk among the young) and that most separations, after lasting about one year, ended in divorce. Since the separation period is known to cause severe stress, manifesting itself in many forms of disorders and disease, the authors of this study concluded that community services were sorely needed (Bloom, Hodges, et al., 1977). Social scientists, politicians, and educators all express concern over the increasing divorce rate. Some emphasize what they perceive as a decline in the quality of life and the weakening of family bonds. Others see greater opportunities for self-expression, the exercise of choices, and greater individual freedom. These facts and figures tell more of the divorce story:

•Although, of course, equal numbers of men and women divorce, the number of divorced women at any one time is greater than the number of men because men are more likely to remarry, and to do it more quickly, than women. About five out of every six divorced men remarry, compared to about three out of every four divorced women.

•The median age for divorce (after a first marriage) is twenty-seven for women and twenty-nine for men. However, the median age for those currently in the divorced category is about forty-five. Since young divorcees are more likely to remarry, more older divorcees remain in the divorced category.

•The earlier the average age of the partners at marriage, the greater the likelihood of divorce. Most divorces occur at young ages, typically twenty to twenty-four for women and twenty-five to twenty-nine for men.

•The most typical ages for remarriage after a first divorce are twenty-five to thirty-four for men and twenty to thirty-four for women. For both men and women, thirty-five to forty-four is the most typical age for a second divorce.

•If present trends continue, about 40 percent of Americans in their late twenties and early thirties who remarry after a divorce may expect their second marriage to end in divorce as well.

However high the divorce rates climb, they do not indicate a disillusionment with marriage itself. The story the statistics tell seems to be one of couples disenchanted with their present marriages, searching for the ideal marriage somewhere else, with someone else.

In their article "Marital Instability: Past, Present, and Future" Arthur Norton and Paul Glick use Census Bureau statistics to analyze the state of marriage in this country. They describe how the tendency to marry, divorce, and remarry is influenced by world conditions; how the success of marriage is related to age, education, and income; and how past birth rates have caused the "marriage squeeze" that affects many young women today. The statistics may indicate the end of family life to some, but these authors lean toward a more hopeful interpretation: that the period of adaptation and resocialization of women's roles, though bringing current hard times, will mean long-term gains for the family and society. They anticipate that expectations for relationships will become more in tune with reality and that adjustments by marriage partners will bring less emotional strain. Can the reader agree with this optimistic view? How might current and future world conditions affect marriage trends? What does the declining fertility rate mean for the future of the family? And what does all this mean for the reader's own future?

For those who experience separation at first hand, emotional distress seems unavoidable. Society may be relaxed about divorce, but the individuals involved—whether or not they want out—will grieve when the split does occur. "The Emotional Impact of Marital Separation," by Robert S. Weiss, suggests that marriages do contribute to the well-being of the partners. Though the marriage may have caused years of unhappiness, contemplating its end is likely to make the couple anxious or frightened. The author paints a poignant picture of "separation distress," which makes its effects felt in every area of the separating individual's life. Why is a "clean break" so difficult to achieve? How does the presence of children affect the separation process? How can support networks help individuals deal with separation?

Like the divorced in their loneliness, but unlike them in other fundamental ways, are the widowed. While divorce affects an equal number of women and men, the death of a spouse affects many more women than men. This is due to a difference in life expectancy of women over men of about eight years; to a tendency for women to marry older men; and to the fact that more men die in combat and from diseases such as heart attacks. As a result, wives outnumber husbands as survivors by a ratio of about five to one. To add to the inequality, many more widowers than widows remarry. Fewer than a third of widows ever remarry.

Important differences emerge between divorced and widowed women which are reflected in the way they cope with their social and personal lives. Widows are generally older; they do not have young children; they have completed less formal education; and they are less likely to have been employed. Starr Roxanne Hiltz sums up the social problems of the widow in the title of her article: "Widowhood: A Roleless Role." She describes widowhood as a "collapse of old roles and structural supports—a negatively evaluated social category in which the individual loses the central sources of identity, financial support, and social relationships."

Comparing a number of recent studies, Hiltz points out several interesting facets of widowhood. First is the importance of the widow's working through of grief to be able to build a new identity. Another is learning to cope with financial problems; often a widow's income falls far below the family's previous standard of living. Dealing with loneliness, social isolation, and feeling like a "fifth wheel" is involved in the widow's adjustment as she works out new relationships with children, relatives, and old friends. The importance of establishing supportive relationships with understanding friends, neighbors, or counselors is stressed.

To help the troubled widow, many communities have developed intervention programs. These programs may employ interaction with other widows, professional counselors, or both. Why should it be necessary for widows in our society to forge a total emotional, financial, and social reorganization of their lives at a time when their resources for such a task are generally inadequate? What private and public efforts can be made to replace financial and emotional distress with opportunities for a satisfying life?

REFERENCE

Bloom, Bernard, William Hodges, Robert Caldwell, Laura Systra, and Antonia Cedrone. "Marital Separation: A Community Survey," *Journal of Divorce*, 1:1, Fall, 1977.

5/ MARITAL INSTABILITY IN AMERICA: Past, Present, and Future

Arthur J. Norton and Paul C. Glick

A demographic analysis of trends in marital instability may be made with better factual support if the study features divorce rather than separation. Annual statistics on divorce for the country as a whole are published from vital records, but corresponding statistics on "separation events" are not available. Moreover, the annual statistics on currently separated persons that are published by the Bureau of the Census regularly show a far larger number of women than men reported as separated. In addition, the statistics on separation would be much more meaningful if there were a way of identifying, at a given point in time, the separated persons who would eventually become divorced, those who would become reconciled in their existing marriages, and those who would remain separated. Accordingly, the present discussion focuses attention primarily on probable connections between changes in dissolution of marriage by divorce and concurrent changes in social and economic variables that tend to have an impact on divorce in the United States.

HISTORICAL PERSPECTIVE

Historical trends in American marriage can be traced in terms of patterns of change in vital rates since the early twentieth century. The historical movement of the incidence (or rates) of first marriage, divorce, and remarriage is well documented in the publications of the National Center for Health Statistics (Plateris, 1969; Hetzel and Cappetta, 1971) and in the publications of the U.S. Bureau of the Census (1976, 1977c). Table 1 and Figure 1 show the estimated annual rates of first marriage, divorce, and remarriage in terms of three-year averages for the periods 1921–1923 through 1975–1977. The first marriage rates were calculated with single women under forty-five years old as the base, the divorce rates with married women under forty-five as the base, and the remarriage rates with widowed and divorced women under fifty-five as the base. These bases include about 99 percent of all single women who marry, 85 percent of all married women who became divorced, and 80 percent of all women who remarry in a given year. (When observing trends

---

TABLE 1

NUMBER AND RATE OF FIRST MARRIAGE, DIVORCE, AND RE-
MARRIAGE: UNITED STATES, THREE-YEAR AVERAGES, 1921-1977

Period	First Marriage		Divorce		Remarriage	
	Thousands	Rate[a]	Thousands	Rate[b]	Thousands	Rate[c]
1921–23	990	99	158	10	186	98
1924–26	992	95	177	11	200	99
1927–29	1,025	94	201	12	181	84
1930–32	919	81	183	10	138	61
1933–35	1,081	92	196	11	162	69
1936–38	1,183	98	243	13	201	83
1939–41	1,312	106	269	14	254	103
1942–44	1,247	108	360	17	354	139
1945–47	1,540	143	526	24	425	163
1948–50	1,326	134	397	17	360	135
1951–53	1,190	122	388	16	370	136
1954–56	1,182	120	379	15	353	129
1957–59	1,128	112	381	15	359	129
1960–62	1,205	112	407	16	345	119
1963–65	1,311	109	452	17	415	143
1966–68	1,440	107	535	20	511	166
1969–71	1,649	109	702	26	515	152
1972–74	1,662	103	907	32	601	151
1975–77	1,508	85	1,070	37	646	134

[a]First marriages per 1,000 single women 14 to 44 years old.
[b]Divorces per 1,000 married women 14 to 44 years old.
[c]Remarriages per 1,000 widowed and divorced women 14 to 54 years old.

Source: Glick and Norton, 1977.

---

in marital behavior over an extended period of years, rates for women are generally used because they present a more consistent population base). . . .

The trend lines for each of the three measures display similar patterns until the late 1950s. Each shows low points during the economic depression years of the 1930s, followed by a gradual climb that accelerates to peak levels in the immediate post–World War II period, succeeded by declines into the 1950s. The first marriage rate continued its rather steady decline through the 1960s and into the 1970s; it has now reached a low level similar to that shown for the latter years of the Depression. However, both the divorce rate and the remarriage rate turned upward around 1960 and increased dramatically during the ensuing decade; by then, the divorce and remarriage rates were higher than any previously recorded for this country. The rising remarriage rate might reasonably be interpreted as a corollary of the rising divorce rate, inasmuch as an estimated four out of every five divorced persons eventually remarry (U.S.

FIGURE 1 RATES OF FIRST MARRIAGE, DIVORCE, AND REMARRIAGE FOR U.S. WOMEN: 1921–1977

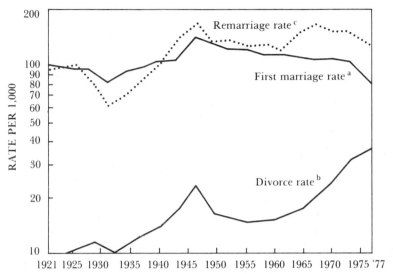

[a]First marriages per 1,000 single women 14 to 44 years old.
[b]Divorces per 1,000 married women 14 to 44 years old.
[c]Remarriages per 1,000 widowed and divorced women 14 to 54 years old.

Bureau of the Census, 1976). Since 1970, however, the divorce rate has continued its steep upward movement while the remarriage rate has declined sharply.

Another measure of the rise in marital disruption was derived from a special survey on marital history conducted by the Bureau of the Census in June 1975. The assumption was made that the future divorce experience of young women will produce future increments in the percentage divorced that are the same as those for successively older cohorts of women in the early 1970s. Using this procedure, a projection was made indicating that four out of every ten marriages contracted by women born between 1945 and 1949 would eventually end in divorce, a figure substantially higher than the estimated three out of every ten for women born just a decade earlier (U.S. Bureau of the Census, 1976). However, the decrease in marriage rates and increase in divorce rates cannot continue indefinitely because the pool of divorce eligibles would eventually be used up.

Inspection of the rates in Figure 1 confirms the undeniable connection between the disposition of people to marry, divorce, or remarry and the contingencies of particular time periods. Apparently the Depression of the 1930s caused a downturn in all of these vital rates, whereas the period of relief and release experienced in the immediate post–World War II era gave rise to a temporary but substantial increase in all these rates. The rapid increase in the level of divorce during the 1960s came at a time when divorce laws were being liberalized and when the social structure at large was in a transitory state, a time when basic social institutions, values, and ascribed roles were being questioned and alternatives were being tested. Some have characterized the 1970s as an era of social uncertainty marked by a movement toward individualism which could be partly responsible for the continued increase of the divorce rate and the overall decline of the marriage rate.

Among the variables that have been shown to have an impact on marital stability are age at first marriage and level of education and income. Reports on several studies have demonstrated that divorce after first marriage was inversely related to age at marriage, education, and income considered separately, but without regard to interaction between these variables (Glick and Norton, 1977; U.S. Bureau of the Census, 1977c). Bumpass and Sweet (1972) reported a high correlation between early age at marriage and marital instability among white ever-married women under the age of forty-five. They also reported that the effect of education on marital disruption is minimal when age at marriage is controlled, but early marriage and low educational attainment are closely correlated among white women (U.S. Bureau of the Census, 1973).

The results of the 1970 census showed that among persons who first married between 1901 and 1970, the proportion of men who were divorced after their first marriage was more than twice as high for those who married before the age of twenty as for those who married in their late twenties; it was more than twice as high for women who married before eighteen as for those who first married in their early twenties (U.S. Bureau of the Census, 1973). A substantial proportion of persons who married at a later age had delayed marriage while attending college. Among both men and women who had ever married, the highest proportion who were known to divorce after their first or last marriage (or both) was of those with an incomplete high school education (U.S. Bureau of the Census, 1972).

Similarly, men on the lower rungs of the income ladder in 1970 had a greater proportion known to have been divorced than those with higher incomes. For females, however, the opposite was true; divorced women with a relatively high personal income level tended to delay remarriage or to remain unmarried, whereas those with relatively low incomes tended to remarry within a short time (U.S. Bureau of the Census, 1972).

The median age at first marriage for men and women in the United States was first computed for 1890 when it was 26.1 years for men and 22.0 years for women (U.S. Bureau of the Census, 1977a). There was a fairly constant decline in the ages at which men and women married from the turn of the century to the mid-1950s. The median ages at first marriage for men and women in 1956 were the lowest recorded in the history of the United States—22.5 years for men and 20.1 for women—and remained at about the same level until the mid-1960s. Since that time, however, the median age at first marriage for both men and women has increased by approximately one year, so that in 1976 the median for men was 23.8 years and that for women 21.3 years.

The increasing tendency during the last decade for men and women to marry at later ages may reflect, in part, the demographic phenomenon referred to as the "marriage squeeze" (Parke and Glick, 1967). This phenomenon depends on the presence of two conditions: (a) a changing level of births, and (b) a traditional differential in the ages at which men and women marry for the first time. In the United States both conditions have been present. Women have traditionally married men a few years older than they are, and the birth rate in this country has been subject to fluctuations that varied from moderate to radical.

The squeeze situation in the mid-1960s arose because more women eighteen and nineteen years old in 1965 were entering the marriage market than were men twenty and twenty-one years old in that year; the women were members of large post–World War II birth cohorts, whereas the eligible or targeted men were members of smaller birth cohorts conceived before the end of the war. In addition, the scarcity of young men was intensified by the large increase in the armed forces during the war in Vietnam and the simultaneous acceleration of college enrollment.

Available data suggest that the squeeze was partially resolved by a process whereby many young women in the vanguard of the "baby boom" either postponed marriage as they moved into adulthood or ultimately married men more nearly their own age.

Thus the marriage squeeze may have been an initial contributor to the establishment of a pattern of delaying marriage, particularly among young women, beyond ages traditionally considered the prime ages for first marriage. The extent of this delay may best be seen by pointing out that in 1960, 28 percent of women twenty to twenty-four years old were single, but in 1976 the corresponding proportion single had increased to 43 percent (U.S. Bureau of the Census, 1977a).

Concomitant developments associated with this delay in marriage among young adults are far-reaching. Especially among young women, postponement of marriage had occurred along with the pursuit of advanced education or career experience, as a prelude to entering into a family living situation, thus providing women with the basis for role expansion beyond that of wife and mother. Increasing postponement of first marriage has been a major aspect of the emerging pattern of transitional living arrangements among many young adults after they leave their parental homes, but before they marry conventionally and form their own families.

College enrollment of both men and women increased markedly during the sixteen years from 1960 to 1976, after being fairly stable during the 1950s. For example, 11 percent of all persons twenty to twenty-four years old in 1960 were enrolled in college as compared to 23 percent in 1976. For men aged twenty to twenty-four, the enrollment rate was more than half again as large in 1976 as in 1960, and for women in their early twenties it more than doubled in those sixteen years (U.S. Bureau of the Census, 1964, 1977b). In addition, there was a sharp upturn in the labor force participation of young women over the past quarter-century, a change almost entirely due to the participation rates of young married women. Among women twenty to twenty-four years old who were married and living with their husbands, about 26 percent were members of the labor force in 1950, as compared to 57 percent in 1975; similarly, for women twenty-five to twenty-nine years old of the same marital status the comparable increase was from 22 percent in 1950 to 50 percent in 1975.

Most of the socioeconomic indicators discussed here which have been traditionally linked to marital discord (young age at marriage, low education, low occupation, and low income) have been changing in directions that would lessen their impact on marital stability. Why, then, has the level of divorce continued to rise? The current period of adaptation and resocialization regarding the roles of women, particularly as they apply to marriage and family living, will not be passed through easily, especially for those who have deeply entrenched traditional views. In the long run, the broadening of work-and-marriage experience seems likely to encourage women to develop a greater self-perception as players of multiple roles and to result in familial and societal gains; however, the short-term effects may be somewhat disruptive. A married woman—especially one who works in a different establishment from that of her husband—may become economically self-sustaining and, therefore, be more in a position to dissolve a marriage that does not seem viable. Likewise, this circumstance can lessen the economic constraints on men confronted with a potential divorce.

Perhaps more important than this practical consideration is the more theoretical and general impact on marital stability of the need for couples to adjust to a traditional institution (marriage) that is in a state of transition. No longer are the roles of husbands (breadwinners) and wives (homemakers) simply conplementary and clearly defined or agreed upon. Marital and familial responsibilities between partners now often overlap; this may generate conflict, which promotes eventual separation. As time goes on, however, expectations regarding marital roles and relationships should become more consistent with "real-world" experiences. In other words, if and when the period of structural transition of the institution of marriage should end, the adjustment to be made by the partners should ideally create less of an emotional strain.

RECENT CHANGES IN DIVORCE

The upsurge of divorce in this country during the past ten years has been stimulated by a growing acceptance of the principle that divorce is a reasonable alternative to an unhappy marriage. While negative sanctions have diminished, so too have the legal and economic constraints of obtaining divorces. The reform of divorce laws has resulted in the shortening of the required period of residence in the state and the required period of separation. Moreover, all but a few states have adopted some form of no-fault divorce and most of the other state legislatures are attempting to incorporate this feature into their legal codes.

Whether or not some of the states have what can be termed "true" no-fault divorce is subject to debate. Yet the fact remains that there has been widespread official recognition of the need to overhaul the legal machinery involved in the granting of divorce decrees so that the demands of citizens will be more equitably accommodated. Implicit in most of the administrative changes is a reduction of the economic costs involved in divorce. In addition, the availability of free legal service has enabled many impoverished families to finalize disrupted marriages by divorce.

The elimination of many barriers previously inhibiting divorce has been relatively recent and rapid. Consequently, it seems reasonable to speculate that at least part of the recent increase in the divorce rate may represent an acceleration in the timing of divorces that, under previous conditions, would have been spread over a longer number of years. If this is the case, one might expect the rate of divorce either to eventually decline or at least to level off. In fact, after a decade of steady annual increases during which the divorce rate per 1,000 population doubled (from 2.5 in 1966 to 5.0 in 1976), the rate has begun to level off. Thus, as of February 1978, the twelve-month divorce rate had remained stable at 5.0 for twenty of twenty-three consecutive months.

At the same time, of course, the argument can be made that the ease with which divorces can now be obtained will likely continue to bring an early termination of many marriages that are near the borderline of viability.

The increased incidence of divorce in this country has occurred at all socioeconomic levels; yet data from the 1970 census (U.S. Bureau of the Census, 1972) for ever-married persons thirty-five to forty-four years old showed the proportion of persons ever-divorced remains clearly the highest for relatively disadvantaged groups. This age group is used for comparative purposes because its members are old enough to have experienced most of their lifetime marriages and divorces and yet are young enough to reflect much of the impact of the recent changes discussed above.

Men thirty-five to forty-four with low incomes and with a low level of educational attainment were more likely to have been divorced than men with higher incomes and educational attainment. Women of this age range with low educational attainment showed the same pattern of greater likelihood of divorce. Also, a higher proportion of women thirty-five to forty-four years old who were in the labor force in 1970 were known to have been divorced than were women of the same age who were not in the labor force—although information is not available to show how many of these women had already entered the labor force well before the time they became divorced. The proportion currently divorced at each survey date is relatively small because this measure disregards the fact that about three-fourths of the women and five-sixths of the men remarry after divorce. Furthermore, the 1970 census shows that 3.8 percent of all ever-married men and 5.0 percent of all ever-married women were currently divorced at the time of the census, but that more than 14 percent of both the men and the women were known to have obtained a divorce. This means that only a small proportion of the adults who had ever experienced a divorce were still divorced at the time of the 1970 census. Nonetheless, revealing comparisons showing the convergence of divorce by social level between 1960 and 1970 can be made by the use of proportions of persons currently divorced.

Between these two dates the proportion divorced among men thirty-five to forty-four years old tended to converge among the educational, occupational, and income groups. As mentioned above, men in the upper status groups continue to have a below average proportion divorced (but not remarried). However, the rate of increase in the proportion divorced was more rapid among men in upper as compared to lower status groups between 1960 and 1970 (U.S. Bureau of the Census, 1967, 1972). These results become even more meaningful when one recognizes that the extent of remarriage among the divorced is greater for men at the upper status levels than for men at the lower levels.

Among women thirty-five to forty-four a general trend toward convergence among status levels of the proportion divorced also occurred between 1960 and 1970, but in the opposite direction from that for men. The proportion divorced among all women thirty-five to forty-four went up by nearly one-half during the 1960s; however, among women who were professional workers or who were in the highest income categories (where the proportion divorced for women, unlike men, has been characteristically quite high), the percentage divorced rose by a smaller proportion than among other women. Thus, for upper-status women the percentage divorced was converging with that for other women by increasing more slowly than the average, whereas for upper-status men the percentage divorced was converging with that for other men by increasing more rapidly than the average.

Data from the June 1975 marital history survey indicate that the trend toward convergence in the proportion divorced among different levels of educational achievement for both men and women has continued through the first half of this decade (U.S. Bureau of the Census, 1977c). In fact, by 1975 the proportion divorced for men with one or more years of college had risen to the level for all other men. However, men and women with four years of college still had the lowest proportions divorced.

The important conclusion that can be drawn from these trends is that the recent increase in divorce has been pervasive with regard to social and economic level, but that socioeconomic differences in divorce are now smaller than they used to be.

Although blacks and whites display generally similar patterns of divorce by social and economic characteristics, the incidence of divorce is uniformly higher for blacks than for whites. In 1975, 25 percent of ever-married black men and women thirty-five to forty-four years old were known to have had a divorce. The comparable figures for white men and women in 1975 were 19 percent and 21 percent, respectively.

A further indication of the higher rate of marital disruption among blacks than among whites is the difference in the proportions of people reporting themselves as separated but not divorced. In 1976, 10 percent of all black men thirty-five to forty-four and 15 percent of all black women thirty-five to forty-four were reported as separated, whereas 2 percent of white men and 4 percent of white women of the same age were separated. Between 1960 and 1976, the proportion separated and the proportion divorced increased among both black and white men and women thirty-five to forty-four years old; however, the rate of increase for each race and sex group was larger for the proportion divorced (Glick and Mills, 1975; U.S. Bureau of the Census, 1977a). This finding brings out the significant fact that decreasing proportions of those with marital problems are leaving them legally unresolved and increasing proportions are resolving them by becoming divorced.

Despite an increasing similarity in the form of marital disruption displayed by the two racial groups, major differences continue to exist. These differences seem to be linked with both the overall level of disruption and the promptness with which divorce and remarriage follow separation. Findings from the 1975 marital history survey showed that although whites and blacks had similar durations of first marriage before divorce, white men and women remarried much sooner than their black counterparts (U.S. Bureau of the Census, 1976). But even though blacks have a generally higher rate of disruption through marital discord than whites, the estimated rates of disruption for those with racial intermarriages is even greater. Using data from the 1960 and 1970 censuses, Heer (1974) reported "clearly the black-white marriages are shown to be less stable than racially homogeneous marriages."

Another characteristic reflecting recent changes in divorce is the presence of children among couples involved in a divorce. The U.S. National Center for Health Statistics (1977a) reports that an estimated 1,123,000 children were involved in divorces and annulments in 1975, an average of 1.08 children per decree. Although the estimated number of children involved in all divorces has been increasing steadily (logically enough, given the overall increase in divorce), the average per decree has been declining in recent years; in 1964 the average reached a peak of 1.36 children per decree. Perhaps the main reason for the decline is the recent decrease in the birth rate. Other reasons include a slight increase in the proportion childless at divorce, although six out of ten divorces in 1975 were among couples who had children and the estimated interval between marriage and divorce decreased from 7.2 years in 1960 to 7.0 years in 1968, and to 6.5 years in 1975. The estimate of the percentage of divorcing couples who were childless was published by the U.S. National Center for Health Statistics on the basis of data reported for the divorce-registration area (DRA) which in 1975 was composed of 29 participating states, each of which used closely conforming certificates of divorce or annulment and cooperated in testing for completeness and accuracy of divorce registration.

The recently declining fertility rate may have contributed to the rise in the divorce rate. Women with small families are more likely to be in the labor force and, therefore, financially independent of their husbands. And as family size has declined, the proportion of children in the family who are of preschool age has declined. This additional development has tended to free the time of the potential divorcee for work outside the home.

Among other factors which may have influenced the recent rise in divorce are an increase in premarital conceptions and the so-called "incentives" toward family disruption found in the present welfare system. As Davis (1972) points out, premarital conception is conducive to divorce, and an increase in family formation in such circumstances tends to increase the divorce rate. The impact of the welfare system on family and marital disruption is open to debate. Various social scientists have studied this problem and have arrived at conflicting or opposing conclusions (Cutright and Scanzoni, 1973; Honig, 1973).

Other possible contributors to the rising level of divorce include the prevalence of intergenerational divorce, the effects of intergenerational mobility up and down the socioeconomic ladder, and the problems faced by veterans returning from the war in Vietnam. The returnees are of special interest because they came back from an unpopular war and were sometimes made to feel that they personified the official war policy. This atmosphere must have affected their ability to adjust to traditional life styles.

Since divorcing has always been largely confined to relatively young adults, the lifetime behavior of persons born during the high fertility years that spanned the period between 1947 and the early 1960s will be of major import in this context. As we have pointed out, "the experience of this population subgroup—largely because of its size—is different from that of any other in the age spectrum. During their lives they have faced, and will continue to face, greater competition for fewer opportunities than their predecessors did or their successors will. They are finding that traditional institutions have not been able to respond effectively to their needs, and their patterns of action have begun to deviate in certain ways from past norms" (Norton and Glick, 1976). Thus, it is clear that their decisions involving marriage, divorce, and living arrangements will have a profound and lasting impact on future life styles. As the vanguard of this group has reached adulthood, patterns of change have already become evident. Along with a postponement of first marriage has been an increased tendency to leave parental homes in favor of setting up nonfamily households either as lone individuals or as sharing partners. The latter group includes the often-discussed "living together" couples who have more than doubled in number since 1970 (Glick and Norton, 1977). Whether these developments represent a prelude to entering into more traditionally conventional family living arrangements or herald the beginnings of a new concept of family living is not clear.

Speculations regarding the future of marriage and divorce in this country are tenuous; nonetheless, the authors have called attention to those factors which seem likely to have an impact on marital behavior over the next several years. Additional observations of marital behavior from year to year will surely provide the students of marriage and the family with better explanations of the current situation than anyone can give with confidence today.

REFERENCES

Bumpass, L., & Sweet, J. Differentials in marital instability: 1970. *American Sociological Review*, 1972, *37*, 754–766.

Cutright, P., & Scanzoni, J. *Income supplements and the American family* (Joint Economic Committee Paper No. 12, The Family, Poverty and Welfare Programs). Washington, D.C.: U.S. Government Printing Office, 1973.

Davis, K. The American family in relation to demographic change. In C. F. Westoff & R. Parke, Jr. (Eds.), *Report of the U.S. Commission on population growth and the American future: Demographic and social aspects of population growth* (Vol. 1). Washington, D.C.: U.S. Government Printing Office, 1972.

Glick, P. C., & Mills, K. M. Black families: Marriage patterns and living arrangements. *Proceedings of the W.E.B. Dubois Conference on American Blacks*, 1975.

Glick, P. C., & Norton, A. J. Frequency, duration, and probability of marriage and divorce. *Journal of Marriage and the Family*, 1971, *33*, 307–317.

Glick, P. C., & Norton, A. J. Marrying, divorcing, and living together in the U.S. today. *Population Bulletin*, 1977, *32*(5).

Heer, D. M. The prevalence of black-white marriage in the United States, 1960 and 1970. *Journal of Marriage and the Family*, 1974, *36*, 246–258.

Hetzel, A. M., & Cappetta, M. *Marriages: Trends and characteristics* (National Center for Health Statistics, Vital and Health Statistics, Series 21, No. 21). Washington, D.C.: U.S. Government Printing Office, 1971.

Honig, M. *The impact of welfare payment levels on family stability* (Joint Economic Committee Paper No. 12, The Family, Poverty and Welfare Programs). Washington, D.C.: U.S. Government Printing Office, 1973.

*Norton, A. J., & Glick, P. C. The changing American household. *Intercom*, 1976, *4*(10), 8–9.

Parke, R., Jr., & Glick, P. C. Prospective changes in marriage and the family. *Journal of Marriage and the Family*, 1967, *29*, 249–256.

Plateris, A. A. *Divorce statistics analysis: United States 1964 and 1965* (National Center for Health Statistics, Vital and Health Statistics, Series 21, No. 17). Washington, D.C.: U.S. Government Printing Office, 1969.

U.S. Bureau of the Census. *1960 census of population: School enrollment* (Final Report PC(2)-5A). Washington, D.C.: U.S. Government Printing Office, 1964.

U.S. Bureau of the Census. *1960 census of population: Marital status* (Final Report PC(2)-4E). Washington, D.C.: U.S. Government Printing Office, 1967.

U.S. Bureau of the Census. *1970 census of population: Marital status* (Final Report PC(2)-4C). Washington, D.C.: U.S. Government Printing Office, 1972.

U.S. Bureau of the Census. *1970 census of population: Age at first marriage* (Final Report PC(2)-4D). Washington, D.C.: U.S. Government Printing Office, 1973.

U.S. Bureau of the Census. *Number, timing, and duration of marriages and divorces in the United States: June 1975* (Current Population Reports, Series P-20, No. 297). Washington, D.C.: U.S. Government Printing Office, 1976.

U.S. Bureau of the Census. *Marital status and living arrangements: March 1976* (Current Population Reports, Series P-20, No. 306). Washington, D.C.: U.S. Government Printing Office, 1977(a).

U.S. Bureau of the Census. *School enrollment—social and economic characteristics of students: October 1976* (Current Population Reports, Series P-20, No. 309). Washington, D.C.: U.S. Government Printing Office, 1977(b).

U.S. Bureau of the Census. *Marriage, divorce, widowhood, and remarriage by family characteristics: June 1975* (Current Population Reports, Series P-20, No. 312). Washington D.C.: U.S. Government Printing Office, 1977(c).

U.S. National Center for Health Statistics. *Monthly Vital Statistics Report* (Vol. 25, No. 13). Washington, D.C.: U.S. Government Printing Office, 1977(a).

U.S. National Center for Health Statistics. *Monthly Vital Statistics Report* (Vol. 26, No. 8). Washington, D.C.: U.S. Government Printing Office, 1977(b).

6/ THE EMOTIONAL IMPACT OF MARITAL SEPARATION

Robert S. Weiss

In Goode's (1956) survey of divorced mothers, about two-thirds said that some level of trauma had been associated with the disruption of their marriage, for the most part occurring either at the time of final decision or at the time of actual separation. Goode's approach relied on survey interviews, in many cases held years after the point of separation. Insofar as retrospective reconstructions may be expected to err in the direction of minimization of distress, we might assume Goode's respondents to have understated the regularity with which marital separation gives rise to distress.

As yet there have been no survey studies comparable to Goode's in which men as well as women were interviewed. But on the basis of group discussions with separated men and women it appears that marital separation is as likely to be distressing for men as for women (Weiss, 1975).

Being the spouse who initiated the separation does not seem to be especially important in deciding whether the separation will be accompanied by distress. Goode's data suggest that it helps a bit to be the one who first suggested the divorce, but it does not help a great deal. Both those respondents who defined themselves as having been left by the spouse and those who defined themselves as having been the leavers appeared to be distressed by the end of the marriage.

A recent study of recovery from bereavement provides further evidence that marital disruption almost uniformly gives rise to distress, irrespective of the quality of the marriage. In this study fifty-two widows and twenty-two widowers were interviewed within the first three weeks after the death of their spouse, again a month later, and again about a year later (Glick, Weiss, & Parkes, 1974). These widows and widowers, all forty-five or younger, included all individuals bereaved within the study period in the age category of interest who lived in the Boston metropolitan region and were willing to cooperate with the study. Only three of these widows and widowers appeared not to have experienced marked grief. Only one seemed not to have suffered grief at all: a woman whose alcoholic husband had several times left her and had moved in with another woman at the time of his death.

Except for disproportionate representation of alcoholic husbands, the marriages dealt with in this study appear to have been the usual run, some very good, some adequate, and some unhappy. The near universality in this sample of distress on loss of the spouse suggests that within American society virtually all marriages, happy or unhappy, make an important contribution to the well-being of the partners.

This study found no simple association between the intensity of grief and the happiness attributed to the marriage. Grief appeared to be somewhat less intense than typical in instances where there had been estrangement between the spouses but also in instances where the marriage had been extremely close. Apart from minor variations, however, nearly disabling grief was the rule even among individuals who could say about the preceding marriage, as one widow did, "Ours wasn't the best marriage in the world."

A PERSISTENT MARITAL BOND

The (Harvard) Laboratory of Community Psychiatry, during the three years beginning in 1971, provided a program of eight educationally oriented meetings for recently separated individuals. This program, called "Seminars for the Separated" (Weiss, 1975), contained both a didactic (or instructive) component and an opportunity for group discussion. Participants included individuals of widely varying educational attainment, but were for the most part college-educated. About 150 recently separated individuals at some point participated in this program. The participants, although self-selected, did not differ from Goode's survey respondents in the kind of distress they reported, and their more detailed descriptions may provide a basis for better understanding of the nature of that distress.

Several participants in the seminars said that even though their marriage had become unhappy, contemplating its end had made them anxious, even terrified. A woman about thirty years of age reported, "When the idea occurred to me that I could live without Dave and be happier, my immediate next feeling was just gut fear. It's really hard to explain. It was just terror."

This suggests that even though a marriage may have become burdensome, it may nevertheless continue to provide security at least to the extent of fending off anxiety. Other participants in seminars for the separated reported that after their separation they now and again felt impelled by anxiety to reestablish contact with their spouse: to telephone or to see the spouse. In a few cases anxiety was reduced simply by driving by where the spouse now lived.

Some among the separated felt drawn to the spouse without being able to account for the feeling. One man whose wife worked in a bookstore repeatedly visited there, even though his wife was rude to him when he encountered her. Another man reported that although he was angry with his wife and resented what he felt to be mistreatment by her, he was disappointed if she was not at home when he visited his children. A woman who was exasperated by her continued yearning for her husband said, "It is like the battered child syndrome. You never find a battered child that does not want to be back with its parents, because they are the only parents it has. I just have very much this feeling."

Most among the separated continue to feel drawn to the spouse even when a new relationship is established which appears in many respects satisfactory. There may be exceptions to this generalization, especially among individuals who left their marriages for relationships that had already become emotionally important to them. But by and large another figure is not easily substitutable for the original partner, and individuals may continue to pine for the spouse even after they have established new relationships. A man whose wife had left him as the final scene in a stormy marriage and who thereupon traveled across the continent to see a former girl friend said, "Here I was, three days with someone of the opposite sex, trying to start rebuilding, and I just got overwhelmed with panic at being three thousand miles from Laura. And these waves built up until I was just white. It is an unbearable feeling."

The marital bond whose characteristics we are noting appears to be unrelated to liking, admiration, or respect. Some among the separated reported that they could continue to like their spouses, even though they or their spouses had decided that they would no longer live together. But even those who now disparaged their spouses felt drawn to them. One woman said of her ex-husband, "I don't like him. As a man I find him boring. If I met him at a party

I'd talk with him for about two minutes and then I'd say, 'I'll see you.' But the emotional tug is still there. He is still attractive to me."

To summarize, there persists after the end of most marriages, whether the marriages have been happy or unhappy, whether their disruption has been sought or not, a sense of bonding to the spouse. Some feel anxious, fearful, or terrified both when contemplating a prospective separation from the spouse and when experiencing the spouse's absence. Others feel drawn to the spouse after separation, even though they may have decided against a continued relationship with the spouse. Pining for the spouse may continue despite the availability of alternative relationships and despite absence of liking, admiration, or respect. In all these ways this persisting bond to the spouse resembles the *attachment bond* of children to parents described by Bowlby (1969). Indeed, it seems reasonable to surmise that the bond we observe to persist in unhappy marriages is an adult development of childhood attachment. I will, in consequence, refer to it as attachment (Bowlby, 1969, 1973; Cohen, 1974).

An issue of some interest is the relationship between attachment and love. Most people would seem to think of love as a condition combining positive regard for another with urgent desire to maintain the other's accessibility. Rubin (1973) has shown that love is ordinarily a syndrome including a number of components such as trust, idealization, and liking which can exist independently of one another. Attachment would be one such component. It would appear that in unhappy marriages most of the components of love fade, sometimes to be replaced by their opposites. In this way trust may change to mistrust, idealization to disrespect, liking to disdain. Attachment, however, seems to persist. It appears that most components of love are modifiable by negative experience, but that attachment once developed can be sustained by proximity alone and fades only slowly in response to absence.

Data collected in a study of early marriage[1] suggest that a significant minority of marriages may be entered by individuals whose attachment to one another is not yet firm, who remain in some degree attached to a parent. Continued attachment to a parent is displayed by separation distress on contemplating departure from the parental home and homesickness while on the honeymoon. Yet it appears from our study of bereavement that loss of a spouse almost uniformly produces intense distress. It seems reasonable to conclude that the marital relationship sponsors attachment even in couples who were not attached to one another when they married. It might perhaps do so through the intensity of shared emotional experiences (which may facilitate the spouses becoming emotionally charged for one another), through the nearly continuous intimate contact with one another required by marriage, and through the barriers established by marriage to other intimate relationships.

RESPONSES TO LOSS OF ATTACHMENT

The disruption of attachment is a major source of emotional disturbance following separation, but it is far from the only such source. Marital separation is an extensively disruptive event, not only ending the continued accessibility of the spouse but also producing fundamental changes in an individual's social role and in his or her relationships with children, kin, and friends. Reactions to the loss of the spouse as attachment figure become intermeshed with reactions to these other disruptions.

The loss of attachment may, however, be seen as the primary cause of the "separation distress" syndrome described by Parkes (1972). It includes the organization of attention around the image of the lost figure, an urge to make contact with the lost figure, anger toward the lost figure, guilt for having produced the loss, and the presence of an "alarm reaction" (Parkes's term), including hyper-alertness to indications of the lost figure's return, great restlessness, and feelings of fear or panic. Difficulties in sleeping and, to a lesser extent, loss of appetite are also expressions of heightened vigilance.

The symptoms of separation distress in adults are very similar to those exhibited by young children who have lost attachment figures. One list of reactions among children to loss of a parent includes, among others, rage and protest over desertion, maintenance of an intense fantasy relationship with the lost parent, persistent efforts at reunion, anxiety, and a strong sense of narcissistic injury (Crumley & Blumenthal, 1973; Bowlby, 1973). Some among the separated themselves recognize the similarities between their current experience of marital separation and an earlier experience in which they were separated from parents.

> When my husband left I had this panicky feeling which was out of proportion to what was really happening. I was afraid I was being abandoned. I couldn't shake the feeling. I remembered later that the first time I had that feeling was when I had pneumonia and my mother left me in the hospital, in a private room, in the winter. And this picture came back of this hospital and these old gray rooms, and it was winter and every night at five o'clock, when the shadows would come across my bed, my mother would put on her coat and say: "Goodbye, I will see you tomorrow." And I had such a feeling of panic and fear at being left.

In what would at first appear to be a very different sort of reaction from this, some recently separated individuals are euphoric for varying intervals. They report not a diminution in self-confidence and self-esteem but rather an increase. They may insist that the separation was wholly for the best, that they feel that by separating they have opened the world for themselves, that their lives have suddenly become adventures in which they are totally engaged. Individuals experiencing this euphoric mood may be untroubled by minor reverses that would once have upset them: by a parking ticket, for example, or a missed appointment. They may become more active and outgoing than they had been previously.

It seemed unusual, at least among participants in Seminars for the Separated, for euphoria to be reported as a dominant mood throughout the period following separation. Much more often it alternated with separation distress or only briefly interrupted separation distress, a circumstance which suggests that it may be another approach to managing a loss of an attachment figure. The following excerpt from one man's diary suggests what may be the process involved:

> I woke about four, thinking about [a further rejection by his wife]. I wondered what I might have done to provoke it. I couldn't get back to sleep. I got out of bed and made myself follow my morning routine . . . [Later] I got dressed and went out. It was still early so I started to walk, instead of taking the bus. It was a brisk, snowy morning, just after dawn. I suddenly felt happy. I had gotten myself through the night. I was going to see people during the day. I was all right. It was a fine world.

What we see in this quotation is a shift from the insecurity of separation distress to the self-confidence of euphoria. The early waking and the agitation suggested by "I couldn't get back to sleep" suggest tension stemming from rejection by the figure whose accessibility had been security-providing. But then the individual's recognition that he had been able to manage alone seems to have convinced him that he would be able to care for himself in the future. When he says "I had gotten myself through the night," he seems to be saying that he had provided himself with reassurance, just as, if things had been different, another person might have provided such reassurance. He felt that he could serve as the guarantor of his own security and in consequence needed no one else. My surmise is that the mechanism responsible for euphoria is the establishment of just such a narcissistic attachment.

Corroboration for this surmise is furnished by the observation that euphoria can be ended by a demonstration that the self is in some significant respect inadequate. Euphoria is likely to disappear suddenly should the individual suffer rejection or serious failure—should he or she, for example, be rejected by a potential date. The individual thereupon is likely not to feel only a bit sadder or to sustain only slightly reduced self-esteem, but to experience the full impact of unmitigated separation distress.

Separation distress, as a syndrome of symptoms one of which is continued pining for the spouse, seems to fade as time passes without contact with the spouse. However, those who do not form a new attachment-providing relationship are likely to discover, when separation distress fades, that its place is taken by loneliness. Loneliness too produces feelings of restlessness, vigilance, anxiety, even panic. But there is in loneliness no image of a particular figure whose accessibility would return the individual to security. Instead there is only a vaguely developed image of a satisfying relationship that would allay the loneliness—often together with the conviction that the world is barren of anyone with whom such a relationship could be established. Lonely individuals sometimes also feel a barrenness of internal community which they may describe by saying that they feel "hollow" or "empty" (Weiss, 1973). Loneliness of this sort can be characterized as "separation distress without an object."

ANGER AS A RESPONSE TO LOSS OF ATTACHMENT

Since loss of attachment produces the intense discomfort of separation distress, it might be expected to give rise to anger. In bereavement there is ordinarily no clear object for anger, although anger is sometimes expressed toward medical personnel and more rarely toward the spouse or the self (Glick, Weiss, & Parkes, 1974). In marital separation, in contrast, the spouse is ordinarily seen as bearing responsibility for the separation. This attribution is particularly likely if the spouse has initiated the separation and refused pleas for reconciliation. But anger with the spouse may also be felt by individuals who themselves initiated the separation, since they may feel that they were forced to do so by the spouse's faults.

Separating spouses may be angry with each other not only because they blame each other for their distress but also because of genuine conflicts of interest. Such conflicts are most likely to occur in relation to property division, support payments, custody of the children, and visitation. Except in relation to visitation, resolutions of all these issues are zero-sum: What one spouse gets, the other loses. As a result, each spouse may be led to view the other as an antagonist in relation to issues of vital importance.

Anger toward the spouse can become intense. In some individuals the feeling is one they had never before experienced. One young woman said, "In separating from someone you discover in yourself things that you had never felt before in your life. That's one of the things that really freaks you out. I've always used my mind to keep down anything I didn't like. And now I discover, wow, I can hate!"

Occasional individuals have murderous fantasies about their spouses. One man said that after reading a newspaper story about an estranged husband who had shot his wife with a rifle, he decided that he could do that too. Some feel their anger to be entirely justified and may be willing to act to hurt the spouse. But others feel their anger as alien from their genuine selves and wish to disown it. The latter was illustrated by a young woman who said: "In many respects I really do hate my husband. But I don't want to think nothing but hate. You know, when I see him walking down the street, I don't want to think, 'I hope when you step off the corner you get run over.' "

Yet even when an individual seems most enraged with his or her spouse, the suppression of positive feelings rarely seems complete. Often it is possible to discern within the expression of hostility an attempt to maintain proximity. One man telephoned his wife at two in the morning to tell her that he would kill her if she did not permit him to see his children. To be sure, he was terrorizing her; but he was also keeping in touch. Quarrels over property, money, and custody sometimes appear to have as one aim keeping the relationship alive through transfusions of hostility. An older woman said:

> I call him up about everything—if the child is sick and I want him to pay for a doctor, or I need money for a baseball glove. I haven't money for taxes, for anything. He is purposely torturing me and making me do this. He wants me to call up. So he can hang up the receiver. Because that's what he does. He curses at me, he hangs up on me.

THE MANAGEMENT OF AMBIVALENCE

Continued attachment produces both desire to rejoin the spouse and, because of the spouse's role in the production of separation distress, intense anger with the spouse. There are also likely to be additional motives for rejoining the spouse, such as shared responsibility for children, and, as has been noted, additional motives for anger.

Because they remain attached to each other and are simultaneously angry with each other, the relationship of separated spouses is intensely ambivalent. One of the problems the separated must deal with is the management of this ambivalence. Some suppress their positive feelings, some suppress their negative feelings, some manage by alternating the feelings they express or by compartmentalizing their discrepant feelings.

The suppression of either positive or negative feelings rarely seems complete. Desires for rejoining, as has been noted, often are discernible in the most hostile of actions. By the same token, rejoinings frequently are marred by the sudden eruption of anger. One young man reported, "There are some times when I sleep with her or I'm at her apartment and she does something that bothers me like it did when we were married, and I feel like yelling and doing a whole big thing again."

Some among the separated express positive feelings in one setting and negative feelings in another. It is not unusual for a couple to battle with one another through their lawyers, even to testify against one another in court, yet to see one another in the evening as friends or lovers (see Baguedor, 1972).

Couples who establish postmarital relationships in which their discrepant feelings are allocated to separate settings sometimes try to keep the positive aspects of their relationship secret from all but their most intimate friends. Having told their family and their lawyers how much they have suffered at each other's hands, a husband and wife can hardly admit that they now look forward to evenings together. As a result, some couples may temporarily adopt a bizarre variation of the marital practice of hiding fights from public view; now they may be estranged in public but affectionate in private.

Some couples find that a period apart permits them to be loving to one another, but after an interval of good feeling they again become hostile. In this way their positive and negative feelings seem to alternate. A man reported, "I was gone for a week and I came back . . . . And we had the most fantastic weekend, really. It was great, it was fantastic. And then things started up again. The bickering, the whole thing, started up Sunday."

Ambivalence makes separated individuals uncomfortable with any resolution of their separated state. Reconciliation may result not only in relief at the ending of separation distress, but also in dismay at the return to an unsatisfactory relationship. The decision to divorce may also have mixed implications: not only gratification that freedom appears within grasp but also sorrow that the spouse will be irretrievably lost. Lawyers who specialize in divorce work sometimes express their frustration with clients who do not seem to know their own minds (O'Gorman, 1963): "Maybe it is first love or whatever, but I'm still attracted to him. There is a basic something, and I can't seem to get rid of that. I do want a divorce and I don't want a divorce."

CONCLUSIONS

Emotional responses to marital separation frequently appear paradoxical, even to those experiencing them. Individuals who feel themselves to have been left may be desolate at the absence of a spouse they can no longer respect or trust. Individuals who have shared in the decision to separate may alternate between deep depression accompanied by lessened self-esteem and euphoria accompanied by heightened self-confidence, and in each state feel that the other state was a temporary mood. Individuals who urgently sought the separation may, after having obtained it, report as one woman did: "I wouldn't want to go back, but I hadn't expected to feel as bad as I do." No matter how decided the individual appears on a particular course of action, there is apt to be intense ambivalence regarding the spouse.

On the basis of these observations we might offer as counsel to the recently separated and to those who may interact with them that they attempt to tolerate the emotional upset that appears to be a nearly inevitable accompaniment to marital separation. And we might warn the separated that at least in the short run they may not be able to resolve their ambivalent feelings about their spouse. Whatever they decide—whether it is to reconcile or to continue their separation and, perhaps, move on to divorce—they will leave one set of feelings unsatisfied.

NOTE

1. The study of early marriage was sponsored by the Laboratory of Community Psychiatry and directed by Rhona Rapoport.

REFERENCES

Baguedor, E. *Separation: Journal of a marriage.* New York: Simon & Schuster, 1972.

Bowlby, J. *Attachment and loss, I: Attachment.* New York: Basic Books, 1969.

Bowlby, J. *Attachment and loss, II: Separation.* New York: Basic Books, 1973.

Cohen, L. J. The operational definition of human attachment. *Psychological Bulletin,* 1974, *81,* 207-217.

Crumley, F. E., & Blumenthal, R. S. Children's reactions to temporary loss of the father. *American Journal of Psychiatry,* 1973, *130,* 778-782.

Glick, I. O., Weiss, R. S., & Parkes, C. M. *The first year of bereavement.* New York: Wiley-Interscience, 1974.

Goode, W. J. *After divorce.* New York: Free Press, 1956.

O'Gorman, H. J. *Lawyers and matrimonial cases.* New York: Free Press, 1963.

Parkes, C. M. *Bereavement.* New York: International Universities Press, 1972.

Rubin, Z. *Liking and loving.* New York: Holt, Rinehart & Winston, 1973.

*Weiss, R. S. *Loneliness.* Cambridge, Mass.: MIT Press, 1973.

Weiss, R. S. *Marital separation.* New York: Basic Books, 1975.

7/ WIDOWHOOD: A Roleless Role

Starr Roxanne Hiltz

The death of a spouse is one of the most serious life crises a person faces. The immediate emotional crisis of bereavement, if not fully worked through, may result in symptoms of mental disorder. During the first few days of bereavement, sacred and secular guidelines define the proper mourning role for the widow. Over the longer term, however, there is generally a need for total restructuring of the widow's life, as she finds herself much poorer, socially isolated, and left without a meaningful life pattern.

Widowhood can thus be defined more by a collapse of old roles and structural supports than by norms and institutions which specify or provide new role relationships and behavior patterns. Lopata (1975a) concludes from her data that American society has been phasing out the traditional status role of "widow" as an all-pervasive lifelong identity: "Usually, widowhood is a temporary stage of identity reconstruction, and this is the major problem. The direction of movement out of it is not clearly specified" (1975a, p.47). Widowhood is best conceptualized as a negatively evaluated social category where the individual loses the central source of identity, financial support, and social relationships. It is a "roleless role."

This article reviews selected works by sociologists, psychologists, and social workers on widowhood in American society. Emphasis is upon studies which examine the factors related to the change or dissolution of old role relationships and their replacement by new

* Indicates selections included in this volume.

ones; aspects of widowhood which are related to the structure and functioning of the American family as a whole; and the recent emergence of social service programs aimed at aiding widows in reshaping their lives and identities.

DEMOGRAPHIC CHARACTERISTICS

Widowhood is shared by a very large number of women. In 1976 there were about 10,020,000 widows in the United States, and their numbers have been increasing by about 100,000 a year (Bureau of the Census, Note 1). This is about 13 percent of all women over the age of eighteen. Growth in the number and proportion of women who are widows is certain to continue for the rest of this century, since Census projections (Note 2) indicate an increase of 43 percent in the size of the total population over sixty-five by the year 2000.

The genesis of widowhood as a social problem in America can be traced to the combined operation of demographic changes and the persistence of a set of values which defines a married woman mainly in terms of her role as a wife.

Currently, American women have a life expectancy of seventy-nine, about seven years longer than American men. If demographic patterns were used to suggest marital arrangements, it would make sense for older women to marry younger males. However, our cultural norms and opportunities are such that the intitial mortality differences are compounded by the tendency for women to marry older men. Since only about 5 percent of previous cohorts of American women never married at all, the inevitable result is that ever larger proportions become widows and remain so for an increasing number of years.

Though the modal age for widowhood is above fifty, a recent detailed study by the Bureau of the Census shows that the majority of women whose first husbands die are widowed before the age of fifty. The younger the age at widowhood, the more likely a woman is to marry, but overall, less than a third of these widows ever remarry.

WIDOWHOOD ROLES

Most preindustrial societies have very clear roles for widows. For example, in traditional Indian society, a Brahmin widow was supposed to committ *suttee* by throwing herself on her husband's funeral pyre. If she did not do this, she was condemned to live out her life dressed in a single coarse garment, with shaven head, eating only one meal a day, and shunned by others as "unlucky." Another extreme solution, practiced in many African societies, was an immediate (automatic) remarriage, in which the wife and children were "inherited" by a younger brother of the deceased or by some other heir, and the widow became one of his wives in a polygamous family. (See Lopata, 1972, for further descriptions of these customs and those of many other societies in regard to widows.) Even if such prescribed actions and roles were not particularly desirable from the widow's point of view, at least it was clear what she was to do with the rest of her life.

The new widow in American and other (Western) industrialized societies has lost not only a husband, but her own main functions, reason for being, and self-identity. In spite of the emergence of "women's liberation," most women who are becoming widows today have defined themselves primarily as wives and mothers. Lopata sums up the situation in *Widowhood in an American City,* a study of Chicago widows:

> In spite of the rapid industrialization, urbanization, and increasing complexity of the social structure of American society, the basic cluster of social roles available to, and chosen by, its women has been that of wife-mother-housewife. This fact imposes some serious problems upon the last stage of their lives, similar to the problems of retirement in the lives of men who had concentrated upon their occupational roles. The wife-mother-housewife often finds herself with children who are grown, absent from her home, and independent of her as a basic part of their lives; her husband has died, and her household no longer contains a client segment (Lopata, 1973c, pp. 87-88).

Caine, in her poignant account of her own bereavement and eventual readjustment with professional help, has written a most moving description of the effects of the wrenching away of one's social and self-identity that occurs with the death of a husband:

> "Widow" is a harsh and hurtful word. It comes from the Sanskrit and means "empty." . . .
>
> After my husband died, I felt like one of those spiraled shells washed up on the beach. Poke a straw through the twisting tunnel, around and around, and there is nothing there. No flesh. No life. Whatever lived there is dried up and gone.
>
> Our society is set up so that most women lose their identities when their husbands die. Marriage is a symbiotic relationship for most of us. We draw our identities

from our husbands. We add ourselves to our men, pour
ourselves into them and their lives. We exist in their reflection. And then . . . ? If they die . . . ? What is left? It's
wrenching enough to lose the man who is your lover, your
companion, your best friend, the father of your children,
without losing yourself as well (Caine, 1974, pp. 181, 1).

It should be noted that Caine had a fine job for many years before
her husband died, but yet this did not alleviate the necessity and
pain of totally restructuring her social role.

Remarriage is not a likely solution. There are fewer than two
million widowers in the United States, one for every five widows,
and they are likely to marry younger women. Cleveland and Gian-
turco (1976), in a retrospective study of North Carolina data, for
instance, concluded that less than 5 percent of women widowed after
age 55 every remarry.

As Lopata points out:

Life styles for American widows are generally built upon
the assumption that they are young and can soon remarry
or that they are very old and removed from the realm of
actual involvement. The trouble is that most widows are
neither, but the society has not taken sufficient cognizance
of this fact to modify the facilities and roles available to
them (Lopata, 1973c, p. 17).

A woman is likely to spend as much time as a widow as she does
raising children. Although she was socialized all through her early
life for the wife-and-motherhood role, she typically has had no preparation at all for the widowhood role. The whole subject has been
taboo, and few women prepare ahead of time for widowhood.

Despite the statistical data and personal tragedies that make widowhood a major social problem "encompassing increasing numbers
of women and their families and indirectly affecting many others"
(Berardo, 1968, p.200), until recently there has been little sociological research or social service resources to deal with it.

There was only some early work by Elliot (1930, 1933, 1946, 1948)
and a study of British widows (Morris, 1958). However, several
large-scale and/or long-term research projects on widowhood have
appeared in the late 1960s and early 1970s, and will form the main
basis for the findings surveyed here:

1. Two major studies by Lopata. *Widowhood in an American City*
(1973c) was based on interviews with 301 Chicago widows and examined the role behavior of widows as mothers, in-laws, friends, and in
the wider community. Her most recent study of support systems for

widows draws on a survey of 1,169 Chicago area widowed Social Security beneficiaries (Lopata, Note 4). It describes the present and needed personal, economic, and social service supports available to the widowed. Lopata's work on the widowed is by far the most extensive. (See also Lopata, 1969, 1970, 1971, 1973a, 1973b, 1975a, 1975b, Note 3, Note 5, Note 6.)

2. The work of members of the Laboratory of Community Psychiatry at Harvard Medical School includes: (a) studies of bereavement as a set of psychological and medical symptoms (Glick, Weiss, & Parkes, 1974; Maddison, 1968; Parkes, 1964a, 1964b, 1965, 1975); (b) a widow-to-widow program (Silverman, 1966, 1969, 1970, 1972; Silverman & Cooperband, 1975; Silverman & Englander, 1975); and (c) Weiss's work on widowhood as a "transitional state." Similar to separation and divorce, widowhood requires not only resolution of "unfinished business" in old role relationships, but also the construction of a new self-identity. Weiss has developed seminars for the bereaved (1969, 1973, 1976).

3. Another major project is on crisis intervention with families of the bereaved aged in the Bronx, New York, at Montefiore Hospital, which focuses on the impact of professional intervention upon physical and psychiatric health (Gerber, Rusalem, Hannon, Battin, & Arkin 1975; Gerber, Wiener, Battin, & Arkin, 1975; Schoenberg at al., 1975).

4. A program of research on the Widows Consultation Center in New York City (Hiltz, 1974, 1975, 1977) focuses on social service programs designed to help widows rebuild their lives, and how these services were helpful to the clients.

There are also some smaller scale studies based on analysis of a single set of survey or other data. Adams (1968) studied strains between middle-class widows and their grown sons. Chevan and Korson (1972, 1975) document the unwillingness of American widows to live with children or others rather than head their own household. Results of a sample survey of widowed and married Los Angeles women ages forty-five to seventy-four suggest that the lower income and employment status of widows accounts for their lower morale, since differences in morale scores disappeared when these status factors were removed (Morgan, 1976). Secondary analysis by Harvey and Bahr (1974) examined the relationship between the morale of widows and their various "affiliations," or roles, and included an examination of the effects of moving from a full-time housewife role to full-time work for widows who also have to cope with children at home. A report by Lucy Mallan for the Social Security Administration (1975) focuses on the contribution of Social Security benefits to the economic status of widows and their families.

GRIEF AS A KIND OF ILLNESS: EFFECTS ON ROLE PERFORMANCE

The emotional and psychological traumas of grief and mourning involve "letting go" of the emotional ties and roles centered on the husband. If this working through of grief is successfully accomplished, the widow can face a second set of problems having to do with building a new life, a new set of role relationships, and a new identity.

Much of the psychological literature on grief represents an elaboration of Freud's theories. For Freud, grief or "grief work" is the process by which bereaved persons struggle to disengage the loved object. The emotional bond is fused with energy, bound to memories and ideas related to former interactions with the loved person. The mourner has to spend time and effort to bring to consciousness all of these memories in order to set free the energy, to break the tie (Freud, 1917/1957).

Building on the Freudian theory is the classic study by Lindemann in 1944. Based on a study of survivors of the Coconut Grove fire, it established the theory that "normal" bereavement consists of the following stages:

1. Numbness and disbelief, a tendency to deny the death, not to accept the fact that "he is *really* dead, gone forever." This numbness often extends for several weeks beyond the funeral.

2. This is followed by emotional reactions such as crying, often accompanied by such psychosomatic symptoms as headache and insomnia; feelings of guilt, "If I had done so-and-so, maybe he wouldn't have died"; expressions of anger, "Why me! It is so unfair!"; hostility or blame, "The doctors killed him"; and often preoccupation with memories of the deceased and an idealization of him.

3. Feelings of sadness and loneliness, which are often incapacitating, depression, loss of customary patterns of conduct and of motivation to try to go on living, is another stage. This may be followed by a recovery phase.

At one time "grief," as in the extended "pining away" of the third stage, was recognized as a cause of death and listed on death certificates. As Glick et al. (1974) have concluded from their extensive studies of bereavement, "the death of a spouse typically gives rise to a reaction whose duration must be measured in years rather than in weeks"(1974, p. 10).

A variety of grief reactions may occur when the mourner does not express emotion or refuses to deal with the loss. These include delay of the grief reactions for months or even years; overactivity without a sense of loss; indefinite irritability and hostility toward others; sense of the presence of the deceased; acquisition of the physical symptoms of the deceased's last illness; insomnia; apathy; psychosomatically based illnesses such as ulcerative colitis; and such intense depression and feelings of worthlessness that suicide is attempted (Parkes, 1972, p. 211; Van Coevering, Note 7, p. 6).

One tendency is to reconstruct an idealized version of one's deceased husband and of the role relationship with him before the death. Referring to this as "husband sanctification," Lopata (Note 6) reports that three-quarters of the Chicago area current and former beneficiaries of Social Security define their late husband as having been "extremely good, honest, kind, friendly, and warm" (Note 6, p. 4-5). Sanctification is especially likely among women who rank the role of wife above all others. It is an attempt to continue defining oneself primarily in terms of the now-broken role relationship. Lopata views this as an effort to "remove the late husband into an other-worldly position as an understanding but purified and distant observer" (Note 6, p. 30), so that the widow is able to go about reconstructing old role relationships and forming new ones.

There are several factors related to severe or prolonged grief. Sixty-eight widows and widowers under the age of forty-five were interviewed shortly after the spouse died and again a year later in the Harvard Bereavement Study. An "outcome score" was obtained from depth interview material and answers to questions on health; increased consumption of alcohol, tranquilizers, and tobacco; self-assessment as "depressed or very unhappy"; and "wondering whether anything is worthwhile anymore." Three classes of strongly correlated and intercorrelated variables predict continued severe bereavement reactions thirteen months after the death (Parkes, 1975, pp. 308-309):

1. Low socioeconomic status, i.e., low weekly income of the husband, Spearman's rho correlation of .44; low occupational status, .28.

2. Lack of preparation for loss due to noncancer deaths, short terminal illness, accident or heart attack, or failure to talk to the spouse about the coming death, correlations of .26 to .29.

3. Other life crises preceding spouse's death, such as infidelity and job loss, correlations of .25 to .44.

It is interesting that a poor outcome is likely if the marriage relationship was troubled before the death; folk wisdom would have it that the widow would be "glad to be rid of him." Psychologically debilitating guilt over having wished the death of the husband seems to be very strong in such cases, however. Another problem is the amount of "unfinished business" (Blauner, 1966) left by the removal of the husband through death. Parkes concludes that for his young respondents, including widowers as well as widows, "When advance warning was short and the death was sudden, it seemed to have a much greater impact and to lead to greater and more lasting disorganization" (Parkes, 1975, p. 313).

However, a British study of mostly older widows and widowers (Bornstein, Clayton, Halikas, Maurice, & Robin, 1973) did not show a similar relationship. Perhaps, in old age, death, even "without warning," is not shocking, since it has commonly been encountered previously among one's reference group of friends, relatives, and their spouses. In a study of "anticipatory grief" among the elderly, an extended period of chronic illness of the spouse was associated with poorer medical adjustment six months after death for widowers (Gerber, Rusalem, Hannon, Battin, & Arkin 1975). This suggests that any intervention should be introduced during such a period.

Emotional problems related to grief or bereavement were by far the most prevalent problems reported by the clients of the Widows Consultation Center, both initially and at the time of the follow-up about one year later (see Table 1). These are not independent of the problems relating to income, friends, and family. Disturbance and dissolution of the widow's main social relationships and removal of the main source of income require finding new friends and activities, a job, often less expensive housing; and similar adjustments. Any major change in role relationships and living patterns is stressful, and causes emotional disturbance. But many changes in one's life circumstances and behavior patterns simultaneously are especially likely to be associated with extreme emotional stress and such symptoms as mental illness, heart attacks, and suicide.

Given the severe and persistent emotional, psychological, and psychosomatic aspects of even "normal " grief, it becomes impossible for a widow to carry out her usual role relationships and to cope with the problems of change in financial and social status that are thrust upon her.

FINANCIAL PROBLEMS

The subsequent life changes and problems faced by the widow indicate that widowhood is a role for which there is no comparable role among males. Glick and associates (1974) summarize the difference between their samples of widows and of widowers: "Insofar as the men reacted simply to the *loss of a loved other,* their responses were *similar* to those of widows, but insofar as men reacted to the *traumatic disruption of their lives,* their responses were *different*" (Glick et al., 1974, p. 262). This differential impact is found in the financial impact of the death. For the widow, it almost always means the loss of the main source of financial support for the family and a consequent lowering of the standard of living. Overall, widows in 1970 constituted 19 percent of the female population over fourteen, but 24

TABLE 1

SELF-REPORTING OF PROBLEMS BY WIDOWS IN RESPONSE TO
STRUCTURED QUESTIONS AT TIME OF FOLLOW-UP INTERVIEW

Problem Area	Problem When Came to Center	Problem Now	N^a
Emotional upset	80%	68%	174
Relations with family	39	32	221
Finding a job	49	39	230
Living quarters	32	31	227
Friends	53	49	220
Government agencies	19	15	222
Managing finances	68	51	218
Relations with men	30	44	146

N^a includes only those who responded to the structured question.

Source: Follow-up interviews, N=259.

percent of those with an income under $1,000 and 36 percent of those living on between $1,000 and $2,999 (U.S. Bureau of the Census, Note 2). In Lopata's sample of Chicago widows, 60 percent had annual family income under $3,000 (1973c, p. 37).

Mallan's 1975 study found that Social Security benefit increases between 1967 and 1971 have "lessened the likelihood that young widows, with one to three children, would be poor" (1975, p. 18). However, three quarters of old widows around the age of sixty, not yet eligible for retirement benefits but not working, were found to be in poverty.

The dynamics of their situation is partially explained by a survey of 1,744 widows whose husbands had died in 1966, conducted by the Life Insurance Agency Management Association in 1968-69 and published in 1970 (Note 8). They found that for 28 percent there was at least a year between the onset of the final illness or disability and the death. This is a financially and emotionally draining experience. Only two-thirds of all widows with medical bills received any health insurance payments, and for them the health insurance paid an average of 77 percent of the bill. Final expenses were $3,600, on the average, with life and health insurance combined covering only 64 percent of the final expenses. For the remainder, the widows had to deplete savings or use income from their Social Security, earnings, or other sources.

By two to three years after the onset of widowhood, the incomes of the widows' families were down an average of 44 percent from previous levels, and 58 percent had incomes that fell below the amount that would have been necessary to maintain their family's former standard of living. This occurred even among those who received life insurance benefits. After final expenses, 44 percent had used up part of this for living expenses, and 14 percent had consumed all of it.

In addition to financially devastating final expenses which wipe out savings, widows are entitled to no Social Security benefits at all unless they have dependents or are over sixty. After sixty years of age, they are entitled only to a portion of what would have been their husband's benefits. The final explanation for the high probability of poverty among widows is that because of age, low level of skill and education, and lack of experience, they are often unable to obtain employment. In other words, neither the private economy nor the public welfare system is currently structured to provide economic support to widows in late middle age.

FINDING NEW SOCIAL ROLES

Before widowhood, a married woman defines herself and relates to others mainly in terms of her status as somebody's wife. At widowhood, most of her role relationships will have to adjust and some will terminate. She will have to establish new role relationships if her life is to be a satisfying one. For example, she is unlikely to maintain close ties with friends and relatives who belonged to social circles maintained with her husband. Changes in finances can require changes in other spheres of life, such as movement into the work force. A change in residence may result in loss of contact with neighbors. Often, in settling her husband's estate, she has to deal with lawyers and insurance agents and has to take on the role of businesswoman (Lopata, 1975a, p. 48).

The difficulties an older woman in our society is likely to encounter in establishing such a new set of role relationships are affirmed by Professor Lopata. She found that half of the widows in her sample considered loneliness their greatest problem, and another third listed it second. Social isolation was listed by 58 percent, who agreed with the statement "One problem of being a widow is feeling like a 'fifth wheel' " (Lopata, 1972, pp. 91, 346).

Lopata's work focuses on the widow's role relationships in regard to motherhood, kin relationships, friendship, and community involvement, including employment. Among her findings are that "women who develop satisfactory friendships, who weather the transition period and solve its problems creatively, tend to have a higher education, a comfortable income, and the physical and psychic energy needed to initiate change" (Lopata, 1972, p. 216). These women are not the "average" widow, who is likely to have a high school education or less, low income, depleted physical energy due to advancing age, and depleted psychic energy due to the trauma of bereavement and its associated problems.

The importance of maintaining or establishing supportive role relationships with an understanding "other" such as an old friend, neighbor, or supportive professional or paraprofessional has been emphasized in many studies. For instance, Maddison and Raphael (1975) emphasize their "conviction that the widow's perception of her social network is an extremely important determinant of the outcome of her bereavement crisis" (1975, p. 29). "Bad outcome" women had no one to whom they could freely express their grief and anger.

DISRUPTION OF FAMILY RELATIONSHIPS

The death of the husband tends to cause strain in relationships with children, in-laws, and even one's own siblings and other relatives. Thirty-nine percent of the clients of the Widows Consultation Center reported that relationships with family members were a problem at the time they came to the Center. Problems with children were reported by more clients (31 percent), compared to in-laws (8 percent) and siblings (6 percent).

The problems with children were twofold: a perceived coldness or neglect to give the widow as much "love" and support and time as she thought she was entitled to (17 percent), and what the widow considered serious behavioral problems with the children, such as taking drugs or withdrawing from employment and from communication with the mother (15 percent) (Hiltz, 1977, pp. 64–65).

What is seen as "neglect" or "coldness" by the widow may be viewed as an unfair and unpleasant burden by the child, especially sons. For example, Adams (1968) found that grown middle-class sons perceived their obligations to their mother as a "one-way" or unreciprocated pattern of aid and support-giving. This typically results in a son's loss of affection for the mother and his resentment of her dependence upon him.

For younger widows with dependent children, there are difficulties in maintaining the maternal role of effectively responding to the child's needs. Taking a sample of nineteen cases of widows with children under sixteen from follow-up three years after bereavement, Silverman and Englander found that most parents and children avoided talking about the death to one another. Common reactions of the child were fear that they would lose the surviving parent, too; the assumption by the child of new family responsibilities; and poor school work related to rebellion and social withdrawal (Silverman & Englander, 1975, p. 11).

Role relationships to in-laws may be cut off entirely if the widow does not find them pleasant and supportive. As Lopata (Note 4) points out, this is a unique kind of institutional arrangement, since the patriarchal family traditionally had vested rights over the wife and the offspring of a marriage. However, "American widows are free to move away from their in-laws, if they were living nearby, and even to lose all contact with them. They are free to cut the ties between their children and that side of the family and even to remarry and change the name of the unit" (Note 4, p. 3). However, none of the studies seem to include the impact of such decisions on the role relationship between paternal grandparents and grandchildren, and on the emotional pain that may be caused if the relationship is severed.

INTERVENTION STRATEGIES AND THEIR EFFECTIVENESS

Findings from recent research projects have sustained the premise that social service or intervention programs to help the widow cope and build a satisfactory network of role relationships do work. One such project involving intervention in the life of the widow is the "Widow-to-Widow" program. Five widows were originally recruited as aides, chosen as having personal skills in dealing with people and as representatives of the dominant racial and religious groups in the community. The aide wrote the new widow a letter saying that she would call on her at a particular time. This usually occurred three weeks after the death, unless the widow telephoned and requested no visit. Of the ninety-one widows located in the first seven months of the program, sixty-four accepted contact, half by visit and half by telephone, an overall acceptance rate of 60 percent. The aides offered friendship as well as advice and assistance with specific problems. In addition, group discussion meetings and social events such as a cookout were organized to which all of the widows were invited (Silverman, 1969, pp. 333–337). As Silverman describes the role of the aid, she "encourages, prods, insists, and sometimes even takes the widow by the hand and goes through the motions with her" (1972, p. 101).

On the basis of this project and one other, Silverman and Cooperband conclude that "the evidence points to another widow as the best caregiver . . . . This other widow . . . can provide a perspective on feelings; she provides a role model; she can reach out as a friend and neighbor" (Silverman & Cooperband, 1975, p. 11).

Some psychiatrists and social workers question the advisability of using untrained recent widows to give aid to other widows, without available referral to professionals. For instance, they point to abnormal grief reactions experienced by widows visited by aides, including two who died, who may have responded to professional intervention. Also, unresolved elements of her own grief might lead the widow-aide to excessive reliance upon her own methods of coping, over-looking or negatively responding to other possibilities (Kahana, 1975). "The danger is that unresolved or unrecognized grief may adversely influence the aid in trying to assist the newly bereaved widow . . . . Some of the people who say 'I know how you feel' may really mean 'I know how I feel' " (Blau, 1975, pp. 36-37).

The Widows Consultation Center's casework service was to pro-vide a single central source of help to eliminate the frustration and despair experienced by clients in going from one agency to another in a search for information, directions, and assistance. Individual counseling with a caseworker included referrals or assistance in deal-ing with agencies such as the Social Security Administration or the New York Housing Authority, or on emotional, social, or family problems. For problems best dealt with by referral, counseling rarely went beyond one session. For emotional problems, however, counseling generally involved many meetings.

Group discussion or therapy sessions, with groups of three to ten widows, met weekly with a professional leader. They varied, depend-ing upon the participants, from fairly casual sharing of experiences as widows to explicitly therapeutic groups. (See Hiltz, 1975, for a description of these groups.)

Social activities and recreational events were organized for the Center's client's. These social get-togethers were initiated slowly, with the first year's activities most typically a monthly tea at the Center preceded by a brief lecture on some topic of apparent inter-est to widows, such as a book on widowhood. By the third year, a part-time social worker was hired to organize and conduct social activities, such as Sunday afternoon sessions at the local "Y," wee-kend bus trips, and free theater parties.

Special professional consultation about legal or financial problems was arranged through caseworkers, who made appointments for cli-ents who seemed to need expert advice. The financial consultant was a well-known writer on personal finance, who did not recommend specific investments but gave generalized advice on types of invest-ments, budgeting, and allocation of funds.

The main criterion of effectiveness used in this study was the widow's own feelings about whether or not the WCC had helped them with each problem area identified by each widow at the time she came to the Center. Widows felt the Center had been most helpful with emotional problems. Overall, 53 percent of widows questioned about this area said that the Center had been helpful to them, and this increases to 80 percent for those with five or more visits to the Center.

When asked "Overall, would you say that the Widows Consultation Center was a great deal of help to you, of some help, or no help at all?" 36 percent of all clients said the Center had been a "great deal of help"; 33 percent said "of some help"; and 30 percent said "no help." These results become more favorable as the number of private interviews, group therapy sessions, or social activities attended increases. For example, less than a third of those who had only one or two private interviews felt that the Center had given them a "great deal of help," compared to 79 percent of those who had five or more private consultation sessions. These findings support the feelings of the caseworkers that they achieved much more success in helping their clients with a supportive casework process that extended over some period of time, rather than a one- or two-visit process.

Building on their work with the separated, sociologist Weiss and his colleagues developed a program of eight "seminars" for the bereaved. Each of eight weekly meetings begins with a lecture of about forty-five minutes on some aspect of bereavement. After each lecture, small discussion groups are formed to discuss various subjects according to members' interests. There is a wine and cheese party at the last meeting and then a "reunion" of the group about six weeks after the last meeting (Weiss, 1976, Note 9). This program is monitored and evaluated with follow-up interviews of participants.

The Widows Consultation Centre in Winnipeg, built upon the experiences of the New York WCC, modified the service model in several respects, resulting in greater economy. It provides a more financially feasible model for the majority of communities than the original WCC, and incorporates techniques developed by Silverman and Weiss. Rather than creating a completely new and independent agency, it was decided by the Winnipeg WCC that "it would be preferable that such a service should be developed as an expansion of an existing agency. The Y.W.C.A. was thought to be most appropriate for this purpose because of its community acceptability and because it had already done some work in the area of programming for widows" (DeGraves, Note 10, Note 11). The Winnipeg WCC operates with only one professional social worker, who does all the counseling, supervises twice-a-month social programs, supervises three visiting widows in a widow-to-widow program, and serves as the group leader for a therapeutic discussion group which is now modeled on Weiss's seminars at the Harvard Medical School (DeGraves, Note 12). Since this is a service-oriented agency, there are no reliable data on the effectiveness of the various components of the program.

The Montefiore Hospital Project with the bereaved aged is the only controlled experiment on the effectiveness of therapeutic intervention. A large number of the elderly are assigned for primary medical care to an internist at the hospital. Therefore, there was an opportunity to work with medical records of a large population in designing an intervention program. The families of all persons who died in the hospital were assigned, on a two to one basis, to brief therapeutic intervention of six months or less by a psychiatric social worker and a psychiatric nurse; or to no treatment. In addition, every third bereaved spouse was matched by age, sex, and number and sex of children with a nonbereaved patient of the hospital. The intervention consisted of client-centered treatment over the telephone or in person with helping the bereaved to express their feelings and understanding their emotional reactions, and assisting with current problems and future plans. Dependent variables were almost entirely medical indicators, such as visits to doctors, major and minor illnesses, and prescription of medicines. In reporting the results of the experiment, Gerber, Wiener, Battin, and Arkin (1975) conclude:

> The results for 75 percent (five of the seven) of the measures of therapeutic outcome tend to suggest that the type of brief therapy we offered was to some extent medically beneficial . . . . From our experience it appears that a therapeutic service to the bereaved will begin to have a positive impact approximately three months after the intervention begins (Gerber et al., 1975, p.330).

However, the authors caution, "We actually have limited knowledge about which type of service (individual versus group therapy), which intervention orientation (long-term versus lay support), produces the most effective result" (1975, p.312). I would add to this list a distinction between socially oriented peer groups and professionally led therapeutic groups, and the distinction between projects which systematically seek out all widows in a community and those which depend on client initiative. What is needed at this point is a large-scale project which systematically experiments with the effectiveness of various individual and combined techniques for widows of various ages, life situations, and severity of grief.

SUMMARY

Studies of widowhood during the last decade have given us an understanding of the fact that widows in American society must forge a total emotional, financial, and social reorganization of their lives, at a time when their resources for such a task are generally inadequate. There are many areas in which the "broad picture" of the problems faced by widows must be filled in by much more detail. Strategies to prevent deterioration in communication and quality of relationship between the newly widowed mother and her dependent or grown children is one example of an area in which such research would be particularly valuable. At the societal level, we need to explore what mix of private and public efforts can replace the likelihood of poverty created by the current Social Security "blackout period" and lack of job opportunities for older widows with some assurance of financial security. Finally, we need to forge a stronger relationship between social service programs and social research, so that knowledge of successful and unsuccessful strategies in helping widows to build a socially and financially supportive set of role relationships becomes cumulative and shared.

NOTES

1. U.S. Bureau of the Census. Marital status and living arrangements, March 1976. In *Current population reports: Population characteristics,* Series P-20, No. 36. Washington, D.C.: Author, 1977.

2. U.S. Bureau of the Census. Population characteristics, marital status and living arrangements, March 1972. In *Current population reports,* Series P-20, No. 42. Washington, D.C.: U.S. Government Printing Office, 1972.

3. U.S. Bureau of the Census. Number, timing and duration of marriages and divorces in the U.S., June 1975. In *Current population reports,* Series P-20, No. 297. Washington, D.C.: U.S. Government Printing Office, 1976.

4. Lopata, H. Z. *Support systems involving widows in a metropolitan area of the United States.* Unpublished manuscript, Loyola University Center for the Comparative Study of Social Roles, 1977.

5. Lopata, H. Z. *Widowhood: Societal factors in lifespan disruptions and alternatives.* Paper presented at the Fourth Lifespan Developmental Psychology Conference, Morgantown, W. Va., May 1974.

6. Lopata, H. Z. *Widowhood and husband sanctification.* Paper presented at the 71st annual meeting of the American Sociological Association, New York City, August 1976.

7. Van Coevering, V. *Developmental tasks of widowhood for the aging woman.* Paper presented at the annual meeting of the American Psychological Association, September 1971.

8. Life Insurance Agency Management Association. *The widows study* (Vol. 1, *The onset of widowhood;* Vol. 2, *Adjustment to widowhood: The first two years).* Author, 1970.

9. Weiss, R. Personal communication, August 1976.

10. DeGraves, D. *The widow-to-widow program.* Unpublished manuscript, 1975. (Available from the Widows Consultation Centre, 447 Webb Place, Winnipeg, Manitoba, Canada.)

11. DeGraves, D. *The widows consultation centre.* Unpublished manuscript, 1975. (Available from the Widows Consultation Centre, 447 Webb Place, Winnipeg, Manitoba, Canada.)

12. DeGraves, D. Personal communication, 1977.

REFERENCES

Adams, B. The middle-class adult and his widowed or still-married mother. *Social Problems*, 1968, *16*, 50–59.

Berardo, F. M. Widowhood status in the United States: Perspective on a neglected aspect of the family life cycle. *The Family Coordinator*, 1968, *17*, 191–203.

Blau, D. On widowhood: Discussion. *Journal of Geriatric Psychiatry*, 1975, *8*, 29–40.

Blauner, R. Death and social structure. *Psychiatry*, 1966, *29*, 387–394.

Bornstein, P. E., Clayton, P. J., Halikas, J. A., Maurice, W. L., & Robin, E. The depression of widowhood at 13 months. *British Journal of Psychiatry*, 1973, *122*, 561–566.

Caine, L. *Widow.* New York: Wm. Morrow & Co., 1974.

Chevan, A., & Korson, H. The widowed who live alone: An examination of social and demographic factors. *Social Forces*, 1972, *51*, 43–53.

Chevan, A., & Korson, H. Living arrangements of widows in the United States and Israel, 1960 and 1961. *Demography*, 1975, *12*, 505–518.

Cleveland, W. P., & Giranturco, D. T. Remarriage probability after widowhood: A retrospective method. *Journal of Gerontology*, 1976, *31*, 99–103.

Elliot, T. D. The adjustive behavior of bereaved families: A new field for research. *Social Forces*, 1930, *8*, 543–549.

Elliot, T. D. A step toward the social psychology of bereavement. *Journal of Abnormal and Social Psychology*, 1933, *27*, 380–390.

Elliot, T. D. War bereavements and their recovery. *Marriage and Family Living*, 1946, *8*, 1–6.

Elliot, T. D. Bereavement: Inevitable but not insurmountable. In H. Berker & A. Hill, *Family, marriage and parenthood.* Boston: D. C. Heath, 1948.

Freud, S. Mourning and melancholia. In J. Strachey (Ed. and trans.), *The Standard Edition of the Complete Psychological Works of Sigmund Freud* (Vol. XIV). London: The Hogarth Press and the Institute for Psycho Analysis, 1957. (Originally published, 1917.)

Gerber, I., Rusalem, R., Hannon, N., Battin, D., & Arkin, A. Anticipatory grief and aged widows and widowers. *Journal of Gerontology*, 1975, *30*, 225–229.

Gerber, I., Wiener, A. Battin, D., & Arkin, A. M. Brief therapy to the aged bereaved. In B. Schoenberg, I. Gerber, A. Weiner, A. Kutscher, D. Peretz, & C. Carr (Eds.), *Bereavement: Its psychosocial aspects.* New York: Columbia University Press, 1975.

Glick, I. O., Weiss, R., & Parkes, C. M. *The first year of bereavement.* New York: John Wiley & Sons, 1974.

Harvey, C. D., & Bahr, H. M. Widowhood, morale, and affiliation. *Journal of Marriage and the Family,* 1974, *36,* 97–106.

Hiltz, S. R. Evaluating a pilot social service project for widows: A chronicle of research problems. *Journal of Sociology and Social Welfare,* 1974, *1,* 217–224.

Hiltz, S. R. Helping widows: Group discussions as a therapeutic technique. *The Family Coordinator,* 1975, *24,* 331–336.

Hiltz, S. R. *Creating community services for widows: A pilot project.* Port Washington, N.Y.: Kennikat Press, 1977.

Kahana, R. J. On widowhood: Introduction. *Journal of Geriatric Psychiatry,* 1975, *8,* 5–8.

Levin, S. On widowhood: Discussion. *Journal of Geriatric Psychiatry,* 1975, *8,* 57–59.

Lindemann, E. The symptomatology and management of acute grief. *American Journal of Psychiatry,* 1944, *101,* 141–148.

Lopata, H. Z. Loneliness: Forms and components. *Social Problems,* 1969, *17,* 248–262.

Lopata, H. Z. The social involvement of American widows. *American Behavioral Scientist,* 1970, *14,* 41–57.

Lopata, H. Z. Widows as minority groups. *Gerontologist,* 1971, *11,* 67–77.

Lopata, H. Z. Role changes in widowhood: A world perspective. In D. Cowgill & L. Holmes (Eds.), *Aging and modernization.* New York: Appleton-Century-Crofts, 1972.

Lopata, H. Z. Living through widowhood. *Psychology Today,* July 1973, pp. 87–92. (a)

Lopata, H. Z. Self identity in marriage and widowhood. *Sociological Quarterly,* 1973, *14,* 407–418. (b)

Lopata, H. Z. *Widowhood in an American city.* Cambridge: Schenkman Publishing Co., 1973. (c)

Lopata, H. Z. On widowhood: Grief, work, and identity reconstruction. *Journal of Geriatric Psychiatry,* 1975, *8,* 41–55. (a)

Lopata, H. Z. Widowhood: Societal factors in life-span disruption and alternatives. In N. Datan & L. H. Ginsberg (Eds.), *Life span development psychology: Normative life crisis.* New York: Academic Press, 1975. (b)

Maddison, D. Relevance of conjugal bereavement for preventive psychiatry. *British Journal of Medical Psychology,* 1968, *41,* 223–233.

Maddison, D., & Raphael, B. Conjugal bereavement and the social network. In B. Schoenberg, I. Gerber, A. Wiener, A. Kutscher, D. Petetz, & C. Carr (Eds.), *Bereavement: Its psychosocial aspects.* New York: Columbia University Press, 1975.

Mallan, L. B. Young widows and their children: a comparative report. *Social Security Bulletin* (U.S. Department of Health, Education and Welfare Publication No. SSA-75-700), May 1975, pp. 3–21.

McCourt, W. F., Bornett, R., Brennan, J., & Becker, A. We help each other: Primary evaluation for the widowed. *American Journal of Psychiatry*, 1976, *133*, 98–100.

Morgan, L. A. A Re-Examination of widowhood and morale. *Journal of Gerontology*, 1976, *31*, 687–695.

Morris, P. *Widows and their families.* London: Routledge & Kegan Paul, 1958.

Parkes, C. M. Effects of bereavement on physical and mental health: A study of the medical records of widows. *British Medical Journal*, 1964, *2*, 274–279. (a)

Parkes, C. M. Grief as an illness. *New Society*, 1964, *80*, 11–12. (b)

Parkes, C. M. Bereavement and mental illness: a clinical study. *British Journal of Medical Psychology*, 1965, *38*, 1–26.

Parkes, C. M. *Bereavement: Studies of grief in adult life.* New York: International Press, 1972.

Parkes, C. M. Determinants of outcome following bereavement. *Omega: Journal of Death and Dying*, 1975, *6*, 303–323.

Schoenberg, B., Gerber, I., Wiener, A., Kutscher, A., Peretz, D., & Carr, A. (Eds.). *Bereavement: Its psychosocial aspects.* New York: Columbia University Press, 1975.

Silverman, P. R. Services for the widowed during the period of bereavement. *Social work practice.* New York: Columbia University Press, 1966.

Silverman, P. R. The widow-to-widow program: An experiment in preventive intervention. *Mental Hygiene*, 1969, *53*, 333–337.

Silverman, P. R. The widow as a caregiver in a program of preventive intervention with other widows. *Mental Hygiene*, 1970, *54*, 540–547.

Silverman, P. R. Widowhood and preventive intervention. *The Family Coordinator*, 1972, *21*, 95–102.

Silverman, P. R., & Cooperband, A. On widowhood: Mutual help and the elderly widow. *Journal of Geriatric Psychiatry*, 1975, *8*, 9–27.

Silverman, P. R., & Englander, S. The widow's view of her dependent children. *Omega: Journal of Death and Dying*, 1975, *6*, 3–20.

Weiss, R. S. The fund of sociability. *Trans-ACTION*, 1969, *6*, 43–63.

*Weiss, R. S. *Loneliness.* Cambridge, Mass.: The M.I.T. Press, 1973.

Weiss, R. S. Transition states and other stressful situations: Their nature and programs for their management. In Caplan & Killilea (Eds.), *Support systems and mutual help.* New York: Grune & Stratton, 1976.

*Indicates selections included in this volume.

PART THREE

FRIENDSHIP, COURTING, AND SEXUALITY

All human beings need intimacy. Sexuality and friendship are two major paths that adults may follow in meeting this need. Yet the experiences of intimacy vary between single and married people, and among singles themselves. Where sexuality is concerned, society today is undergoing a well-publicized revolution. This is not only a sexual revolution but a gender-role revolution as well, liberalizing behavior and ideas about the equality of men and women. One product of this change is society's increasing acceptance of sexual relationships outside of marriage, which increases the options that single men and women may choose.

Some single men and women choose celibacy. This may be a long-term voluntary state or a temporary, perhaps difficult, state between relationships. Celibacy may be a religious requirement, a moral conviction, or a means of conserving energy for creative endeavors. It may also be a flight from intimacy. A celibate person's satisfaction depends on motivation and on freedom of choice.

For many singles, sexual experimentation is a part of their identity, enjoyed for itself or used as a stage leading to marriage or choice of a single sexual partner. Those who try a variety of relationships can learn much about the world and about themselves. They may avoid commitment in order to work on a career or personal growth, or to recover from a painful relationship in the past. Some set up a hierarchy of relationships involving special obligations to a primary partner and lesser responsibilities to others. Personal enrichment is a possible benefit of this style of relationships, but the stress of managing conflicting commitments and lack of clarity about one's role are potential problems.

Many singles believe that an individual cannot love more than one person at a time. Those who adhere to this Judeo-Christian value may prefer a monogamous relationship—a single sexual partner—without the obligations and daily responsibilities of marriage. As needs and desires change, couples may move on to new partners—serial monogamy.

Cohabitation is more than a living arrangement; it qualifies as a style of sexuality as well. As a source of intimacy, living together ranks high for growing numbers of singles. Most cohabitors consider their relationships important, affectionate, supportive, and excluding of outside sexual involvements. Those who live together claim to gain deeper self-understanding and emotional growth. Many homosexual as well as heterosexual couples choose cohabitation as a shorter or longer term alternative to marriage.

Homosexuality is a term that encompasses a wide range of attitudes and behavior. Same-sex relationships may be just as diverse as heterosexual relationships. Some gay people prefer a permanent partner in a marriage-like arrangement, some prefer singlehood. Public acceptance of homosexuality is an increasingly important issue for gays, as is active participation in the gay subculture. Political consciousness of the gay community is growing and is certain to have important repercussions for the future of society at large.

Within the described major categories of sexuality there are two other types of behavior that bear mention. Casual sexuality—whether heterosexual or homosexual—is preferred by some singles. Even today this style is still more frequently practiced by men, and less commonly by women. Many women find it difficult to be aggressive enough to find varied partners, and women's idea of love is also more likely to be violated by this seeming promiscuity. "Relationship" sexuality is a more popular choice with women, whether as part of a monogamous or a sexually experimental life style. A relationship is considered to be "leading somewhere" and sexual intercourse symbolizes a degree of caring between the partners (Lews and Schwartz, 1977).

Social supports are crucial to singles' lives. These supports improve life chances and increase life-style options. Friendship networks are a major source of social support that for many singles may fill the gap left by traditional family structures. Close, caring friendships can provide the basic satisfactions of intimacy, sharing, and continuity.

Intimacy may come from opposite or same-sex friendships. Groups of friends—formal or informal—are especially well suited to meeting the needs of single people, helping them to deal with life choices and to spur personal growth. For some single people, friendships may mean survival.

My own study of men's friendships found that "in difficult times and in trouble-free times, friendships are indeed crucial sources of support" (Stein, 1981). Although friendship "has its own subjective rationale, which is to enhance feelings of warmth, trust, love, and affection between two people" (Parlee, 1979), it is also a fragile role for which fewer norms and expectations exist. In these men's groups (similar to women's consciousness-raising groups) where many of the traditional barriers to close relationships between men were dissolved, an atmosphere of sharing and openness existed that allowed the development of friendship. The result was a growing sense of commitment among group members who offered each other support for work, for interests, and for life in general.

Why are traditional styles of friendship so different for men and for women? Hess explores biological, social, and historical forces behind these differences in "Friendship and Gender Roles over the Life Course." From prehistoric hunting parties to modern football teams, boys and men are taught the value of teamwork and surface good will toward many others. In contrast, women are encouraged to form close, confiding friendships with few others, reserving their most intimate bond for children and family. Hess points out that childhood socialization and the resulting friendship patterns adopted by boys and girls are highly functional to the adult roles they will assume; these are adaptive behaviors in terms of the major life tasks of women and men, and highly preservative of societies. The virtues of these sex-differentiated bonding patterns—male to male and female to child—for the society or for personal intimacy needs are most obvious in the early and middle adult years. But what about friendship in the later years, when the major roles of parent and worker are past? Traits which are beneficial at one life stage can be liabilities at another. Men may suffer great loss when they retire and lose contact with workmates, and women may not be able to adapt to the loss of a husband through intimacy with a friend. But the author contends that the future can bring a society of enriching friendships and marriages based on reciprocal vulnerability and mutual trust.

The search for intimacy goes on in many places. A most interesting place is the singles bar. Allon and Fishel observed the New York City singles bar scene for their paper "Singles' Bars as Examples of Urban Courting Patterns," noting behavior patterns and raising questions. Among their observations are the importance of physical appearance, the prevalence of touching, the elaborate cues used to single out possible partners. How does the singles bar experience reflect traditional male/female gender roles encountered in the larger society? The authors found that the structured patterns of interaction in singles bars seem based on stereotypical sex-role behavior. Men pursue; women wait. Those who visit singles bars—to escape boredom, for companionship, for affection, or for social acceptance—what do they really gain? How do communications there rely on traditional sex-role definitions? What are the differences in form and content of verbal and nonverbal messages these singles send? And to what extent do the bars fulfill the singles' need to meet others?

The middle years are a time when each of us must confront our own sexuality. At this time of life men seem to need more tenderness and intimacy and to focus more on close relationships. Women often feel stronger, more self-assured, and more sexually assertive than before. Martha Cleveland, in "Sexuality in the Middle Years" observes that middle-years confrontation with sexuality is likely to be more difficult for divorcing people than for those whose marriages remain intact. At the same time, the stimulation of the need to redefine one's identity, a changed living situation, or new partners may yield an increase in sexual feelings and erotic behavior. The author explains the main avenues of sexual outlet and the motivations behind them, including rebellion and the need to validate masculinity or femininity, and to blot out feelings of failure. Cleveland's exploration of middle-years sexuality raises interesting questions: How does the double standard for men and women affect chances for satisfying sexual involvement? Why does the developing sexuality of their adolescent children create problems for divorcing people? What options are available to women who are bound for long-term singlehood?

The search for loving relationships by gay people parallels that by straight singles in its variety and in its problems. In "Forbidden Colors of Love: Patterns of Gay Love" John Alan Lee outlines the major styles of loving relevant to homosexuals and relates the changing fashions in gay love styles to gay liberation and the gay subculture. Lee's typology of relationships begins with Eros, the search for the ideal physical image, and ends with Pragma, an approach to love based on considerations of social and personal compatibility. Using personal advertisements from gay newspapers, he identifies categories of desirable characteristics of gay partners and finds in them many prejudices also found in heterosexual relationships. He also describes gay life styles such as communal living and group marriage that provide intimacy and support as well as sexual opportunities. How does the existence of the gay subculture improve the life chances of gays? Can homosexuality act as a sufficient bond in relationships, overriding other social differences? How can an understanding of the homosexual world help heterosexuals solve problems of traditional relationships and family life styles?

Women homosexuals also have many different life styles from which to choose. But no matter what the choice, there is an omnipresent shadow: prejudice. J. Lee Lehman, describing "What It Means to Love Another Woman," reviews the history of lesbianism, noting that even today lesbianism remains an enigma. Part of the reason, the author believes, is that lesbianism has been viewed as a sexual activity rather than a sexual preference; something a woman does in bed rather than the way she lives her life. Lehman stresses that the important distinction is not that lesbians have sex with other women, but that they love them, and it is this love that profoundly affects their lives and, in this society, sets lesbians apart. Lesbian love is no harder or easier than any other romantic love. However, a lesbian may find herself falling in love with a woman who has no lesbian inclinations. Like gay men, gay women try to change the odds in their favor by separating from society into their own subculture or community. Unlike many gay men, lesbians emphasize relationships—monogamous, group, or friendship—rather than one-night stands. Whatever their type of relationship, the building of woman-to-woman intimacy is a challenge and an opportunity for creative interaction. How may acknowledging lesbianism help women to become stronger individuals? Why is society so reluctant to see lesbianism and so ready to suspect males of being homosexuals? What is the societal cost a woman must pay for emotional support from other lesbians?

REFERENCES

Lews, Judith Long, and Pepper Schwartz. *The Sexual Scripts.* New York: Holt, Rinehart & Winston, 1977.

Parlee, Mary. "The Friendship Bond," *Psychology Today,* October, 1979.

Stein, Peter. "Men and Their Friendships," in Robert Lewis (Ed.), *Men in Troubled Times.* Englewood Cliffs, N.J.: Prentice-Hall, 1981.

8/ FRIENDSHIP AND GENDER ROLES OVER THE LIFE COURSE

Beth B. Hess

There is little question that girls and boys, women and men display very different friendship behaviors. There is a great debate about why this is so. Georg Simmel, writing early in this century, summed up the traditional view of nineteenth-century evolutionists by proposing that real and lasting friendships are a sign of higher personality development, and that such individualization is characteristic only of men. That male friendships appear to be deeper and truer than those of women—the very stuff of epic literature and grand opera—receives a more modern, scientific explanation from the American anthropologist Lionel Tiger (1970). Tiger proposes that the earliest masculine associations—small hunting parties, say—depended for success upon deep, unquestioning trust (not so much individual skills but the capacity to work together), and that over the millennia there has been a selective process in favor of those males who have the ability to bond with one another. By now—two million or so years later, when few men hunt wild beasts for food—the capacity, need, and wish to bond with other males is built into the biology of men. Women, on the other hand, because evolutionary selective forces favor the most reproductively successful, have an innate need to bond with their children. Alice Rossi (1977) urges consideration of the case for a maternal attachment to the child stimulated and reinforced through the physiological processes of pregnancy, birth, and lactation.

Tiger draws our attention to the idea of a "gentlemen's agreement," for which no feminine counterpart exists; to the evident enjoyment that men derive from association with other men (rather than with the lower-status individuals such as children and women, except for sexual purposes), and to the obvious ability of men to conduct together the important business of the world. Thus there may be some biologically based predisposition for men to feel comfortable with other men in a way they cannot with women, and for women to feel closest to their own children above all other relationships. This may be why the institutionalization of marriage as the only legitimate sexual arena has been so necessary for societal survival.

We must consider these social-historical forces if we are to understand patterned variations in behavior, even such seemingly "natural" phenomena as male and female friendships. Sex-role socialization—that is, learning the appropriate behaviors for the sexes—and the norms or rules of male-female relationships of a given epoch in a particular society will tell us more about friendship than will the study of evolution or genetics. For example, there is evidence from anthropology that women's groups are as viable as men's in certain societies (Leis, 1974). Our own history demonstrates that deep, trusting relationships between women were not uncommon in the nineteenth century (Smith-Rosenberg, 1975). The social structural characteristics that seem most conducive to such relationships are sex-role rigidity at the level of culture, and the relative isolation of a "world of women" at the societal level. By the same token, extreme individual competitiveness can inhibit the bonding of men, as much recent data suggests. Taking the contemporary American scene, then, let us see how friendship patterns vary by age and sex, and try to see why this is so.

Beginning at the beginning, in childhood, Maccoby and Jacklin (1974) report that most studies have found boys tending to congregate in larger peer groups than girls, but that the smaller friendship networks of girls, often simple pairs or cliques, are characterized by greater intimacy than boys' groups. A review of the literature on "self-disclosure," a willingness to receive and to communicate highly personal details (Cozby, 1973), indicates that childhood differences persist into adulthood: half the studies show greater female than male self-disclosure, and the other half show no difference by sex, but none shows men more disclosing than women.[1] In preadolescence, for instance, both girls and boys disclose information about sex-typed behaviors to same-sexed friends, but the girls are more willing than the boys to reveal emotionality, anxiety, and dependence—which may say more about growing up female than about self-disclosure (O'Neill et al., 1976). Among male undergraduates, Komarovsky (1974) found that the closest *female* friend was the recipient of more disclosure than male friends, and that these men were also more disclosing to their mothers than their fathers (as did Bender et al., 1976, in their sample of homosexual and heterosexual college students of both sexes).

In adulthood, single men and women appear to confide more in cross-sex than in same-sex friends (Stein, 1976; Booth and Hess, 1974), and there is conflicting evidence about whether singles are more confiding than marrieds (Hacker, forthcoming), but in all cases women are more likely to confide in a friend than are men. Since the great majority of women are married, the salience of female friendships is striking.

Sidney Jourard, in his influential volume *The Transparent Self* (1971), makes much of the reciprocal nature of female self-disclosure: that women receive as well as give highly personal communications, which provides experience in sensitivity to others. Conversely, Jourard considers men's relative inability to share intimacies with either men or women one of the more "lethal aspects" of the male role. Robert Bell (1976, 1977) suggests that lack of disclosing and disclosures makes men less accurate perceivers of others and less responsive to subtle emotional cues. Men prefer to deal and be with other men, but this does not necessarily indicate deep affection. On the contrary, to ackowledge deep feelings would be "feminine," and if there is one thing to be avoided at all cost by American males it is to be like women. Homophobia, the fear of femaleness or homosexuality, operates to keep male friendships at a surface level, either business-centered or joking. At the same time these friendships offer a surcease from the demands of the women in their lives to feel or respond or share intimacies.

Such friendship patterns can be seen to derive from differential sex-role socialization. Girls are encouraged to be specialists in human relations, to develop few but highly emotional relationships—and thus prepare to become mothers and wives who will invest much in a very limited set of others. Boys are expected to have extensive networks of buddies; to share all kinds of team experiences, typically goal-directed; to be gregarious—precisely the type who should do well in the American occupational structure. While we socialize males for extreme competitiveness, so that self-disclosure would generate vulnerability, we also expect them to be "good fellows," and these are not incompatible goals when most business settings require a modicum of teamwork and willingness to accept the rules of the game. In this sense, childhood socialization and the resulting friendship patterns adopted by boys and girls are highly functional to the adult roles they will assume, and highly preservative of societies.

The argument over whether such adaptations are biologically based or socially learned rages on. If these tendencies are inherent (biologically based), individuals will not be able to adapt to modern social life with ease. On the other hand, if friendship patterns are dysfunctional in some important ways, and these are simply a matter of training and practice, then changes in socialization mechanisms and cultural-level expectations and norms are required.

Much has been made, especially in England, of social-class differences in contemporary friendship patterns. Elizabeth Bott (1957) first proposed a distinction between close-knit and loose-knit friendship networks. The former are those in which most friends of one person are friends of one another as well, a characteristic of working-class members, who typically have minimal social or geographic mobility, and remain in the same neighborhood with childhood and adult friends. Furthermore, working-class marriages are often associated with a high degree of sex-role segregation. Few social activities are shared: he has his pub, she has her gossip chums. A recent observation of the "regulars" at a blue-collar bar in Milwaukee finds much the same behavior (LeMasters,1975). These men seek a refuge from their homes in the masculine turf of the Oasis Tavern, where they openly express their deep contempt and fear of homosexuals, blacks, commies, and, above all, women.[2]

All of which may be very functional for maintaining a sense of superiority among men whose employment is often deeply alienating and dehumanizing, and also for their wives, whose needs for intimacy are not being met by their husbands. However, when the wives are exposed to and influenced by middle-class norms of marital relations—from their own employment, or through their children, or from the media—traditional sex-role segregation can create new sources of strain (Rubin, 1976; Marciano, 1974; Jacoby, 1973).

Middle-class, white-collar couples, on the other hand, are presumed to have adapted to the social and geographic mobility requirements of modern managerial occupations, by weaving an extensive but loosely knit network of friends; by developing the ability to integrate quickly into neighborhoods and communities; and, above all, by turning to one another for affection, personal stability, and emotional nourishment. This is the heralded "companionate" couple, whose "togetherness" and emphasis upon the marriage bond stand in marked contrast to the sex-segregated, kin-oriented world of the working class and traditional cultures in general. That these conjugal goals are so difficult to achieve, may account for the very high rate of marital disruption often cited as evidence of the "end of the family." It may be claimed that the lack of rootedness in a close-knit network leaves the unhappy middle-class spouse more isolated and bereft of intimacy than his or her counterpart in the working class. However, Helena Lopata (1973) found that while the death of the husband created greater personal disruption in the life of her more-educated respondents than was the case for less-educated women, and also greater dislocation of the friendship network since it had been based on couple companionship, the better educated women had greater emotional and financial resources. They were able to move about and meet others whom they could choose as friends, and also had less stressful relationships with their children than did the less-educated women. The same advantages may characterize reintegration in friendship networks after separation or divorce.

It is probably true that modern marriages are high-risk relationships which also offer the highest prize. Friendships that are most supportive or least competitive with such marital expectations are adaptive by definition. An American version of the British study found that close-knit friendship networks were functional alternatives to companionate family life; and that the same proportion of women were "satisfied with their husband's understanding of them" in both the companionate and traditional marriages, provided that the friendship network was appropriate to the marital orientations— a tight-knit "clique" for the traditional, and loose-knit "individualistic" for the companionate (Nelson,1966). An additional advantage of the loose, individualistic network is, of course, its greater resistance to dislocation if one member defects or moves away; and the interpersonal skills associated with being able to maintain a varied set of friends can be used to construct another such web in another place, if necessary (cf. Fellin and Litwak, 1963).[3]

While there appears to be general agreement that working-class or traditional husbands and wives maintain premarital friendships and associate on a typically sex-segregated basis, there is some question about who chooses friends for whom in the middle-class marriage. On the basis of a very small sample of young marrieds in the Midwest in the late 1950s, Babchuk and Bates (1963) announced findings of "male dominance"; though their tables show that fully half the couples were not in full agreement over friend choice. Two later replications included couples married longer and in a less parochial setting, with fairly similar findings regarding the husbands' more active role in initiating friendships for the couple and in deciding who their "best" friends should be (Babchuck, 1965). The researchers also found that husbands were more likely than wives to confide in the chosen friends (but this might be because many weren't of her choice).

My own researches (Hess, 1972) found that among middle-class, middle-aged managerial migrants currently living in an affluent suburban community, there was almost no overlap between those designated by husband and wife separately as their two "best" friends. Nor, surprisingly, were the wife's choices restricted to wives of business friends of the husband, although their colleagues provided the largest pool of "best friends" for the men. Further, the women did not use voluntary associations, churches, or their kin network to meet people after a move. They simply kept up with their old friends from the previous residence(s) and made new ones in the neighborhood, with the proportion of old to new diminishing with years in residence. The husbands, in addition to friends made at work, kept some from the last neighborhood, and very gradually added new neighbors to their "best" list. The women were twice as likely as the men to talk about "personal problems and feelings" with friends. Half the men did not communicate on this with either friend, 20 percent communicated with only one and 29 percent with both. On the other hand, 50 percent of the women communicated with both friends, and an additional 33 percent with one; 19 percent did not discuss personal feelings and problems with either best friend.

Cultural-level proscriptions regarding same-sex relationships may deter males from investing in friendship those energies best devoted to home, country, community, or company. Thus the homophobia generated by fear of male homosexuality actually functions to inhibit male closeness and to direct men to seek intimacy only within marriage. But through the marriage relationship they are more surely bound to the other institutional spheres of a society. For women, we propose precisely the opposite effect: the same-sex friendship draws her out of the isolation of the home and into a wider social network, serving an integrative function for both individual and society. Nor do female friendships compete with or detract from the mother-child bond. Rather, female friends often reinforce their involvement in the world of child rearing.

Whatever the virtues of sex-differential bonding patterns—male to male, female to child—for the society or for personal intimacy needs, they are most clearly demonstrated in the years of preparation for adulthood and those of assuming the major roles of parent and worker. In societies where mortality rates limited life expectancy for most members, and where kinship obligations governed most relationships, the story would end here. But today most men and women can expect to outlive these major roles and to enter an extended period of postparenthood and postemployment.

What of friendship in the later years?

In many ways, the data on friendship in later life is continuous with that on earlier ages: men are reported to have a wider range of social contacts (including family and civic/neighborhood activities), but the women have more stable, long-lived, and intense friendships (Powers and Bultena, 1976; Moss, Gottesman, and Kleban, 1976; Lowenthal et al., 1975; Cantor, 1976; Rosenkaimer et al., 1968). But here a very important variation in friendship patterns reflects the differential life expectancy and marriage ages of men and women. At older age levels, the proportions of men with a living spouse far exceed those of women. Not only do men typically marry women a few years younger than themselves, but female mortality rates are more favorable throughout adulthood, which ultimately creates a gross imbalance in marital status: In the United States today, at age sixty-five and over, 77 percent of men live with a wife, but only 38 percent of women have a living husband; and even among men over seventy-five, 68 percent still have a living spouse. Most surveys that ask "Do you have someone to talk over personal problems with?" find that these older men most often indicate their wives, while the women cite children or close friends (NCOA, 1974; Lowenthal and Haven, 1968; Rosenkaimer et al., 1968; Rutzen, 1977; Blau, 1973; Huyck, 1976).

While clearly adaptive in many respects, these friend/confidant(e) patterns have some hidden problems. For example, what of the working-class men whose fears of women and female behaviors have kept them from confiding in their wives (Lowenthal and Haven 1968), whose workmates are often lost in retirement, and whose buddies may have died? Their old age life space is severely reduced. And what of those who had considered their wife their best friend? When widowed, these men become prime candidates for mental illness and suicide (Lowenthal and Haven 1968; Bock, 1972; Bock and Webber, 1972; Gove, 1973; Rutzen, 1977). The paradox is that while marriage is a mental and physical preservative for men, it is also an "all the eggs in one basket" proposition. Bereft of the one relationship, they have little else to fall back on. They may, however, have money and other material resources, which in at least one extensive study (Atchley, 1976) were sufficient to give widowers a morale advantage over widows. But the weight of the evidence suggests that the female's well-socialized skill in personal relations gives her more flexibility in constructing social support networks, and may account for some of her enhanced life expectancy, even under conditions of material deprivation.

Nevertheless, for many women, especially those who invest heavily in the marriage relationship, widowhood can be as devastating as it is so often for men (Lopata, 1973a). Margaret Huyck (1976) has proposed that women's greater openness and responsiveness to others may place them under extraordinary stress in later life, as these important others die or move or otherwise withdraw their support. On the other hand, much research, reviewed by Kline (1975), indicates that women have been socialized for role discontinuity—not to pursue a single unchanging commitment, but to pick up and drop, acquire and relinquish—and that such experiences prepare women to deal with the role changes of later life. It has even been suggested that because women have had little experience in independence, the dependencies of old age will be less ego-stressful, making it easier for them to call upon family and friends for support (Berghorn et al., 1978).

Whatever the reason, women, and especially educated women (Lopata, 1973a), do seem to have reserves of interpersonal sensitivity in later life, as well as at earlier stages. Social participation is often associated with satisfaction and happiness in life or in marriage (Graney, 1975; Hess and Waring, 1978; Phillips, 1967). These advantages may not always accrue to women, since at certain life stages men will have a wider range of involvements. But to the extent that intimacy is more important than the number or variety of social contacts, women's friendships will have enhanced value in old age (Candy, 1976). Age, or life stage, may affect the needs for certain kinds of friendships, but individuals who find intimacy easy to achieve can make the most of available resources. There are always some people who have been lifelong "loners" and for whom the isolation of old age is a comfortable condition (Stephens, 1976), and many others who welcome the "disengagement" which old age permits or encourages (Cumming and Henry, 1961). But for most old people there is a great survival value in having someone who provides emotional support with whom to share the world.

Studies of friendship at various life stages all highlight the complex, even paradoxical nature of social relationships: family systems change, technology intervenes, history unfolds. What do they tell us of friendship among men and women today?

To the degree that male and female bonding patterns are built into the species—biosocially determined—it would appear that same-sex friendships for men will continue to support that world view which sees women as outsiders (we must take seriously the idea of a Little League team as the last vestige of a hunting party) and which ties men to the arena of civic and economic life. For women, the training to self-disclosure and intimacy makes both close friendship and mother-child bonding possible, and encourages sensitivity to the needs of husband and lovers—with the difference that close friendships are expected to involve reciprocity and the giving to children and husbands must be unconditional. But the picture is not so clear when we look at the later years of the life span, years which were not in the original evolutionary equation. Males who are incapable of self-disclosure with either men or women may be enormously successful in some forms of competition and achievement and become relatively disadvantaged in old age. The remarkable resilience and adaptability of older women may have its roots in their socialization to self-disclosure, expressiveness, and other-orientation—characteristics which have been perceived as barriers to success in economic and political roles at younger ages.

To the degree that we are dealing with socialized traits, however, it is possible to envision a society in which mutual trust and openness will characterize a variety of relationships among men and women, enriching friendships, marriages and personality development throughout the life course.

NOTES

1. The studies showing no difference often do not distinguish between very personal items and all other topics of conversation, so that men's greater range of interests may mask a qualitative difference in disclosure. (See Morgan, 1976.) There is also some evidence of response bias in findings on

friendship. Phillips and Clancy (1972) report that "social desirability" was more important than sex status in many surveys. Having a lot of friends was desirable to men, while intimacy with friends was seen as appropriate by women, and these perceptions did affect questionnaire responses.

2. Two interesting exceptions, both primarily middle-class samples, are Komarovsky's college men already cited, and Peter Stein's (1976) single adults. The Stein respondents displayed our by-now familiar sex differences in the meaning and depth of relationships, but also a sizable number of men who had female confidantes. Single women found other women easier to relate to than the men found other men; and where cross-sex relationships were formed, more men than women found these easier than same-sex friendships. Stein concluded that, overall, it's easier to be friends with women than with men.

3. Granovetter (1973) points out "The Strength of Weak Ties," namely that nonoverlapping networks allow for wider and more varied contacts, and receiving "new" information from a number of sources. Strong ties, on the other hand, are time-consuming, emotionally intense, and likely to be sustained among those who already share similar attitudes and beliefs.

REFERENCES

Atchley, Robert C., "Selected Social and Psychological Differences between Men and Women in Later Life, " *Journal of Gerontology* (1976), 31(No.2): 204–211.

Babchuk, Nicholas, "Primary Friends and Kin: A Study of the Associations of Middle-Class Couples," *Social Forces* (1965), 43: 483–493.

Babchuk, Nicholas, and Alan P. Bates, "The Primary Relations of Middle-Class Couples: A Study in Male Dominance," *American Sociological Review* (1963), 28 (No. 3): 377–384.

Bell, Robert R., manuscript paper, Philadelphia, Temple University, 1977.

Bell, Robert R., and Wendy Jones, "The Adult Male Sex Role and Resistance to Change," paper at National Council on Family Relations Annual Meeting, New York City, October, 1976.

Bender, V. Lee, Yvonne Davis, Oliver Glover, and Joy Stapp, "Patterns of Self-Disclosure in Homosexual and Heterosexual College Students," *Sex Roles* (1976), 2(No. 2): 149–159.

Berghorn, Forrest J., Donna E. Schafer, Geoffrey H. Steere, and Robert F. Wiseman, *The Urban Elderly: A Study of Life Satisfaction.* Montclair, N.J.: Allanheld, Osmun, 1978.

Blau, Zena Smith, *Old Age in a Changing Society.* New York: Franklin Watts, 1973.

Bock, E. Wilbur, "Aging and Suicide: The Significance of Marital, Kinship and Alternative Relations," *Family Coordinator* (1972), 21 (No.1): 71–79.

Bock, E. Wilbur, and Irving L. Webber, "Suicide Among the Elderly: Isolating Widowhood and Mitigating Alternatives," *Journal of Marriage and the Family* (1972), 34: 24–31.

Bott, Elizabeth, *Family and Social Network*. London: Tavistock Publ., 1957.

Candy, Sandra E. Gibbs, "A Developmental Exploration of the Functions of Friendship in Women," paper at Gerontological Society Annual Meeting, New York City, October, 1976.

Cantor, Marjorie, "The Configuration and Intensity of the Informal Support System in a New York City Elderly Population,"paper at Gerontological Society Annual Meeting, New York City, October, 1976.

Cozby, P. C., "Self-Disclosure: A Literature Review," *Psychological Bulletin* (1973), 79: 73–91.

Cumming, E., and Henry, William E., Jr., *Growing Old: The Process of Disengagement*. New York: Basic Books, 1961.

Fellin, Phillip, and Eugene Litwak, "Neighborhood Cohesion under Conditions of Mobility," *American Sociological Review* (1963), 28 (No. 3): 364–376.

Gove, Walter, "Sex, Marital Status and Mortality," *American Journal of Sociology* (1973), 79 (No. 1): 45–67.

Graney, Marshall J., "Happiness and Social Participation in Aging," *Journal of Gerontology* (1975), 30 (No. 6): 701–706.

Granovetter, Mark S., "The Strength of Weak Ties," *American Journal of Sociology* (1973), 78 (No. 6): 1360–1380.

Hacker, H. M. "Blabbermouths and Clams: Sex Differences in Self Disclosure," *Psychology of Women Quarterly*, forthcoming.

Hess, Beth B., "Friendship," in Matilda White Riley, Marilyn Johnson, and Anne Foner, eds., *Aging and Society, Vol. 3: A Sociology of Age Stratification*. New York: Russell Sage Foundation, 1972.

Hess, Beth B., and Joan M. Waring, "Changing Patterns of Aging and Family Bonds in Later Life," *The Family Coordinator*, (Oct. 1978), 27 (No. 4): 303–314.

Huyck, Margaret Hellie, "Sex, Gender and Aging," paper at Gerontological Society Annual Meeting, New York City, October, 1976.

Jacoby, Susan, "What Do I Do for the Next 20 Years?" *New York Times Magazine*, June 17, 1973.

Jourard, Sidney M., *The Transparent Self*. New York: D. Van Nostrand Co., 1971.

Kline, Chrysee, "The Socialization Process of Women: Implications for a Theory of Successful Aging," *The Gerontologist* (1975), 15 (No. 6): 486–492.

Komarovsky, Mirra, "Patterns of Self-Disclosure of Male Undergraduates," *Journal of Marriage and the Family* (1974), 36 (No. 4): 677–686.

Leis, Nancy B., "Women in Groups: Ijaw Women's Associations," in Michelle Z. Rosaldo and Louise Lamphere, eds., *Women, Culture and Society*. Stanford, California: Stanford University Press, 1974, pp. 223–242.

LeMasters, E. E., *Blue Collar Aristocrats*. Madison, Wisconsin: University of Wisconsin Press, 1975.

Lopata, Helena Z., "The Effect of Schooling on Social Contacts of Urban Women," *American Journal of Sociology* (1973a), 79 (No. 3): 604–619.

Lopata, Helena Z., *Widowhood in an American City*. Cambridge, Mass.: Schenkman Publishing Co., 1973b.

Lowenthal, Marjorie Fiske, and Clayton Haven, "Interaction and Adaptation: Intimacy as a Critical Variable," *American Sociological Review* (1968), 33 (No. 1): 20–30.

Lowenthal, Marjorie Fiske, Majda Thurner, David Chiriboga, and Associates, *Four Stages of Life*. San Francisco, California: Jossey-Bass Publishers, 1975.

Maccoby, Eleanor E., and Carol N. Jacklin, *The Psychology of Sex Differences*. Stanford, California: Stanford University Press, 1974.

Marciano, Theresa Donati, "Middle Class Incomes, Working Class Hearts," *Family Process* (1974), 13 (No. 4): 489–502.

Morgan, Brian S., "Intimacy of Disclosure Topics and Sex Differences in Self-Disclosure," *Sex Roles* (1976), 2 (No. 2): 161–166.

Moss, M. S., L. I. Gottesman, and M. H. Kleban, "Informal Social Relationships among Community Aged," paper at Gerontological Society Annual Meeting, New York City, 1976.

National Council on Aging, *The Myth and Reality of Aging in America*. New York: L. Harris and Assoc., 1974.

Nelson, Joel I., "Clique Contacts and Family Orientations," *American Sociological Review* (1966), 31 (No. 5): 663–672.

O'Neill, Sylvia, Deborah Fein, Kathryn McColl Velit, and Constance Frank, "Sex Differences in Pre-Adolescent Self-Disclosure," *Sex Roles* (1976), 1 (No. 1): 85–88.

Phillips, Derek L., "Social Participation and Happiness," *American Journal of Sociology* (1967), 72: 479–488.

Phillips, Derek L., and Kevin J. Clancy, "Some Effects of 'Social Desirability' in Survey Studies," *American Journal of Sociology* (1972), 77 (No. 5): 921–940.

Powers, Edward A., and Gordon L. Bultena, "Sex Differences in Intimate Friendships of Old Age," *Journal of Marriage and the Family* (1976), 38 (No. 4): 739–747.

Rosenkaimer, Diana, Avalie Saperstent, Barbara Ishizaki, and Stacy Mong MacBride, "Coping with Age-Sex Differences," paper at Gerontological Society Annual Meeting, New York City, October, 1968.

Rossi, Alice S., "A Biosocial Perspective on Parenting," *Daedelus*, April, 1977, pp. 1–31.

Rubin, Lillian B., *Worlds of Pain: Life in the Working Class Family*. New York: Basic Books, Inc. 1976.

Rutzen, Robert, "Varieties of Social Disengagement Among the Aged: A Research Report on Correlates of Primary Socialization," paper at Eastern Sociological Society Meeting, New York City, March, 1977.

Simmel, Georg, "Friendship, Love and Secrecy," translated by Albion Small, *American Journal of Sociology* (1906) 11: 457–466.

Smith-Rosenberg, Carroll, "The Female World of Love and Ritual: Relations between Women in Nineteenth-Century America," *Signs* (1975), 1 (No. 1): 1–29.

Stein, Peter J., "On Same-sex and Cross-sex Friendships," paper at National Council on Family Relations Annual Meeting, New York City, October, 1976.

Stephens, Joyce, *Loners, Losers, and Lovers*. Seattle: University of Washington Press, 1976.

Tiger, Lionel, *Men in Groups*. New York: Random House, 1970.

9/ SINGLES' BARS AS EXAMPLES OF URBAN COURTING PATTERNS

Natalie Allon and Diane Fishel

One of the most significant additions to social opportunities for singles has been the establishment of singles' bars. With the advent of these bars, singles had a place of their own to go, where they could feel comfortable and meet other single people. Once the need for singles-only gathering places was recognized by entrepreneurs, hotels and resorts organized singles' weekends, and singles-only "country" clubs and apartment complexes were established as well. The singles' bar is, however, still the most popular singles' establishment, since it is the most easily accessible.

Basic participant observation and interviews on the scene were the research methods. One hundred persons (plus several bartenders) were interviewed at eight singles' bars in Manhattan that stressed cross-sex relationships. Specific questions about age, occupation, and education were asked, and open-ended questions allowed participants to talk about their feelings and attitudes.

SITUATIONAL CHARACTERISTICS

SEX RATIO

The sex ratio in the singles' bars we visited was about 65 percent men and 35 percent women. One woman explained the sex ratio this way:

> There are definitely more males than females in the singles' bars. Men drink more than women and are more apt to go to a bar just to drink, to mingle or be with their friends, and maybe meet a few new females to possibly date. Females will almost never go to a bar just to drink, they go primarily to meet men, and if they are not in the mood to meet new people they won't go at all, whereas men will.

AGE

The age range in the singles' bars visited was about twenty-two to thirty for women; twenty-five to forty for men. The mean age is about twenty-five for women, twenty-eight for men.

SOCIAL BACKGROUND, EDUCATION, AND OCCUPATION

The overwhelming majority were from middle-class backgrounds. Most of the men said they had completed college and slightly less than half were taking graduate courses or had completed graduate school. Most had white-collar jobs.

Slightly more than half the women had completed college. Many of the women were teachers or secretaries/administrative assistants, and many were flight attendants. There were few professionals in the dating bars, and patrons did not anticipate meeting any there. The consensus among the women was that they wanted to meet men who had at least a college degree. The first thing the women were interested in finding out when they met a man was where he went to college and what his occupation was. In contrast, the men wanted to know if a woman lived alone and where she lived. They generally wanted a woman to have at least some college education, but that was not very important.

There were other conflicts in values. Most women were interested in finding a man they would want to marry. They did not seem to want a passing affair. Most men, on the other hand, were living strictly in the present.

INTERACTION AS SINGLES

For most bar attenders, single implies the legal and social status of being single—not married, living together, or going steady. A constant, steady relationship for these people implies "nonsingleness." For a minority of bar attenders, singleness seems to be wish fulfillment: Such people seem to yearn for singlehood and act out their desires by attending a singles' bar, despite their formal status as spouse.

Men more often than women entered singles' bars by themselves. The men often went to the bar to meet their friends, but did not necessarily come with them. Most women entered with female friends in order to feel more "secure."

Behavior in the singles' bar frequently showed an eagerness to form a relationship. Gazing with intense eyes, whispering, stroking hair, hugging, kissing, and displaying one's body were cues of readiness to be "coupled."

Other behavior indicated a meticulous concern with the self. During a conversation one would often see either the speaker or the listener checking to make sure a sweater was on straight or every hair was in place. In some dating bars, participants seemed so involved with their own and others' bodies that there was little opportunity to begin to develop empathy for another. And a cardinal principle seemed to be that first impressions do count.

STARING

Staring was a game people played with each other's eyes; it is a basic singles' bar cue that a person wants to initiate a relationship. Women would stare when they saw a man they wanted to meet, but would not actually approach him. As in the traditional sex-role stereotypes, women still seemed to feel that the man should initiate the relationship.

A man often would stare at a certain woman to single her out of the crowd. Then she would know that he wanted to meet her and not any number of other women around her. Mutual staring seemed to show that a man and woman wanted to start their own party.

TOUCHING

We observed that people in the singles' bars had a habit of touching each other. It could be a hand or a shoulder, a pat on the head, a hand steadying a hand to light a cigarette, or an entire body touch. Touching happened not only in crowds but also when there was plenty of room to pass without having body contact.

Touching was often a simple gesture to start a conversation. "What an attractive necklace you're wearing," one man said to a woman, while stroking her neck. "It must have taken you years to grow your hair that long," another man said as he ran his fingers through a woman's hair. The touching seemed to reinforce what they were saying and at the same time establish intimacy.

Touching might be a sign of approval or a gesture of affection, or of course have sexual connotations. Touching might also be a pompous way of assuring oneself of being noticed.

SEX-ROLE STEREOTYPES

The people in the singles' bars seem to conform to traditional stereotyped sex roles. Men light women's cigarettes, buy them drinks, offer them bar stools, and so on. Women try to be superfeminine; they expect the men to light their cigarettes and buy them drinks. The men play to women's egos and vice versa.

The division of sex roles is perhaps even more clearly defined in the bar environment than elsewhere. Most women expect a man to take their phone number or ask them out; most men do not expect a woman to call them or ask them out. When a woman in a dating bar says that she is liberated, she generally means sexually liberated only.

ALIENATION AND SOCIABILITY

Alienation and sociability are both clearly identifiable in word talk, body talk, and eye talk. Bar participants frequently give the impression of being "all over the place," relating to different people on different levels at the same time. Typically, silent communication occurs between two bar attenders in a different section of the room, each somewhat involved in a verbal conversation with someone nearby.

An initiator acts tentative enough so that if he is rejected he can maintain that no overture was intended. When the recipient encourages an overture, it is in a way that can be viewed as mere friendliness, should the need arise to fall back on that interpretation.

SOCIAL MOTIVATIONS FOR GOING TO SINGLES' BARS

The two most frequent explanations were "companionship" and "escape from boredom."

Bar participants expressed a strong need and desire for companionship. For them it connoted various kinds of sociability:

Intimacy. I'm here because I'd really like to find a man to love, to get married and settle down (woman).

Social Integration. I'm just looking for a gal of similar interests—a buddy. Sure we both might enjoy sex—it's fun—but I like sports and all kinds of music. It's fun to do things with somebody who likes your thing too (man).

Nurturing. I really feel that I want a kid and I sure want the right father for it. I know I need a father sometimes too, so I want a strong man who knows who he is (woman).

Reassurance of Worth. I want a gal who'll build me up, pat me on the back. She can do her own thing too, but I'm not a woman's libber, so if I have a hard day at work she'll understand—at least I know I have a good little woman (man).

Assistance and Guidance. I'm looking for a guy who'll help me find myself even more. Like I'm not really sure what I

> want to do with my life and I figure I can get a better perspective by finding a guy I really like. You do find yourself through somebody else (woman).

Most participants admitted to being lonely. Some wanted temporary companionship. Some sought short-term but steady companionship. Others were looking for somebody to date occasionally or on a long-term basis. Still others wanted to begin relationships that might lead to marriage.

There is much pressure and tension connected with finding such companionship at the singles' bar. Alienation and sociability operate hand in hand. The greater the show of sociability, the greater may be the sociopsychological distance of people from each other.

The atmosphere is strained and forced. Because people are trying very hard to meet people, they seem to smile all the time so that no one will think they're bored or uninterested, and they try to create the impression that they always know the correct thing to do. There is a lot of competition in a singles' bar.

Everyone seems defensive and on guard, not at all natural. A number of people commented that they were surprised to see how different someone they met in a singles' bar acted on a date.

> Everyone knows why you're here; you want to meet people. But at the same time no one wants to seem over-anxious. You have to be very cool about it, and the tougher you act the cooler people will think you are (man).

> I do want to meet new men to go out with, but I don't want them to think I'm hard up for a date. I try not to seem too excited if a guy asks for my number or asks to take me out . . . . Guys can be real smartasses, especially if they think you really want them (woman).

When we asked bartenders why people went to their bars, they all said that people were there because they were lonely and wanted to meet old and new friends. But the bartenders added that these people still seemed lonely and discontented even at the bar.

Next to companionship, boredom was most often cited as the reason for attending singles' bars. Many singles want a diversion from the daily humdrum and a place to relax from the tensions of the working day. Other people go to the singles' bars to break up a dull evening:

> I come home from work, have dinner, take it easy for a while, maybe watch a little TV or read the paper, then I

go out for an hour or so. Going to a singles' bar is a good way to end the day. Maybe I'll meet some new people. In any event, it's a nice change of pace (man).

Bar participants talked about feeling isolated in jobs at which they had only superficial and fragmented relations with others. In the dating bar they could talk about life experiences, exchange information about social gatherings, and join in sexual banter.

FURTHER STUDY OF SINGLES' SOCIAL LIFE

Since we visited a limited number of bars, all on the Upper East Side of Manhattan, we cannot speculate whether differences or similarities can be found in dating bars elsewhere, in other neighborhoods and other cities. Most of the people we saw and talked with were middle- and upper-middle class, white and young. Our study did not compare relationships among same-sex companions, since the dating bars we visited put a premium on opposite-sex relationships and "antagonistic cooperation" between same-sex associates. A comparative study of other singles' establishments such as singles-only apartment houses, country clubs, organizations, summer retreats, and resorts holding singles' weekends would also be useful. Dating bars are only one aspect—though in metropolitan areas an increasingly important one—of increasing options for life-style choices among singles.

NOTE

1. This article is a revised version of a paper presented at the annual meetings of the American Sociological Association. A different and much longer version appears in *Urban Life Styles*, by Natalie Allon (Dubuque, Iowa: Wm. Brown Co., 1979).

REFERENCES

Goffman, Erving. *Behavior in Public Places: Notes on the Social Organization of Gatherings.* New York: The Free Press, 1963.

Laing, R. D. *The Divided Self: An Existential Study in Sanity and Madness.* Baltimore, Md.: Penguin Books, 1965.

Scheflen, Albert E. *Body Language and the Social Order.* Englewood Cliffs, N. J.: Prentice-Hall, Inc., 1972.

Simmel, Georg. "The Metropolis and Mental Life," trans. Gerth and Mills. In *Man Alone: Alienation in Modern Society,* edited by Josephson and Josephson. New York: Dell Pub. Co., 1962.

———."The Sociology of Sociability," trans. Everett C. Hughes, *American Journal of Sociology* LV (November 1949).

10/ SEXUALITY IN THE MIDDLE YEARS

Martha Cleveland

This paper examines the sexual dimension in the lives of middle-aged men and women who have been recently divorced or who are in the process of divorcing. The conclusions presented do not result from a specific research project; rather, they have been developed from clinical impressions gained through counseling with such individuals. The clinical observations have been made in a midwestern metropolitan location and may not, therefore, be typical of national norms or other geographical areas.

The middle years are a time when each of us must confront our own sexuality (Sheehy, 1974). They are the years when physiological factors result in an undeniable change in our sexual behavior and raise new questions about our feelings of masculinity and femininity. Middle-aged men often report increasing emotional needs for tenderness and intimacy, less sexual aggressiveness, and a tendency to become more relationship-oriented than they have been in the past. Women in their middle years often report feeling stronger, more sure of themselves, more in control of relationships, and more sexually aggressive than ever before. These changing feelings are difficult to deny and tend to force us, in the middle years of our lives, to reevaluate our own sexuality.

The middle-years confrontation with sexuality is probably more difficult for divorcing people than it is for men and women whose marriages remain intact. Sexual attitudes and behaviors of the married are primarily tied to the spouse, and when separation and divorce take place these attitudes and behaviors may no longer seem desirable or even relevant. The new social and emotional status thrust upon divorcing men and women makes a redefinition of the sexual self imperative.

SEXUAL BEHAVIOR IN MIDDLE-YEARS DIVORCE

Although some couples retain satisfactory sex lives with deteriorating marriages, this is rare. More common is a sex life that, in microcosm, reflects the dynamic problems of the marriage. In most cases sexual interaction between spouses almost ceases for an appreciable period before separation. Either or both spouses may have alternative sexual partners during this time.

In a previous article the author has discussed the physiological, behavioral, and emotional realities of sex in middle-years marriage (Cleveland, 1976). Following separation, the physiological reality of the middle-aged divorcing man or woman is the same as that of his or her married counterpart. However, the stimulation of the need to redefine one's identity, a changed living situation, and new partners may yield an increase in sexual feelings and erotic behaviors. On the other hand, the tension and anxiety engendered by the situation may result, for some, in impotence or in problems with ejaculation or orgasm. No male clients and very few female clients indicate that sex is not an issue in their adjustment to divorce.

For divorcing men and women, there seem to be four main avenues of sexual outlet. These outlets are not mutually exclusive: at any given time any individual may choose one or more of them.

1. *Sexual interaction with the spouse.* It is not uncommon for a separated couple to have sexual relations with each other. However, clients are reluctant to disclose this behavior because in many states it is legally defined as "contamination" and may jeopardize the legal process of divorce.

2. *Masturbation.* Masturbation is commonly reported by men. Fewer women disclose masturbation, but most report having erotic dreams that result in orgasm.

3. *Short-term partners (either serial or concurrent).* During any period of redefinition of self, gender-related concerns are an important component of that definition. Separation or divorce may traumatize an individual's sense of masculinity or femininity. As a result, for many divorced or divorcing men and women it seems crucial to be able to attract a new partner. Sexual encounters and "conquests" may become goals for their "new" postdivorce self. This goal seems to be particularly elusive for mid-life individuals who have been culturally conditioned to feel that physical aging is not sexually attractive. As a result, some mid-life divorcing people become involved in frantic efforts to appear and act younger than they are. In order to prove that sexual responsiveness has not been affected by the aging process, they are apt to set up unrealistic performance goals for themselves which, when not met, yield anxiety and therefore difficulty in subsequent performances. The individual becomes

a victim of the need to "prove" his or her sexual identity. The effort at youthful behavior most often results in tension and a distorted sense of reality that delays the individual's emotional acceptance of the objective situation and the reality of a middle-years self.

In terms of gender-related difficulties, there seem to be interesting differences between men and women. Client responses indicate that men want to prove their sexual virility to themselves and to society. Women, on the other hand, want to prove their sexual desirability to themselves and to their ex-spouse. The male wants to prove his ability to perform, the female her ability to attract. The male wants to prove himself to himself and society, the female to herself and her ex-partner.

Some divorcing men and women who choose short-term partners as their avenue of sexual outlet seem to do so as a kind of acting out or rebellious behavior. They report it as an aggressive action aimed directly at their former spouse or as rebellious behavior directed against "everyone and everything." When the resistance is worked through, rebellion against spouse or "everyone and everything" turns out to be rebellion against their own feelings of disappointment, frustration, and failure, and an attempt at protection against their own despair.

A special group that may choose short-term partners for sexual outlet is made up of women who have experienced long-term sexual dysfunction within the marital relationship. After separation or divorce, and with a changed life situation and emotional outlook, their dysfunction may disappear. These women, perhaps for the first time in their lives, experience good sexual relations, and many feel the need to "make up for lost time."

In choosing short-term sexual partners, both men and women tend to choose people younger than themselves. Men often pick younger women for reasons that point to upholding a facade of youthfulness and to avoid the threat they seem to feel from women their own age. They indicate that this threat arises from either of two sources: (a) the physical similarity of middle-aged women to their ex-wife; and/or (b) women of middle years seem to them to be more aggressive than younger women. Men report having expectations for ongoing monogamous relationships with younger women.

Middle-years divorcing women also seem to pick younger short-term sexual partners. The reasons they give for this choice indicate a revitalization of feelings of youthful desirability and excitement. Women do not seem to have expectations that lasting relationships will grow out of these encounters.

Divorcing men and women both seem to have realistic expectations concerning the possibility of ongoing relationships with younger partners. It is culturally acceptable for men to have wives significantly younger than they, but it is not acceptable for a woman to be married to a significantly younger man. Physiologically, however, the man with the younger wife is in a potentially difficult situation. Over time, as the novelty of sex with a new and younger woman decreases and his physiology catches up with his emotions, his sexual "youthfulness" will prove to be illusory, and there is a high probability that the couple may become sexually less compatible.

For people who use short-term relationships as their sexual outlet, loneliness tends to become an increasing problem. Most middle-years divorced and divorcing people report that loneliness is more of an issue in the development of heterosexual relationships than is sex. Once the newness and novelty of changing short-term partners wears off, continuing isolated sexual encounters tend to increase the sense of isolation. These encounters are reported to be empty and meaningless. Women indicate that they expected that sex without a sense of ongoing intimacy would be meaningless over the long run. Men, on the other hand, are often confused and frightened by their reaction. They do not understand the rising needs for tenderness and intimacy that come with their middle years, and they tend to classify these feelings as weak and unmanly.

4. *Ongoing monogamous partners.* It is most common to find that men or women who use an ongoing monogamous relationship as their sexual outlet during and immediately following divorce were involved in this relationship before they separated from their spouse. In fact, the relationship is often the immediate catalytic factor in the decision to terminate marriage. In cases where spouses separate because of another man or woman, added pressure seems to be felt by the "deserted" spouse to show that he or she is still sexually desirable and competent. "I'll show him [or her]" becomes a central theme in post-separation sexual behavior.

The ongoing monogamous relationship pattern seems to be the most ultimately desirable outlet for middle-aged divorcing people. The great majority of both men and women report that finding an ongoing relationship, inside or outside of marriage, is their sexual goal.

No matter which of the above patterns of sexual outlet a man or woman chooses, analysis of the sexual behaviors of the middle-aged divorced and divorcing indicates five basic motivational elements: (a) a need to "act out" or rebel; (b) a need to validate their masculinity or femininity; (c) a need for companionship, intimacy, and affectional outlet; (d) a need to blot out the emotional sense of failure and "last chance"; and (e) a need to find an ongoing monogamous relationship. At any one time, any one or any combination of these motivations may predominate for a given individual.

USE OF SEX DURING THE DIVORCE PROCESS

Cohabitation (sexual relations) between separated spouses is fairly common and may confuse the resolution of separation and, finally, the resolution of divorce. Postseparation cohabitation may raise hopes of reconciliation for either or both spouses. These hopes are particularly difficult for the middle-aged divorcing to handle; their senses of failure and "last chance" combine to make them frantic in their attempt to come to a final resolution "before it is too late." Also, cohabitation is often used by a spouse as a part of a manipulative double message: "I want a divorce, leave me/We are so attracted to each other we must stay together" or "I can't stand you any longer, I want a divorce/I find you sexually irresistible." The double messages may raise unrealistic hopes for reconciliation for a spouse who wants to maintain the marriage or may be confusing and frightening to a spouse who is unsure of his or her decision to divorce.

In addition to the negatives, there may be positive aspects to cohabitation. It may be useful in that for one spouse the recognition of the other spouse's manipulative use of the double message, and/or the raising and dashing of unrealistic hopes for reconciliation, may ultimately be helpful in reaching a realistic definition of the situation. Also, cohabitation can, for some individuals, come to be a validation of separation. These men and women find the sexual interaction satisfying, but it brings on no desire to remain in the relationship.

Following separation, some individuals use their sexual relationship with a new partner as a tool to hurt or enrage their former spouse. They may flaunt their new relationship by bringing the new partner when picking up children for visitation or having the new partner present to be with the children during the period of visitation. The ploy is usually successful, and the ex-partner, whether or not he or she also has a new partner, experiences feelings ranging from "qualms" through "hurt" to full-scale rage when he or she becomes aware of the old spouse's new sexual relationship.

OPPORTUNITIES FOR SEXUAL INTERACTION

Although it is decreasing, for many middle-age divorcing people there still exists a double standard for postseparation sexual involvement; such involvement is acceptable for men, but not for women. This double standard exists both externally (normatively in the greater culture) and internally (on an intrapersonal level). The result is that it is far more difficult for divorcing women to find opportunities to develop heterosexual relationships than it is for divorcing men.

Statistics show that previously married people tend to remarry those of their own marital status; widows and widowers intermarry, and divorced women find remarriage with divorced men. The problem, then, is to find socially acceptable situations in which divorced people may meet. Most mid-life divorcing men and women complain of the difficulty of finding ways in which to meet new people. The efforts of married friends do not seem to fill this need, and many of the groups and places utilized for this purpose (e.g., Parents Without Partners, divorce adjustment groups, singles' bars, and health clubs) seem to the middle-aged to consist of twenty- and thirty-year olds, groups with whom they feel they have little in common and by whom they do not feel welcomed. The end result is that they are left very much on their own in terms of finding opportunities for sexual interaction.

CHILDREN AND SEXUAL BEHAVIOR IN MIDDLE-YEARS DIVORCE

Many "after forty" divorcing families contain adolescent offspring. For these mothers and fathers their children's developing sexuality is often particularly difficult to handle, a constant reminder of their own sexual insecurities.

Another problem is that parents' sexual relations in divorce are very hard for adolescents to deal with. Research shows that most adolescents do not visualize their middle-aged parents as sexual beings (Pocs, Godow, Tolone, & Walsh, 1977), nor do the parents want them to do so. This poses a real problem both during and following the divorce process. Parents are resentful when their children question or disapprove of their dating patterns or partners. Children often feel resentful and rejected by their parents' overt need for heterosexual companionship. This problem is exacerbated by the adolescents' feelings concerning their own sexual development and the adolescent tendency to project their own sexual confusion, fears, desires, and fantasies onto the dating parent.

In sum, a middle-aged divorcing mother and her teenaged daughter may each be dating, but motivations and behaviors involved in the dating will be very different. Unless the mother and daughter are able to recognize and discuss these differences, the whole area of sexual behavior may become a fertile area of conflict between them.

LONG-TERM SINGLEHOOD

Older divorced men are statistically much more apt to remarry than are older divorced women. The probability for a single woman's remarriage at the age of forty is three in five (Hunt & Hunt, 1977);

by the age of sixty-five it is one in thirty-two (Nye & Berardo, 1973). Middle-aged divorce, like middle-aged widowhood, results in a large number of aging women who remain single. In terms of ongoing sexual behavior, these women seem to have five possibilities open to them:

1. They can deny their need for sexual outlet on the basis of their age and can validate their femininity in the traditional female roles of mother to their married children and grand-mother to their grandchildren.

2. They can develop autoerotic patterns and define themselves as self-sufficient sexually.

3. They can attempt to maintain ongoing sexual relationships with younger men.

4. They can have short-term or concurrent affairs as long as they can find partners.

5. They can develop lesbian relationships.

Until the present, Numbers 1 and 4 seem to have been the most typical patterns. Although this is highly speculative, it is possible that in the future the traditional normative acceptance of females' affec-tion to each other may combine with the rise in the women's move-ment and the gay movement to yield an increasing number of les-bian relationships among aging single women.

CONCLUSION

At present there is no indication that the number of divorces among couples over forty will decrease. On the contrary, as social accep-tance of divorce grows, as no-fault divorce laws are implemented, and as social alternatives for divorced men and women increase, the number of marital dissolutions in the middle years may continue to climb. It is evident that sexual behavior is an important dimension in the lives of divorced and divorcing middle-aged people; this paper is a report of clinical impressions concerning that dimension. What is needed next is rigorous research to validate or reject the impressions that have been presented here. Only then can we draw a true picture of a situation in which many men and women will find themselves in the years to come.

REFERENCES

Cleveland, M. Sex in marriage: At 40 and beyond. *Family Coordinator*, July 1976, pp.223–240.

Hunt, M., & Hunt, B. *The divorce experience.* New York: McGraw-Hill, 1977.

Nye, F., & Berardo, F. *The family: Its structure and interaction.* New York: Macmillan, 1973.

Pocs, O., Godow, A., Tolone, W., & Walsh, R. Is there sex after 40? *Psychology Today,* June 1977, p.54.

Sheehy, G. *Passages.* New York: E. P. Dutton, 1974.

11/ FORBIDDEN COLORS OF LOVE: Patterns of Gay Love

John Alan Lee

My title combines two other titles—*Forbidden Colors*, a novel about Japanese gay life by Yukio Mishima, and *Colors of Love* (Lee, 1973), a typology of love styles. Mishima's (1970, p. 90) hero, Yuichi, sits in a Tokyo gay bar: "Whenever a man entered, all the guests would look up. The man coming in would be instantly bathed in glances. Who could guarantee that the ideal sought for so long would not suddenly take shape and appear through that glass door?"

Similar scenes are familiar in gay bars from Toronto to Stockholm, San Francisco to Munich. After interviewing over 200 heterosexuals and homosexuals for my typology of love styles, I am convinced that gay and straight alike face the sad truth of Erich Fromm's (1963, p. 4) remark: "There is hardly any activity, any enterprise, which is started with such tremendous hopes and expectations, and yet which fails so regularly, as love."

The parallel problem of "single" men and women, gay or straight, encountering suitable partners for intimacy and possible mate selection is emphasized by the convergence of life-styles of single people in the large city. Judith Rossner's (1975) *Looking for Mr. Goodbar* might have as easily and credibly been written about gay men or women.

Morton Hunt (1966, pp. 96–98) describes the search for love, but to which sexual orientation does the following refer? "A loosely integrated, semi-secret society within a society . . . seeking out places where they can receive a given service . . . mingling with potential mates . . . on the lookout . . . at the local pickup bar." The description is that of divorced people in America's *World of the Formerly Married,* not homosexual males. But the fear that "you're nobody till somebody loves you" motivates gay and straight alike to exclaim, "I want a lover!" (Belkin, 1975).

In this paper I will outline very briefly some of the major styles of loving relevant to male homosexuals, and relate the changing fashions in gay love styles to gay liberation and the gay subculture. The method by which the types or styles of loving were developed is rather complicated and can only be summarized here (cf. Lee, 1973, for detailed explanation). A quota sample of men and women of various ages and social classes, in England and Canada, were interviewed on their experiences of intimate adult affiliation ("love" or "being in love"). The interview instrument was an original one devised by the author, consisting of an omnibus love story, which combines into one set of card selections all the possible varieties of basic intimate events of every conceivable love story. This "Love Story Card Sort" was developed out of an exhaustive review of the fictional and nonfictional literature of love. Using its 1,500 cards, each respondent could compose and reconstruct his or her own experience of love with another person. The Sort was produced in appropriate variations for sex, multiple relationships, and special situations such as illicit affairs. In the occasional event for which no card was supplied, the respondent provided the details by using an "other" card. Since all the anticipated events were already precoded, further coding required only the classification of "other" unanticipated events.

Several methods of data processing were used to sort the variety of relationships described by the respondents into certain basic sequences of events. There was clearly no single, universal pattern, and thus no one "true" style of loving. However, the varieties in styles of loving are surprisingly small, just as are the number of primary colors necessary to an artist, from which all other hues and shades may be constructed. Thus a small taxonomy of types of loving was developed, each type characterized by its most salient features. As will be seen below, it is as easy to recognize each love style, and distinguish it from the others, as to recognize red, blue, or yellow. There are six primary styles of loving, but one of them, altruistic, self-sacrificing *agape* (commonly called "Christian love"), is not very relevant to this study, and is not described below. As in colors, it is possible to mix primary love styles to produce secondaries—for example, eros and ludus to produce ludic-erotic love.

A TYPOLOGICAL APPROACH TO LOVE

How long should a relationship last before it qualifies for the name of love rather than infatuation? How exclusive is the experience of "real love"? How jealous should "true love" be? Capellanus (1941, p. 53), the codifier of twelfth-century courtly love, argued that the lover who is not jealous is not a true lover. Margaret Mead, however, believed that "jealousy is not a barometer by which depth of love can be read, but merely records the degree of the lover's insecurity" (Krich, 1960, p. 94).

Various observers of love have argued its "true" nature for 2,000 years, and littered our fictional and nonfictional literature with various definitons of love. Indeed, the idea of love is considered the most complex in Western ideologies (Hazo, 1967, p. xi). My approach is that of constructive typology (McKinney, 1966). Rather than attempt a definition of love, I have accepted any consistently definable pattern of positive, intimate adult affiliation related to mate selection as a "style" of loving, and endeavored to produce a typology that distinguishes each love style by its most salient characteristics (Lee, 1974).

A taxonomical approach to love has important advantages. It ends the frustrating debate about whether "you *really* love me," or "love me *as much as* I love you," and directs attention instead to the ways in which each of us love "after our fashion." We may then determine to what extent our love styles are compatible or congruent. The search for a suitable mate becomes that for a partner with an appropriate love style. The derogatory definition of discordant love styles, by such labels as "puppy love," infatuation, mere sexual attraction, or "only an affair" is discouraged. The temptation to rewrite our own biographies through alternation (Berger, 1963, p. 54) is reduced; instead we can learn from each love experience, and more clearly define our preferences in love styles, just as a variety of experiences enables us to choose more aptly a satisfying life-style.

One cautionary note is always necessary when introducing a theory of love styles. The typology is one of relationships, not of lovers. An individual may move through a love career in which one preferred love style gives way to another; and a relationship itself, over time, may be altered in predominant love style. When I refer, for example, to a "manic lover" I mean simply a lover who, in the relationship in question at the time in question, was enacting a manic love style. Some lovers, of course, remain within the same love style for a lifetime.

EROS

This love style is the search for a partner whose physical presentation of self—visually, orally, tactilely, and so forth—conforms with an ideal image held in the mind of the lover. The definition of this image varies with individuals, and almost any would-be lover has some notion of what attracts him, but in the erotic love style first priority is given to this image. The lover is not interested in becoming acquainted with candidates who do not hold out the promise of conformity with the image.

The erotic lover is usually aware of the rarity of individuals conforming to his ideal, among the persons he encounters daily. When a hopeful encounter occurs, there is a surge of anticipation and excitement. Stendhal (1957, p. 53) called it a "sudden sensation of recognition and hope."

Any statistician could tell an erotic lover how poor his chances are for even a short list of desired qualities that must all occur in the same person. The odds must be awesome indeed for an erotic lover who advertised in a gay paper: "White male seeks lover. You should be 19 to a youthful 30, good-looking, no beard or mustache, blond hair and brown eyes, slender, under six feet, well endowed, well shaped very hairy legs, masculine, straight-looking. Write with photo to———."

A gay male who consistently pursues a narrowly defined ideal image becomes known among his friends for "his type." The type, or ideal image, becomes a screening mechanism. He walks into a bar, looks over scores of men, and grumbles, "There's no one here tonight."

When he does meet a possible incarnation of the ideal image, there is an urgency that may spoil his management of front and presentation of self. He is in danger of "rushing" the prospective partner to bed, because usually intimate tactile contact and full revelation of the body are necessary to assure the lover that the ideal image is fully actualized. The discovery, for example, that the candidate has a very hairy back, when the ideal image demands smoothness of skin, would promptly disqualify an otherwise suitable partner.

LUDUS

The ludic lover (the term comes from Ovid, *amor ludens*) has a playful style, as the name indicates. While aware of the differences between bodies, he considers it foolish to restrict one's chances by specializing in only one type. As in *Finian's Rainbow*, when he doesn't find a face he fancies, he fancies the face he finds. Love is expected to be pleasant and noncommittal, lasting as long as the two parties enjoy the relationship, and no longer. Ludus is not merely one-night stands or casual sex; on the contrary, it may become an elaborate ritual of behavior, as in the courtly love style of seventeenth-century France.

At some periods in history ludus has been depreciated as exploitation, manipulation, even seduction, but a playful style of love like that proposed by Ovid twenty centuries ago is again gaining widespread currency. An example of a gay advertisement for a playful partner reads: "Adventuresome 27-year-old, not sick of the bar and bath scene, charming and attractive, likes fun, travel and love and affection. Seeks man with lots of money who is fun to be with. Age not important. We can bring much warmth into our lives if you are ready."

Sometimes a gay couple who have established a more committed love style for their own relationship will seek playful relationships with others outside the pair. An ad titled "Three is no crowd" sought "fun-loving companions" for such a couple. This emphasizes the point that a lover may enact different styles in different, concurrent relationships.

STORGE

This ancient Greek term (rhymes with "more gay") for affectionate companionship arising out of gradual acquaintance, as between cousins or childhood friends growing up together, is appropriate for the style of loving in which an individual "grows accustomed to" the partner, rather than "falling in love."

Storge is not the sort of love in which one can advertise for a partner, obviously, so I will refer to interview reports instead.

> Andy and Alan have been together for 15 years. They first met and became friends while at college.
>
> It was more than 2 years before each discovered the other was gay. Indeed, it was in relation to the other that each realized his own gayness. Andy and Alan are not so much homosexuals as they are homosexual in relation to each other. Neither has had a gay relationship with any other man.

A love relationship does not require two individuals with identical love styles, though in most cases that would assure the greatest agreement.

> Barry is a balding professor of 40 years, whose charm and sophistication compensate for homely appearance. His preference in love styles is eros, and his ideal image is the tall, blond Scandinavian youth. This is a type generally in great demand in North American gay places, and considering Barry's looks, his chances of mating with such an ideal seemed slim.
>
> But Barry was lucky. He met Alan, a handsome Scandinavian new in town and looking for friends. Alan grew up in a small town and had the typical rural manner—shy, dependent, and reserved. He was turned off by the "pretty boys" who fell all over him, but was drawn to Barry's self-

assured, steady, and gentle style. Alan has no ideal image of a sought-for partner; his style of loving is storge. Barry nicely fulfills Alan's prescription, and Alan, Barry's.

The typical storgic lover prefers a gradual process of self-disclosure, especially of the physical body in sex. Thus Barry could easily have ruined his chances by rushing Alan to bed. Fortunately, his long years of searching had taught him to respect the potential partner's love style. Even luckier, he met Alan in the shower room of a swimming pool, so he knew that Alan's body fully conformed to the desired ideal.

MANIA

A lover who feels lonely and discontented with life anxiously seeks a partner—almost anyone will do—to fill the void left by his own lack of self-esteem. He will likely act out a manic style of loving. The symptoms are all too familiar: intense mental preoccupation with the beloved, who is often an unlikely and even unwilling choice, jealous possessiveness, repeated demands for assurances of love by the partner, dramatic scenes, even violent expressions of love.

The manic lover has no ideal image but becomes obsessed with whoever is chosen as the object of fixation. A gay ad reads: "Wanted desperately, a friend for long-lasting companionship. Size/looks unimportant. Am new to gay scene."

A common theme among those whose style of loving is mania is the fatigue and despair resultant from repeated rejection in the bar scene. The playful, noncommittal style of ludus works well in the bar, especially for those who are self-assured, even vain. If one has good looks to be vain about, so much the better. The typical manic lover, by contrast, "has had it with bar people" and is "tired of tricks and insincere people."

The sociopsychological factors that predispose some heterosexuals to mania, especially discontent with life and low self-esteem (Reik, 1949, p. 96), are even more likely to occur in homosexuals coping poorly with homophobic social environments, disapproving parents, the anxieties of living "in the closet," and similar factors. If the lover has internalized society's disapproval as a form of self-oppression (Hodges & Hutter, 1974), then he may also despise any partner, who becomes an unconscious accomplice in the lover's homosexuality. This condition facilitates the familar love-hate ambivalence so typical of mania.

PRAGMA

The Greek root for pragmatic or practical refers to an approach to love in which considerations of social and personal compatibility are paramount. The education, race, social class, vocation, religion, politics, or similar characteristics of candidates are of first concern to the pragmatic lover. If the lover's social norms of mate selection include certain prescriptions of physical appearance (such as considering excess weight a stigma), these will form part of the pragmatic lover's shopping list, but he will be otherwise relatively indifferent to considerations of physical attractiveness.

Pragma is a style of loving easily converted to utilitarian manipulation, whether through "arrangements" by a marriage broker or by computer dating and similar facilities. The object is a compatible union; if compatibility goes out of the relationship through change of one or both parties, this style of loving defines disengagement as perfectly reasonable—in contrast to mania, for example, in which a threat of separation may even lead to counterthreats of suicide.

Social stigmatizations of homosexuality have made pragmatic mate selection difficult. While an increasing number of heterosexual computer dating agencies flourish in large cities such as Toronto, using the most sophisticated technology such as closed-circuit television, several attempts to establish a gay introduction service have failed. In the United States, such services seem rapidly to degenerate into sources of sexual assignation and one-night stands.

An alternative pragmatic method is the use of newspaper advertising. Even the use of photographs does not provide much assurance for the erotic lover, but a lengthy, detailed description of one's own social and personal characteristics, together with a list of those desired in the partner, can perform much the same function as a computer dating service. If there is a hazard for the pragmatic advertiser, it is in the exploitation of the same medium by playful, ludic lovers who do not share the pragmatic lover's earnest desire for a long-term, committed relationship (assuming a compatible partner is located).

A probable pragmatic advertisement reads: "Looking for mature male, who is easygoing, sincere, faithful, to share my interest in theater, books, art, quiet evenings at home, music; for friendship which hopefully can lead to a permanent relationship. I am 38, quiet, reserved, professional. If you are seriously looking for a lover, looks are not important."

A determination of which personal advertisements in a gay newspaper originated from lovers preferring a pragmatic love style, in contrast to those preferring eros, ludus, or mania, would be somewhat arbitrary. While an element of desperation, loneliness, and indifference to type of partner would indicate mania, and a playful, permissive (or pluralistic), nonjealous attitude would indicate ludus, with eros suggested when there is a great emphasis on physical appearance, together with the insistence on a photograph, there are many ads that lack the necessary clues . . . .

GAY COMMUNES AND GROUP MARRIAGE

Heterosexual speculation on the future of marriage has recently been turning toward various extensions of the married pair/nuclear family formation (Constantine, 1973; Kammeyer, 1975; Libby, 1973; Rimmer, 1973). As James Ramey (1972) notes, the communal or group marriage, which combines commitment to the group with multiple pair-bonding among members, is the most complex form of marriage.

In terms of the typology of love styles, a group marriage would probably function with the least friction arising from jealousy if there were an appropriately balanced mixture of two love styles: storge and ludus. Storge would supply the communal loyalty and companionship between pairs, while ludus would provide a sufficient degree of playful detachment from excessively intense or passionate involvement within any dyad. In the traditional romantic union, the necessary social limitations on libidinal withdrawal into the dyad are provided by a system of family and community obligations centered on kinship and procreation (Slater, 1963). These are often lacking in the new forms of group marriage, such as the "corporate marriage" (Rimmer, 1968, 1973).

Since the same traditional controls described by Slater are also lacking in the gay commune, it provides a useful model for resolution of some of the problems likely to face heterosexual group marriages. Westley and Leznoff (1956) reported that gay friendship groups commonly functioned with social controls on intimacy akin to an "incest taboo." Such friendship groups continue to exist. For example, in Toronto a group of business and professional gay males living in the affluent suburb of Forest Hill enforce a strict requirement to "be married" in order to participate in the group's parties and dinners. Each gay couple in the group is expected to maintain what George and Nena O'Neill (1972) have called a "closed couple front."

However, one of the important products of the gay liberation movement has been the breakdown of the "incest taboo" on having sex with friends. On the contrary, there is now a positive emphasis on sex (one or several encounters) as a legitimate and desirable part of the process of becoming better acquainted.

A sociology student under my supervision has completed a participant-observer study of a circle of fourteen gay males who define themselves as a friendship group. If this were a group of the type described in Forest Hill, there could be only seven acceptable sexual relationships, in pairs.

Other relationships among the fourteen members would be expected to be nonsexual friendships. If any of the fourteen felt the need for sexual variety, he would be expected to seek it outside the group, in a covert and nonaffective manner—for example, at the gay baths (Westley & Leznoff, 1956).

In the group of young gay males my student observed, there was much more varied expression of sexual affection alongside friendship expression. Relationships ranged from "being married" to "having an affair" to "occasionally having sex." None of the "married" members were exclusively faithful; indeed, two of them were rather promiscuous, or, to use a less derogatory word, pluralistic.

Not all the members of this group shared a "gay liberation" consciousness, and some of the pluralism was creating tensions between those who defined it as immoral, or at least troublemaking, and those who defined the *objections* to pluralism as old-fashioned and moralistic.

In a gay commune, the process is taken one step further: The acceptance of sexual interaction as a legitimate expression of various dyadic relationships crosscutting the membership of the commune is combined with common residency. This can lead to really complex problems of interaction, such as those Rimmer (1968, p. 276) attempted to solve for his corporate family, by a new type of housing. In one Toronto commune, for example, six gay males lived together as a close, almost familylike group but also enjoyed sleeping with each other. However, the complications arising from bed hopping led to the posting of a list of "who will be in each bed" for the week.

While these communes as corporate entities have shown a surprising ability to survive over a period of years, there has been a tendency for members to pair off and move off on their own, so that few members of the commune remain in it for the whole of its life. But some do, and in the case of one surviving commune they continue to make it work.

Gay males who have fully internalized the gay consciousness and are truly "proud to be gay" are less likely to suffer the lack of self-esteem that is a common predisposing factor toward a manic love style. There is clearly an ideological relationship between gay liberation and a less jealous, less possessive, more playful love style. For example, Carl Wittman's (1972, p. 162) *Gay Manifesto* urges:

> The things we want to get away from are
>   1. exclusiveness, propertied values toward each other, a
> mutual pact against the rest of the world;
>   2. promises about the future, which we have no right to
> make, and which prevent us from growing.

These values are synonymous with those advocated by George and Nena O'Neill (1972) for the heterosexual "open marriage." Clearly a gay commune, in which such values find social support within a legitimating ideology, can help each individual member to enjoy an intimate paired relationship without converting this to closed couple marriage.

The second pattern occurring in the interplay of gay liberation and styles of loving is that of a more honest intimacy in the gay subculture, whether intensely passionate dyadic unions ("gay marriages") are involved or more casual "seeing someone" relationships.

When an *Advocate* advertiser pleaded, "Isn't there anyone who is tired of the phony games in the bar scene, and ready to settle down to a sincere, loving relationship?" he was voicing a complaint often heard among gay males. Many gay liberationists deliberately eschew the bar scene, finding it oppressive and dishonest, and even destructive of integrity. Of course much of this is a function of self-oppression, as noted by *Downcast Gays* (Hodges & Hutter, 1974).

The problem of the gay bar and similar environments is that of an intersection of social environments most conducive to two different, and often fundamentally opposed, love styles: eros and ludus. The emphasis on physical appearance is a natural consequence of the diversified constituency of most gay bars. Perhaps all that the guests have in common is their sexual orientation. Their educational qualifications, vocations, incomes, political and religious views, and indeed their moral values in general, may cover the gamut of social possibilities. All that the guests may have to go on, in deciding (and it is often a painful and hesitant decision) to make the first move in initiating acquaintance, is the other person's "looks."

Thus there is a strong social pressure to maintain a casual, easily detached, noncommittal manner in the bar—in short, a pressure toward a playful or ludic style of love. One must learn to avoid overoptimistic evaluations such as follow on the sudden, exciting encounter with someone who seems to be the ideal partner. Bar people are all too familiar with the syndrome "Lovers who just met tonight, and tomorrow are not even friends."

A successful mixture of ludus and eros is a tightrope act (Lee 1973, p. 112, 1974, p. 49). The art of passionate caution is not easily acquired. The ludic-erotic lover must combine the ecstatic intimacy of eros with the playful pluralism of ludus. He must be truly with the present partner in the here and now, fully enjoying today's intimacy, yet capable of detaching himself from the partner painlessly.

Paul Rosenfels (1971, p. 101) captures the paradox nicely: "The ability to make romantic attachments as if they were permanent and complete, and at the same time to retain the capability of dissolving such an attachment. . . . If an individual cannot dedicate himself to

romance without reserve, he imposes qualifications which undermine the experience he seeks to have."

What is advocated here is definitely *not* a Don Juan syndrome of
manipulative exploitation (Rosenfels, 1971, p. 94). Don Juan conned
his victims into intimacy by persuading them that he was willing to
marry. Rather, the ludic-erotic lover is fully open and honest about
his intention to engage in a noncommitted relationship. There can
be mutual enjoyment, trust, and comradeship, but without a promise
about the future. . . .

The ideology of gay liberation groups, at least in Toronto, is
clearly that of intimacy among friends, including erotic ecstasy and
sexual playfulness, without the necessity of lifetime commitment in
imitation of heterosexual marriage. Likewise, the separation of intimates is not expected to be a bitter divorce, but a friendly disengagement in which the partners can continue to relate to each other as
fellow members of the gay liberation movement.

As Andrew Hodges and David Hutter (1974, p. 8) note in one of
the most emphatic British statements of gay liberation:

> Gay people have no reason to envy the institutionalized
> sexuality available to heterosexuals, cluttered as it is with
> ceremonies of courtship and marriage . . . [Our] hetero-
> sexual detractors betray their limited vision by their mis-
> taken assumption that promiscuity is incompatible with
> lasting relationships. Homosexuals are in the happy posi-
> tion of being able to enjoy both at once.

However, they suggest that intimate roles that combine "promiscuity" (I prefer the term pluralism) with intimate relationships lasting
(at least as continued friendship) for a long period of time are roles
that come easier to homosexuals than to heterosexuals. I think they
are mistaken. Both gay and straight share socialization into the same
"romantic" heritage that emphasizes the search for one fulfilling
relationship, a possessive coupling with that person, and a residual
bitterness if the relationship does not work out. Gays need liberation
from this traditional world view before they can enjoy satisfying
ludic-erotic relationships.

Heterosexuals need such liberation too, and as George and Nena
O'Neill (1974) admit in their second book, *Shifting Gears,* the transition will not be an easy one. It may well be that gay liberation is
pioneering a new model of intimate relationship on the margins of
society, which will eventually resolve the problems of a larger society.
"The love which has no name" may give new names for love, new
love styles to all humanity.

REFERENCES

Belkin, A. I want a lover. *The Body Politic,* October 1975, p. 15.

Berger, P. *Invitation to sociology.* New York: Anchor, 1963.

Capellanus, A. *The art of courtly love* (J. J. Parry, Ed.). New York: Columbia University Press, 1941.

Constantine, L. and J. *Group marriage.* New York: Macmillan, 1973.

Fromm, E. *The art of loving.* New York: Bantam, 1963.

Hazo, R. *The idea of love.* New York: Praeger, 1967.

Hodges, A., & Hutter, D. *Downcast gays.* London: Pomegranate Press, 1974.

Hunt, M. *The world of the formerly married.* New York: McGraw-Hill, 1966.

Kammeyer, K. *Confronting the issues.* Boston: Allyn & Bacon, 1975.

Krich, A. M. (Ed.). *Anatomy of love.* New York: Dell, 1960.

Lee, J. A. *Colors of love.* Toronto: New Press, 1973.

Lee, J. A. Styles of loving. *Psychology Today,* October 1974, pp. 43–51.

Libby, R. *Renovating marriage.* San Ramon, Calif.: Consensus Publications, 1973.

McKinney, J. *Constructive Typology.* New York: Meredith, 1966.

Mishima, Y. *Forbidden colors.* New York: Avon, 1970.

O'Neill, G., & O'Neill, N. *Open marriage.* New York: Evans, 1972.

O'Neill, G., & O'Neill, N. *Shifting gears.* New York: Evans, 1974.

Ramey, J. W. Emerging patterns of behavior in marriage. *Journal of Sex Research,* 1972, *8*(1).

Reik, T. *Of love and lust.* London: Farrar, Straus, Cudahy, 1949.

Richmond, L., & Noguera, G. (Eds.). *The gay liberation book.* San Francisco: Ramparts Press, 1973.

Rimmer, R. *Proposition 31.* New York: Signet, 1968.

Rimmer, R. *Adventures in loving.* New York: Signet, 1973.

Rosenfels, P. *Homosexuality, the psychology of the creative process.* New York: Libra, 1971.

Rossner, J. *Looking for Mr. Goodbar.* New York: Simon & Schuster, 1975.

Slater, P. Social limitations on libidinal withdrawal. *American Sociological Review,* 1963, *28,* 339–345.

Stendhal (H. Beyle). *De l'amour* (H. Martineau, Ed.). Paris: Le Divan, 1957.

Westley, W., & Leznoff, M. The homosexual community. *Social Problems,* April 1956.

Wittman, C. Refugees from Amerika: A gay manifesto. In J. McCaffrey (Ed.), *The homosexual dialectic.* New York: Prentice-Hall, 1972.

12/ WHAT IT MEANS TO LOVE ANOTHER WOMAN

J. Lee Lehman

What is a lesbian? She is a female homosexual. She is a woman who prefers other women on many levels: psychologically, emotionally, psychically, sometimes politically, and sexually. A lesbian may form lasting emotional and sexual bonds with another woman or women or she may form satisfying friendships with other women which are never acted out sexually. There are many different life styles selected by the millions of lesbians in this country. No matter what the choice, however, there is an omnipresent shadow: prejudice.

In different times and cultures, lesbianism has been seen in different ways. It may be totally acceptable (even expected), acceptable (or expected) up until a certain age, or unacceptable. In Western society lesbianism has been flaunted by some (such as Sappho and her disciples), encouraged for pragmatic reasons (such as keeping the illegitimacy rate down), discouraged as sinful (by the Catholic and some other churches), or even presumed to be nonexistent (what can two women do in bed together anyway?). Homosexuality was punishable by burning during the Reformation, death in the Nazi concentration camps, and commitment to mental institutions in the United States. It is only in the seventies that health professionals—psychologists and psychiatrists—are recognizing that there is nothing inherently bad or "sick" about lesbianism.

Even today, lesbianism remains an enigma. No psychologist, no physician, no scientist, has been adequately able to explain whether there is a "cause," genetic or environmental. The best statistics on its incidence are nearly thirty years old. Of course, "science" hasn't explained the "cause(s)" of heterosexuality either, but this fact has been generally overlooked. Part of the reason, I believe, is that lesbianism has been viewed as sexual activity rather than sexual preference; something a woman does in bed rather than the way she lives her life. Lesbianism is a very complex behavior pattern which is not readily accessible to simplistic analysis. The important distinction is *not* that we have sex with other women, but that we love them, and it is this love that profoundly affects our lives and, in this society, sets us apart.

Love is something that none of us understands fully, but most cherish. Lesbians fall in love: love at first sight, a friendship that develops into something more, an intuitive flash that says, "Get to know this woman!" The effect of falling in love may have different ramifications. If both women have already "come out" (acknowledged their lesbianism), then the process is much easier. It can be disconcerting for a woman who has acknowledged the strength of her feelings for other women. She may say to herself, "What a wonderful friend!" and then wonder why she gets tongue-tied in that woman's presence, or jealous of anyone the woman sees, or just why she is obsessed with thinking about her. Few of us have been raised to be more than vaguely aware that lesbianism exists, much less that it could be a viable alternative. As a result, it may never occur to her that she is "in love" with the other woman. This realization can take years. In my own case, I had a habit of becoming extremely attached to whoever was my best friend. In high school I suffered through jealousy attacks whenever one of my friends started dating. (Why is she wasting her time on him? What does she see in him?) I freely acknowledged that I preferred women, and I vaguely knew I wasn't going to change. But I didn't recognize any of these feelings as sexual in nature. Finally, in my late teens, it took the prodding of a straight friend who realized I had a crush on her to push me into exploring my sexuality, but not with her!

If, on the other hand, the woman is aware of her preferences, the path of love is more direct, though not necessarily easy. The feelings may not be mutual, may not be of the same intensity, or may not follow the same time sequence. Lesbian love is no harder or easier than any other romantic love. However, there is an additional twist. A lesbian may find herself falling in love with a woman who has no lesbian inclinations. Many of us have experienced this at some point, and it can be very painful to realize that one is "stuck" with unrequited love. We may try to rationalize that the other woman just hasn't come out yet, but this is not always so. The impossibility of love because of circumstance is a theme familiar enough, but as a minority of the population, it can be exasperating to be surrounded by a majority that is unavailable.

The fact that the law of averages is not in our favor introduces one of the major differences in our life styles. Unlike heterosexual men, we cannot assume that all women around us are potential partners. Like gay men, we have to do something to change the odds to our favor. For this reason we separate from the mainstream of society into our own "subculture" or "community." In this world, we can drop the "straight" disguise that many feel the need to wear "outside." In our own places, we are assured that the other women we meet are lesbians. Whether the need is for light conversation, a friendship, a relationship, or a night of sex, we know we aren't going to be hassled. Of course, our subculture serves two very different functions: providing a place to meet other lesbians and providing an escape from the pressures of a frequently hostile world. Sometimes these may be blurred: many lesbians are so completely separate in the "straight" and "gay" worlds that they are almost two separate women.

The lesbian subculture differs in some essential ways from the gay male one. The two are seldom completely separate. Depending on the location, for example, there may be separate women's and men's bars or the bar(s) may be mixed. Many lesbians have gay male friends, and their social circles may be separate or mixed. No matter what the choice, lesbian spaces tend to be much less "cruisy" than gay male ones. Cruising, the process of surveying one's surroundings with hope to pick someone up, usually for a one-night stand, is much more common in the gay male community. Some lesbians do cruise, but the process is less acknowledged, that is to say, more subtle. To complicate matters, many lesbians use the word "cruising" to simply denote looking. At any rate, the emphasis on "tricking" (one-night stands) so common in gay male situations is much less evident in lesbian ones. For better or worse, there is a much heavier stress on "relationships" in lesbian circles.

The name of the game, then, is relationships. The meaning of this word is almost as difficult to define as love. Instead of being fool enough to try, I will simply list some of the more common kinds.

1. Monogamous relationships. This is the closest equivalent to the heterosexual marriage concept. The women usually don't go through a wedding ceremony (they can have a religious ceremony in some churches), but they may pool their incomes, buy property together, live together, and share their lives for years.

2. Nonmonogamous relationships. This is probably closest to the heterosexual "open marriage" idea. The women may define their relationship as primary, with each free to develop relationships with others, sexual or otherwise. As with monogamous relationships, the women may live together, own property together, or share the greater part of their lives. Like other nonmonogamous relationships, this type has pitfalls as well as advantages: While it can take the pressure off a relationship since it frees the women from trying to fill 100 percent of each other's needs, it can also add jealousy.

3. The affair. A relationship between two women can be primarily or exclusively sexual in nature. It is satisfactory when both partners are comfortable with the idea that no one person can (or should) meet all their needs.

4. Friendships. Many lesbians put special emphasis on friendships. Sometimes the friendship may have a sexual element, but this is not the only possibility. For some, the combination of affairs with

some and friendships with others is quite satisfactory; for others friendships are an additional bulwark besides more involved relationships. In any case, friendships provide insight, fun, and emotional support regardless of any sexual content. However, the fear of sexual involvement can impair one's ability to have friends when one is involved in a monogamous relationshp.

5. Groups. Some lesbians choose to live communally with a group of other lesbians. The main definition of the group is as a household; sexual relationships may or may not be present between members of the household. In either case, this is one very good method of obtaining multiple viewpoints and a strong emotional support structure, provided that the women involved are compatible.

WOMAN TO WOMAN: LESBIAN INTIMACY

No matter what the choice of relationship(s), lesbians have had to tread on publicly unexplored territory: the building and maintenance of intimacy between two women. There are certain advantages to two women relating to each other. In a society that has placed such emphasis on separating the sexes, there is considerable empathy possible within each camp. I know another woman intuitively in ways I cannot know a man, because to know another woman is (partially) to know myself. Women have been encouraged to develop their emotional sides, and two women together usually don't have to waste as much time trying to get the other to admit to having feelings. A lesbian does not have to explain to another woman what it means to *be* a woman. Because the woman-woman relationship has been left comparatively undefined, there is more latitude to develop a unique relationship based on meeting needs rather than fulfilling roles.

Within the lesbian community, there is considerable support for relationships, but far less for intimacy. The "goal" is to find Princess Charming and live happily ever after with her, but no one is telling how to do either. One of the side effects of this emphasis on relationships, I believe, is the very common situation of many lesbians in their late teens and early twenties. Many get involved in (usually) monogamous relationships, begin to live together, and then break up after two years or less. Within six months, both of the former "partners" are in similar relationships with someone else. Their goal is to be involved, but in the midst of dreams of togetherness, they do not learn how to relate to each other. When they reach a crisis in their relationship, they break up. Fortunately, many lesbians acquire the necessary relationship and intimacy skills as they grow older.

Feminism in general and lesbian feminism in particular encourages women to become stronger individuals. Like most women, we have been raised to put all of our energy into relationships; when the relationship fails, we believe that we have failed. This tendency to practically define oneself in terms of one's relationships puts an undue stress on the relationship. The development of a stronger sense of self—frequently a beneficial side effect of the process of coming out—allows many lesbians to build their relationships between two strong people. For some, consciousness-raising groups, cocounseling situations, or therapy may be ways to further this process. While most lesbians do not choose these alternatives, they are available in most larger cities and many smaller ones where there are feminist and/or lesbian therapists willing to set up or facilitate these groups.

There is some doubt whether a successful relationship necessarily requires large doses of intimacy. More probably it requires a proper ratio of personal space and intimacy. Certainly many women find the right balance, because many spend the greater part of their lives in one relationship. When two women live together for years, the neighbors may choose to accept them as good friends, two "old maids" who get what little comfort they can from each other, relatives, or afraid to live alone. When I came out to my parents several years ago, they told me that they didn't know any other lesbians. I couldn't help thinking of the "roommates" and "friends" I had been introduced to, and the "best friends" with whom my parents used to play bridge! In this respect, it appears to be much easier for two women to live together without raising straight eyebrows than for two men to do the same thing.

The difference in "blind spot" between two women living together and two men doing the same is quite interesting. In the case of two men, everyone seems capable of imagining what they can do together, even if it is the "love that dare not speak its name." With women, all aspects of the relationship are granted as acceptable except any sexual dynamic, which is either unimaginable or unthinkable. Women are almost expected to be intimate emotionally with each other. It is a well-recognized fact that communication is different between two women, a woman and a man, and between two men. A rather amusing illustration was provided by the early attempts to form all-male consciousness-raising groups using the model of the CR groups that have been so helpful to many women. In one case the men were told that they could talk about anything except business, sports, cars, politics, and religion. There was silence for ten minutes! Women are far more used to discussing feelings with each other than men are. As a result, it is scarcely surprising that society has recognized that two women are very capable of giving each other emotional support. After all, women have been defined almost exclusively as emotional. To carry the point a bit further, since men are given less credit for being able to give each other such support, it is hardly surprising that straight people's minds wander to other topics when two men live together. The difference is easily demonstrated: In most communities two women can walk down the street holding hands and few people will notice. (Kissing may be another matter!) If two men do it, they may be arrested for inciting a riot!

This does not mean that lesbians suffer less discrimination than gay men. Once the label "lesbian" is applied, one is seen almost exclusively as a sexual being. In fact, studies have shown that lesbians are believed to be far more sexual than other women. There is no scientific evidence to support this belief, but that hasn't stopped many people from thinking that lesbians are sex-crazed. This misinformation has led to a host of other myths, including:

1. "Lesbians are child molesters." Lesbians are no more guilty of this offense than heterosexual women. Women in general are rarely child molesters. More than 90 percent of child molestation is committed by *heterosexual men.*

2. "All a lesbian needs is sex with a man to 'cure' her." In fact, many if not most of us have had sex with men and it obviously hasn't done a thing for us! Isn't this idea an interesting commentary on men's perceptions of their own sexuality? Sex with a man is supposed to be so great that lesbians would willingly give up their assumed greater sexual appetite for it! Needless to say, this idea isn't true, in fact the *opposite* is true if one is strictly looking at sexual performance standards. According to Masters and Johnson, a woman is most likely to have an orgasm while masturbating, with lesbian sex a close second and heterosexual intercourse a poor third. Of course, the most important consideration in sexual pleasure is the psychology of the situation, and a lesbian is going to prefer having sex with a woman and a heterosexual woman is going to prefer having sex with a man.

3. "Lesbians are 'that way' because they are afraid of or hate men." While this may be true of some lesbians, there is no evidence that it is true of a large proportion. It is probably just as true that heterosexual women are "that way" because they fear or hate other women. But since straight scientists think that heterosexuality is the norm, which doesn't have to be explained, there hasn't been any research on the subject.

4. "All two lesbians want from each other is sex, sex, sex!" (And to think of all the times I have avoided sex at all costs with another lesbian in order to preserve the friendship.)

Garbage, garbage, garbage! Lesbians are "that way" because they prefer other women for love and emotional support. It's as simple as that.

The need for emotional support from other lesbians is increased considerably by the societal "cost" of being a lesbian. To be a lesbian is to reject the most basic thing one has ever been told about the definition of "woman." We are faced with how to come to grips with this situation during the process of coming out. Coming out can be on several levels, including:

1. Coming out to oneself: the process of discovering and accepting one's lesbianism.

2. Coming out sexually: going to bed with another woman.

3. Coming out to friends and/or family.

4. Coming out publicly: making one's lesbianism a generally known fact.

5. Coming out politically: becoming involved with lesbian feminism, the gay movement, or the women's movement in order to change the status of lesbians in society.

Besides the decisions about whether to open the closet door, keep it closed, or dynamite it, one has to define a self-identity which encompasses the various places. As a lesbian one does not fit the ideal of wife and mother. Lesbians have generally tried three different ways of adapting to this situation. The first two solutions are based on the traditional model of the straight marriage; while these patterns are diminishing in importance, they should still be mentioned.

1. The "femme" role. This is an attempt to keep all the definitions intact except the lover choice. The femme is usually indistinguishable from the average heterosexual woman, at least to the straight world. However, she is likely to be more aware that she is playing a "role" than a straight woman would be. (A friend of mine described it as "being in drag and knowing it.")

2. The "butch" role. This is a rejection of all definitions of "woman" and to varying degrees becoming its antithesis. The classic butch dresses in a motorcycle jacket or a suit and tie, swears a lot, and swaggers. Few lesbians go this far, but their appearance and behavior may approximate that of men to a greater or lesser degree.

3. By attempting to redefine "woman." Few lesbians (and few other women as well) totally fit the stereotypic roles of the ideal woman or its antithesis without a lot of pushing and shoving. The women's and gay movements have encouraged all women (and men as well) to redefine themselves as persons, not as halves to be completed by the opposite half. As a result, an increasing number of lesbians are defining themselves as having both "sides": the rational/aggressive and the nurturing/emotional. A lesbian relationship then becomes the meeting of two equals, not a contest in mutual leaning. Lesbians are increasingly discovering that it is easier—as well as more honest—to be themselves rather than a character in someone else's play.

Lesbians are a very diverse group, and I have barely scratched the surface in this article. I have probably come closer to defining what lesbians are *not* than to defining what we are. Lesbianism defies simple explanations. We are complex human beings in search of many things. In recent years, as we have begun to define ourselves instead of allowing others to do so, we have been struck by our differences. If it weren't for the discrimination against us, we would have much less in common. Yet through all the variables, in our love and caring for women we are united.

PART FOUR

EMOTIONAL AND PHYSICAL HEALTH

Historically, studies have shown that married people live longer than unmarrieds and that they use health care facilities less often. The complex cause and effect relationship between marital status and better health has been acknowledged, but more recent studies suggest that this relationship is less strong today.

In a comprehensive review based on data from two national health surveys, Verbrugge (1979) writes that "the rates of limiting chronic and work-disabling conditions are rather low for noninstitutionalized single people." Among singles, the divorced and separated have the worst health status followed by the widowed and then the never-married. One survey suggests that noninstitutionalized never-marrieds "are the healthiest of all marital groups. . . . They take the least time off for health problems and have lowest utilization of physician and hospital services." However, institutionalization rates for the never-married are relatively high, and the *total* singles population is, in fact, less healthy than the total married population. "People with serious congenital or childhood health problems are not attractive for marriage. The most seriously ill enter institutions when quite young; those who remain outside institutions are often limited in their social involvement," according to Verbrugge.

What happens to singles when they are ill? The lucky ones have a support group they can turn to: family, neighbors, fellow communalists, roommates. Indeed, the crucial issue may not be marriage versus singlehood, but the strength of the support network. As the single state becomes less deviant, and more friends and groups become available to single adults, their general health and well-being should improve. Today, however, as single people grow older and their health deteriorates, they more readily than marrieds enter institutions, having fewer opportunities for home care and fewer social responsibilities (Verbrugge, 1979).

A recent study of 400 single adults found no differences between marrieds and singles in terms of reported nightmares or crying spells, but "more singles worry, more are likely to feel guilty, despondent, worthless, or lonely. However, when [we] separate the divorced from the never-married, it is the divorced that report feelings of despondency, worthlessness, sexual apathy, and loneliness more often than the never-married and the married. On a different

149

measure, frequent contemplation of suicide, the figures are highest for the divorced (20 percent), [then] the never-married (10 percent), and the married (7 percent) (Melko and Cargan, 1980).

The three articles in this section examine the connections between singlehood and good or poor health. "The Study of Loneliness," by Robert Weiss, is one of few pieces of research on this subject. "Many of us severely underestimate our own past experience with loneliness," says Weiss, "and as a result underestimate the role it has played in the lives of others." Who are the lonely? He reports that severe loneliness appears to be unusual among married men, somewhat more prevalent among married women, and quite prevalent among the unmarried of both sexes. Are women truly more lonely, or just more open about admitting loneliness? What can be done to replace the social ties lost with aging and illness?

Leonard Pearlin and Joyce Johnson, in "Marital Status, Life-Strains, and Depression," take a new approach to the connections between marital status and health. This link has traditionally been interpreted as reflecting the unmet inner needs and emotional frustrations of never-married and formerly married people. In contrast, this study looks at the consequences of economic hardship, social isolation, and parental obligations. These are three basic conditions to which unmarried people are both more exposed and more vulnerable. Yet the authors find that the greater life hardships of the unmarried only partly explain their greater depression. For even when hardships of married and unmarried people are equally severe, their effects are more penetrating among the unmarried: "The combination most productive of psychological distress is to be simultaneously single, isolated, exposed to burdensome parental obligations, and—most serious of all—poor." To what extent does marriage help fend off the psychological assaults of economic and social problems? Is its protective function the reason why marriage remains a stable institution?

History has shown that married persons live longer on the average than unmarried persons and that they generally make less use of health care services. In "Marital Status, Health, and the Use of Health Services" Anne R. Somers explores current perceptions of health, illness, and need for health care. She points out that as the family's role in health has declined, there has been a concurrent rise in the "need" for, and cost of, the external health care system, and she offers some new data. For example:

•For divorced American men under the age of sixty-five, compared with the married, the rate is almost double for coronary heart disease and cancer; double for lung cancer and strokes; almost three times as high for hypertension; four times as high for car accidents; nearly five times as high for suicide.

•For single men the hospital admission rate is 230 percent higher than for married men; for the separated, the rate is 2,100 percent higher.

Somers studies such questions as "Are young persons, who are postponing marriage and children until their late twenties and after, and who are making increased use of community health services, healthier or less healthy than their parents were at the same age? Is the middle-aged, divorced, and childless professional woman . . . healthier or less healthy than her mother? How about the retired widow, with enough income to live alone rather than in her daughter-in-law's back bedroom, but totally lacking in routine family contacts?" We may ask ourselves, after reading these articles, how the changing role of the family, and changing social perceptions, are changing both the provision of care and the demands of those who are being cared for.

REFERENCES

Melko, Matthew and Cargan, Leonard. "In Sickness and in Health." Unpublished manuscript, Wright State University, Dayton, Ohio, 1980.

Verbrugge, Lois. "Marital Status and Health," *Journal of Marriage and the Family* (May, 1979), 41:2, pp. 267–285.

13/ THE STUDY OF LONELINESS

Robert S. Weiss

Loneliness is a condition that is widely distributed and severely distressing. Yet only a handful of psychiatrists, psychologists, and sociologists have studied the ordinary loneliness of ordinary people. Sullivan, the great American psychiatrist, is among the very few who have done so and among the very few in any of the social sciences who have attempted a description of the symptomatology of loneliness. His description is brief and sketchy, but nevertheless notably perceptive. In particular he commented on the "driving force" of loneliness—a force great enough, he pointed out, to cause people who were normally painfully shy to aggressively seek social activity. He concluded that "the fact that loneliness will lead to integrations in the face of severe anxiety automatically means that loneliness in itself is more terrible than anxiety."[1] Others who have observed the pressures under which the lonely seem to act by and large have agreed with Sullivan's appraisal.[2]

Why, then, has there been so little research on loneliness? Loneliness is much more often commented on by songwriters than by social scientists. One psychiatrist has suggested that we neglect loneliness because we have no theory with which to begin to cope with its manifestations.[3] There may be some merit in this position; scientific attention may be directed in part by the emphases of theory and the established preoccupations of the field. But Frieda Fromm-Reichmann noted that at least one reason that we have no very good theory about loneliness is that we have studied it so little. She suggested that the absence of attention to loneliness was to be explained not by the challenge loneliness presented to understanding but rather by the threat it presented to well-being. She said that loneliness is "such a painful, frightening experience that people will do practically everything to avoid it."[4]

Fromm-Reichmann's explanation is appealing but seems not to go far enough. There has for some time now been active research interest in the sometimes excruciatingly painful phenomena of grief and the intensely anxiety-provoking phenomena of dying,[5] and loneliness would not seem to be more frightening than these conditions. There would seem to be some additional quality in loneliness that leads to its neglect.

Many of us severely underestimate our own past experience with loneliness and as a result underestimate the role it has played in the lives of others. The observation that times of loneliness are later difficult to recall has been made by both Sullivan and Fromm-Reichmann. Sullivan believed that loneliness was an experience so different from the ordinary that its intensity could later not be entirely credited. He said it was "an experience which has been so terrible that it practically baffles clear recall."[6] Fromm-Reichmann believed that there was active rejection of the memory of loneliness, and not simply passive inability to recall. She believed that many of those who had once been lonely were aware that memory of that state would be threatening to their current well-being. She said, "It is so frightening and uncanny in character that they [those who have once suffered loneliness] try to dissociate the memory of what it was like and even the fear of it."[7]

I have occasionally asked individuals who were not at the moment lonely to recall for me times when they had been. If I knew that a year or so earlier they had moved into a new community where they had had no friends, or that until the last few months they had been without an intimate, I pressed them to remember how they had felt during these periods of relational insufficiency. More than once I have been told something like, "Yes, I suppose I was lonely. But I wasn't *myself* then." I think this is a most suggestive response. It implies that an individual when lonely maintains an organization of emotions, self-definitions, and definitions of his or her relations to others which is quite different from the one he maintains when not lonely. Asked at a time when he is not lonely to remember back to when he was lonely, he may protest that the person he is at the moment has never been lonely and that in the lonely past "I wasn't myself." The self associated with the absence of loneliness is a different one from the self associated with loneliness: it is more engaged by a range of interests, more confident, more secure, more self-satisfied. To someone in this state the earlier lonely self—tense, restless, unable to concentrate, *driven*—must seem an aberration.

As an implication of the foregoing we might expect that those who are not at the moment lonely will have little empathy for those who are, even if in the recent past they had been lonely themselves. If they had earlier been lonely, they now have no access to the self that experienced the loneliness; furthermore, they very likely prefer that things remain that way. In consequence they are likely to respond to those who are currently lonely with absence of understanding and perhaps irritation.

Professionals in research and treatment, if they have dealt with their own past experiences of loneliness in this way, might also prefer not to disturb their current emotional arrangements. To maintain their current feelings of well-being, they too might be impatient with the problem of loneliness. They might be willing to consider loneliness in an exotic form—the loneliness of the mentally ill or of the Arctic explorer or the alienation of marginal man. But they would be made uncomfortable by the loneliness that is potential in the everyday life of everyone.

The frequency and intensity of loneliness are not only underestimated but the lonely themselves tend to be disparaged. It seems easy to blame their loneliness on their frailties and to accept this fault-finding as explanation. Our image of the lonely often casts them as justifiably rejected: as people who are unattractive, shy, intentionally reclusive, undignified in their complaints, self-absorbed, self-pitying. We may go further and suppose that chronic loneliness must to some extent be chosen. Surely, we might argue, it is easy enough to be acceptable to others. All that is necessary is to be pleasant, outgoing, interested in the others rather than in oneself. Why can't the lonely change? They must find a perverse gratification in loneliness; perhaps loneliness, despite its pain, permits them to continue a self-protective isolation or provides them with an emotional handicap that forces handouts of pity from those with whom they interact. Thoughts like these may justify professional as well as lay impatience with the lonely.[8]

There may be some small merit in this characterological theory of loneliness, as we shall later note. But there is also implicit in it a rationalization for rejection of the lonely and of the problem of loneliness. Each is pictured as easy to understand: the lonely are people who move against others or away from others and of course they then feel bad because they are alone. Along these lines, advice for the lonely would seem obvious: be pleasant, outgoing, interested in others; meet people; become part of things. If the lonely cannot behave in these ways, then they ought to enter psychotherapy, change, learn to be more outgoing.

Yet for those who suffer from loneliness, advice of this sort often seems oddly beside the point. There may seem to them to be something in loneliness that is "uncanny," to use Fromm-Reichmann's word. It is peculiarly insistent; no matter how much those who are lonely would like to shake it off, no matter how much they may berate themselves for permitting it to overcome them, they find themselves possessed by it. No matter how devotedly they may count their other blessings, no matter how determined they may be to put their minds to other things, the loneliness remains, an almost eerie affliction of their spirits.

Loneliness is not simply a desire for company, any company; rather it yields only to very specific forms of relationship. Loneliness is often uninterrupted by social activity; the social activity may feel "out there," in no way engaging the individual's emotions. It can even make matters worse. However the responsiveness of loneliness to just the right sort of relationship with others is absolutely remarkable. Given the establishment of these relationships, loneliness will vanish abruptly and without trace, as though it never had existed. There is no gradual recovery, no getting over it bit by bit. When it ends, it ends suddenly; one was lonely, one is not any more.

LONELINESS AND OTHER CONDITIONS

What do we mean by loneliness? The word has been used to describe a number of different conditions, even as other words, including *depression* and *grief,* have been used to describe conditions that would seem to have some affinity with loneliness.

Sometimes the term *loneliness* has been used to describe a not at all disagreeable condition in which a sense of one's separateness from others offers "a way back to oneself."[9] This sort of loneliness refers to a time in which one is not only alone but also able to use one's aloneness to recognize with awesome clarity both one's ineradicable separateness from all else and one's fundamental connectedness. It is a time of almost excruciating awareness in which one sees clearly the fundamental facts of one's small but unique place in the ultimate scheme, after which one can recognize one's true self and begin to be that true self.

I do not doubt that this experience occurs: that there are times when being alone gives rise to this awesome awareness of oneself and one's world. Some individuals may be able to transmute the intense discomfort of ordinary loneliness into this exalted state. But the state, even if it begins in ordinary loneliness, is different from the experience described to my colleagues and me in our studies of loneliness in ordinary life. The loneliness we have been told of is gnawing rather than ennobling, a chronic distress without redeeming features.

Another condition that may be described as loneliness is unwanted individuation: being separated off from parents and others to fend for oneself, not just in the sense of becoming responsible for oneself but also in the sense of being and developing as a separate self.[10] Again, although this condition may be related to what most of us experience as loneliness, it does not appear to be quite the same thing. Nor is the existentialist notion of the ultimate loneliness of each of us in deciding and evaluating our course in life the same thing.

The condition discussed in this book is the one Sullivan described as "the exceedingly unpleasant and driving experience connected with inadequate discharge of the need for human intimacy."[11] This common, if perplexing, condition is the only one we have had reported to us in our studies of loneliness in ordinary life. The other forms of loneliness I have just noted would appear from our studies to be fairly rare states. They are not the loneliness experienced by those who are bereaved or divorced or uprooted.

Ordinary loneliness is uniformly distressing. It may be useful to distinguish it from other forms of distress. To begin with, it is different from what is usually described as depression. In loneliness there is a drive to rid oneself of one's distress by integrating a new relationship or regaining a lost one; in depression there is instead a surrender to it. The lonely are driven to find others, and if they find the right others, they change and are no longer lonely. The depressed are often unwilling to impose their unhappiness on others; in any event their feelings cannot be reached by relationships, old or new.[12]

Loneliness is also distinct from grief. The term *grief* may be used in a number of ways but perhaps is best used to describe the syndrome of shock, protest, anger, and painful, searing sadness, which is produced by traumatic loss.[13] Loneliness often is a component of this syndrome; however it is a reaction to the *absence* of the cherished figure rather than to the experience of its loss. We would expect every other aspect of grief to subside as time goes on: shock might be expected to disappear, protest to be muted, anger and sadness to diminish. But loneliness, so long as no new relationship is formed to replace what has been lost, might be expected to continue.

ORDINARY LONELINESS

Research on the nature of ordinary loneliness is as yet fragmentary. Surveys have generated useful statistics regarding the proportions of individuals in various demographic categories who declare themselves to be lonely, but to my knowledge none has investigated the reasons for loneliness, the conditions under which loneliness occurs, or the subjective experience of loneliness. We do have, however, case studies of individuals living in conditions likely to give rise to loneliness. These describe individuals who have been widowed, who have separated from or divorced a spouse, who have entered into a new community, or who have suffered the loss of intimates which is one of the afflictions of advanced age. On the basis of these studies we can develop some initial understandings of loneliness.

The dictionary definition of loneliness is not very useful. This is how Webster's defines the term: ". . . A state of dejection or grief caused by the condition of being alone. . ."[14] To be sure, no one who is lonely would consider himself happy, and to this extent Webster's is correct in associating loneliness with dejection and grief. But the definition is misleading in asserting that loneliness *is* dejection or grief; loneliness is quite different from these conditions, as has been noted earlier. More important, the definition is misleading in asserting that loneliness is "caused by the condition of being alone." On this point the case study materials we have collected are unambiguous. Loneliness is caused not by being alone but by being without some definite needed relationship or set of relationships.

Only those who are not lonely suppose that loneliness can be cured merely by ending aloneness. Not only is random sociability no antidote to loneliness, but under some circumstances it can exacerbate it; someone who is not married and in consequence feels outside the society of settled family life may find that being with married couples only intensifies his or her feelings of marginality, of having no valid place. A widower said about an evening with married friends, "It's like being a fifth wheel."

Loneliness appears always to be a response to the absence of some particular type of relationship or, more accurately, a response to the absence of some particular relational provision. In many instances it is a response to the absence of the provisions of a close, indeed intimate, attachment. It may also be a response to the absence of the provisions of meaningful friendships, collegial relationships, or other linkages to a coherent community. These seem to be the most common forms of loneliness, but there may be others as well; conceivably, some parents whose children have left home may feel the absence of the distinctive provisions of the relationship one maintains with those one has nurtured. And at Christmas time, especially, many of those who are unable to join with kin feel distressed by the separation, for Christmas is a time of reaffirmation by kin of their fundamental commitment to one another.[15]

All these instances of conditions giving rise to loneliness support the presumption that loneliness is a response to relational deficit. Although each syndrome of response to specific relational deficit appears to be unique in some respects, each appears to include certain common symptoms, just as any infection may have both unique symptoms by which it can be distinguished from other infections and also shared symptoms such as fever. All loneliness syndromes would seem to give rise to yearning for the relationship—an intimacy, a friendship, a relationship with kin—that would provide whatever is at the moment insufficient. All may be able to produce the driving restlessness of which Sullivan spoke. And all may induce impatience or irritability with relationships that seem to impede access to the desired relationship. Insofar as those symptoms seem to be part of any experience of loneliness one may speak of "loneliness" as a single condition.

Different forms of loneliness are, however, responsive to different remedies. We have repeatedly found in our studies that a form of loneliness that appears in the absence of a close emotional attachment, which we characterize as "the loneliness of emotional isolation," can only be remedied by the integration of another emotional attachment or the reintegration of the one that had been lost.[16] Evidence that the loneliness of emotional isolation cannot be dissolved by entrance into other sorts of relationships, perhaps especially new friendships, is repeatedly rediscovered by new members of the Parents Without Partners organization. New members often are attracted to that organization because they are lonely and hope membership will allay the loneliness. Within the organization they may form new friendships or take on new responsibilities, but unless they also form a single intense relationship, one which in some ways makes the same provisions as the marriage they no longer have, they remain lonely.

Conversely, we have found that the form of loneliness associated with the absence of an engaging social network—the "loneliness of social isolation"—can be remedied only by access to such a network. This was demonstrated for us in a pilot study of couples who had moved to the Boston region from at least two states away.[17] The wives in these couples tended for a time to have "newcomer blues"; they felt out of place and unwanted in their new community and were deeply homesick for their former one. Their husbands, no matter how close the marriage, were of little help. The husbands did not share their wives' distress since they had entered a ready-made community at their workplace. Furthermore, the husbands' attention and energies were absorbed by their efforts to become established in their new jobs. But even when the husbands did seem able in a limited way to understand and to sympathize, the wives continued to be lonely for friends and acquaintances who would share their interests as their husbands did not. They wanted access to a network of women with whom they might establish and then discuss issues of common concern: shopping, home management, the developing lives of their children and, of course, one another. Though the newcomer wife might be content in her marriage, social isolation nevertheless made her painfully lonely, and her loneliness ended only when she found an accepting—and acceptable—community.

The complex of symptoms of the loneliness of emotional isolation are in the main different from those of the loneliness of social isolation, although there is in each the same driving restlessness and the same yearning for the missing relational provisions. The complex of symptoms associated with the loneliness of emotional isolation is

strongly reminiscent of the distress of the small child who fears that
he has been abandoned by his parents. On the other hand, the
symptoms associated with the loneliness of social isolation are like
the boredom, feelings of exclusion, and feelings of marginality of
the small child whose friends are all away. We might reasonably
suspect that the loneliness states of adults are developments of the
earlier childhood states. They may have been modified by the new
strengths and understandings of maturation, but still they seem like
the childhood syndromes in fundamental ways.

Many of the symptoms of the loneliness of emotional isolation
seem to stem from a re-experiencing of the anxiety produced by
childhood abandonment. This is a central theme, and gives rise to a
sense of pervasive apprehensiveness—one of our respondents called
it "a nameless fear"[18]—that may prevent concentration on reading or
television and almost force the individual into some sort of motor
activity as a channel for his or her jumpiness.

Associated with apprehensiveness is sometimes vigilance to threat,
a readiness to hear sounds in the night, which keeps one tense,
unable to relax enough to sleep. Often though, vigilance seems less
to be directed to threat than to possible remedy; the individual is
forever appraising others for their potential as providers of the
needed relationship, and forever appraising situations in terms of
their potential for making the needed relationships available. The
lonely individual's perceptual and motivational energies are likely to
become organized in the service of finding remedies for his or her
loneliness.

Finally, those experiencing the loneliness of emotional isolation
are apt to experience a sense of utter aloneness, whether or not the
companionship of others is in fact accessible to them. This sense of
utter aloneness may be phrased in terms of the absence of anyone
else in the environment, in which case the individual may describe
the immediately available world as desolate, barren, or devoid of
others; or the sense of utter aloneness may be phrased in terms of an
empty inner world, in which case the individual may say that he or
she feels empty, dead, or hollow.

Occasionally, the hyperalertness of the individual suffering from
the loneliness of emotional isolation produces an oversensitivity to
minimal cues and a tendency to misinterpret or to exaggerate the
hostile or affectionate intent of others. This oversensitivity can make
the individual seem to be awkward or foolish.

The dominant symptoms of the loneliness of social isolation are
different from these. Feelings of boredom or aimlessness, together
with feelings of marginality, seem to be central themes, rather than
anxiety and emptiness. Boredom seems to come about as the tasks
that make up one's daily routines, because they are inaccessible to

the affirmation of others, lose their meaning and begin to be simply busy work. The day's duties then are a burdensome ritual which one can hardly persuade oneself to observe. Again there is restlessness and difficulty in concentration, preventing the individual from becoming engaged in a distraction such as a book or television. And again the individual may feel impelled to leave the home, to move among people, at least to come into the vicinity of sociable warmth. Yet here the individual seems driven not to find that one other person with whom he or she may feel at ease but rather to find the kinds of activities he or she can participate in, the network or group that will accept him or her as a member.

We know less about other loneliness syndromes than we do about the two just described. From the intensity of the desire for an adoptive child displayed by some childless couples (the wife, especially[19]), we might suspect that childlessness too is experienced by some as an uncomfortable driving force, with its own object and very likely its own symptomatology. As we have noted, there undoubtedly are other, although less frequently experienced, types of loneliness as well.

THE PREVALENCE OF LONELINESS

By the "prevalence" of a condition we mean the proportion of the population who experience the condition during a particular period.[20] One problem in estimating the prevalence of loneliness is that loneliness is not a condition like a broken leg, which one has or one doesn't have, but is nearer to fatigue, a condition that can vary from the barely perceptible to the overwhelming. How much loneliness must one feel for it to be counted?

Survey studies leave it to respondents to answer this question. At least two survey studies have been conducted to determine the prevalence of ordinary loneliness, each of which asked respondents whether during a particular time period they had felt "very lonely or remote from other people." Presumably including the phrase "remote from other people" amplified what had been intended by the word "lonely" but did not add to it some foreign syndrome. In any event it was in each case the responsibility of respondents to decide whether they had experienced loneliness or remoteness and, if so, whether the experience had been sufficiently severe to justify the adverb *very*. We might suspect that the more introspective, the more sensitive, and the more candid respondents may have over-reported in comparison with others. We might also suspect that those who considered that a certain amount of loneliness might be normal for their situation—the unmarried or the aged for example—might have under-reported. Nevertheless, these are the only statistics we have, and despite their limitations we must make the best of them.

In the first survey the full question was, "During the past few weeks, did you ever feel very lonely or remote from other people?" Twenty-six percent of a national sample responded that they had. The loneliness clearly had mattered to them: those reporting themselves to have been "very lonely or remote from other people" were likely also to have reported themselves to have been "depressed or very unhappy."[21]

In another survey, one in which a national sample was interviewed by telephone, respondents were asked whether *during the past week* they had ever felt very lonely or remote from other people. Because the time frame was narrower than that in the first survey, and perhaps because telephone interviewing leads to more limited rapport than face-to-face methods, the percentage of respondents answering that they had been very lonely or remote from others dropped to 11 percent[22]—still an appreciable proportion of the population.

In this study women were more likely to report loneliness than men: 14 percent compared with 9 percent. Whether this was because women actually suffered greater loneliness or because it is easier for women to admit to loneliness cannot be known.

Marital status was of even greater importance than sex. Of those who were not married, 27 percent of the women and 23 percent of men reported severe loneliness in the preceding week, whereas among the married the percentages were 10 percent for women and 6 percent for men. Severe loneliness appears to be unusual among married men, somewhat more prevalent among married women, and quite prevalent among the unmarried of both sexes.

One might expect loneliness to be especially prevalent among the widowed and divorced. Over half of the small number (16) of widowed men in the telephone survey reported severe loneliness in the preceding week. The proportion for widowed women was much smaller, though still very high: 29 percent. In another study, however, Lopata found 48 percent of a sample of widows reporting loneliness to be the leading problem in their lives and another 22 percent reporting that loneliness was an issue for them.[23] There were too few cases of presently divorced individuals in the telephone survey to provide reliable figures. But on the basis of a rather impressionistic study of those who had just separated from a spouse, Hunt writes: "Of all the negative feelings of the newly separated, none is more common or more important than loneliness. Only a minority fail to suffer from it, and even those who most keenly desired the end of the marriage often find the initial loneliness excruciating."[24]

It is significant that among the unmarried the percentage of women who were severely lonely is not appreciably greater than the percentage of men. Women on their own sometimes suppose that loneliness is a woman's affliction. They envy what they perceive as the ability of men to get out of the house to theaters or bars or sporting events without having first to arrange for an escort or at least a protective friend. They sometimes wish it was socially permissible for them as well as for men to take the initiative in exploring new ties. But women may exaggerate the worth of the right to make the first move: courtship is a two-person game and the primary problem of courtship, which men share with women, is that of finding a partner with whom to play. Women also tend to overlook the lesser accessibility of same-sex friendships to men past early adulthood: it seems far easier for women in our society to establish close friendships with other women than for men to establish such friendships with other men. It also seems easier for women than for men to keep in touch by telephone or lunches or evening get-togethers with an extended network of not-quite-so-close friends. Kin ties, too, are more often retained in good repair by women than by men.

The telephone survey study also showed that those who were poor were especially likely to be lonely.[25] Why this might be the case can only be surmised, but perhaps with low income there is a tendency to social withdrawal. In addition there may be different social patterns at different income levels, and the patterns maintained by the poor may be more vulnerable to failure. Furthermore, aging may be productive of both poverty and loneliness and so responsible for some of the apparent connection between the last two. In partial corroboration of this surmise, some correlation does exist between loneliness and age and we know from other data that a correlation exists between age and poverty. Ill health may also produce both poverty and loneliness. A fairly strong correlation exists between loneliness and ill health and again we know from other data that ill health and poverty are associated.[26]

The telephone interview study found that if respondents were divided into three age groups, with ages thirty-five and fifty-five being the points of division, little difference in reported loneliness occurred among men in the various age groups, but some difference did occur among women.[27] Those women over age fifty-five were somewhat more likely than other women to report loneliness: more than 16 percent among the older women compared with less than 13 percent among the younger. This slight bulge in the category of older women may result not only from widowhood but also from children having left home, an event that may perhaps produce a form of loneliness distinct from those discussed here. We might suspect that had the telephone survey interviewed an appreciable number of individuals of more than seventy years, much more loneliness would have been found. It seems probable that both men and women who are very old are especially vulnerable to the loss of critically important social ties and, therefore, to loneliness. However, we cannot as yet demonstrate this with survey data.[28]

NOTES

1. Harry Stack Sullivan, *The Interpersonal Theory of Psychiatry* (New York: W. W. Norton, 1953), p. 262.

2. Sullivan saw loneliness as uniformly painful. Not all later writers agree. Among those who do are: Frieda Fromm-Reichmann, "Loneliness," *Psychiatry* 22, no. 1 (January 1959): 1; Henry D. Witzleben, "On loneliness," *Psychiatry* 21 (1968): 37–43; Klaus W. Berblinger, "A psychiatrist looks at loneliness," *Psychosomatics* 9, no. 2 (1968): 96–102. Among those who find redeeming features in loneliness, while also recognizing that it carries potential for pain, are Clark E. Moustakas, *Loneliness* (Englewood Cliffs, N.J.: Prentice-Hall, 1961) and *Loneliness and Love* (Englewood Cliffs, N.J.: Prentice-Hall, 1972).

3. P. Herbert Leiderman, "Loneliness: a psychodynamic interpretation," in *Aspects of Depression,* edited by Edwin S. Shneidman and Magno J. Ortega (Boston: Little, Brown and Co., 1969), p. 155.

4. Fromm-Reichmann, "Loneliness," p. 1.

5. For studies of both grief and dying, see the collection of papers, *Death and Identity,* edited by Robert Fulton (New York: John Wiley, 1965). See also in regard to grief, Colin M. Parkes, *Bereavement* (New York: International Universities Press, 1972). And in regard to dying, see Barney G. Glaser and Anselm L. Strauss, *Awareness of Dying* (Chicago: Aldine, 1965).

6. Sullivan, *The Interpersonal Theory,* p. 261.

7. Fromm-Reichmann, "Loneliness," p. 6.

8. Even those who recognize the potential intensity of the distress of loneliness may be condescending to "ordinary loneliness." See, for example, Witzleben, "On loneliness."

9. Moustakas, *Loneliness and Love,* p. 22.

10. See Arthur Burton, "On the nature of loneliness," *American Journal of Psychoanalysis* 21 (1961): 34–39.

11. Sullivan, *The Interpersonal Theory,* p. 290.

12. Magno J. Ortega, "Depression, loneliness and unhappiness," in *Aspects of Depression,* edited by Edwin S. Schneidman and Magno J. Ortega (Boston: Little, Brown and Co., 1969), pp. 143–153.

13. Parkes, *Bereavement.* See also James R. Averill, "Grief; its nature and significance," *Psychological Bulletin,* 70, no. 6 (1968): 721–748.

14. *Webster's Third New International Dictionary* (Springfield, Mass.: G. and C. Merriam Company, 1968).

15. For a category system of relational provisions, see Robert S. Weiss, "Fund of sociability," *Trans-action*, July/August, 1969. For the problems of those away from kin over the Christmas holiday, see Mark Benney, Robert S. Weiss, Rolf Meyersohn, and David Reisman, "Christmas in an apartment-hotel," *American Journal of Sociology* (November 1959): 233–240.

16. See Weiss, "After the breakup: Mrs. Graham"; "Relying on one's community: Mrs. Davis"; and "Parents without partners as a supplementary community," in *Loneliness: The Experience of Emotional and Social Isolation* (Cambridge, Mass.: The M.I.T. Press, 1973), pp. 131–141; 197–211; 212–224.

17. See Weiss, "Fund of sociability." Also see "An uprooted woman: Mrs. Phillips" in Weiss, *Loneliness*, pp. 165–174.

18. See "After the breakup: Mrs. Graham" (Note 16).

19. H. David Kirk, *Shared Fate: A Theory of Adoption and Mental Health* (New York: Free Press, 1964).

20. Gartly Jaco, *The Social Epidemiology of Mental Disorders* (New York: Russell Sage, 1960), p. 12. To be precise, the definition I offer is of prevalence *rate*, rather than prevalence.

21. Norman Bradburn, *The Structure of Psychological Well-Being* (Chicago: Aldine, 1969), pp. 56–61. The correlation between "very lonely" and "depressed" was .71 for women and .72 for men. See page 60.

22. Based on data provided by Richard Maisel. For study design and other results see Richard Maisel, *Report of the Continuing Audit of Public Attitudes and Concerns* (Harvard Medical School: Laboratory of Community Psychiatry, 1969), mimeographed.

23. Helena Z. Lopata, "Loneliness: forms and components," in Weiss, *Loneliness*, pp. 102–115. The open style of interviewing used by the Lopata study seems more likely to elicit evidence of loneliness than the pre-categorized questionnaires used by the Bradburn or the Maisel studies. In addition, the time period under consideration in her study was not so limited. These differences in method may account for the greater apparent incidence of loneliness in the Lopata study.

24. Morton Hunt, "Alone, alone, all, all, alone," in Weiss, *Loneliness*, pp. 125–133.

25. Maisel, *Report*. Correlation of income with loneliness was .15. A correlation of .04 or greater was statistically significant at the .05 level.

26. The correlation between loneliness and health in the Maisel study was −.13.

27. The linear correlation between loneliness and age was small when the sexes were grouped together. There was more loneliness among the very young than among the middle-aged, undoubtedly because of the lesser frequency of marriage in the former category, and still more loneliness among the aged. The relationship of loneliness and age is in fact curvilinear.

28. Some evidence for this surmise that the very old are especially vulnerable to loneliness is offered by Peter Townsend's article, "Isolation and loneliness in the aged," in Weiss, *Loneliness*, pp. 175–188.

14/ MARITAL STATUS, LIFE-STRAINS, AND DEPRESSION

Leonard I. Pearlin and Joyce S. Johnson

Occasionally important relationships between social structural factors and mental disorders are discovered far in advance of our learning how these relationships are forged. This has been the case with regard to the psychological impact of such fundamental features of social organization as social class (Kohn, 1972; Mechanic, 1972) and sex roles (Gove, 1972; Gove and Tudor, 1973; Pearlin, 1975) as well as for marital status, the concern of this report. For many years, at least since Durkheim's (1966) work, it has been recognized that the unmarried are more disposed than the married to emotional problems. There is now an accumulation of studies showing with rare, though not perfect (Dupuy et al., 1970), consistency that people with spouses are more likely to enjoy psychological well-being than those without (Blumenthal, 1967; Bradburn, 1969; Briscoe and Smith, 1974; Gurin et al., 1960; Knupfer et al., 1966; Radloff, 1975; Srole et al., 1962).

Although there is relatively little research aimed directly at understanding how these differences arise, three major explanatory themes can be extrapolated from existing writings. The first, discussed by Bachrach (1975:6–7) in her extensive review of the literature, pertains exclusively to the formerly married. It views the very transition from marriage to singleness as a stressor event entailing a variety of psychic traumas. Self-conceptions may be assaulted in the course of becoming single, social networks often become unraveled, and established habit patterns frequently must be abandoned. It also has been suggested (Hunt, 1966) that the formerly married have the difficult task of accommodating to the new role definitions that are more ambiguous than those that gave meaning and direction to their behavior as married men and women. Sexual problems, too, may be especially severe for those newly single who had been accustomed to sexual gratification (Bell, 1966). But regardless of the particular problem identified by different observers, each emphasizes essentially the same process: becoming unmarried is itself a condition imposing difficult and often unclear demands for change, and it is these demands that lead to psychological disturbance.

A second interpretation, perhaps less convincing now than in earlier years, attributes the psychological distress of the unmarried to the powerful norms defining marriage as the most desirable state adults can attain. According to this view, the single who remain single are moving against the grain of these norms, eventually running the risk of being treated as people either unwilling or unable to conform to accepted practice. They are considered as being outside the normative pattern of living (Lee, 1974; Udry, 1974; Gurin et al., 1960) and come to be seen as unfit and deviant. Their disposition to psychological problems, therefore, is a consequence of being objects of contempt because of their failure to conform to prized norms.

Finally, it has been proposed that the psychological problems of the unmarried are not a consequence of their marital status but, rather, a cause of it. This explanation argues that people who are depressed or who suffer other personality debilities are selectively less able than others to be married and to stay married. Such an interpretation is especially favored by epidemiologists and clinicians who have observed the disproportionate number of unmarried people among those suffering from psychoses (Ødegaard, 1946; 1960; Malzberg, 1964; Garfield and Sundland, 1966). Because interpretations of selectivity usually are made from observations of psychiatric populations, we cannot be sure how applicable they are to more representative populations. Nevertheless, while such interpretations may be limited in their generality, they underscore the difficulties in determining whether the marital status or the onset of the psychological disturbance comes first (Bachrach, 1975:2–3).

The present analysis emphasizes the stress-provoking problems of daily life which, with rare exception (Warheit et al., 1976), are ignored by prevailing perspectives. A comprehensive understanding of the relationship between marital status and mental functioning must recognize more than transitional traumas, normative violations and the possibility of psychological selectivity. The part played by structured, persistent life-strains also must be considered. Three such conditions concern us here: the economic resources of people, isolation from social networks, and parental responsibilities. We shall see that these conditions do, in fact, contribute to differences in the psychological functioning of the married and the unmarried, because the unmarried are more frequently exposed to them and are more vulnerable to their effects.

BACKGROUND AND METHODS

The data presented here are part of a larger investigation into the social origins of personal stress and were gathered through scheduled interviews with a sample of 2,300 people representative of the population of the Chicago area, which includes sections of North-western Indiana as well as some of the surrounding suburbs.

The interview dealt extensively with the strains experienced by people—the conflicts, frustrations and threats that earlier explora-tory interviews revealed to be quite common. It particularly focused on strains occurring in the roles of occupation, marriage, childrear-ing and economic life. Second, the interview sought to identify the coping repertoires people employ in dealing with the strains they experience in these roles. Third, it inquired into people's emotional stresses and their symptoms of disturbances such as depression and anxiety. The present analysis, while focusing on marital status, in-cludes information from a number of different areas covered by the interview.

DEPRESSION

Although fundamentally we are interested in the relationship of marital status to all manifestations of emotional well-being and dis-tress, we shall limit our examination to depression. This is partly for ease and partly because it is a state experienced to some de-gree by everyone under ordinary conditions of life. Indeed, it has been described as the "common cold of psychiatric practice" (Silverman 1968:131). Its commonness suggests that it may be a fairly sensitive psychological barometer of life-strains, and it is largely for this reason that it is selected for use here. But it is important to recognize that depression is only one of several indi-cators of distress that are related to marital status. Thus, measures of anxiety, happiness, psychosomatic disturbances and self-esteem each are associated with marital status at a level of statistical sig-nificance. Our emphasis on depression, therefore, should not ob-scure the fact that marital status also is relevant to other dimen-sions of well-being and distress.

The measure of depression adopted for use here, developed by Lipman et al. (1969) and Derogatis et al. (1971), asks respondents the frequency with which they experience each of eleven symptoms.[1]

MARITAL STATUS AND DEPRESSION

For much of our analysis, two groups will be delineated: the married and the unmarried. However, in order to show the pivotal relation-ship between marital status and depression in greatest detail, Table 1 further subdivides the unmarried into the widowed, the divorced and, although they are still legally married, the separated. The re-sults clearly show that the presently married are most free of depres-sion, the formerly married are most burdened by it, and the never

TABLE 1
MARITAL STATUS AND DEPRESSION (PERCENT)

Depression	Married	Never Married	Formerly Married	Types of Formerly Married		
				Widowed	Divorced	Separated
High 1	12	20	27	22	27	32
2	14	18	20	22	14	25
3	18	23	17	15	16	23
4	29	24	18	21	22	10
Low 5	27	16	18	20	21	10
N=	(1,589)	(288)	(415)	(172)	(141)	(102)

married fall squarely between these extremes. Among the groups making up the formerly married category, the separated are outstandingly most susceptible to depression, with no appreciable difference existing between the divorced and the widowed.

Because several important social characteristics are associated with marital status, the relationship between marital status and depression may be spurious, shaped not by marital status but by its attendant social characteristics. Sex, age and race are particularly implicated in this regard, for each of these characteristics is differentially distributed among the marital statuses. For example, women and blacks are markedly overrepresented in all categories of formerly married. With regard to age, the never married have the youngest mean age and, unsurprisingly, the widowed the oldest.

In order to determine if the relationship of marital status and depression persists after taking account of sex, age, and race, we have partialed out the effects of these characteristics. . . . We can be confident, then, that the results of Table 1 do not spuriously stem from ascribed characteristics that are related to, but different from, marital status itself, for the results persist after the possible influences of such characteristics are removed. Nevertheless, as we observe some of the conditions that do link marital status and depression, the potential relevance of these characteristics will surface again. Consequently, they will be considered throughout the course of the analysis.

MARITAL STATUS AND LIFE-STRAINS

The life-strains we shall be examining—economic hardships, social isolation and parental role overloads—have in common a resistance to rapid amelioration. They are persistent problems, and persistent problems can have deleterious psychological effects over time. These three life-strains do not account for all of the differences in depression between the married and the unmarried, but they do illuminate how adverse circumstances built into the structure of daily life contribute to the differences. Two mechanisms will be shown to underlie this contribution: differential exposure and differential vulnerability. Each of these will be in evidence as we consider the three life-strains one by one.

Economic hardship. Our evaluation of economic strains relies on a three-part question asking people about their difficulties in acquiring the necessities of life: How often does it happen that you do not have enough money to afford (1) the kind of food you (your family) should have? (2) the kind of medical care you (your family) should have? (3) the kind of clothing you (your family) should have? Each item was answered by "never," "once in a while," "fairly often" or "very often" and a score ranging from 3 to 12 was formed by summing the values of the three responses. . . .

Table 2 divides people according to economic strain, with those scoring 3 being classified as being "free" of strain, from 4 to 6 as under "moderate" strain and from 7 to 12 as experiencing "severe" strain. The unmarried are more likely than the married to experience economic strains: only 73 (5 percent) of all married people are under severe strain compared to 13 percent of the unmarried. Correspondingly, 74 percent of the married are free of strain compared to 55 percent of the unmarried. Within the unmarried group, the separated experience the most hardship, followed by the divorced, widowed and never married. The table also points to a connection between the intensity of economic strain and the level of depression, for regardless of marital status, the proportions high on depression vary directly with the severity of economic strain. Thus, economic hardship links marital status and depression by (1) being more prevalent among the unmarried and by (2) being a condition disposing people to depression.

However, their greater *exposure* is not the only reason that unmarried people are more depressed by economic strain; they also appear to have a greater *vulnerability* to the effects of limited resources. This is suggested by comparing the married and the unmarried who are exposed to economic strains of the same severity. The pattern revealed by this comparison appears repeatedly throughout the analysis: the differences in depression between the married and the unmarried are greatest under conditions of greatest strain; as strains diminish, differences in depression among people of different marital status also diminish, although they remain appreciable. . . . Whereas we saw earlier that unmarried people are more likely to experience economic deprivation, we see now that they also may be more readily depressed by such deprivation. Both differences are reflected in the relationship of marital status and depression.

TABLE 2
ECONOMIC STRAINS, MARITAL STATUS, AND
DEPRESSION (PERCENT)

Depression	Severe Strain		Moderate Strain		No Strain	
	Married	Unmarried	Married	Unmarried	Married	Unmarried
High 1	26	50	19	29	9	15
2	17	15	22	21	12	18
3	8	12	16	27	19	17
4	26	16	27	13	30	26
Low 5	23	7	16	10	30	24
N=	(73)	(92)	(335)	(220)	(1,175)	(383)

Is the effect of economic hardship on the relationship of marital status to depression attributable to extraneous social characteristics? This question is especially pertinent with regard to race; for a disproportionate number of blacks experience severe economic hardships, thus raising the possibility that race more than economic strain is the influential condition in Table 2. However, for blacks and whites alike, the association between marital status and depression is closest under conditions of greatest strain, with the association being reduced appreciably with each reduced level of economic strain. . . . Furthermore, these relationships are found in the same order among men and women, among those less than forty years of age and those forty and over. While there are variations from one group to another in the magnitude of the association, invariably the unmarried, regardless of their race, sex or age, differ most from the married when under greatest strain and the difference is considerably diminished when strain is minimal. Thus, it is economic strain that is the pertinent condition, not race, sex or age.

The same patterns of association emerge when comparisons are made of the married with the never married, widowed, divorced and separated. Except in the case of the separated . . . differences in depression between the married and each sub-type of unmarried are most pronounced where there is most deprivation and are markedly less with improved economic circumstances. Regardless of the circumstances leading to the absence of a spouse, therefore, it is a condition especially likely to be associated with depression under adverse economic conditions.

The unmarried, then, are doubly disadvantaged with regard to economic circumstances. First, they are unequally exposed to a hardship conducive to depression; second, such hardship, even when equally severe among people of different marital statuses, is still more likely to result in depression among the unmarried. Severe economic strains thus are more heavily concentrated in the unmarried population and, in addition, they take a greater psychological toll from the unmarried.

Social isolation. The apparent inability of the unmarried to withstand hardship as well as the married is not necessarily because of a greater psychic fragility on their part. It is equally reasonable to suppose that marriage itself is a barrier standing between outside strain and inner depression. When faced with adversity, married persons may have the advantage of being able to draw emotional support and concrete help from their partners. Of course, supportive and helping relations between people are not limited to marriage; unmarried people often establish interpersonal ties that serve as partial functional alternatives to marriage. This suggests that when one has neither a spouse nor surrogate relations one will be especially open to depression.

Several items are indicative of the extent and stability of people's social affiliations. One question asks respondents how long they have lived in their present neighborhoods; another inquires into membership in voluntary associations; and a third asks about the number of "really good friends" who live within an hour's drive. These indicators were pooled to form a measure of isolation from extrafamilial relations. The highest possible score indicates neighborhood residence for less than two years, having either only one or no friends close by, and not belonging to a voluntary association. As judged by this measure, the unmarried are more likely than the married to experience isolation, a result consistent with observations that single people, especially the formerly married, have greater difficulty than couples in establishing a durable and extensive social life (Gove, 1972). Moreover, as the extent of isolation from extrafamilial relations increases, so do the tendencies to depression. Thus, marital status is related to isolation and isolation to depression.

Since isolation is related both to marital status and to depression, it also may be one of the circumstances linking marital status and depression. As in the case of economic deprivations, however, differential exposure alone does not bear the burden of explanation. In Table 3, the married and the unmarried are divided into three groups according to the degree of social isolation they experience. Once again, the findings show the unmarried to be doubly susceptible to depression: first, a larger proportion lives in considerable isolation and, next, they are more likely to be depressed by equivalent conditions of isolation. Indeed, married people are virtually unaffected by isolation from extrafamilial contacts. For this reason, the differences in depression between the married and unmarried who are considerably or fairly isolated stem entirely from the impact of isolation on the latter. Evidently, the absence of social ties can

TABLE 3
SOCIAL ISOLATION, MARITAL STATUS, AND DEPRESSION (PERCENT)

Depression	Considerably Isolated		Fairly Isolated		Not Isolated	
	Married	Unmarried	Married	Unmarried	Married	Unmarried
High 1	13	28	11	24	11	21
2	15	19	13	15	14	16
3	18	19	18	20	19	22
4	28	21	30	21	29	20
Low 5	26	13	28	20	27	21
N=	(270)	(200)	(315)	(135)	(957)	(343)

represent a more complete isolation for the unmarried than for those with spouses, making the depressive consequences of isolation singularly severe for unmarried people.

Again, it is necessary to ask if the results of Table 3 are being shaped by extraneous social characteristics, for blacks substantially more than whites and the older slightly more than the younger are isolated. Among both blacks and whites, isolation is most likely to have depressive consequences for the unmarried. Interestingly, however, the decline in the magnitude of the association with decreased isolation is greater among whites. . . . Thus, the results of Table 3 arise not because blacks are more often isolated from extrafamilial ties but in spite of their being somewhat less adversely affected by isolation. Moreover, we find that, regardless of the age or sex of respondents, vulnerability to depression is greatest among the unmarried who are separated from social contacts. We can be assured, then, that the relationships in Table 3 are being conditioned by isolation, not by extraneous characteristics associated with isolation.

With regard to the different subgroups of unmarried, it can be noted that there are differences in the degree of isolation they experience: the widowed are least isolated, followed in order by the never married, divorced and separated. However, when these groups are treated separately, we find in each case that the association between marital status and depression is closest among people experiencing either a considerable or fair degree of isolation, dropping off sharply among those not isolated. Isolation, it can be noted, makes least difference to depression among the separated, many of whom are immersed in the first steps of marital dissolution where the peak emotional crises of this period may overshadow the more low-keyed problems of life.

The absence of a spouse, therefore, is most apt to result in depression when it is in combination with isolation from contacts outside the family. Under any condition, isolated or not, the unmarried are consistently more disposed than the married to depression; but the difference between the two groups is considerably reduced in the absence of social isolation. Being without a mate apparently leaves one open to the depressive consequences of life-strains, especially so when one is also lacking alternative supports.

Parental responsibilities. Economic hardships and social isolation, while seemingly very different conditions of life, have a very important property in common. It is the rather relentless constraints each typically imposes on behavior and experience, the kind of life-strains that remain constant across a range of life-situations. The burdens and responsibilities of parenthood, to which we turn now, also may impose persistent strains having depressive consequences.

The most direct indicator of parental burdens is the number of children for whom the parent has responsibility. There is one respect, however, in which this feature of parental responsibility is quite different from the other strains we have examined. Although 38 percent of the unmarried people in our sample have the daily care of at least one child, it is the married who are much more likely than the unmarried to have the larger number of children at home. Unlike their greater exposure to economic hardship and social isolation, single people are less exposed than the married to this potential source of strain. If parental responsibilities have a part in the relationship of marital status and depression, therefore, it is not because these responsibilities are more concentrated among the unmarried, but because such responsibilities, where they do exist, are more onerous for the unmarried.

The unmarried do, in fact, have a greater sensitivity to these burdens. Table 4 reveals that as the number of children in the household increases to three or more, there is a corresponding increase in the proportions of unmarried parents who are highly depressed. By contrast, there is a slight tendency in precisely the opposite direction among the married. The net result . . . is that the difference in depression between the married and the unmarried having three or more children at home is substantial, while the difference between those having no children in the household is considerably smaller. Thus, marital status and depression are most closely connected when parental responsibilities are most demanding. The never married who are parents, it should be pointed out, are somewhat more affected by these responsibilities than are the formerly married groups.

Because the social characteristics of people are closely interwoven with the magnitude of their parental responsibilities, it is again necessary to examine their potential part in producing the results in Table 4. Sex is especially salient in this regard, for almost all unmarried people with responsibility for the care of children are women.

TABLE 4
NUMBER OF CHILDREN AT HOME, MARITAL STATUS, AND
DEPRESSION (PERCENT)

| | Number of Children | | | | | |
| | Three or More | | One or Two | | None | |
Depression	Married	Unmarried	Married	Unmarried	Married	Unmarried
High 1	12	34	12	26	11	20
2	12	18	14	20	17	19
3	16	17	19	24	20	19
4	31	16	28	18	27	23
Low 5	29	15	27	12	25	19
N=	(458)	(89)	(715)	(179)	(416)	(435)

Only 18 single men have any parental responsibility, four of whom have the care of three or more children. It is difficult, therefore, to separate fully the possible effects of sex from those of parental responsibility on the relationship of marital status and depression. It is instructive, however, to focus on the 18 single men who have responsibility for children. Although few in number, they are entirely similar to their female counterparts, for they are much more disposed to depression than are married men having the same parental responsibilities and more depressed, too, than those men who are also single but free of these responsibilities. Although this is by no means conclusive, it suggests that sex is not responsible for the results in Table 4.

Race, too, is intertwined with the magnitude of parental responsibilities, with unmarried blacks more likely than unmarried whites to have children and to have them in larger numbers. However, when the relationships in Table 4 are examined separately for blacks and whites, the pattern of associations is parallel. . . . Finally, it is the younger parents who are likely to have the care of children at home, making it necessary to distinguish the effects of family size from the possible effects of parental age. When the relationships in Table 4 are examined separately for people younger than forty years and those older, equivalent results appear. The results in the table, therefore, cannot be attributed to race or age or, judging from the 18 unmarried male parents, to sex.

The age of children, like family size, is also a dimension of family composition indicative of parental responsibilities. Briefly, we find that the younger the children in the household, the greater is the association between marital status and depression. . . . Thus, depression is most likely to exist among unmarried parents of very young children, the arc of the life cycle in which the burden of parental responsibility is greatest. By the time children reach 18 years and beyond, ages of greater independence, differences between the married and unmarried parents shrink to insignificance. It is apparent that the burdens of caring for young children are felt most keenly by the parent who faces the task alone.

Being a parent, then, entails very different obligations, has very different meanings, and yields very different experiences for the married and the unmarried, regardless of their other social characteristics. The greater the number and the younger the ages of children for whom unmarried parents have responsibility, the greater these differences become. For single parents, the joys of parenthood are most likely to be aroused when the number of their children is small and their ages large.

THE LIFE-STRAINS: THEIR INDEPENDENT AND JOINT EFFECTS

The foregoing analysis has succeeded in identifying the ways in which some key life-strains contribute to the association between marital status and depression. It is apparent that persistent problems, unequally concentrated among and having an unequal effect on the unmarried, forge the links between marital status and depression. Being unmarried increases one's chances of experiencing hardship and of being psychologically hurt by such experience.

But there are certain issues that remain unaddressed. For example, we have not yet taken into account the overlap that exists in being poor, being isolated and being burdened by parental responsibilities. In order to know the order of importance among these conditions, it is necessary to weigh the effect each has when independent of the others. Second, a direct assessment of the greater vulnerability of the unmarried to life-strains requires that we sort out the interactions of strains and marital status and observe the effect they have on depression in conjunction with each other. Finally, we have not yet dealt with the magnitude of the combined influence of the life-strains on the relationship between marital status and depression. Each of these issues can be dealt with by regression analysis.

. . . It can be seen that economic strain is preeminently more important to depression than any other variable. Because, as we saw, the unmarried are much more likely to be exposed to economic deprivation, it is by far the major contributor to the association of marital status and depression. But what about the differential vulnerability of the unmarried to life-strains? Some of the depressive effects of strains were found to be conditional on the marital status of people experiencing them, suggesting that life-strains and marital status jointly produce effects uniquely different from those created by each separately. . . . Parental responsibilities in conjunction with marital status are more closely associated with depression than the other combinations. This is consistent with our earlier observation that the number of children is positively related to depression among the unmarried, but is slightly negatively related among the married.

Overall, being without a spouse is more likely to result in depression when one is also enmeshed in a context of unrelenting strains, especially strains of an economic nature. It is apparent that single people withstand these conditions of hardship less well than do married people. Indeed, marriage is the more beneficial arrangement under all conditions, since being single is somewhat disposing to depression even when strains are absent. Nevertheless, the advantages of marriage are especially apparent when life circumstances are most difficult, not when they are most benign.

NOTE

1. Respondents were asked to reply "never," "once in a while," "fairly often," or "very often" to the following items: During the past week how often did you: lack enthusiasm for doing anything? have a poor appetite? feel bored or have little interest in things? lose sexual interest or pleasure? have trouble getting to sleep or staying asleep? cry easily or feel like crying? feel downhearted or blue? feel low in energy or slowed down? feel hopeless about the future? have any thoughts of possibly ending your life? feel lonely?

REFERENCES

Bachrach, Leona L. 1975. Marital Status and Mental Disorder: An Analytical Review. DHEW Publication No. (ADM) 75-217. Washington, D.C.: U.S. Government Printing Office.

Bell, Robert R. 1966. Premarital Sex in a Changing Society. Englewood Cliffs, N.J.: Prentice-Hall.

Blumenthal, Monica D. 1967. "Mental health among the divorced: a field study of divorced and never divorced persons." Archives of General Psychiatry 16:603–8.

Bradburn, Norman M. 1969. The Structure of Psychological Well-Being. Chicago: Aldine.

Briscoe, C. William and James B. Smith. 1974. "Psychiatric illness—marital units and divorce." Journal of Nervous and Mental Disease 158:440–5.

Derogatis, L. R., R. S. Lipman, L. Covi and K. Rickles. 1971. "Neurotic symptom dimensions." Archives of General Psychiatry 24:454–64.

Dupuy, H. J., A. Engel, B. K. Devine, J. Scanlan and L. Quereck. 1970. Selected Symptoms of Psychological Distress. National Center for Health Statistics. Public Health Service Publication 1000, Vital and Health Statistics Series 11, No. 37. Washington, D.C.: U.S. Government Printing Office.

Durkheim, Emile. 1966. Suicide. New York: Free Press.

Garfield, S. L. and D. M. Sundland. 1966. "Prognostic scales in schizophrenia." Journal of Consulting Psychology 30:18–24.

Gove, Walter R. 1972. "The relationship between sex roles, marital status and mental illness." Social Forces 51:34–44.

Gove, Walter R. and Jeanette F. Tudor. 1973. "Adult sex roles and mental illness." American Journal of Sociology 78:812–35.

Gurin, Gerald, Joseph Veroff and Sheila Feld. 1960. Americans View Their Mental Health. New York: Basic Books.

Hunt, Morton. 1966. The World of the Formerly Married. New York: McGraw-Hill.

Knupfer, Genevieve, Walter Clark and Robin Room. 1966. "The mental health of the unmarried." American Journal of Psychiatry 122:841–51.

Kohn, Melvin L. 1972. "Class, family and schizophrenia: a reformulation." Social Forces 50:295–304.

Lee, G. A. 1974. "Marriage and anomie: a causal argument." Journal of Marriage and the Family 36:523–32.

Lipman, R. S., K. Rickles, L. Covi, L. R. Derogatis and E. H. Uhlenhuth. 1969. "Factors of symptom distress." Archives of General Psychiatry 21:328–38.

Malzberg, Benjamin. 1964. "Marital status and the incidence of mental disorder." International Journal of Social Psychiatry 10:19–26.

Mechanic, David. 1972. "Social class and schizophrenia: some requirements for a plausible theory of social influence." Social Forces 50:305–9.

Ødegaard, Ø. 1946. "Marriage and mental disease: a study in social psychopathology." Journal of Mental Science 92:35–59.

———. 1960. "Marriage rate and fertility in psychotic patients before hospital admission and after discharge." International Journal of Social Psychiatry 6:25–33.

Pearlin, Leonard I. 1975. "Sex roles and depression." Pp. 183–98 in Nancy Datan and Leon Ginsberg (eds.), Proceedings of Fourth Life-Span Developmental Psychology Conference: Normative Life Crises. New York: Academic Press.

Radloff, Lenore. 1975. "Sex differences in depression: the effects of occupation and marital status." Sex Roles 1:249–65.

Silverman, Charlotte. 1968. The Epidemiology of Depression. Baltimore: Johns Hopkins Press.

Srole, Leo, Thomas S. Langer, Stanley T. Michael, Marvin K. Opler and Thomas A. C. Rennie. 1962. Mental Health in the Metropolis: The Midtown Manhattan Study. New York: McGraw-Hill.

Udry, J. R. 1974. The Social Context of Marriage (3rd edition). Philadelphia: Lippincott.

Warheit, George J., Charles E. Holzer, III, Roger A. Bell and Sandra A. Arey. 1976. "Sex, marital status and mental health: a reappraisal." Social Forces 55:459–70.

15/ MARITAL STATUS, HEALTH, AND THE USE OF HEALTH SERVICES: An Old Relationship Revisited

Anne R. Somers

> Health and demography form an intertwined system in which demographic factors may reflect health trends, while health trends simultaneously may reflect demography.
>
> —*J. Lipman-Blumen (1977)*

A generation ago the relation between marital status, health, and the use of health services was generally taken for granted. This was clearly demonstrated in the positive association between marriage and longer life expectancy and between marriage and less use of health care services.

During the 1960s and early 1970s, interest in this subject apparently declined except in the field of mental illness; major traditional sources of information dried up, and little new was added to earlier knowledge. In more recent years, however, interest has revived, in part, because of the ever-rising cost of health care, which has led to study of every conceivable contributing factor, and in part, because of the decline in the proportion of married persons in the population and speculation as to whether this may be contributing to increased morbidity and the use of health services.

MARITAL STATUS AND DEATH RATES

The National Center for Health Statistics and its predecessor offices published information on mortality by marital status periodically from 1890 to 1970. Numerous reports and studies based on these data (especially those for 1940, 1949 through 1951, and 1959 through 1961) concluded that among both men and women at every age (white and nonwhite), married persons, on the average, live longer than the single, widowed, or divorced.[1-6] For example, the 1959 through 1961 mortality for single and widowed white men were each about 1.5 times that of white husbands (for divorced white men more than double that for white husbands).[3] For widowed men of other races, the mortality was 1.8 times that for husbands.

The consistency of the findings is striking. In 1956, for example, Kraus and Lilienfeld[5] of the Johns Hopkins Medical School concluded:

> For both sexes and colors combined, the ratios of the age-adjusted death rates in these nonmarried groups were 1.47, 1.46, and 1.84 respectively. . . . The relative excess mortality in the non-married categories compared to the married group was greater at the younger ages. . . . The relative excess mortality in the nonmarried categories was consistently greater in males than in females.

In 1957 the Metropolitan Life Insurance Company concluded:

> The married have a [health] advantage at every period of life, particularly prior to age 45. . . . Among males 20–44 the death rate for the married is only about half that for the single, and an even smaller fraction of that for the widowed or divorced.[4]

Unfortunately, these were the last reports by either Metropolitan or the National Center for Health Statistics on the subject. Metropolitan, despite its position as leader of the insurance business with respect to biostatistics, is now unable to provide similar information, even for its own insureds (Clarence Pearson, Metropolitan Life Insurance Co., written communication, Feb. 10, 1978). The center no longer collects information on marital status from death certificates (A. J. Klebba, Division of Vital Statistics, National Center for Health Statistics, oral communication, Feb. 6, 1978).

In 1978, however, the Council of Life Insurance and Health Insurance Institute, in a publication designed for the general public,[7] prominently featured a 1977 book by Lynch[8] of the University of Maryland School of Medicine, which, drawing heavily on the earlier data, took as its central thesis the relationship between marital status, loneliness, and health outcomes. Emphasizing the excess deaths among divorced American men younger than sixty-five years of age compared with the married, Lynch pointed out that the rate was almost double for coronary heart disease and cancer; double for lung cancer and strokes; almost three times as high for hypertension; four times as high for car accidents; nearly five times as high for suicide; seven times as high for cirrhosis of the liver, pneumonia, and homicide; and ten times as high for tuberculosis (Table 1). "The statistics for women are similar," he said, "although in some categories they are slightly lower."

MARITAL STATUS AND MORBIDITY

Some Relevant British Data: A 1951 census of all patients in all National Health Service hospitals (including psychiatric institutions) in England and Wales found the distribution shown in Table 2 as between young patients, those fifteen years and older who were married, and those fifteen years and older who were single, widowed, or divorced. The corresponding distribution for the entire population is also given.

These figures led Abel-Smith and Titmuss,[9] two of Britain's leading health economists, to conclude:

> Marriage and its survival into old age would seem to be an important safeguard against admission to hospitals in general and to "chronic" and mental hospitals in particular. . . . In relation to their numbers in the total adult population [of England and Wales] the single, widowed,

TABLE 1
DEATH RATES, DIVORCED AND MARRIED MEN, UNITED STATES, 1959–1961*

| | White Males | | Nonwhite Males | |
Cause of Death	Married	Divorced	Married	Divorced
Heart disease	176	362	142	298
Motor vehicle accidents	35	128	43	81
Cancer of respiratory system	28	65	29	75
Cancer of digestive system	27	48	42	88
Stroke	24	58	73	132
Suicide	17	73	10	21
Cirrhosis of liver	11	79	12	53
Hypertension	8	20	49	90
Pneumonia	6	44	22	69
Homicide	4	30	51	129
Tuberculosis	3	30	15	54

*Per 100,000 population, ages 15 to 64 years. Data from Lynch.[8]

TABLE 2
HOSPITAL POPULATION AND TOTAL POPULATION, DISTRIBU-
TION BY SEX, AGE, AND MARITAL STATUS, ENGLAND AND
WALES* 1951† AND 1975‡

	Males		**Females**	
	Hospital Census, %	Total Population	Hospital Census, %	Total Population
April 1951, yr				
< 15	15	23	10	21
≥ 15, Single	47	21	40	19
≥ 15, Widowed or divorced	8	4	16	11
≥ 15, Married	30	52	34	49
1955				
< 15	12	23	6	22
≥ 15, Single, widowed, or divorced	36	24	55	29
≥ 15, Married	51	52	40	50

*From Abel Smith and Titmuss[9] and from Abel Smith (written communication,
March 21, 1978).
†All hospitals.
‡Nonpsychiatric hospitals only.

and divorced make about double the demand on hospital
accommodations.

Comparable figures are not available for the 1970s. However,
Abel-Smith has provided the data shown in Table 2, based on a 1975
hospital inpatient enquiry of nonpsychiatric hospitals in England
and Wales.

Comparing the two surveys taken nearly a quarter-century apart,
following are some noteworthy findings: the reduced use of hospitals by children despite a constant proportion of the total population; the persistence of a lower rate of use, in relation to population,
by married women but not by married men; and the persistence of a
marked excess use by unmarried men but less extreme, 50 percent
in 1975, than in 1951, when it was 120 percent.

Unfortunately, the 1975 data do not permit distinction between
the never married and the formerly married. This failure and the
absence of age-adjusted data, which would help us to distinguish
between elderly widows, young unmarried couples, and middle-aged
divorcees, preclude definitive analysis. Still it seems fair to conclude
that married persons in England continue to make fewer demands
on the health services than the unmarried, even when psychiatric
services are excluded.

MENTAL ILLNESS

The latter exclusion is important. Nowhere in the entire health field is the differential demand more striking than in mental health. Pollack,[10] writing in 1975, concluded:

> The relationship between marital status and mental disorders has been studied extensively over the years. In the large number of studies that have measured the rate at which persons in specific marital status categories have come under psychiatric care, the patterns have been remarkably similar. The rate for married persons has been consistently the lowest, while the rates for separated and divorced persons have been the highest, with rates for single and widowed persons somewhere between these extremes.

Kramer[11] studied the resident population of all U.S. mental hospitals in 1960 and found that 48 percent had never been married, 13 percent were divorced or separated, and 12 percent were widowed.

Rednick and Johnson compared admission rates to U.S. mental hospitals and outpatient psychiatric clinics for the total population fourteen years of age and older in 1970 and found the differences reported in Table 3. For single men the hospital admission rate was 230 percent higher than for married men; for the separated, the rate was 2,100 percent higher. For clinic admissions the differences were not as large but were still striking: 192 percent and 862 percent, respectively. The differences for women were less extreme, but the same relationship prevailed in all categories.

Such statistics have led leading psychiatrists and officers of the National Institute of Mental Health to conclude that "the single most powerful predictor of stress-related physical as well as emotional illness is marital disruption."[12]

NURSING HOMES

Further corroboration of the high-risk status of the unmarried comes from examination of the nursing home population in the United States from 1973 through 1974; only 12 percent were married.[13] Sixty-four percent were widowed, 19 percent had never been married, and 5 percent were divorced or separated. The difference in this distribution and that of the noninstitutionalized population is dramatic. For example, while only 12 percent of institutionalized persons sixty-five years of age or older were married, the proportion for the noninstitutionalized was 54 percent. While

TABLE 3
ADMISSION RATES TO STATE AND COUNTY
MENTAL HOSPITALS AND TO OUTPATIENT
PSYCHIATRIC CLINICS, BY FAMILY STATUS
AND SEX, UNITED STATES, 1970*

	Mental Hospitals		Outpatient Clinics	
	Male	Female	Male	Female
Total	331	212	493	579
Single	439	242	806	743
Married	133	125	276	423
Separated	2,976	1,066	2,654	2,835
Divorced	2,168	759	1,366	1,622
Widowed	630	249	311	286

*Per 100,000 population, ages 14 years and older. From
Rednick and Johnson.[23]

15 percent of the institutionalized elderly were never married, the
figure for the noninstitutionalized was less than 6 percent.

GENERAL ILLNESS

For general illness in the noninstitutional population, the U.S. picture is less clear. Recent data from the National Center for Health
Statistics (1971 through 1972 and 1976; Table 4) comparing selected
health measures by marital status and by age adjustments indicate
that the never married make the least demand on the health care
system. (The figures include maternity care, which obviously affects
the results for women, but the lesser use is also true of never married men.) The formerly married of both sexes and in all the categories continue to have the most illness and continue to make the
greatest demand, with the highest rates experienced consistently by
the separated. For example, the latter reported a 30 percent higher
incidence of short-term conditions than the married and averaged
30 percent more visits to a physician. Again there is the same conclusion: the disruption of marriage, whether by death, divorce, or separation, appears to be one of the major risk factors influencing both
physical and mental illness and use of health services.

GROWING PROPORTION OF SINGLES

The relation of marital status to health and use of health services is
relevant not only to the person involved but to national health policy. Estimates of future health need and demand will have to take

TABLE 4
SELECTED HEALTH MEASURES, NONINSTITUTIONAL CIVILIANS, BY MARITAL STATUS, UNITED STATES*

	Restricted Activity, Days per Person per Year	% Limited in Activity Because of Long-term Conditions	Incidence of Short-term Conditions per 100 Persons per Year	Physician Visits per Persons per Year	% With 1 Short-stay Hospital Episode or More During Past Year
1971–1972					
All persons	18.8	17.0	174.4	5.4	13.0
Married	17.6	15.7	174.4	5.6	14.8
Formerly married					
Widowed	28.1	21.7	165.3	6.2	....
Separated	30.5	24.6	223.5	6.8	18.5
Divorced	26.2	21.7	216.4	6.6	14.6
Never married	17.0	20.6	161.2	4.6	9.1
1976					
All persons	21.2	18.6	182.9	5.3	12.7
Married	20.2	17.5	175.6	5.4	13.5
Formerly married					
Widowed	28.2	24.9	170.7	6.4	16.5
Separated	38.8	27.0	227.6	7.0	17.3
Divorced	30.7	24.4	221.4	6.5	14.5
Never married	19.3	19.8	184.3	4.7	9.3

*Aged 17 years and older. Age-adjusted rates include maternity care. Data from National Center for Health Statistics[24] and unpublished data from the Health Interview Survey.

into account the growing proportion of "singles" in the U.S. population—both the never married and the formerly married.

With the ever-growing disparity in life expectancy between men and women, more women are living on into widowhood. Among men older than sixty-five years, nearly 80 percent are married; among women of the same age, less than 40 percent are married.[14] Adding together the widowed, the divorced, and the never married, 60 percent of all women older than sixty-five years are now living without a spouse. Most continue to live with children or other family members, but 41 percent of all noninstitutionalized elderly women are living alone or with nonrelatives.

Among younger persons as well, the lack of traditional family supports is increasing. The disappearance of the extended family is now followed by the apparent decline of the nuclear family. Although 84 percent of U.S. families were still of the husband-wife variety in 1975, the percentage has been falling at an accelerating pace since 1960.[15] Among black families, only 61 percent were of this pattern compared with 75 percent in 1960. As a result of the falling marriage rate (10/1,000 population in 1976) and the rising divorce rate (5/1,000), the ratio of divorced to married persons has increased sharply. In 1960 there were 35 divorced persons per 1,000 married persons; in 1977 the figure was 84.[16] For those younger than forty-five years of age, the figure tripled from 30 to 91 persons.

The following trends, dominant throughout the 1960s and the first half of the 1970s, appear to corroborate, at least temporarily, the popular impression of the decline of the nuclear family:[16,17]

1. Later age of marriage;

2. Fewer children per family;

3. Growing proportion of never married persons in the population: for males 14 years and older the percentage rose from 25 percent in 1960 to 30 percent in 1977; for women, from 19 percent to 23 percent;

4. Growing proportion of individuals who live alone or with unrelated persons: up nearly 50 percent from 1970 through 1977, to nearly 18 million, compared with a rise of only 10 percent for family households;

5. Growing number of unmarried adults living with a person of the opposite sex: more than 1.5 million in 1977, more than twice as many as in 1970;

6. Dramatic rise in single-parent families, especially those headed by a woman: up by one third since 1970 to more than 9 million and 16 percent;

7. Declining proportion of children living with two parents: 79 percent in 1977 compared with 85 percent in 1970.

During the twelve-month period ending in March 1978, there

were several developments that suggest a possible reversal or at least stabilization in some of these trends: the marriage rate rose fractionally, the divorce rate leveled off, and the fertility and birth rates rose 1 and 2 percent, respectively. The data are too recent and the time period too brief, however, to be sure of the meaning.[18]

A HEN-AND-EGG RELATIONSHIP

A 1977 publication of the Institute of Medicine, *Perspectives on Health Promotion and Disease Prevention,* states:

> Changes in marital status are not commonly viewed as conditions predisposing the individual to disease and death. Nevertheless some research indicates significant correlations. . . . At every age level the relationship of people to their families is an important influence on health. In general, persons who experience conflict with or isolation from social groups, such as the family, are less healthy than those who have family support.[19]

A similar statement was endorsed by the 1975 National Conference on Preventive Medicine:

> People who are isolated from family support, single people, the divorced and the widowed, have rates of morbidity and mortality which are higher than those who are married. . . . Children who grow up in families from which either parent is missing are reported to have less good health than those who grow up in intact nuclear families.[20]

The explanation for the relationship between marital status, health, and use of health services is, of course, complex. Twenty years ago, Metropolitan had this to say:

> In part, the generally higher mortality among the unmarried reflects the reduced chances of marriage or remarriage for those with serious chronic illness . . . . also the more healthful way of life that marriage provides.[4]

A generation later, Abel-Smith said:

> Some of the factors related to high utilization of hospital beds, for example, old age, severe handicap, are also related to marital status. Therefore, although married peo-

ple may use fewer hospital beds, this could be caused by other factors which also explain their marital status (B. Abel-Smith, Department of Health and Social Security, London, written communication, March 21, 1978).

In general the explanations appear to fall under two broad categories: (1) the absence of marriage, with its traditional physical, emotional, and social supports, results in more illness and use of health services, and (2) poor health, reflected in physical, mental, or emotional disability, results in the absence or disruption of marriage.

William J. DeMaria from Blue Cross–Blue Shield of North Carolina illustrates the first approach. Exploring the "fundamental blocks to optimal personal health care" as well as the rising costs, DeMaria lists as the primary factor "change in structure and function of the nuclear family" and identifies three special subfactors: loss of proximity to grandparents, high divorce and separation rate, and the working mother:

> Mothers remain the single most important factor in determining success or failure of providing optimal health care for family members. The mother is the primary health provider for family members. She is the person of first contact for the children, spouse, and others. . . . She must decide when, how, and where to make entry into the health service arena. After medical advice has been given, she is the major influence in determining the successful application of drugs and procedures and continuity of care for both acute and chronic problems (W. J. DeMaria, written communication, Nov. 7, 1977).

Some authorities maintain that sheer loneliness is a major contributor to illness and premature death. C. H. William Ruhe of the American Medical Association emphasized the second approach:

> The underlying conditions causing the marital disruption might be identical with or might have been caused by the "illness," rather than the reverse. If so, the disruption of marriage may simply have been an early manifestation of the physical and/or mental illness. . . . (written communication, July 31, 1978).

A CHANGING RELATIONSHIP?

It is possible that the influence of both these factors is now in decline. Referring to the changes in the structure of the family, Leona Bachrach of the National Institute of Mental Health says:

It is not unreasonable to speculate that such profound normative changes in the institution of the family may be accompanied by changes in the long-established association between marital status and mental disorder. Divorce, in short, may no longer necessarily reflect personal disorganization as once it did, nor marriage personal stability.[21]

This view, inconsistent as it is with traditional American values, could help to explain the reduced differential in health status and in use between the married and single as well as the simultaneous increase in the proportion of single persons in the population and the overall drop in mortality. The decline in family supports is increasingly being compensated for by the rise in public and community supports, including emergency room, psychiatric, and counseling services. The lesser stigma now attached to single status has probably reduced the degree of adverse selection.

It is too soon to be sure of any conclusions, however. In the complex web of conflicting developments influencing the health and marital status of the American people, we do not really know all that is happening.

Are young persons, who are postponing marriage and children until their late twenties or after and who are making increased use of community health services, healthier or less healthy than their parents were at the same age? Are today's children, raised in the typical one- to two-child family, healthier or less healthy than their parents, raised among more siblings? Is the middle-aged, divorced, and childless professional woman, virtually free of family chores and responsibilities, healthier or less healthy than her mother? How about the retired widow, with enough income to live alone rather than in her daughter-in-law's back bedroom, but totally lacking in routine family contacts?

Despite our limited knowledge, two facts stand out. They are summarized in the following quotations:

We can no longer usefully consider health disorders as fixed, defined entities with known biological expression, for they are also an expression of . . . changing social patterns. Social and economic factors cause health disorders; they alter the numbers of people at risk of being affected; and they create a variety of new pathways for the transmission of disorders of all kinds. Social factors also affect the expression and visibility of health disorders. . . . Social perceptions and definitions influence both the provision of care, and the demands of those who are being cared for.[22]

> As the family's role in health activities has declined, there has been a concurrent rise in both expectations of, and dependence on, the external medical system.[19]

Thus, even if the association between marital status and health is not as clear as it used to be, the persistent differential in life expectancy and use of services and the growing proportion of widowed, divorced, and separated persons in the population and of children living in single-parent families suggest a continued rise—from these factors alone—in the perception of need for health care, the demand for such care, and the cost of such care. These are factors over which neither the health professions nor health planners have any control.

This development is one aspect of a much larger issue: the future of the family. As has frequently been pointed out, the individual is too vulnerable to survive without some form of easily accessible social supports. In Lynch's[8] words, "Quite literally, we must either learn to live together or face the possibility of prematurely dying alone. . . . Nature uses many weapons to shorten the lives of lonely people."

Either we will see a revival of the traditional family and a return to greater family responsibility in health matters, or some new form of social organization—some new type of "family"—will emerge to take its place. The implications of the latter for individual health, the cost of health services, and the role of the physician are unknown.

REFERENCES

1. Moriyama IM: *Deaths From Selected Causes, by Marital Status, by Age and Sex: US 1940,* special reports 23:118–165. Vital and Health Statistics Series, Public Health Service, 1945.

2. Shurtleff D: Mortality among the married. *J Am Geriatr Soc* 4:654–655, 1956.

3. Klebba AJ: *Mortality From Selected Causes by Marital Status US, parts A and B,* No. 1000. Series 20-No. 8. Rockville, Md, Public Health Service, 1970.

4. Mortality lowest in married population, Metropolitan Life Insurance Co. *Stat Bull* 58:4–7, 1957.

5. Kraus AS, Lilienfeld AM: Some epidemiologic aspects of the high mortality rate in the young widowed group. *J Chronic Dis* 10:207–217, 1959.

6. Carter H, Glick PC: *Marriage and Divorce: A Social and Economic Study.* American Public Health Association, Vital and Health Statistics Monograph, Cambridge, Mass, Harvard University Press, 1970.

7. *Loneliness Kills,* American Council of Life Insurance and Health Insurance Institute, Washington, DC, Feb 15, 1978, p 1.

8. Lynch J. J.: *The Broken Heart: The Medical Consequences of Loneliness.* New York, Basic Books, 1977.

9. Abel-Smith B, Titmuss RM: *The Cost of the National Health Service in England and Wales.* Cambridge, England, Cambridge University Press, 1956, p 145.

10. Pollack ES: Mental health indices of family health. *World Health Stat Rep* 28:280–281, 1975.

11. Kramer M: Statistics of mental disorders in the US: Current status, some urgent needs, and suggested solutions. *J R Stat Soc* 132:373, 1969.

12. Rosen BM, Goldsmith HF, Rednick RW: *Demographic and Social Indicators From the US Census of Population and Housing: Uses for Mental Health Planning in Small Areas.* Rockville, Md, National Institutes of Mental Health, 1977, p 24.

13. *Characteristics, Social Contacts, and Activities of Nursing Home Residents US 1973–74,* No. (HRA) 77-1778. National Center for Health Statistics, US Dept of Health, Education, and Welfare, 1977.

14. *Facts About Older Americans 1976,* No. (OHD) 77-20006. Administration on Aging, US Dept of Health, Education, and Welfare, 1977.

15. *Social Indicators 1976.* 041-001-00156-5, Bureau of the Census, 1977, p 62.

16. *Current Population Reports: Marital Status and Living Arrangements March 1977,* P-20, No. 323. Bureau of the Census, 1978.

17. *Current Population Reports: Some Recent Changes in American Families.* P-23, No. 52. Bureau of the Census.

18. *Births, Marriages, Divorces, and Deaths for March 1978,* 78-1120. National Center for Health Statistics, US Dept of Health, Education, and Welfare, 1978.

19. Nightingale EO, Cureton C, Kalmar V, et al.: *Perspectives on Health Promotion and Disease Prevention in the US.* Washington, DC, National Academy of Sciences Institute of Medicine, 1978.

20. Hinkle LE: *Preventive Medicine USA,* Task Force on Social Determination of Human Health. New York, Prodist, 1976, p 646.

21. Bachrach LL: *Marital Status and Mental Disorder: An Analytical Review.* No. (ADM) 75-217, p 12. US Dept of Health, Education, and Welfare, 1975.

22. Susser M: The public health and social change: Implications for professional education in public health in the US. *Int J Health Ser* 1:60–70, 1971.

23. Rednick RW, Johnson C: *Marital Status, Living Arrangements and Family Characteristics of Admissions to State and County Mental Hospitals and Outpatient Psychiatric Clinics, U.S. 1970,* statistical note 100, (ADM) 74-6. National Institute of Mental Health, 1973.

24. *Differentials in Health Characteristics by Marital Status, U.S. 1971–1972,* (HRA) 76-1531. National Center for Health Statistics, US Dept of Health, Education, and Welfare, 1976, p 2.

PART FIVE

LIVING ARRANGEMENTS

Among the important decisions single men and women face is where to live. This involves not only such fundamental matters as one's financial resources and the availability of housing, but also such questions as with whom to live, for what period of time, and what these decisions say to the world about oneself. Living arrangements are a crucial issue of single life, since each alternative involves many possibilities and limitations.

A single person may live alone, with friends or family, as head of a household, or as a part of an unmarried couple. He or she may choose a commune, a single-family home, an apartment, or a dormitory. These recent data show the most common living arrangements for singles:

•Living alone: In 1978 there were 17 million people living alone, a 65 percent increase from the 11 million of 1970. Over those years the number of single residences maintained by persons under the age of thirty-five nearly tripled (from 1.5 million to 4.3 million). A majority of these men and women are living in urban areas—New York City, Chicago, Los Angeles, and San Francisco are the most prominent. In each of these cities, and others, there are areas which are occupied primarily by single adults living alone. But the greatest number of people living alone are not younger singles; older ones are more numerous. The largest group was elderly widows; of all women living alone, more than half were widows over sixty-five.

•Heading households: About six out of ten households headed by single adults are headed by single women. The number of single-parent households headed by women is now about 8.2 million, or 10.6 percent of the population, while only 1.6 million (2.1 percent of the population) are headed by men with no woman present.

•Cohabiting couples: Some 2.3 percent of all "couple households" are unmarried men and women living together. In 1978 there were 1,137,000 unmarried couples living together—twice as many as in 1970. For couples under twenty-five this represents an eightfold increase; for couples under forty-five, a sixfold increase.

While ideally single adults might choose living arrangements that precisely reflect their needs and values, it is more likely that their household situation will primarily reflect their economic status. For example, census data show that in 1977 the median income of women

191

living alone was $3,412, which means that half of these women actually received less than that figure. Since "housing choices will be somewhat limited even for those with incomes up to $8,000 . . . the wonder is not that so few aged parents share a home with an adult child, but that so many do not" (Hess and Markson, 1980).

Yet in 1975 the overall category of lone householders had an average income of $6,688, compared to income (per member of household) of the general population of $4,767. Obviously some singles are living alone with the kind of money to live the way they want to.

Why are so many singles choosing to live together as unmarried couples? Cohabitation is defined as "a more or less permanent relationship in which two unmarried persons of the opposite sex share a living facility without legal contract" (Cole, 1977:67). Cohabitation has been around a long time, but has become increasingly popular recently. Apparently more people are willing to be open about their life style, but these social trends are also influential:

- greater social tolerance of alternative living arrangements;
- financial considerations—the higher cost of living;
- housing shortages in urban areas;
- greater tolerance and support for cohabiting among undergraduate and graduate students and postcollege adults;
- greater acceptance of premarital sex;
- changing gender-role definitions;
- a sheer greater number of singles.

Paul Glick and Graham Spanier used data from the U.S. Bureau of the Census to estimate the prevalance of "Cohabitation in the United States." "Rarely does social change occur with such rapidity," they write. "Indeed, there have been few developments relating to marriage and family life which have been as dramatic as the rapid increase in unmarried cohabitation." They mention the trend toward smaller families and the increase in age at which women begin childbearing as contributing to this phenomenon. The authors found that unmarried cohabitation was more common in large cities, more likely for blacks than for whites, and most likely to end for any given couple within two years. The reader may agree with the authors' interpretations of this information, or draw his or her own conclusions from the wide-ranging data. Where is the trend toward unmarried cohabitation leading young people? What does it mean for older couples? What are the legal implications? Consider the case of Marvin *v.* Marvin, for instance, in which the appellate court of the state of California ruled in favor of Michele Triola Marvin's claim to her cohabitator's earning and property—a claim based on an unwritten agreement. The court announced that "the fact that a man and woman live together without marriage and engage in a sexual relationship does not in itself invalidate agreements between them related to their earnings, property, or expenses" (Foster and Freed, 1978).

College students are by all accounts the greatest practitioners of living together. Eleanor D. Macklin studied a group of eighty-six Cornell University students to find out the nature of the cohabitating relationship and the reasons behind it. She noted many variations in the couples' living arrangements, in the amount of time spent together, and in the management of chores and finances. But there was much common ground in the students' reasons for living together: their search for meaningful relations; attempts to deal with the loneliness of a large university; and questions about the institution of marriage. Despite their many problems—from jealousy to fear of parental disapproval—most participants gave their relationship high marks. They listed many benefits, particularly the growth of emotional maturity and self-confidence. The author sees these students not as consciously testing a marriage but as enjoying the cohabitating experience for itself, and she asks such questions as "Will cohabitation lead to healthier marriages or more fully functioning persons?" and "What is the relationship of commitment and identity formation?"

According to Margaret Adams, a successful single way of life depends on a support system—"good neighborliness." She strongly disagrees with a popular view that "by virtue of their solitary style of life, single people are in a conspicuously isolated, lonely, and therefore vulnerable situation." Instead she found many single people involved in groups devoted to helping one another. These groups included commune dwellers, neighbors in an apartment house, and owners of separate houses, all exchanging services and company and all offering "a useful opportunity for combining an enjoyable, satisfying, and often stimulating style of living . . . with flexible scope for change in the future." Adams emphasizes the benefits of shared tenancy and the power of a comfortable home to deter desperate marriages. Her enthusiastic description of the "blessed" single life gives the reader opportunity to question the majority's preference for the traditional married life style.

REFERENCES

Cole, Charles Lee. "Cohabitation in Social Context," R. W. Libby and R. N. Whitehurst (eds.), *Marriage and Alternatives*. Glenview, Ill.: Scott, Foresman, 1977.

Foster, Henry and Doris Freed. "Nonmarital Partners: Sex and Serendipity," *Journal of Divorce*, 1:195–211, 1978.

Hess, Beth and Elizabeth Markson. *Aging and Old Age*. New York: Macmillan, 1980.

16/ COHABITATION IN THE UNITED STATES

Paul C. Glick and Graham B. Spanier

This article presents estimates of the prevalence of three forms of living arrangements of adults in the United States: married couples living together, formerly married individuals currently living with an unrelated adult of the opposite sex, and never-married individuals currently living with an unrelated adult of the opposite sex.

. . . .

The present analysis primarily uses data from the current Population Survey conducted by the United States Bureau of the Census in June of 1975. These data were collected for persons age fourteen and over and were weighted by the Census Bureau to represent the adult population in the United States. This article describes the recent trend in "informal joint residence," referred to here as unmarried cohabitation of two (and no more) unrelated adults of opposite sexes, even though some of the individuals involved were actually still married but separated and living in a household apart from their spouse with another partner; thus "unmarried" cohabiting may include some "married" persons.

. . . .

Previous discussions of unmarried cohabitation have noted the profound increase in the phenomenon in recent years (Bower and Christopherson, 1977; Clayton and Voss, 1977; Glick and Norton, 1977; Glick, 1978b; Macklin, 1978). Figure 1 shows the sustained increase since 1960 in the total number of unmarried couples living together in the same house or apartment outside marriage; these couples were living in households that contained only two adults, a man and a woman. It is evident that the most dramatic increase in this form of living arrangement has occurred since 1970, when the number of such couples was 523,000. Advance tabulations from the March 1978 Current Population Survey indicate that 1,137,000 unmarried couples of opposite sex—more than double the number in 1970—maintained living quarters which they shared. Thus more than 2 million adults among the 1.1 million unmarried couples were

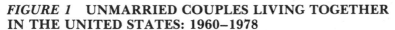

FIGURE 1   UNMARRIED COUPLES LIVING TOGETHER IN THE UNITED STATES: 1960–1978

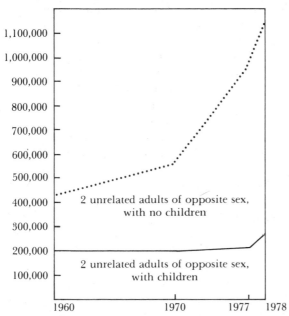

Source: Paul C. Glick and Arthur J. Norton, "Marrying, Divorcing, and Living Together in the U.S. Today," Population Bulletin, No. 5, Vol. 32, Population Reference Bureau, Inc., Washington, D.C., 1977; and U.S. Bureau of the Census, unpublished Current Population Survey data for June, 1975.

reported to be living in such households in 1978. About 76 percent (865,000) of these couples were living in a household with no other persons present, and the remaining 24 percent (272,000 households) had one or more children present. From 1977 to 1978, there was a very substantial increase in the number of unmarried couples living together—19 percent. Rarely does social change occur with such rapidity. Indeed, there have been few developments relating to marriage and family life which have been as dramatic as the rapid increase in unmarried cohabitation.

The present analysis of the trend of unmarried cohabitation indicates that the number of unmarried couples in households *with children present* has not varied much over the seventeen-year period for which data are considered. The increase is accounted for, therefore, primarily by *young couples without children.*

This significant trend has developed at the same time as other important changes in the social structure. There has been an increase in the ages at first marriage for both men and women in recent years (U.S. Bureau of the Census, 1976), and it is likely that the implied postponement of marriage may be related to increased cohabitation among young adults. This delay in marriage may in turn be related to the increased sexual freedom among adolescents and young adults (Zelnik and Kantner, 1977; Spanier, 1979). Access to a sexual partner may be decreasingly a reason for marriage. Other changes, such as the trend toward smaller families and the increase in the age at which many women begin childbearing (Glick, 1978b), may also indirectly promote living together while unmarried by delaying the need for marriage for the sake of legitimizing children. Moreover, the increasing liberalization of norms relating to life styles, the relaxation of social pressures to marry during the period of highest marriage rates (ages eighteen to twenty-four for females and twenty to twenty-six for males), and the decrease in social stigma associated with divorce undoubtedly make cohabitation a relatively attractive and plausible temporary life style for some (Glick, 1978a).

It is probable that the increase in unmarried cohabitation is the result, in part, of more honest reporting of marital status and living arrangements. It is likely that unrelated adults of the opposite sex who share a household increasingly are willing to divulge that fact to interviewers. Furthermore, part of the increase in the number of persons in such living arrangements is due to the larger cohort of individuals born during the postwar baby boom years who are now in their twenties and early thirties—ages during which unmarried cohabitation is most prevalent for those who have never married. Nevertheless, the changes seen in recent years cannot be explained alone by variations in cohort size or frankness of response. Surely the most likely explanation of this increase is that young Americans are becoming increasingly attracted to this life style, and their parents are becoming less critical of this behavior as long as it does not result in childbearing and as long as those involved directly are economically independent.

Clayton and Voss (1977) found that, among the young men they studied, 18 percent had lived with a woman for six months or more outside of marriage. Only 5 percent of these men, however, were cohabiting at the time of their survey. They found that blacks were more likely to choose this living arrangement than whites, and that unmarried cohabitation was more common in large cities. Higher proportions of formerly married than never-married men had lived with an unrelated female. Clayton and Voss were able to infer from their data that for about 37 percent of the men with one experience in cohabitation and one marriage, cohabitation led to marriage. Thus, in about 63 percent of the cases, cohabitation did not lead to— or at least was not immediately followed by—marriage to the same person up to the time of the survey. Cohabitation was less likely to result in marriage among those who had been previously married.

Glick and Norton (1977) concluded that the majority of unmarried couples live together a relatively short time before they marry or separate. Data from the 1977 Current Population Survey indicate that 63 percent of unmarried couples had shared the same house or apartment for less than two years and the other 37 percent for two years or longer. However, it is not known what proportion of the couples who no longer reside in a given household have married and how many have split up.

Data from the June 1975 Current Population Survey allow for the most complete examination in recent years of data pertaining to the marital history of American adults. Thus, the cross-tabulations presented in the remainder of this article feature the June, 1975 data. In that month, there were an estimated 886,000 unmarried cohabiting couples in the United States, involving 1,772,000 adults. This number is a small but significant portion of the adult population. It is estimated that there were 49,316,000 male-female couples who were living together in June, 1975, most of them married couples. Thus the approximately 886,000 unmarried couples comprised about 1.8 percent of all couples living together. Among the men involved in these relationships, 432,000 (49 percent) had never been married and 454,000 (51 percent) had been previously married. Among the women, 369,000 (42 percent) had never been married and 517,000 (58 percent) had been previously married. Thus females were more likely than males to have been married at some time before the current living-together relationship.

When one considers that these figures are based on persons currently living together, and that an unknown proportion of the population of the same age has previously lived with an adult of the opposite sex outside marriage, or will do so in the future, it is clear that this form of household arrangement deserves attention. Even if reporting becomes more frank, there may continue to be some underreporting of this phenomenon. Unmarried cohabitation, then, applies to a significant minority of the American population and involves many more never-married as well as previously married males and females during a lifetime than those reported upon in this cross-sectional study.

At the same time, some important limitations also deserve attention in evaluating the data presented here. Since these figures are estimates based on sample data, they are subject to sampling and nonsampling variability. Estimates are least reliable for groups which involve small numbers of unmarried cohabitants or for small percentage differences between groups.

One additional descriptive note about these couples is in order. It is reasonable to assume that most unmarried couples of opposite sexes with no other adults in the household are living together because there is some romantic or affectional involvement. However, a small minority of these persons may have landlady-tenant, landlord-tenant, or employer-employee relationships without being intimately involved. Available data do not allow for discerning how many are maintaining one of the latter relationships, but careful study of the following information about unmarried couples leaves a distinct impression that a large majority are not living in the same house or apartment for strictly financial reasons. Moreover, it is reasonable to suspect that the number of unmarried couples with no romantic involvement is more than offset by the number of unmarried couples who report themselves as married.

PROFILE OF SOCIAL CHARACTERISTICS

Table 1 presents a profile of selected social characteristics of persons according to living arrangements. Individuals are classified by sex and age, and are cross-classified by education, metropolitan-nonmetropolitan residence, and race.

Most *never-married* individuals who live with an unrelated person of the opposite sex are young. About 85 percent of such persons are under age 35, 8 percent are between thirty-five and fifty-four years of age, and 7 percent are fifty-five or older. Corresponding percentages are quite different for unmarried persons living together who have been *previously married*. Approximately 38 percent of such individuals are under age thirty-five, 30 percent are ages thirty-five to fifty-four, and 32 percent are fifty-five or older. Thus unmarried cohabitation is found about equally among all three age categories examined for persons who were previously married. Although unmarried cohabitation has been studied mostly in relation to young adults (Bower and Christopherson, 1977), the data presented here for 1975 demonstrate that the number of persons thirty-five and older living in unmarried arrangements (719,000) was about two-thirds as large as the number under age thirty-five (1,052,000).

How do the small minority of persons who choose to live together outside marriage differ with respect to education, metropolitan or nonmetropolitan residence, and race from the vast majority who are married? The educational differences are particularly noteworthy for the younger women who are involved. Only three in ten of the married women continued their education after graduation from high school, whereas one-half of the never-married cohabiting women had attended college. The difference is particularly great among women who started into college but did not graduate; 31 percent of the never-married cohabiting women reported having had some college education as compared with only 16 percent of the married women. No doubt more of the former than the latter were still enrolled in college. In fact, the number of college students living together as unmarried couples may exceed the level implied by these findings. Some students may maintain separate residences while living with someone else. Response problems of this nature deserve to be considered when examining the living arrangements of students.

The educational classification in Table 1 shows that formerly married cohabitants are less well educated than either never-married or currently married (spouse present) cohabitants. For example, among those thirty-five years old and over (the age range in which a substantial majority of previously married cohabitants are concentrated), about half again as large a proportion of previously married as currently married cohabitants had not completed high school. The available data do not explain this finding; however, it could reflect a generally greater difficulty on the part of poorly educated persons than better educated persons to find a satisfactory partner before their first marriage and/or a willingness on the part of many of the poorly educated divorced persons to opt for unmarried cohabitation instead of remarriage—at least for a while. The much larger proportion of cohabiting persons without a full high-school education among those fifty-five years old and over than among those in younger age groups obviously reflects the lower educational expectations of the older group.

Where do unmarried couples live? About half of cohabiting couples live in large metropolitan areas with populations above one million. This finding is in contrast to about 37 percent of married couples who live in communities of this size. Whereas about one in three married couples in the United States live in rural areas, small towns, and other communities outside metropolitan areas, only about one in five cohabiting couples can be found in these areas. Younger cohabiting couples are more likely to reside in larger cities than are older cohabiting couples.

There are substantial racial differences with regard to living arrangements. About one in thirteen or fourteen married couples in the United States are black, but about one in four unmarried couples are black. Thus, although the *number* of cohabiting couples is heavily concentrated among whites, the cohabitation *rate* among blacks is three times that of whites. To some extent this situation is associated with the fact that the proportion of black adults with less than a full high-school education is half again as large as that of white adults, and with the fact noted above that unmarried cohabitation among those thirty-five years old and over is most prevalent among the poorly educated.

TABLE 1

SELECTED SOCIAL CHARACTERISTICS OF ADULTS ACCORDING TO LIVING ARRANGEMENTS BY SEX AND AGE

| | Living With Unrelated Person of Opposite Sex | | | | | | Married, Living With Spouse | | |
| | Never-Married | | | Ever-Married | | | | | |
Characteristic[a]	Under 35 Yrs.	35–54 Yrs.	55+ Yrs.	Under 35 Yrs.	35–54 Yrs.	55+ Yrs.	Under 35 Yrs.	35–54 Yrs.	55+ Yrs.
MEN									
Education									
0–11 years	18.9	58.6	74.0	23.2	46.1	68.9	19.2	31.0	55.2
12 years	35.5	15.8	5.3	40.5	28.2	15.6	39.8	36.6	24.4
13–15 years	23.8	8.9	–[b]	22.5	5.7	6.0	20.0	13.2	9.2
16 years or more	21.8	16.7	20.7	13.9	19.9	9.5	20.9	19.1	11.2
SMSA Size									
1 million or more	51.1	58.8	34.6	57.2	50.8	42.5	36.3	39.0	36.1
250,000–999,999	22.7	7.6	28.8	27.2	23.1	24.3	21.7	20.6	19.4
Less than 250,000	5.7	3.7	5.0	4.5	4.9	10.2	9.5	8.5	8.1
Not in SMSA	20.4	30.0	31.6	11.1	21.2	23.0	32.5	31.9	36.4
Race									
White	77.7	59.5	63.9	81.8	66.2	63.6	90.4	90.5	91.7
Black	18.1	40.5	36.1	18.2	33.8	36.4	8.2	8.1	7.2
Other	4.1	–[b]	–[b]	–[b]	–[b]	–[b]	1.4	1.4	1.1
N (in thousands)	361	39	31	170	144	140	14,633	19,201	14,626
Total (in thousands)	432			454			48,460		

WOMEN

Education									
0–11 years	18.0	46.2	46.7	21.3	47.3	68.6	21.3	29.4	50.8
12 years	29.4	30.8	46.7	50.8	44.1	19.6	49.4	48.3	32.3
13–15 years	30.9	7.7	6.7	18.9	6.5	5.9	16.0	12.0	9.6
16 years or more	21.6	15.4	—b	9.0	2.2	5.9	13.2	10.3	7.3
SMSA Size									
1 million or more	56.3	65.6	33.9	52.2	50.7	36.5	35.8	38.9	35.7
250,000–999,999	21.7	—b	47.1	21.9	25.3	30.0	22.0	20.3	19.8
Less than 250,000	4.3	6.6	5.8	6.9	4.0	8.2	9.4	8.7	8.0
Not in SMSA	17.7	27.8	13.2	19.1	20.0	25.2	32.8	32.1	36.5
Race									
White	78.0	54.0	58.7	83.1	66.2	64.4	90.2	90.6	92.8
Black	18.8	30.3	41.3	13.0	31.7	32.1	7.9	7.9	6.3
Other	3.3	15.7	—b	3.8	2.2	3.5	1.9	1.6	.9
N (in thousands)	323	22	24	198	150	169	17,726	18,990	11,685
Total (in thousands)		369			517				48,401

aTotal for each characteristic is 100 percent.
bZero or rounds to zero.

Source: U.S. Bureau of the Census, unpublished Current Population Survey data for June, 1975.

PROFILE OF ECONOMIC CHARACTERISTICS

Table 2 presents data on three economic correlates of living arrangements by sex and age of the respondent. The table reveals some interesting contrasts between married and unmarried cohabitants. In 1975, 92 percent of married men and 44 percent of married women under age thirty-five were employed. The other 8 percent of the married men and 56 percent of the married women were unemployed or not in the labor force. For unmarried couples, however, a different profile emerges. A far greater proportion of never-married men in this age group (29 percent) and a much smaller proportion of the never-married women (32 percent) were unemployed or not in the labor force. Thus, whereas cohabiting men were much less likely to be employed than married men, cohabiting women were much more likely to be employed than married women.

Table 2 also considers the living arrangements of persons by broad occupational groups. Married men had larger proportions in the category of white-collar workers than did their unmarried counterparts. The reverse distribution was found among cohabitants in the service worker category. There was a negligible proportion of farm workers among the young never-married cohabitants, but a greater proportion among the older unmarried cohabiting adults.

Finally, Table 2 demonstrates the relatively low income levels among unmarried cohabiting couples within each age group. Although information in a later section will show a greater likelihood of a dual income among the unmarrieds (higher unemployment rates notwithstanding), low income seems to be much more characteristic of unmarried than married cohabiting couples. Among those under thirty-five years of age, about one-third of the never-married and one-fifth of the ever-married cohabitants had incomes below $5,000. (Among unmarried couples, the incomes of the man and the woman are not combined into "family" income as is done for married couples.) The corresponding percentage reached a majority for unmarried cohabitants age fifty-five and over. By contrast, only 8 percent of the married couples under age thirty-five had family incomes below $5,000 per year, and this percentage reached only 21 percent for the oldest age group. Similar economic differentials persist for the other income categories presented. Yet many of the unmarried couples had a reasonably high income between the two persons involved. Thus either the man or the woman (or both) in one unmarried couple out of every five had an annual income of $15,000 or more.

JOINT CHARACTERISTICS OF MARRIED AND UNMARRIED PARTNERS

This section considers the results of cross-tabulations between selected demographic characteristics of married and unmarried partners for couples in which the woman was under thirty-five years old. The race, age, education, employment status, and marital history of men in each type of living arrangement are compared with the same characteristics of the corresponding women. This analysis is limited to the younger couples in order to feature the most rapidly increasing category of informal cohabitants and for the sake of brevity and clarity.

RACE

As with married couples, most young adults who live with someone of the opposite sex outside marriage choose partners of the same race. However, interracial couples are found in a considerably greater proportion of unmarried than married couples. In 1975, about 200,000, or 1.2 percent, of the married couples in which the woman was under thirty-five involved persons of different races. Close to 50,000 were black male/white female relationships, whereas about 30,000 were white male/black female relationships. The majority (120,000) were couples with a white man or woman married to a person who designated a race other than black or white.

Census data show that black men in unmarried relationships, whether never-married or previously married, were about four to five times as likely as married black men to have a white woman as a partner. Taking into account all three racial groups, about 7 percent of the couples in which the man had never been married and about 2 percent of the couples in which the man had been previously married consisted of interracial relationships (U.S. Bureau of the Census, 1975). A reasonable speculation is that interracial couples violate strongly held social norms; and therefore some of them may be reluctant to formalize their relationship by marriage. Furthermore, social support for an informal relationship may be greater among peers or acquaintances if the couple does not marry.

Again the reader is cautioned that because the number of interracial couples found in the Current Population Survey is quite small, comparisons among these groups must be tentative. The general pattern of results shown here, however, is similar to that in the 1970 census.

AGE

In comparing the ages of women under thirty-five in different types of living arrangements with corresponding ages of their partners,

WOMEN

Employment Status									
Employed	67.8	95.5	20.8	59.1	48.7	27.8	43.9	47.7	22.5
Unemployed or not in labor force	32.2	4.5	19.2	40.9	51.3	72.2	56.1	52.3	77.5
Occupational Group									
White collar	50.2	36.4	—[b]	37.4	21.3	7.7	32.0	31.6	12.7
Blue collar	11.8	27.3	8.3	10.6	11.3	7.7	7.4	17.1	4.6
Service workers	17.3	27.3	12.5	19.7	22.7	12.4	8.9	9.0	5.4
Farm workers	—[b]	—[b]	—[b]	2.5	2.0	1.2	0.6	1.4	0.9
Never worked or not in labor force	20.7	9.0	79.2	29.8	42.7	71.0	51.1	40.9	76.4
Family Income									
Less than $5,000	30.8	35.6	74.2	21.4	29.5	50.9	8.0	5.1	22.7
$5,000–$9,999	26.1	21.1	—[b]	33.9	35.3	14.6	24.2	14.2	27.7
$10,000–$14,999	20.2	15.7	—[b]	21.3	11.3	16.6	31.8	24.5	18.7
$15,000 and over	23.0	27.6	25.8	23.3	23.9	17.9	36.0	56.3	31.0
N (in thousands)	323	22	24	198	150	169	17,726	18,990	11,685
Total (in thousands)		369			517			48,401	

[a]Total for each characteristic is 100 percent.
[b]Zero or rounds to zero.

Source: U.S. Bureau of the Census, unpublished Current Population Survey data for June, 1975.

data indicate that although the two partners generally are in the same age group or an adjacent one, the ages of the partners tend to be most widely dispersed if the man had previously married and least widely if the man had never married, with married couples being intermediate.

Only 30 percent of never-married cohabiting men were in an older age group than their partner, whereas the corresponding percentages for married men and previously married men were 45 percent and 60 percent, respectively. These findings are heavily weighted by the relative concentration of never-married cohabitants among those under twenty-five, and of previously married cohabitants among those twenty-five years old and over. The far greater proportion of previously married than currently married men who were in an older age group than their partner is consistent with the tendency for men to select a younger woman (or for women to select an older man) "the second time around."

EDUCATIONAL ATTAINMENT

For couples in which the woman is under age thirty-five the two partners were generally in the same education level or in an adjacent one, but the degree of consistency varies with the type of living arrangement. Approximately one-half of both the married couples and the cohabiting couples in which the man had previously been married were in the same educational level, but the corresponding proportion for couples with the man never married was 40 percent.

Young married couples included the largest proportion (55 percent) of partners both of whom ended their schooling without attending college. Young couples with the man never married included the largest proportion (36 percent) of partners both of whom had some college education. And young couples with the man previously married included the largest proportion (28 percent) of partners in which the woman exceeds the man in educational attainment. Both types of unmarried cohabitants include relatively large proportions with an incomplete college education and the generally younger cohabitants with the man never married include a relatively large proportion of college graduates (U.S. Bureau of the Census, 1975).

Among other things, these findings suggest that young adults who are well educated tend to be more willing to accept the possible risks associated with living together outside marriage than are the less well educated who tend to choose the more conventional married life style. Unmarried liaisons tend not to last very long on the average, among the more affluent informal unions (Glick and Norton, 1977: 35); the affluent couple may choose to marry, the persons involved may choose to revert to living alone, or they may enter liaisons with other unmarried persons.

EMPLOYMENT CHARACTERISTICS

Census data indicate that both of the partners were much less likely to be in the labor force if they were married than if they were unmarried. Thus only 48 percent of the married couples included a husband and a wife who were workers, as compared with 64 percent of the two partners with the man previously married and 75 percent of the two partners with the man never married. As would be expected, however, a far larger proportion of the married couples (46 percent) reported that the man, but not the woman, was employed; for couples with a previously married man, the corresponding proportion was only 17 percent, and for those with a never-married man it was 6 percent. Conversely, only 4 percent of the married women were employed while living with someone who was not employed as compared with about 15 percent of the women among unmarried couples (U.S. Bureau of the Census, 1975). Obviously more of the wives than of the female unmarried cohabitants devoted their time at home to caring for children.

Neither partner was employed among 12 percent of the unmarried couples with the man never married; for couples with a married or previously married man, the corresponding proportion was only half as large. Most likely, the nonworking couples with a never-married man consisted largely of students living on incomes transferred to them from their parents or of young poor couples living on welfare payments.

MARITAL HISTORY

Information about the marital history of unmarried couples with the woman under thirty-five years of age shows that a majority of the unmarried couples living together have the same marital history, primarily because of the very large proportion of never-married men and never-married women living together. This combination accounted for 43 percent of the entire 524,000 unmarried couples in 1975 with the woman under thirty-five years of age. Actually, all other unmarried couples with the same marital history add up to only about one-third as large a proportion (8 percent with both divorced, 3 percent with both separated, and 2 percent with both remarried). Although the frequencies are small, they suggest that about one-fourth again as many never-married women (17.3 percent) as never-married men (13.9 percent) were living with a separated or divorced partner.

Another frequently occurring combination of marital histories among unmarried couples included a divorced person who had not remarried but who was living with a never-married person (21 percent of all couples). A less frequently occurring combination included separated persons (really still in their first marriage) living with someone who had never been married (10 percent of all couples) (U.S. Bureau of the Census, 1975).

Thus young unmarried couples bring together a diverse array of marital histories; but aside from couples neither of whom have ever married, persons of a given marital history were more often sharing the living quarters of a partner with different rather than an identical marital history.

TRENDS

. . . Unpublished data from a 1978 survey show that an estimated 1.1 million couples, or 2.3 percent of all man-and-woman couples living together in the same household in 1978, were not married to each other. This number represents a 19 percent increase between March 1977 and March 1978. Information from the 1975 survey on which most of this article is based showed that one-half of the unmarried men and three-fifths of the unmarried women in couples of this type had been previously married. The previously married persons were found in about equal numbers in the young, middle, and older categories that were used. In contrast, 85 percent of the never-married cohabitants were in the young category, under thirty-five years of age.

. . . .

The rapid increase in the number of adults who choose to live with an unrelated person of the opposite sex has been showing no signs of diminishing. Moreover, the cross-sectional count of unmarried couples is certain to be much smaller than the count of actual lifetime experiences of persons with informal living arrangements. Increased freedom in adult behavior, less pressure to marry at traditionally normative young ages, and greater acceptance of unmarried cohabitation as a life style are evidently providing a context in which this way of living is becoming increasingly accepted as an alternative to marriage or as a temporary arrangement preceding or following marriage.

NOTE

Each month the United States Bureau of the Census conducts a survey consisting of a national probability sample of about 100,000 adults living in approximately 50,000 households. These surveys are used to estimate national employment and unemployment patterns, characteristics of the labor force, education, migration, fertility, and other important demographic characteristics of the population.

The 1975 CPS sample was based on updated 1970 census files that reflected new construction of housing units and other residential changes. It is a sample of households spread over 461 areas, with coverage in all fifty states and the District of Columbia. A household is defined as all the persons who occupy a housing unit. A house, an apartment or other group of rooms, or a single room, is regarded as a housing unit when it is occupied or is intended for occupancy as separate living quarters. A household includes related family members and all unrelated persons, if any. A person living alone in a housing unit, or a group of unrelated persons sharing a housing unit as partners, is also counted as a household.

REFERENCES

Bower, Donald W., and Victor A. Christopherson, 1977. "University student cohabitation: A regional comparison of selected attitudes and behavior." Journal of Marriage and the Family 39 (August):447–454.

Clayton, Richard R., and Harwin L. Voss. 1977. "Shacking up: Cohabitation in the 1970's." Journal of Marriage and the Family 39 (May):273–284.

Glick, Paul C. 1978a. "The future of the American family." Statement prepared for the Select Committee on Population, U.S. House of Representatives, May 23.

———. 1978b. "Social change and the American family." The Social Welfare Forum 1977:43–62.

Glick, Paul C., and Arthur J. Norton, 1977. "Marrying, divorcing, and living together in the U.S. today." Population Bulletin 32 (5). Washington, D.C.: Population Reference Bureau, Inc.

Macklin, Eleanor D. 1978. "Nonmarital heterosexual cohabitation: A review of the recent literature." Marriage and Family Review 1 (March/April):1–12.

Spanier, Graham B. 1979. "Human sexuality in a changing society." Pp. 1–9 in Graham B. Spanier (Ed.), Human Sexuality in a Changing Society. Minneapolis: Burgess.

U.S. Bureau of the Census, 1975. "Marital status and living arrangements: March, 1976." Current Population Reports, Series P-20, No. 306. Washington, D.C.:U.S. Government Printing Office.

———. 1978. The Current Population Survey: Design and Methodology. Technical Paper 40. Washington, D.C.:U.S. Government Printing Office.

Zelnik, Melvin, and John F. Kantner. 1977. "Sexual and contraceptive experience of young unmarried women in the United States, 1976 and 1971." Family Planning Perspectives 9 (March/April):55–71.

17/ COHABITING COLLEGE STUDENTS

Eleanor D. Macklin

This study was undertaken because little was known about the current patterns of cohabitation among college youth. This report summarizes the pilot phase of the research. To obtain a more complete picture of the various forms which living together might assume, a fairly inclusive definition of cohabitation was adopted: to share a bedroom for at least four nights per week for at least three consecutive months with someone of the opposite sex.

The objectives of this phase of the research were to gain an estimate of the prevalence of this experience, and an understanding of the nature of the relationship, the reasons for involvement, and the problems and benefits experienced. A series of four-hour semistructured interviews was conducted with fifteen junior and senior female students at Cornell University, Ithaca, N.Y., who had experienced heterosexual cohabitation. A questionnaire based on the interview schedule was given to 104 junior and senior women in a course on adolescent development at Cornell. Of the 86 who responded, 29 had experienced cohabitation. The fifteen interviewees had been involved in a total of 20 such relationships (eleven had experienced one such relationship, three had had two, and one, three). The 29 questionnaire respondents had experienced a total of 35 cohabitation relationships (24 had had one, four had had two, and one had had three).

The following discussion is based on the information obtained from the combined group of 44 cohabitants. Questionnaire data will serve as the basis for all quantitative reporting, but it should be understood that interview data were generally corroborative.

PREVALENCE

From the present data one can only surmise the frequency with which cohabitation occurs at Cornell. Of the 86 junior and senior women who completed the questionnaire,[1] 34 percent had already had such an experience. When these 86 students were asked to predict what percentage of Cornell undergraduates probably experience cohabitation prior to graduation, almost three-quarters predicted that 40 percent or more would do so. When asked how many of their close friends had experienced or were experiencing cohabitation, only 7 percent said "none," and over 40 percent said "many" or "most."

Of the 57 respondents who had not experienced cohabitation as defined, almost two-thirds checked that they had stayed with someone but not for as long as indicated in the definition. When asked why they had not cohabited, the large majority indicated that it was because they had not yet found an appropriate person. A few checked that it would be unwise for them at present due to the stage of their relationship, their immaturity, the possibility of discovery, or physical impracticality. Only one person said she had not because it would be wrong to do so outside of marriage.

Further clues to the frequency of cohabitation come from the questionnaire pretest which was given to two undergraduate classes. Of 150 underclassmen responding, 28 percent indicated having experienced cohabitation. From an upperclass seminar on delinquency taught by the author, 12 of the 20 students volunteered to be interviewed regarding their cohabitation experience. One is led to conclude from all available evidence that cohabitation is a common experience for students on this particular campus and is accepted by many as a "to-be-expected" occurrence.

DESCRIPTION OF THE COHABITATION EXPERIENCE

A wide variety of types of cohabitation experiences were revealed: among them, living with a male roommate in a co-op (with no sexual involvement and with both roommates having other romantic attachments), living in a tent while traveling in Europe, sharing a dormitory or a fraternity room, or sharing a room with another cohabiting couple. However, the most common pattern was for the girl to move into the boy's room (or vice versa) in an apartment or house which he was sharing with several other males (one of whom might also have a girl living in). Graduate student pairs are more likely to live alone in an apartment or a house; freshman couples are more likely to share a dormitory room. Very few couples shared their bedroom with a third person.

In the majority of cases, living quarters had not been obtained initially with living together in mind (although many men arrange to have a single room in order to allow privacy for any potential entertaining). Living arrangements were not usually jointly arranged until the second year of a relationship. However, even then, couples were hesitant to arrange for a single joint living situation, and planning simply involved ensuring that the potential apartment-mates were willing to have a girl share the premises. Practically all girls also maintained a room in the dormitory or sorority or in an apartment with other girls. Most went back once a day for a few hours to visit, get messages or mail, change clothes, shower, or study. Maintaining a separate residence precludes having to explain to parents, ensures a place to live if the relationship is not working well, helps maintain contact with female friends, serves as a convenient place to study, and provides often necessary storage space (the boy's room being too small to hold both sets of belongings).

In about half of the relationships, the couple spent seven nights a week together. In the remaining half, the girl returned to her own room one or two nights a week in order to see her friends and to allow him time with his friends. It should be noted at this point that spending the night together, even in the same bed, need not imply a full sexual relationship. Aside from the instance of the nonemotionally involved coed roommates, there were couples who had lived together for more than three months without intercourse because they did not yet feel ready for this experience (these were usually virgin women). The irony of this is the frequency with which the older generation refuses to accept that this could be true, or if it is, insists that the male must be a "queer."

There was a wide range in amount of time spent together. The majority reported being together about 16-17 hours a day on weekdays (5 P.M. to 8 A.M. plus lunch). Most couples shared at least two meals a day, although occasionally dinner was eaten separately because of the inconvenience involved in having an extra person at dinner or because her parents had already paid for her meals on campus and funds were tight. There was practically no instance of total pooling of finances in these relationships, although the couple normally shared food and entertainment expenses. Usually the girl paid her way and maintained her own separate finances, either because the couple could not afford otherwise or as a matter of principle. When there were chores involved, the couple generally did them together (e.g., shopping or laundry), although there was a tendency for the girl to assume responsibility for cooking and cleaning. There was a wide range in the degree to which they shared activities (e.g., classes, study, or hobbies) or spent time with others. The tendency was to share the majority of activities, to have many mutual friends, and to spend much of their time with others as opposed to time only with one another.

WHY STUDENTS LIVE TOGETHER

There are three aspects to the question of why students are now living together: the circumstances existing at the particular institution, the broader societal reasons, and the personal motivations of the specific students.

Changes in dormitory regulations and the slow demise of *in loco parentis* have greatly facilitated the development of the new pattern. If one goes back to earlier issues of the campus newspaper, one notes that in 1962 a graduate student was indefinitely suspended from the university for living with a woman in his apartment, and in 1964 a male student was reprimanded for staying overnight at a local hotel with a nonuniversity female. Sexual morality was considered a legitimate concern of the university faculty and "overnight unchaperoned mixed company" was considered by the faculty council on student conduct to be a violation of sexual morality.

Today, Cornell students are free to live in much the same way that nonstudents who are living and working in the outside world are free to live: they are likely to be residing in a structure which also houses persons of the opposite sex (many of the dorms are now coed, with men and women segregated by floors, wings or suites, although there is experimentation with men and women living on the same corridor); if they are sophomores or beyond, they are free to elect to live off campus; and they may entertain someone of the opposite sex in their room at any time during the 24-hour day. Official policy still prohibits "continuous residence" with someone of the opposite sex in the dormitory setting, but this is difficult to police.

These changes in curfew and dormitory policy must be seen as a reflection of broader social changes: a change in the status of women which makes it difficult to justify different regulations for men and for women, youth's increasing demand that they no longer be treated as children, a questioning of the rigid sexual mores which have traditionally governed people's lives, a greater willingness to grant individuals the right to select their own life-style, and the increasing availability of contraception and abortion services.

When students are asked to hypothesize why cohabitation has become more common and more open, they mention youth's search for meaningful relations with others and the consequent rejection of the superficial "dating game"; the loneliness of a large university and the emotional satisfaction that comes from having someone to sleep with who cares about you; the widespread questioning of the institution of marriage and the desire to try out a relationship before there is any, if ever, consideration of permanency; the desire on the part of many to postpone commitment until there is some certainty that individual growth will be compatible with growth of the relationship; the fact that young people mature earlier and yet must wait so long until marriage is feasible; and the fact that the university community provides both sanction and feasibility for such a relationship to develop. Given peer group support, ample opportunity, a human need to love and be loved, and a disposition to question the traditional way, it seems only natural that couples should wish to live together if they enjoy being together. One might almost better ask: Why do students choose *not* to live together?

When one asks students why they personally become involved in a cohabitation relationship, one finds a mixture of enjoying being together and expediency (e.g., too far to drive her home at night, easier to stay than to get up and go back at midnight, less expensive, someone else living with one's roommate, or partner was sick and needed someone to care for him). On occasion, curiosity about what it would be like to live with the opposite sex was involved, and sometimes "to test out the relationship" was mentioned, but it was rarely such a purposeful act.

In fact, living together was seldom the result of a considered decision, at least initially. Most relationships involved a gradual (and sometimes not so gradual) drifting into staying together. The general pattern was to stay over one night; in several weeks, if all was well, to stay for the weekend; in another few weeks to add a week night; in another few weeks, a second week night, and so forth. In half the relationships the couple had begun staying together four or more nights a week by the end of four months of dating.

If and when a decision with conscious deliberation was made, it was usually precipitated by some external force (e.g., need to make plans for the summer or next fall, graduation, unexpected pregnancy, or a necessary housing or room change). Until this time there was only a mutual, often unspoken, recognition of the desire to be together—a natural progression of the relationship.

NATURE OF THE RELATIONSHIP

When asked to indicate the nature of the relationship at the time they began living together four or more nights per week, about half checked that they "had a strong, affectionate relationship, not dating others" (i.e., "going steady"—although they resisted this term). Another large group indicated that they "had a strong affectionate relationship but were also open to other relationships." Only a few indicated tentative engagement; even fewer stated that they were just "friends."

It is interesting to note that the above is very similar to answers given by all 86 questionnaire respondents when asked what kind of relationship they felt should exist before college-aged student cohabit. One is impressed by the fact that cohabitation is more frequently associated with the "going steady" stage of a relationship than with engagement, even tentative engagement.

The initial commitment to the relationship varied greatly. Some saw it as strictly temporary (e.g., "while traveling," "he was planning to leave Ithaca," or "he was already committed to someone else") and a few, at the other extreme, definitely planned "marriage in the future when it is more convenient." But the vast majority entered it either with a "let's see" attitude (i.e., to test the relationship—to stay together as long as it was mutually satisfying), or—a somewhat more definite commitment—planned to do all they "could to develop a lasting relationship, but future marriage was not definite."

This raises some question about the label "unmarried marrieds" which has often been applied in the popular literature to unmarried cohabitation. Most of the undergraduate couples did not consider themselves married in any sense of the word. Not only did they not consider themselves married, they rarely considered marriage as a viable alternative to their present cohabitation. When asked, "Did you consider the possibility of getting married instead?" a frequent response was "Heavens, no!" Marriage might be seen as a possibility for the future, but the distant future. The future seemed too indefinite to plan that far ahead, they needed more time to grow and develop before considering marriage, and it was financially impractical. Moreover, marriage appeared to have some negative connotations for many of these students—it was seen as limiting their freedom and their growth, and they feared falling into the traditional roles they associated with being wives, even though over two-thirds of those interviewed said their parents would consider their own marriage "very successful."

PROBLEMS ENCOUNTERED

As with any real relationship, these were not always blissful. It was encouraging that those interviewed seemed very aware of the problem areas and were able to verbalize about them easily.

Problems could be divided into four major categories: emotional problems, sexual probelms, problems with parents, and problems related to the living situation. (In the interviews, no one had experienced problems with the community; thus the question was not included in the questionnaire.)

The major emotional problem (see Table 1) was the tendency to become overinvolved and to feel a subsequent loss of identity, lack of opportunity to participate in other activities or be with friends, and an overdependency on the relationship. On the basis of the available data, one is tempted to hypothesize that how this issue is dealt with and the success with which it is handled are major determinants of the outcome of the relationship. The problem of how to achieve security without giving up the freedom to be oneself, and how to grow together and yet leave enough space so the individuals can grow also, appears central.

TABLE 1

EXTENT TO WHICH EMOTIONAL, SEXUAL, AND LIVING
SITUATION PROBLEMS WERE EXPERIENCED IN 35 COHABI-
TATION RELATIONSHIPS AS REPORTED BY 29 UPPERCLASS
FEMALE STUDENTS (CATEGORIES ARE ORDERED BY NUM-
BER OF PERSONS REPORTING THE PROBLEM)

Problem Area	Number No Problem	Indicating Some Problem	Averaging Rating Given by Those Indicating Some Problem*
Emotional problems			
Overinvolvement (loss of identity, lack of opportunity to participate in other activities or with friends, overdependency)	14	21	2.7
Jealousy of partner's involvement in other activities or relationships	14	15	3.1
Feeling of being trapped	18	15	2.9
Feeling of being used	19	13	2.6
Guilt:			
at beginning of relationship	20	9	3.7
during relationship	25	5	3.8
at end of relationship	15	2	4.0
Lack of feeling of "belonging" or of being "at home"	22	9	3.4
Other "will have to separate for a while after his graduation"	—	1	3.0
Sexual problems			
Differing degrees or periods of sexual interest	10	23	3.4
Lack of orgasm	11	21	3.6
Fear of pregnancy	15	15	3.1
Vaginal irritation or discharge after intercourse	17	15	3.4
Discomfort of partner during intercourse	18	10	3.7
Impotence of partner	23	6	3.0
Problems related to living situation			
Lack of privacy	15	17	3.4
Lack of adequate space	19	13	3.0
Did not get along with apartment- or housemates	20	6	2.2
Lack of sufficient money	26	6	3.3
Disagreement over use of money, sharing of money, etc.	27	4	3.5

*Respondents were asked to rate each problem. Average ratings are based on ratings from 1 to 4, 1 indicating the greatest amount of problem. Thus, the lower the average rating, the greater the problem for those experiencing it.

Other problems in this category were feelings of being trapped (should break up but afraid to do so), feelings of being used, jealousy of partner's involvement in other activities or relationships, and lack of feeling of belonging (e.g., "When I expect that he will share his money with me now that my parents have cut me off, he reminds me that we are not married"). It should be recognized, however, that although there were a few who indicated that these problems caused them a great deal of trouble, the majority indicated little or no problem. It is also important to note that more than two-thirds indicated no feelings of guilt, and the remainder indicated only a minimal amount. In the interviews, when guilt was stated to be present, it was usually related to having to conceal the relationship from parents or it occurred in those instances where they knew that the relationship could not last.

Sexual problems were common (see Table 1). Only a few indicated "no problem" in this area. Differing degrees or periods of sexual interest, lack of orgasm, fear of pregnancy, vaginal irritations, feelings of sexual inhibition, and less satisfaction with sex as the relationship deteriorated were the more frequently mentioned problems. However, in spite of problems, over three-fourths of the respondents rated the relationship as sexually satisfying. Practically all used contraception (over 80 percent used either the pill or the diaphragm), with about two-thirds of these having started contraception before or at the time of the first intercourse in the cohabitation relationship.

A major problem area was parents. More than one-fourth indicated that parents had caused "some" or "many" problems: parental disapproval of the boy, fear of discovery, guilt because they were deceiving or hurting their parents, rejection by or ultimatums from parents, and, most frequently, sadness at not being able to share this important part of their lives with their parents. Because of fear of disapproval or unpleasant repercussions, more than two-thirds had tried to conceal the relationship from their parents—by not telling them the whole story, by distorting the truth, and by developing often elaborate schemes to prevent discovery. Almost half of the respondents believed their parents to be unaware of their cohabitation, with the remainder divided equally between those who felt they definitely knew, those who thought they probably knew, and those who were unsure. The boy's parents were much more likely to be aware.

Problems related to the living situation were considered minimal. Lack of privacy, lack of adequate space, lack of sufficient funds or disagreement over money, and friction with apartment mates were all mentioned, with lack of space or privacy and tension with others in the living situation the most common. It should be noted that there was practically no problem experienced as a result of the external community, i.e., landlords, local employers, school administration, neighbors, or contemporaries. In fact, the great majority felt their friends strongly approved of and supported their relationship. In cases where this was not true, it was because friends considered this relationship rather than the cohabitation per se undesirable.

BENEFITS

It is important that the problems not be seen as outweighing the values of such relationships. More than half rated their relationship as "very successful," and more than 80 percent checked that it was "both maturing and pleasant." Even in those few cases where the relationship was said to be "painful," they emphasized the personal growth which had occurred, e.g., "I question whether I'd understand myself as well without the hard times." In no case was the experience rated "very unpleasant" or "not at all maturing," and in no case was it considered primarily detrimental to the person involved. In more than 60 percent of the cases, they would do it over again with the same person, even in those relationships which had broken up at the time of the report.

The benefits seen by the participants included a deeper understanding of themselves and of their needs, expectations, and inadequacies; increased knowledge of what is involved in a relationship and of the complexities of living with someone else; clarification of what they wanted in a marriage; increase in emotional maturity and in self-confidence, e.g., "learned not to commit myself too soon," "learned through breaking up how much strength I have," increased ability to understand and relate to others; emotional security and companionship, e.g., "because we have coped with problems and come out topside, I have more faith that we will be able to do so again." The main undercurrent in the data was the many ways in which the experience had fostered growth and maturity. All persons interviewed indicated that they would not consider marriage without having lived with the person first, and all—while hesitant to say what others should do—felt the move toward cohabitation could only be seen as a healthy trend.

OUTCOME OF THE RELATIONSHIP

At the time of the questionnaire, one-third of the relationships had dissolved (having lasted an average of four and one-half months from the time they began staying together four or more nights a week), one-third [of the respondents] were married or planning to be married, and another third were still in the process of defining the relationship (either were still living together but not yet contemplating marriage, or were still "going together" but not living together—either because the partner was away or they sought more freedom than they had when living together). A somewhat larger portion of those interviewed had broken their relationship, but this may be due to the fact that the interview was later in the academic year. The 23 relationships which were still in process had existed an average of 13 months, with five having continued for two or two and one-half years.

IMPLICATIONS

1. It appears that cohabitation has become an increasingly common aspect of courtship on the campus studied and one could predict that the trend will proliferate.[2]

Although the phenomenon of unmarried persons living together is obviously not a new one, either in this society or others, it has certainly not been a common phenomenon among unmarried middle-class youth in the United States until quite recently. Some pass it off by saying it is merely a more open expression of what students have been doing sexually on the sly for years, but this suggests a very narrow interpretation of the present situation. The pattern which is currently evolving appears to be primarily concerned with total relationships and only incidentally with the sexual aspects. It is this concern with getting to know another as a whole person and the emphasis on sharing as openly and as completely as possible with that person, which is probably the major new dimension being added to old courtship patterns.

2. There is some question whether cohabitation as now practiced on the college campus fits the concepts of trial marriage, premarital marriage, companionate marriage, or two-stage marriage which some have sought to apply to it. Trial marriage, for instance, tends to imply a level of commitment usually associated with the engagement portion of the courtship continuum which is not characteristic of the campus relationships studied. These students do not in general see themselves as consciously testing or even contemplating a potential marriage, at least not initially. Instead, in most cases, living together seems to be a natural component of a strong, affectionate "dating" relationship—a living out of "going steady"—which may grow in time to be something more, but which in the meantime is to be enjoyed and experienced because it is pleasurable in and of itself.

3. In addition to the question of whether it does in fact lead to healthier marriages or more "fully functioning" persons, there are other intriguing issues. For instance, what is the relationship between commitment to a relationship and identity formation? To what extent must one have developed a strong identity before one

can achieve a strong intimate relationship (in Erikson's sense)? What chance is there for a mature, mutual relationship when the individual is still so necessarily focused on his own development? How much commitment to a relationship is necessary for it to have a strong chance of success? Alternately, does early commitment to a relationship hinder identity development? When a person should be at a point of maximum identity development, is it healthy for him to be devoting so much of his energy to the development of a relationship or will this simply accelerate the process? These become very real problems as cohabitation inevitably occurs earlier and becomes increasingly common as a freshman experience.

4. There is a great need to help society adjust to the evolving courtship patterns. Parents in particular tend to see cohabitation as antithetical to all that they consider healthy or moral. They need help if they are to understand and to react without alarm, recrimination, and rejection. Consideration will have to be given to legal implications of the new patterns—some present laws conflict and maybe should be changed, and some new protections for the rights of unmarried participants may be necessary. The professions touched by the new trends are myriad. Bankers, for instance, as they seek to help parents write wills and set up trust funds, and as they themselves seek to administer these trusts, find themselves confronted with having to understand and interpret the new patterns. Students in particular need more realistic preparation, both at home and in school, and more opportunity for relationship and sex counseling, if they are to cope as responsibly and effectively as possible with the increased freedom and the new pressures. The first step, which most of the adult population has not yet taken, is to acknowledge that the changes are actually occurring and to be willing to entertain the hypothesis that they may indeed be an improvement on the traditional patterns.

NOTES

1. Of the 104 junior and senior women in the class, 86 completed the questionnaire. Of these, 58 handed it in on the due date and 28 after a follow-up request. Since the percentage of cohabitants was the same for the initial and the follow-up respondents, it is assumed that the percentage would be similar for the 18 nonreturnees.

2. Two recent studies are: Cole, Charles Lee. "Cohabitation in Social Context," in R. W. Libby and R. N. Whitehurst (Eds.), *Marriage and Alternatives.* Glenview, Ill.: Scott, Foresman, 1977; and Macklin, Eleanor D. "Nonmarital Heterosexual Cohabitation," in Marvin B. Sussman (Ed.), *Marriage and the Family: Current Critical Issues.* New York: Haworth Press, 1979.

18/ LIVING SINGLY

Margaret Adams

Accessible neighborliness is a basic prerequisite for everyone's social security, but for single people it is a categorical imperative to compensate for their lack of formally ascribed companionship and the support that is normally supplied through marriage or other dyad relationships. It is also vital to the psychological well-being of single people, in that it permits them to live with the degree of solitary privacy that most of them feel they must have without compromising their safety or leaving them too vulnerable to the emotional, social, and practical dangers of total isolation.

This sort of arrangement is nicely illustrated by my own fortunate experience in settling into New York City, where hospitable colleagues helped me to find and furnish an apartment in the pleasant middle-class minicommunity of Brooklyn Heights, where several of them already lived. In the fullness of time a friend from England moved to the street next to mine, and over the next four years we were gradually joined by four other women (two from Great Britain and two from Eire), whom we met through our respective jobs. From these small beginnings we gradually evolved a very effective nucleus of reciprocal support. When I returned from a spell in hospital for major surgery a rota of these unofficial Good Samaritans supervised my care, taking it in turns to cook an evening meal, do the shopping, and see to the other minutiae of domestic existence. On a different occasion one of the other members of this coterie developed a severe and unexpected attack of asthma at 12:30 A.M. and telephoned one of the group, who was able to go round immediately because of the close proximity of their households and the relative safety of the area. This basic, all-female support system acquired a further dimension by the cooption of a male neighbor, who could be called upon for household tasks for which we lacked skills or necessary physical strength and who, in return, received assistance with more female-focused activities such as upholstering furniture, sewing, and the occasional meal.

An example very like the one I have just cited from New York comes from Washington, D.C., where four professional women in their late fifties occupy separate apartments in a converted brownstone house. By degrees they struck up acquaintance, discovered many interests and needs in common, and have devised an informal system of reciprocal service that provides companionship, helps to reduce the pressures of managing a job and household alone, and is on hand to meet major crises that cannot be weathered alone. This particular arrangement, like all the other informally evolving patterns, came about by chance and was largely dependent on the happy accident of certain sociological conditions that were outside of any single individual's personal control. In this case the community is geographically compact, relatively well-off economically, and has a relatively stable population of middle-aged and older residents.

Encouraged by these experiences of informal good neighborliness, I was interested in learning to what extent my sample of single people were able to incorpoarate this important ingredient of social survival into their living arrangments. The popular view is that by virtue of their solitary style of life single people are in a conspicuously isolated, lonely, and therefore vulnerable situation (Gurin, Veroff, and Feld, 1960:231). I was not convinced of the truth of this stereotype, and my discussions with single people have gone far to disprove it, as the following personal testimonies should demonstrate.

Today there is a much wider choice of living arrangements open to the single person than there was formerly, even in the interwar period when I was growing up. Then, as earlier, the word *home* usually meant either the habitation a woman shared with her husband and family as wife and mother, or the original family establishment in which she (or he, if a bachelor) lived with parents and/or other adult brothers and sisters. In some rare instances the term did encompass modest ménages run by single women, such as the small house of one of the old maids described by Charlotte Brontë in *Shirley,* or the combined basement shop and home of Edith Wharton's "Bunner Sisters" in Stuyvesant Square; and, in the male domain, there were the simple cottage of Silas Marner and the sparsely furnished attics where the struggling writers portrayed by George Gissing in *New Grubb Street* eked out a frugal literary existence. When the parental home became defunct it was usual for the single woman to be absorbed into the family of another relative, like Charlotte Lovel in Edith Wharton's novella "The Old Maid."

During part of my childhood an unmarried second cousin in her mid-fifties came to live with us for two years; after the death of her matriarchal mother she had disposed of the family home, and instead of trying to build up her own ménage she adopted the laissez faire practice of doing the rounds of relatives' houses, shifting her base every two years or so in order not to wear her welcome too thin. Other women who did not fit easily into either of these main pigeonholes—i.e., the nuclear or extended family household—generally had to contrive for themselves a rather precarious and marginal domestic niche either in a boarding house or private hotel or as lodgers (more politely, paying guests) in private homes. When, for instance, the daughter of one of my father's business associates took a secretarial job in my father's firm, which was some two hundred miles away from her home, she came to live with us, because there were then no suitable alternatives for a girl of twenty in our small market town. The boarding house model (which most single women of my generation have savored at some point in their lives) is admirably portrayed in Muriel Stark's vivid novel *The Girls of Slender Means*, and throughout literature there are many examples of lodgers who find a domestic niche in other people's homes, Mr. Dick's long-term accommodation with Miss Betsy Trotwood (in *David Copperfield*) being a prime example.

Of the single individuals I interviewed in depth almost all have some sort of independent ménage, either on their own or sharing with one or more people on a basis of democratic equality. The exceptions to this rule were Geraldine O'Brien and James Lynch, who still occupy their family homes of long standing, and Freda Burns, who boards with an elderly couple and their daughter, to whom she is distantly connected through a relative's marriage. The most modest setting encountered was a furnished room with provision only for making tea or coffee, and the most lavish homes were two houses that their respective owners had purchased on mortgages from carefully husbanded savings. The most common arrangement was an apartment, either with sole occupancy or shared with one other person. This was a predictable finding, because this type of accommodation provides the amount and kind of space that single people generally need and can afford and is the most easily available in the larger cities, where the single population tends to cluster. It has also been the commonly recognized living arrangement for unattached individuals for the last thirty or forty years.

However, an interesting new trend is beginning to transform this old established conventional formula. Sharing an apartment or house has shifted from being exclusive to one sex to, in some cases, accommodating both women and men, who live together as a purely practical business arrangement for home-sharing, with the explicit understanding that this does not include sexual involvement (Santo, 1973). Although still rather a novelty, and not wholly appreciated by either parents or landlords (Dumanowski, 1974), this is a very sensible arrangement on several counts. It resembles other home models, fosters a more varied exchange of living experiences, and increases the household's scope for self-support through the greater diversity of homemaking skills both sexes can contribute. This observation is not intended to suggest that a man is not capable of, nor suitable for, cooking the dinner or seeing to the laundry, or that women will necessarily leave the plumbing and carpentry to their male roommates; but the plain fact is that a good many of both sexes have been raised to develop different skills, and under these circumstances it is often expedient to allocate chores on this realistic basis of greater aptitude and familiarity or personal preference.

Although a good many of the single people I talked to made it very clear that privacy and the feeling of possessing their own exclusive and inviolate domain were very important to them, some were also frank in admitting that they did not relish the lonely aspects of solitary living. One or two of the latter were therefore looking around for an alternative arrangement that would safeguard their privacy as well as providing companionship and some measure of reciprocal commitment. Sylvia Hale, a woman psychologist in her mid-forties, would like to find some modus vivendi that caters to her need to spend time alone after a demanding day's testing while allowing her to be part of a companionable group. Accordingly she has put out a feeler to other solitarily placed people through newspaper advertisements. From the replies, she has brought together a group of men and women in varying statuses of nonattachment to pool their ideas about ways of living other than the solitary single-cell system each presently occupies and to see if they can devise some cooperative venture that would simultaneously accommodate their common needs for separateness and sharing.

This enterprising attempt is just one example of the innovative schemes for experimental living that have been burgeoning at a very rapid pace over the past five years, which, between them, cover a variety of different organizational patterns and underlying ideologies. At one end of this variegated spectrum of possibilities is the commune model, in which all aspects of domestic living are shared and expectations of emotional and social dedication are explicitly articulated and strictly enforced (Davis, 1972; Kanter, 1972). Some of these communal living projects have developed from a firmly articulated common social philosophy, and their objective is to experiment with, and demonstrate, different systems of living that reflect in their minuscule example a new basis for relationships throughout society as a whole. For example, one goal of the commune is to challenge the firmly entrenched belief in the exclusive ownership of private property and to attack the alienation of individuals that this particular social philosophy and system create. In the same way some of the cooperative living situations set up by unattached women represent a desire to reorganize the pattern of female lives on a basis other than dyad marriage or its derivatives. These innovations are attempts to remodel the entire system of societal and sexual exchange away from the exclusive, patriarchal, essentially sexist model now prevailing to one having greater flexibility and more variations, that can emphasize the concept of greater reciprocity and equity between the sexes in all their social dealings with each other.

In contrast to these specifically organized systems are the loose assemblages of unattached individuals who enjoy some measure of corporate living but are not yet prepared to commit themselves either to the formally defined system of marriage and the nuclear household or to the ideological rigors of a strict commune. The practical mechanics of living are the main concern of these latter, more casual models, and their principal rationale is the expedient one of saving on expenditure of money, energy, and time through sharing common tasks of home maintenance. However, even in these hardheaded schemes, the companionable component tends to intrude, often assuming equal importance in the end. With other groups the companionship and shared living are the primary motive forces behind this sort of establishment, and details of its practical organization evolve as the result of these shared intentions.

The individuals I have talked to who live in one or other type of communal situation have suggested that each participant views the system as a useful opportunity for combining an enjoyable, satisfying, and often stimulating style of living in the here-and-now with flexible scope for change in the future, should circumstances dictate need of the latter. Everyone agreed on the importance of thoroughly understanding the nature and extent of emotional commitment that is proffered by, and required of, both the group and individual, and the need to build in options for members to move out if their emotional needs or social circumstances no longer fit them into the group pattern. This felicitous opportunity for having the cake of commitment while eating its crumbs of relative freedom is especially appealing to single people and is made possible by the fact that in such corporate living situations emotional and practical commitment is made to a group of people. In this social situation emotional give-and-take is spread among several people instead of being deeply invested in one or two persons, and interdependence is, therefore, much less intensely focused. Within this emotional framework separation and transfer of emotional resources can be accomplished with less painful, restrictive repercussions.

Judith Bennett, who lives with five others, articulated this point clearly by saying that she appreciated the sense of security the household gave her but also liked the knowledge that she was basically independent and did not have to answer to anyone else for major decisions that would affect her living plans. She said that, if for instance, she decided to take a year's leave of absence from work to travel abroad, she would feel some responsibility toward the house and her fellow occupants, but it would take the essentially practical form of maintaining her share of the house's upkeep or finding a satisfactory person to take her place during her absence. By contrast, she felt that, were she married, this decision would implicate emotional maneuvering of much greater psychological complexity; her husband might resent the summary disruption of his familiar living routine, feel at a loss without her companionship, or even interpret her action as a gesture of emotional abandonment. This hazard is somewhat less now that women are approaching marriage from a more independent standpoint and tend to make clear in the preliminary negotiations the degree of independence they expect to exercise; but old ways of thinking and feeling die hard, and the woman in a ménage established à *deux* (even if on an informal, nonlegal basis) is generally less free than my respondent. Since the latter's original interview with me she has acted on her premise by giving up her job for a four-month tour in Europe and North Africa, following this venture up with a summer camp assignment in a different part of America from her home.

The relatively flexible nature of the domestic arrangements I am describing permits them to be adapted to the diverse needs of individuals of different temperaments, social aspirations, and phases of development. One group of four young women (who are actually below my minimal age criterion of twenty-five) share a rented house in a well-to-do suburb near Boston. The household in common makes it easier for them to enjoy a higher standard of material living than if they lived separately and gives them an opportunity to develop skills in home management that run the gamut from budgeting, house cleaning, and cooking to entertaining. It also fosters the delicate art of getting on with several people and increases insights into individual and group stresses and how to deal with these intangibles of civilized living.

Nevertheless, each girl pursues her own social life apart from the group and with a different circle of friends, and it is my impression that most of the present occupants will eventually move into marriage after an appropriate period of exploratory dating. One of the girls, however, has a very high investment in her professional nursing career and has embarked on a graduate degree, so at this point she is less concerned with furthering her opportunities for marriage or an intimate heterosexual relationship. Within the house she has fallen into the unofficial role of chatelaine and will probably continue to live there longer than her current coresidents, remaining as the stable hub of a group that exchanges its constituent parts every two years or so. She may also marry eventually, but whether or not this happens in the future, in the here-and-now she has a congenial setting that suits her needs, offers a good many practical and emotional satisfactions, and reinforces her status as an independent woman. All of these factors give her a position of independent vantage from which she is actually and psychologically free to shift gears into marriage or stay where she is, without compromising her practical situation, social role, or personal self-esteem.

The inherent flexibility of such group living situations also accommodates another social factor that wields significant influence in the lives of single people. This is their social mobility, which most of them cherish as the gilt-edged asset of their single status and which may manifest itself at very short notice through the unexpected opportunity to move to the far side of the American continent or even the world. The personal conflict that single people have to contend with between their constant urge to be footloose and fancy-free to follow the gleam of fresh opportunities and their equally pressing need for some sort of emotional roots is to some extent resolved in a group situation, which allows for movement without the isolation and alienation that comes from ultradetachment from others. Judith is a case in point, and to show further how corporate living can partially resolve this quandary I shall describe another group living situation, which embodies a more explicit and clearly articulated commitment to common emotional and social concerns than the one I have just referred to but which also has built into its philosophy and organization provision for potential impermanence among its members. This is essential for its success, because all of the members are in types of professions that can be practiced almost anywhere and are at the stage of their careers when movement from job to job in both vertical and horizontal directions is a very likely occurrence.

This group shares a converted nineteenth-century farmhouse, which is owned jointly by two women and run as a cooperative venture by themselves, two other women, and two men. The coopted members were recruited from among friends, colleagues, and individuals who had links with friends, so that there was some assurance of compatibility in tastes and outlook; and when one founding member left, a great deal of trouble and thought was given to selecting a successor, who had to be approved by everyone. The organization of the house is relatively loose. Its financial upkeep, including mortgage repayments, capital expenditure on major repairs or alterations, and ongoing maintenance, is divided equally, and each member has an unfurnished room for which she or he has sole responsibility, plus the use of two common sitting rooms, kitchen, and bathroom and entitlement to the guest room when free. The common rooms have been furnished by the owners, who have imported some old pieces of furniture from their childhood homes in order to create an atmosphere of home, also creating, inadvertently, a sense of continuity through the female line.

One has brought a very old writing desk inherited from her New England great-grandmother and the other a large picture that used to hang at the bottom of the staircase in her home in California. I mention these details because they contribute appreciably to the feeling of shared intimacy that pervades the house and helps to create the conviction that for the people who live there—even if only for a limited period—it is a home, rather than a mere residence, in which they have a vital stake. This bond in living has been very much strengthened by the fact that at the outset the house required a good deal of minor repairs and decorating, which the first occupants set to and did themselves. Since it is an old structure, with more room and ground space than is usual for a city dwelling, this means that there are always upkeep jobs to be done in the yard or house and scope for making improvements to the physical fabric of the home.

The equitable basis for everyone's tenancy does away with the sense of potential exploitation and antagonism that tends to color the normal contractual relationship between landlord and tenant, so that there is a greater sense of physical security as well as the ever-present opportunity for companionship. Every member has the privilege of having guests to meals or staying overnight, on the understanding that he or she must assume full responsibility for their guest's comfort and that other members of the household have no obligations toward them beyond common courtesy. In fact, because of the group's closeknit character, situations of this kind are always worked out amicably, and guests are generally enjoyed by everyone involved.

In the course of its development the household has come to realize that for smooth running there must be a regularly scheduled forum for exchanging views and even airing minor complaints, and a routine mechanism for communication has been established. Aside from the financial arrangements and allotment of individual territorial space, it is the only formal piece of structure that is built into the house's organization. Since everyone is on different and very flexible work schedules and involved in a good many after-work activities, catering tends to be a rather ad hoc arrangement; evening meals are cooked by whoever is at home and usually with enough margin provided to accommodate at least one unexpected extra. Expenses for food are based on general provision of certain common commodities, which are shared by all in return for a fixed levy to the common pool, and ad hoc allocation of other expenditures according to who participated in the meal.

An interesting point that arose in connection with this house is the considerable amount of financial responsibility that the owners had to assume, and I asked whether they feel this to be a social encumbrance that hampers their sense of real and psychological freedom. One of them admitted that at times she feels oppressed by the knowledge that she is responsible for the maintenance of the house's basic structure and fabric, fearing the possibility of some major repair that would require the painful choice between laying out a considerable sum of additional money or selling the house. Against this she enjoys the freedom to do what she likes with the property and the realization that investment of time or money is to her advantage, and both she and the co-owner are happy at being independent of landlords' whims and unstable rents. Since buying the house was a relatively easy venture, once the initial investment of capital had been raised, both owners feel that selling it would be equally feasible, since it is a convenient size and located in an area where property is in demand. To promote a sense of security there is a common agreement among the occupants that any change of ownership and policy will be open to discussion by every concerned member of the incumbent resident group.

I am emphasizing this aspect of ownership because all too often one hears of the problems single people have in acquiring property, the burden of maintaining it, and the perpetual anxiety that such an investment of resources will constitute a tie that will cramp their style. Although there are some realistic grounds for this sort of anxiety—women without the reassuring ballast of a male salary behind them are often regarded as risky candidates for a mortgage or questionable property owners—I am also convinced that this general female reluctance to invest in a solid home base stems from the attitude of mind that is still reluctant, or unable, to perceive the single status in terms of defined substance, social stability, and permanence. My own experience has taught me that such weighty plans are determined by the economic resources one has to play with and that single women, in common with other members of their sex, are still at a grave disadvantage regarding wordly goods, on account of salary differentials (Bird, 1972), discrimination in employment (Epstein, 1970; Komisar, 1971), and—even earlier in their lives—educational choices that are biased against women (Pullen, 1970; Roby, 1973). Underlying these hard facts, however, is the insidious maid-in-waiting myth that continues to bewitch our thinking and plans and the manner in which we attempt to translate the latter into practical action. We need, therefore, to engage in a vigorous redefinition of what I call the problem of independence and substance and to cease seeing and projecting ourselves as socially incomplete beings who have a shadowy identity and equally tenuous style of practical living.

The process of looking at alternate patterns of living for single people has sharpened my awareness of this need for redefinition, because beyond their obvious utilitarian function of offering a wider range of accommodation I have come to recognize that they have an intangible, and therefore often unperceived, secondary value that should be considered. By providing a comfortable, functionally efficient, and emotionally supportive home setting in the here-and-now, these new and flexible communal models of domesticity help to neu-tralize the vestibular climate of thinking evoked by solitary apart-ment or quasi-dormitory living. This experience of domestic security also gives single people an opportunity to form a more realistic pic-ture of the assets of being single as well as the drawbacks (which generally receive more attention), and in the process they have a better chance of redefining their roles and forming a clearer idea of their status.

Because I consider this an important concept I shall try to explain it at slightly greater length. Moving into a group living situation, such as those I have described, exacts some degree of personal com-mitment just to make it work. The investment of emotion that occurs as a by-product of this commitment and its dividend of reciprocal satisfaction means that when someone leaves the setting a corre-sponding amount of emotional effort will be required to deal with the separation; in the course of this process there will inevitably be a careful assessment of the situation being abandoned and the one to which the individual is transferring.

This opportunity for an emotional and social commitment to a particular living plan—even if it is not permanent—can be an impor-tant stabilizing influence for both the single and married person, on a number of counts. Firstly, if unattached women and men are com-pelled to live in lonely, isolated, and emotionally bare circumstances because there are no alternative living arrangements that allow them scope for making a commitment to other people, then there is a much higher chance that they will be forced into marriage—or some other recognized dyad arrangement—by the negative pressures of desperation to escape from being trapped in a vacuum of loneliness and social alienation. With such painful motivation as its broker, marriage is not a valid choice, and the prospect of its turning out a satisfactory experience is seriously diminished.

Contrariwise, if an individual's living arrangement prior to mar-riage has been reasonably happy, there is a good chance that the new pattern of living will be equally satisfying—in the same way that children are able to adjust easily to a fresh phase of social develop-ment if they have found the previous one happy and rewarding. Furthermore, if marriage is approached from the vantage point of satisfaction rather than desperate frustration, there is much less risk that it will be viewed as a vertical move *upward* along a predestined path of social progress, which approximates the current popular view of this institution. Instead it is more likely to be seen as a horizontal shift from one pattern of psychological and practical com-mitment to another, which contains many different features but is not ipso facto superior to the previous mode so much as more appropriate to a particular individual's needs at that juncture of her or his social development. This perspective on married and single living forestalls the unrealistic investment of marriage with impossible hopes that it will miraculously cancel out all previous unhappiness; it also endows singleness with a stature of recognizable feasibility, to which individuals can legitimately commit themselves if it suits their particular book.

A final point of practical import to be mentioned here is that group living provides a sort of neutral respite territory, where the conflicts that most adults experience in regard to choices around marriage can be worked through in a climate of thinking and feeling that is not biased by the societal pressures for marriage nor by the necessarily antithetical stance of the camp of dedicated celibacy. Since it is probable that most, if not all, members of a group household will be engaged in the same task of trying to reconcile freedom with commitment and to discover their positions along the polarized spectrum of options, there is likely to be a high level of consensus support for individual heart searchings, which makes them less painful to deal with and offers greater assurance of a sound solution. This sort of interchange represents a built-in advantage to group living that is missing in single occupancy arrangements. The single person living alone is much more vulnerable to these self-doubts and questionings because she or he does not have anyone at hand to share them with and also because the very circumstances of living alone tend to emphasize the atypical nature of the social position. Within the group living situation, on the other hand, each person is in a safe microcosm of *shared similarities,* and even though this mini-world is conspicuously *different* from the social norm, as a reference point for personal identity and self-esteem it is very reassuring.

Much of this article has been allotted to discussing communal or group living arrangements because they represent one of the innovative social trends that are enabling single women and men to revamp their status in modern society and to cope more effectively with some of the practical frustrations in living that they encounter. However, it is important to remember that these new patterns are neither universally accepted nor specifically available to any one person in any one community and that in general their greatest appeal is to younger members of the unattached population. For older single people, or those who do not have the temperament for group living, even on a minor scale, the separate single dwelling is still the commonest mode.

Of the single people I talked to by far the most either lived alone or shared with one companion, and since my population of informants was drawn from large cities they usually lived in apartments rather than houses. Apart from one or two who felt that loneliness was a marked disadvantage to living alone, the majority of solitary dwellers were obviously contented with this living arrangement, and a substantial number expressed a positive pleasure in having their own home, because of the independence and solitude it provided and because it was a means of expressing their personality and consolidating their social identity. All those living by themselves had found ways of manipulating the practical mechanics of existence so that they could be successfully managed by one person, and most people organized and maintained their households with a minimum of outside help. I do not propose to go into the details of these daily routines because they are in no way remarkable and would read as a boringly familiar catalogue of minutiae exactly similar to those governing the daily existences of the population at large, irrespective of age, sex, and marital status.

Before concluding, however, I do want to pursue the points about status, self-image, and social substance that I raised in regard to group living and to show how they apply also to single individuals whose lives run on more solitary links. The majority of single people I met have a very substantial image of themselves as socially independent people, and they regard their home setting and the life style it embodies as being very essential components of this social identity. This is projected through the type and location of their homes, the disposition and character of their furnishings, and the hundred and one manifestations of individual taste that these reveal.

Most of my informants took an obvious pleasure in describing their homes, and several emphasized the enjoyment they derived from having nice household fittings and beautiful possessions around them. One or two were knowledgeable antique collectors and had acquired some very elegant pieces. At a humbler level, one of the women, Thelma Green, who has very little money or cultural sophistication, demonstrated a similar inclination, eagerly displaying some odd pieces of old, flawed, but very good china that she had managed to pick up at junk stores. Stanley West and Ellen Collins, who had lived in institutions for so much of their adult lives, mentioned with pride the coffee pots and bedspreads that they had purchased for their rooms. Coffee pots and bedspreads are high status symbols in institutions, chiefly because they represent, respectively, the practical opportunity for self-sustaining independence (making a cup of coffee *when you want it*) and a visible embodiment of separate, individual taste and identity. Ellen went to great pains to explain that red was her favorite color and that she was trying to collect red decorations and furnishings for her room.

Several women and men said that they had made a special point of incorporating pictures, ornaments, and pieces of furniture from their family homes into their spinster or bachelor quarters, and one

of them—Althea Webster—made the comment that she derived a
sense of enduring identity and continuity over time and space when
she saw a flower bowl or table that had started life in a large family
house in Rochester, New York, ensconced in her apartment in Washington, D.C. Another woman said that by design or accident she had
found herself living in a neighborhood where the type of houses
recalled the small town she had lived in during her childhood, and I
now realize that I find myself almost unconsciously drawn to the sort
of street and house that rings a faint connecting bell with my past in
England. Brooklyn Heights, for example, bears a strong resem-
blance to parts of Bristol or Chelsea, and my present apartment
complex in Cambridge could have been modeled on the English
almshouses that sat at the end of my aunts' road in a Wiltshire
market town.

For a conclusion I am extending this idea further and suggesting
that just as group living is a tentative exploratory experience by
which younger people are attempting to discover their real identity
and a social pattern most conducive to its growth, so for some individuals at a later stage of life the act of establishing their own clearly
separate and independent home is an explicit affirmation that they
have graduated to a stable phase of singleness, which, if not permanently affirmed, is now officially recognized. For single women this
overt gesture has an important ritualistic significance in that it confirms their own sense of solitary and psychologically independent
destiny in the same way that moving into the shared home of marriage confirms the different social role and personal life style that
the newly married woman assumes. This *rite de passage* is very rarely
acknowledged as either a practical or a psychological reality—probably because society is reluctant to recognize the single status as a
socially viable option unless it is within certain prescribed institutional limits such as the religious vocation—but it is nevertheless an
important social phenomenon, which we should respect.

This point is beautifully illustrated by a spinster cousin of mine,
who, in her mid-forties, was left a modest legacy of money and a
sizable dowry of serviceable furniture by her godfather. Vested with
this financial wherewithal and material belongings she systematically
went to work to set up her own establishment, buying a small country cottage with the money and filling it with the household effects
she had inherited. When her family and friends attempted to dis-
suade her from sinking her resources in this venture and warned
her of the responsibilities of running her own house, with its valuable contents, she countered with the remark that her two sisters had
come into well-furnished homes when they married and that she felt
perfectly justified in following suit when the opportunity came her
way. Although she did not put it in so many words, she was, I think,

voicing the unconscious thought that she had now achieved, by a different route, parity of status with those two matrons and that her new position of material substance, as manifested in her nice home, was the spinster's counterpart to the initiation rites of marriage that ratify a woman's social status. The nineteenth-century short story by Mary E. Wilkins Freeman (1973) entitled "A New England Nun" mirrors the same attitude. Its theme concerns a spinster spoken for in marriage to a man who has been abroad for fourteen years. When he returns to claim her she suddenly realizes that the neatly ordered home she has lovingly built up in his absence has become the outward and visible expression of her real identity; rather than risk losing this she breaks off the engagement and very contentedly resumes her serene life of singleness with her canary, dog, herbs, and homemade jellies.

REFERENCES

Bird, Caroline. "Is Money the Root of All Freedom," *Ms.,* Dec., 1972.

Davis, Karen. "Joining a Commune," *Glamour,* March, 1972.

Dumanowski, Dianne. "Morality Play in Somerville," *Boston Phoenix,* Oct. 8, 1974.

Epstein, Cynthia Fuchs. *Woman's Place.* (Berkeley and Los Angeles: U. of Calif. Press, 1970).

Freeman, Mary E. Wilkins. "A New England Nun," in *Images of Women in Literature,* ed. Mary Anne Ferguson. (Boston: Houghton Mifflin, 1973).

Gurin, Gerald, Joseph Veroff, and Shiela Feld. *Americans View Their Mental Health.* (New York: Basic Books, 1960).

Kanter, Rosabeth Moss. *Commitment and Community: Communes and Utopias in Social Perspective.* (Cambridge: Harvard University Press, 1972).

Komisar, Lucy. *The New Feminism* (New York: Franklin Watts, 1971), Chapter 6.

Pullen, Doris L. "The Educational Establishment: Wasted Women," in *Voices of the New Feminism,* ed. Mary Lou Thompson (Boston: Beacon Press, 1970).

Roby, Pamela. "Institutionalized and Internalized Barriers to Women in Higher Education," in *Academic Women on the Move,* ed. Alice Rossi (New York: Russell Sage Foundation, 1973).

Santo, Carol. "Non-Romantic Cohabitation," *Single,* Nov., 1973.

PART SIX

WORK

One of the first things most people want to know when meeting someone new is what that person's occupation is. This seems to be equally true at suburban parties and singles' bars. "And what do you do for a living?" is a standard opening. Society places a high value on what we do for a living; so do the people we meet; so do we ourselves. Work provides the means for obtaining the goods and pursuing the activities that are the essence of the single life style. Marketing experts recognize the impact of singles' consumption patterns in the marketplace and they create product lines and selling strategies to lure singles' dollars. From town houses to sports cars, from tape decks to vacations in Mexico, goods are created and singles work to obtain the money to enjoy them.

Beyond the marketplace, work provides a crucial source of identity. Power, prestige, and privilege all flow from occupational involvement, as does a sense of self-worth. The psychiatrist Robert Gould argues in "Measuring Masculinity by the Size of a Paycheck" that for men in our society money indicates not only success but masculinity. For some women, this argument is also valid, although for most single women work is an indispensable factor in economic independence. Single people are far more likely to place their career goals above interest in family and in other kinds of personal development. Many devote longer hours to work than some of their married colleagues (Stein, 1976), and many feel that they receive emotional support from their co-workers.

Though it appears that single women and men can be superior employees, many continue to receive lower wages than married colleagues and are often passed over for promotion. A survey of fifty major corporations found that in 80 percent of the responding companies the official corporate position was that marriage was not essential to upward mobility. However, in a majority of the companies only 2 percent of their executives, including junior management, were single. Over 60 percent of the replies stated that single executives tend to "make snap judgments," and 25 percent said that singles are "less stable" than married people (Jacoby, 1974). Discrimination may range from overt cases to more subtle ones, involving the complex networks that exist in every institution: business-related friendships, luncheon conversation, and informal contacts that affect job retention and promotion. Since race, sex, ethnic origin, and religion are also bases for discrimination, discrimination against singles is often hard to isolate. Is a woman not promoted because she is divorced or because she is a woman? Is a man kept back because he has never married, or because his boss suspects he is gay? Whatever its cause, such discrimination victimizes many men and women who hope to get ahead in their work, or even just to get by.

The articles in this section deal with several aspects of the singles work experience, including comparison of careers of single and married women from different socioeconomic backgrounds; a study of the importance of marriage to black women of different classes; an examination of employment discrimination against gay men.

What determines the occupations women choose? Marital status and the socioeconomic status of the woman's family are particularly influential. Natalie Sokoloff studied a sample of female college graduates from the 1960s and from the late 1970s. The earlier study showed that single and married women differed in their early career activities as well as their specific occupations. Most of the differences in early career activities were not between married and single women but between those from different socioeconomic groups. Some of Sokoloff's findings were:

•Almost all single women from all socioeconomic origins were employed; 25 percent were in school (typically while working);
•Far fewer married women were either employed or in school three years after college graduation;
•A larger percentage of women from families of low socioeconomic status than higher status remained single three years after graduation. This was true even when the women had children;
•The largest percentage of the women in the sample were employed in traditional female professions.

Examining 1978 statistics, Sokoloff found that the percentage of college graduates in the labor force had risen from 58 to 66 percent, but that the percentage of employed female college graduates working in professional, technical, and managerial jobs had dropped, while the percentage in clerical and sales work had risen.

What do these findings indicate for women's future career choices? How will the predicted decline in the need for teachers affect women? How can women become better prepared to enter traditionally male occupations? How can the level of discrimination be reduced?

For many women, obtaining a good education and entering a profession take priority over marrying and establishing a family. This is particularly true of black women from lower-middle-class families. Elizabeth Higginbotham studied middle- and lower-middle-class women, comparing the degree to which their families stressed educational attainment and the degree to which they stressed marriage. The upwardly mobile women from lower-middle-class backgrounds had parents who were not assured of upward mobility for their daughter solely through marriage. They focused on educational success to the exclusion of other goals. On the other hand, women from black middle-class homes were expected to integrate careers with family life. For the lower-class women, "The process of being socially mobile necessitates concentrating energy on adjusting to new environments and modes of interaction; consequently it forces many black women from lower-middle-class backgrounds to postpone marriage." What other links are there between social class and marriage in black culture? And how do parental ambitions conflict with personal needs?

Integrating personal and professional life is very difficult for many gay men. Keeping one's job often means hiding homosexuality. How this is accomplished, what happens when gays are found out, and the extent of discrimination throughout the working world are the subjects of Martin Levine's "Employment Discrimination Against Gay Men." Public-opinion polls report strong support for barring gays from high-status occupations; application forms are constructed to weed out gays; there is discrimination even in government licensing and security clearances. The struggle to conceal their sexual orientation from co-workers often leaves gay people feeling artificial and anxious, and if they fail to conceal it, the situation is worse. Many companies' policies require firing. Others will keep an employee at a low level or transfer him to an unsuitable job. Is the author's suggestion of legislation to prevent systematic employment discrimination against homosexuals workable? Would laws be sufficient to stop the practice? What other actions might both straight and gay people take to change the situation?

REFERENCES

Gould, Robert. "Measuring Masculinity by the Size of a Paycheck," in Joseph Pleck and Jack Sawyer (Eds.), *Men and Masculinity* (Englewood Cliffs, N.J.: Prentice-Hall, 1974).

Jacoby, Susan. "49 Million Singles Can't All Be Right." *New York Times Magazine,* February 17, 1974: 13, 41–49.

Stein, Peter. *Single* (Englewood Cliffs, N.J.: Prentice-Hall, 1976).

19/ EARLY WORK PATTERNS OF SINGLE AND MARRIED WOMEN

Natalie J. Sokoloff

In the 1970s, women's participation in employment moved from being front-page news to commonly accepted experience. Studies of this experience began by looking at women's mobility in terms of their marriages (Rubin, 1968; Elder, 1969; Glenn et al., 1974; Chase, 1975; both Glenn et al. and Chase compare women's mobility through marriage with men's mobility through occupational attainment) and then at women's own occupational mobility (DeJong et al., 1971; Tyree and Treas, 1974; Treiman and Terrell, 1975; McClendon, 1976; Featherman and Hauser, 1976).

My own research interest was to look at the influence of mothers and fathers from different socioeconomic strata on the early career activity and occupational experiences of their college-educated daughters. Here the focus is limited to these questions: What difference does being single or married make in the early careers and occupational experiences of college-educated women? How does this vary according to socioeconomic origins?

The increasing rate of employment of married women living with husbands is one of the most impressive changes that has occurred in the United States labor force since World War II. Before 1940 the typical employed woman was young and single. Between 1940 and 1977 the proportion of employed married women rose from 15 to 42 percent, while single women increased their labor force participation rate from 48 to 59 percent.[1] Since married women represent the largest increase and the greatest number of women employed today,[2] there has been a tendency to neglect the work experiences of single women. Little has been done to compare labor force experiences of these two groups of women. And despite the fact that socioeconomic origins are believed to play an important role in educational and occupational achievement (Sewell, 1971; Jencks et al., 1972; Bowles and Gintis, 1976), little has been done to explore the labor force experiences of single and married women from different socioeconomic origins.

The higher the level of education completed by women, the more likely it is that they will be employed in the paid labor force. Today as in the 1960s, much of the literature focuses on the employment experiences of college-educated women, but the impact of socioeconomic origins and of marital status are not usually investigated.

It is widely believed that the career and occupational experiences of educated women who remain single are different than those of educated women who marry. Two assumptions that emerge from other studies, and from popular thought, are (1) that single college-educated women are more likely to be employed than married college-educated women, and (2) that these single women will be more likely than the married women to be employed in higher-status, male-dominated professions. As we will see, single women are more likely than married women to be employed and to be in high-status occupations, but these findings must be qualified in terms of both the type of occupation and the influence of socioeconomic origins.

The data used in this study come from a national stratified random sample of U.S. women who graduated college in 1961 and were reinterviewed in 1964. These data are part of a longitudinal survey of male and female college graduates carried out by the National Opinion Research Center between 1961 and 1968. All numbers in this study are weighted to balance out an oversampling of students going to professional and graduate schools from the original design. Although the weighted sample size was 15, 663, we use the responses of 11,885 women who were reinterviewed in 1964 and who had all the needed information for this analysis. For further description of the entire sample, see Davis (1964) and NORC Codebook (1974).

It was felt that family income would be the most adequate single measure of socioeconomic origins, because family income reflects the relative contribution of *both parents* to the family's socioeconomic position.

In this study, the income of the family of origin is divided into three categories: under $5,000, $5,000 to under $15,000, and $15,000 or more.[3] We classify marital status as single (never married) or married (ever married). Since very few women were either widowed, separated, or divorced, they are included in the ever married category.

The two dependent variables I have chosen to explore refer to (1) career activity, which includes homemaking as well as occupational and school activity, and (2) specific occupational type, which refers to the male- or female-dominated nature of the occupation.

The datedness of the information must be mentioned. Although these data are now fifteen to twenty years old, the fact that they were collected prior to the contemporary women's movement eliminates certain response bias that might otherwise exist in such data today. Moreover, they provide a base line for further research now being pursued in this area.

PROFILE OF THE WOMEN

Of the female college graduates in this 1961 national sample 96 percent are white, U.S. born citizens. The majority (66 percent) are Protestant; about 25 percent are Catholic; 9 percent are Jewish. Forty-four percent went to urban high schools, 34 percent to suburban, and 22 percent to rural schools. Most of the women (80 percent) were either twenty-four or twenty-five years old. Three years after college graduation only one-third of the women in the sample were single; two-thirds were married. Forty percent of the women had one child and 38 percent had no children.

Most of the women in the sample (68 percent) are employed in the paid labor force; 15 percent go to school (postcollege courses); and 26 percent are full-time homemakers (see Table 1).

Among those women who are employed, nine out of ten hold full-time jobs. Full-time and part-time employed women have been combined in analyses since the number of part-time employees is too small for separate analyses. This finding is important in that it reinforces the idea that women with high educational levels are not only very likely to be employed, but they are likely to be employed in rather stable, full-time work. This is true for single and married women alike.[4]

TABLE 1

WHAT ARE 1961 FEMALE COLLEGE
GRADUATES DOING IN 1964?*

Career Activity	Percent Active
Employed only	57
Employed and in school	11
School only	4
Homemaker only	26
No answer given	2
Total	100

*The question on which this information is based was asked in such a way that one can determine only the respondent's *main* activity, whether or not she does it full time. Thus a married woman without children may have indicated that she was "employed only," even though she did homemaking tasks too. A person who said she was in "school only" may or may not have been in school full time. Likewise, the category "homemaker only" is not a perjorative term but means that this woman responded solely to the category "homemaker" and to no others. It can be presumed that such a response implies the person was a full-time homemaker.

TABLE 2

IN WHAT TYPES OF OCCUPATIONS ARE FEMALE COLLEGE
GRADUATES EMPLOYED IN 1964?*

Professions (Male Dominated)	20%
Professional	(11%)
(More than two-thirds of the workers in these occupations are men. This category includes only traditional professionals, e.g., lawyers, doctors, architects, etc.)	
Manager	(4%)
(More than two-thirds of the workers in these occupations are men. This category only includes managers.)	
In-Between Profession	(5%)
(One-third to two-thirds of the workers in these occupations are women.)	
Semiprofessions (Female Dominated)	71%
(More than 50 percent female occupation, e.g., elementary school teacher, librarian, social worker, etc.)	
Clericals (Female Dominated)	10%
(More than 50 percent female nonprofessional occupation, primarily secretarial and clerical workers.)	
TOTAL	101%***
(N = 7,501)	

*Employed women includes women who are employed only (and not in school) as well as women who are both employed and in school.
**In the tables, this general category will be referred to as "professions," even though it includes other high-status male-dominated jobs, like managers.
***Due to rounding.

While a small but significant proportion of women continue in graduate school, the vast majority of those in school are *not* full-time students, but rather are working and going to school simultaneously. Only 4 percent of the entire sample of female college graduates report their main activity in 1964 as attendance in postcollege school.

In looking at the occupations of all employed women it is very clear that female college graduates work predominantly in the traditional female professions, which will here be called the semiprofessions[5] (Table 2), with the largest group working as elementary school teachers. Almost three-fourths of the women (71 percent) are employed in the semiprofessions, while one-fifth (20 percent) are employed in high-status male-dominated occupations (male professionals and managers, as well as in-between professionals). An additional 10 percent are in the low-status traditionally female nonprofessions; they are here called clerical workers. So few women (only

32) were employed in low-status male nonprofessions (e.g., factory workers) in 1964 that this category was dropped from the current analysis.

In terms of the reliability of the data, these findings compare favorably with reports that 90 percent of the female college graduates who were employed in the paid labor force in the 1960s were employed in the professions or semiprofessions (Women's Bureau, 1971).

Among women in high-status male-dominated occupations, the majority are working in the highest status male professions (lawyer, architect, accountant, engineer, etc.), as opposed to either male managerial or in-between professional jobs. The data indicate that most of the women who are attending school in 1964 are also employed in the labor force. From the data, it appears that these women are working to improve their positions within their existing occupational categories, rather than "working their way through school" at undesirable jobs in search of higher-status male-dominated jobs.

CAREERS AND OCCUPATIONS

In general, the data indicate that remaining single has a very definite effect on the early career activity of female college graduates,[6] but that the types of jobs into which single and married women are recruited are actually quite similar.

Table 3 indicates that virtually all of the single women (93 percent) are employed three years after graduation, and 24 percent are in school. In comparison, for 40 percent of the married women homemaking seems to be defined as a viable alternative career. At the same time more than half (56 percent) of all married women are employed in the labor force, and 11 percent are in school. In all cases single women are more likely than married women to be employed only, to be both employed and in school, and to be in school only. The questionnaire provided no category for those women who were unemployed. However, in 1963, white female unemployment was 5.8 percent overall, with 7.4 percent for women twenty to twenty-four years old and 5.8 percent for those twenty-five to thirty-four, the major age group studied here (U.S. Department of Labor, Women's Bureau, 1969).

Both single and married women are most likely to be employed as semiprofessionals and least likely to be employed as clericals (see Table 3B). Though differences are not great, married women are more likely than single women to be employed in the semiprofessions (74 percent married vs. 66 percent single). Single women are a little more likely than marrieds to be employed in high-status male-

TABLE 3

CAREERS AND OCCUPATIONS OF WOMEN THREE YEARS AFTER
COLLEGE GRADUATION—FOR SINGLE AND MARRIED WOMEN
IN 1964

Career Activity Career	Single (%)	Married (%)
Employed only	76	48
Employed and in school	17	8
School only	7	3
Homemaker only	*	40
	100	99 (due to rounding)
	(3,971)	(7,759)

Occupational Type Occupation	Single (%)	Married (%)
Professional	22	17
Semiprofessional	67	74
Clerical	11	9
	100	100
	(3,424)	(4,066)

*Not applicable. None of the single women responded that they were homemakers.

dominated occupations (22 percent singles vs. 17 percent marrieds). There is virtually no difference by marital status for employment in the low-status female nonprofessions.

It appears that those women who are in the more traditional role of marriage are more likely to be channeled into more traditional types of occupations: female semiprofessions. These jobs are believed to be more compatible with the dual role of wage earner and homemaker. Single women are a little more likely to be in high-status male-dominated occupations.

CAREERS OF SINGLE AND MARRIED WOMEN FROM DIFFERENT SOCIOECONOMIC BACKGROUNDS

In Table 4 we find that the careers of *single* women are quite uniform regardless of their family's socioeconomic origins. At least nine out of ten single women from each socioeconomic background are likely to be employed in the labor force; and one-fifth to one-fourth of all single women are in school. Quite clearly, *singlehood is related to employment for women of all socioeconomic origins.* A large minority continue in school. Single daughters of highly educated mothers are most likely of all women to be in school only, in 1964. The situation is clearly different for *married* women. In Table 4 we learn that socioeconomic origins are important in influencing the early careers of married college-graduated women. *The lower the family income, the more likely the woman is to be employed and the less likely she is to be a full-time homemaker.*

Full-time homemaking is more frequently an activity of higher income women. The data suggest that women from high-income origins are channeled into homemaking as a viable career alternative. Married women from low-income origins who have made it through college, however, appear less likely to give up their hard-won educations to full-time homemaking, and it is unlikely that they can afford to do so financially. Further, it appears that women from high-income origins are more likely to be married to men from high-income origins and with more promising future careers (see Funk's 1969 analysis of these data). In this way, women from high-income origins may have found full-time homemaking and marriage to a successful man a substitute for their own potential careers in the female-dominated semiprofessions.

In this sample, low-income-origin married women are more likely than high-income-origin women not only to be employed, but also to be going to school at the same time. Thus, while only 4 percent of the married women from the highest family income origins are in school while they are employed, this figure increases to 12 percent for women from the poorest family backgrounds.

Married women who are full-time students are not more likely to come from high-income families. Among married women, very few (3 percent) are full-time students. Married women from high-income origins are not more likely than women from low-income origins to attend school full time.

How can we explain these findings with regard to early career activity? Let us begin by looking at the *single* women. Almost all college-educated women who have not gotten married by the time they are in their mid-twenties, regardless of socioeconomic origins, work in the paid labor force. They do so for a combination of reasons: to provide for their own support, to gain experience, to establish a career in the labor market, and to establish an independent and single life style, as well as to "keep busy" or to look for the "right husband."

In addition, many single women continue their education, although the majority do this while they are employed. It is primarily the single daughters of graduate-school-educated parents who are the most likely to be in school as their main activity.[7] Parental role models and socioeconomic environments which are conducive to

TABLE 4
EARLY CAREER ACTIVITY OF SINGLE AND MARRIED
WOMEN BY FAMILY OF ORIGIN INCOME

Career Activity	Family of Origin Income			
	Under $5,000	$5,000 to under $15,000	$15,000 or More	Total
Single				
Employed only	80%	75%	76%	76%
Employed and in school	15	18	16	17
School only	5	7	8	7
Overall school	20	25	24	24
	100%	100%	100%	100%
	(839)	(2411)	(721)	(3971)
Married				
Employed only	50%	50%	40%	48%
Employed and in school	8	8	6	8
School only	3	3	4	3
Homemaker only	39	39	50	40
	100%	100%	100%	99%*
	(1276)	(4784)	(1699)	(7759)

*Due to rounding.

educational achievement appear to be important in influencing single women to undertake full-time graduate education. These women are still in school three years after college graduation; thus they will have the greatest likelihood of being employed in elite, high-status male professions such as medicine and law.

With regard to *married* women, the fact that socioeconomic origins play an important role in influencing early career activity receives support from several sources. To repeat, not only are women from upper-income origins more likely to be full-time homemakers and less likely to be employed in the labor force than lower-income-origin married women, but they are also less likely to be in school than lower-income-origin women. In fact, lower-income-origin married women show a clear trend toward being in school when they also work in the paid labor force.

One possible overall explanation for these findings is that since it is much more difficult for children of poor parents to complete college, after graduation these women would be less likely to settle for homemaking as their sole activity. Moreover, financial disadvantages would thrust daughters of poorer parents into the labor force more quickly than daughters of better-off parents. White (1967), Siegal (1976), and

Levine (1968) all suggest that college is a "vocational training ground" for lower-socioeconomic-origin students in contrast to a "broadening experience" for higher-socioeconomic-origin students. In our case, the vast majority of low-socioeconomic-origin women were trained at vocationally oriented teachers' colleges.

An unexpected finding for low-income-origin married women emerges from this data: they appear more likely than high-income-origin married women to go to post-college school *if they are employed* at the same time. Since many of these lower-strata-origin women may have married men from similar origins, they would *both* probably need to work to maintain their newly won middle-class status.

High-income-origin women are often married to men from similarly high socioeconomic origins who have promising careers in business and the professions. These women become full-time homemakers and gain status and rewards through their husbands' careers instead of their own. This is due to the fact that occupational opportunities available to college-educated women are more restricted to low pay and relatively low status (in comparison to their husbands' opportunities) in a sex-segregated labor market (Oppenheimer, 1970; Blaxall and Reagan, 1976; U.S. Department of Labor, Employment Standards Administration, 1976).

Women from higher socioeconomic origins who marry the "appropriate" husbands (usually in terms of class, race, and religion) are more likely to entertain within the home and to pursue leisure, cultural, and community activities that are more prestigious, status-granting, and nonfinancially rewarding (Domhoff, 1970; Funk, 1969). Opportunities and responsibilities to gain status and satisfaction through unpaid, voluntary activities, as well as through "self-improvement" activities (Fidell and Prather, as reported in Tavris, 1976), are more accessible to the wives of higher status men, decreasing these women's labor force activity.

Many daughters of upper- and middle-strata backgrounds are encouraged to attend college to find the "appropriate" husband.[8] College is not only an occupational training ground but also a "marriage broker." This appears to be increasingly true the higher up the socioeconomic ladder one goes.

Cynthia Fuchs Epstein (1971) pointed out that women are faced with the "double bind" when they are in the typically middle- and upper-middle-class environment of college. They have been encouraged to achieve academically all through their early school years. In college they must alter their behavior so they focus on marriage rather than occupational achievement as their "primary" responsibility. Both men and women are sent to college in part to find "appropriate" partners. This takes women out of the labor market while it ensures men their entrance into it. Thus marriage appears to decrease the occupational activities of upper-strata women more than lower-strata women. That this phenomenon is changing with increase of young women twenty-five to thirty-four and mothers of young children in the labor force during the 1970s and 1980s should not obscure the fact that women's responsibilities for home, child, and husband care do not disappear (Vanek, 1977; Poloma and Garland, 1971). Problems emerging from women's dual home and market responsibilities may be intensified as women are encouraged to think of themselves as market workers, as well as housewives and mothers. The inflationary period that has developed since the early 1960s is requiring more than one wage earner in each family (Kolko, 1978; Sokoloff, 1980), at the very same time that more and more women are on their own—as single, divorced, separated, widowed, or married women not living with their husbands (Brown, 1979).

OCCUPATIONS OF SINGLE AND MARRIED WOMEN FROM DIFFERENT SOCIOECONOMIC BACKGROUNDS

In the previous section we indicated that while class origins do not influence the early careers of single women, they do so for married women. In this section we learn that socioeconomic background is important in determining the occupational type of *both* married and single women.

In Table 5 we find the following patterns: (1) In all socioeconomic strata, the majority of women, both single and married, are found in the female-dominated semiprofessions. (2) However, the higher the family of origin income, the less likely a woman is to be found in these semiprofessions; and (3) the more likely she will be employed, first, in high-status male-dominated occupations and, second, in low-status clerical work. What this means is that low-income women are more likely to be employed in more traditional female occupations, the semiprofessions; and high-income women are more likely to be employed in occupations that are atypical for female college graduates: both high-status male-dominated jobs and low-status female nonprofessional jobs (clerical work). Moreover, this is true for both single and married women. Thus socioeconomic origin has an independent effect for the types of occupations female college graduates enter in their early employment activity.

A look at the effect of marital status within each family-income group indicates the following: (1) Within each socioeconomic grouping, married women are more likely than single women to be working in the semiprofessions.[9] (2) Within each socioeconomic grouping, single women are more likely to be employed in high-status male-dominated occupations than married women.[10] (3) With regard to

TABLE 5
EARLY OCCUPATIONS OF SINGLE AND MARRIED WOMEN
BY FAMILY OF ORIGIN INCOME

Occupation Type	Family of Origin Income			
	Less than $5,000	$5,000 to under $15,000	$15,000 or More	Total
Single				
Professional	20%	21%	30%	22%
Semiprofessional	72	69	51	67
Clerical	8	10	19	11
	100%	100%	100%	100%
	(742)	(2078)	(604)	(3424)
Married				
Professional	12	16	20	16
Semiprofessional	82	76	63	74
Clerical	7	8	17	10
	101%*	100%	100%	100%
	(740)	(2589)	(737)	(4066)
Total				
Professional	16	18	24	19
Semiprofessional	77	73	58	71
Clerical	7	9	18	10
	100%	100%	100%	100%
	(1482)	(4672)	(1342)	(7501)

*Due to rounding.

low-status clerical work, however, marital status makes no difference: a small percentage of single and married women in both low- and middle-income-origin families are clerical workers, whereas a larger percentage of both single and married women in high-income-origin families are clerical workers.

In summary, being single appears to be related to being employed in atypical occupations for *female* college graduates: especially in high-status male-oriented occupations. This is true across socioeconomic strata. In contrast, married women from all socioeconomic strata are more likely to be employed in the female semiprofessions.

Socioeconomic origins also independently influence occupational experiences for both single and married women. Coming from higher-income origins predisposes women to be employed in the atypical occupations for college graduates (*both* high-status male-dominated jobs and low-status clerical jobs), and decreases the likelihood that these women will be employed in the female-dominated semiprofessions. Instead, the more traditional occupations (semiprofessions) for female college graduates are most often chosen by low-income-origin women.

Socioeconomic origins and marital status both have independent effects on the types of occupations in which women are employed three years after college graduation in the mid-1960s. First, socioeconomic origins are important for early occupations of women, regardless of their marital status. And second, marital status is important in influencing women to enter the semiprofessions and high-status male-dominated occupations, regardless of the women's socioeconomic origins. Marital status does not influence low-status clerical employment, while socioeconomic origins do. Socioeconomic origins determine the early careers of married women but not the careers of single women, and also help to determine—in the same direction—the occupational experiences of both single and married women.

HOW CAN WE INTERPRET THESE FINDINGS?

How might we explain these findings with regard to female college graduates' early careers and specific occupational employment?

First of all I suggested earlier that being a *single* college graduate means that one is likely to be employed in the labor force. Whether they expect to be married and full-time homemakers or are interested in singlehood and full-time careers in the labor force, highly educated single women from all social strata do work in the paid labor force. Among *married* women—even women with children—employment in the labor force is more common for women from low-income origins and homemaking is more common for women from high-income backgrounds.

When we look at the occupational experiences of employed women with college degrees, we learn that women who are *married* are more likely to work in traditional female jobs: the semiprofessions. Thus women who find themselves in more traditional roles as housewives are employed in more traditional jobs outside the home as well. This is true for women from high- as well as low-income origins. For the low-income-origin women, however, this represents a tremendous amount of upward mobility.

Single women from all socioeconomic origins, on the other hand, are more likely than married women to end up in high-status male-dominated occupations, those that are atypical for women. Several studies document the greater likelihood of women who are in graduate education and in male professional schools to be single (Ginzberg, 1966; Astin, 1971; Trigg and Perlman, 1976; and Bernard, 1975). One theory suggests that whether these women are single voluntarily or involuntarily, single educated women put their energies into developing their higher-status professional lives rather than investing these energies in their families. Jessie Bernard (1964) contends that in the unmarried population, "among women it is often the cream of the crop who are not married; among men, the rejects" (p. 211).

At this point we should note that our initial hypotheses are confirmed: single women are more likely than married women to participate in employment and school; and they are more likely to be found in high-status male-dominated occupations. Moreover, this is true for women from all socioeconomic strata. What is unexpected is that women from well-to-do backgrounds are more than twice as likely as women from poorer backgrounds (see Table 5) to be found working in low-status clerical jobs (18 percent compared with 7 percent). This is true for single women as well as married women. How can we explain this?

First we might test the theory that the best-qualified people will be the most likely to obtain the best jobs in society. Thus some women coming from high socioeconomic origins may have been able to get through college but, according to this theory, are not really able to perform well (based on some measure of intellectual or academic performance) in the professions (male *or* female dominated) and therefore may end up working in lower-status clerical types of jobs. This, however, is simply not the case.

The best available measure of academic performance was that of female college graduates' college grade-point average, which shows no relationship to either early career activity (homemaking, employment, or postcollege schooling) or occupation. What does show a very strong relationship with occupational type is the quality of the school from which the women graduated in 1961. Both married and single women graduating from high-quality schools are much more likely than those graduating from low-quality schools to be employed three years later in *both* low-status clerical *and* high-status male-dominated occupations. And school quality is highly related to socioeconomic origins of the women.

Class origins appear to be critical in determining school quality, which in turn is instrumental in explaining which jobs women enter in the labor force. The women's academic capabilities are not the determining factors in their occupational choice. Rather, schools channel women from different class origins into different types of occupations.

A second possible explanation would be that women of high-income origins would be more likely than women of low-income origins to be found in low-status clerical work because they are either waiting to get married or are working until their husbands are able to support them as full-time homemakers and mothers.

Homemaking as a desired full-time status for upper-income-origin women should be reflected in their long-term career aspirations. Thus we expect high-income-origin women employed as clericals to be more likely than low-income-origin women employed as clericals to *desire* to be full-time homemakers in the future. A look at Table 6 shows that this is precisely the case.

In Table 6 we see that while very few single women aspire to be full-time homemakers (8 percent), it is clearly single women of high-income backgrounds (17 percent) who are the most likely to have such aspirations. And, among married women, the higher the family of origin income the greater the likelihood that women will want to be full-time homemakers (from 13 percent among low-income-origin married women to 38 percent for high-income-origin married women). Clearly, hardly any women aspire to low-status clerical jobs.

Further our hypothesis is confirmed (data not shown) that women employed specifically as low-status clerical workers are more likely than women employed in other occupations to aspire to be home-

TABLE 6
LONG-TERM CAREER ASPIRATIONS IN 1964 OF SINGLE AND MARRIED FEMALE COLLEGE GRADUATES, CONTROLLING FOR FAMILY OF ORIGIN INCOME

| Long-Term Career Aspirations* | Family of Origin Income | | | |
	Under $5,000	$5,000 to $15,000	$15,000 or more	**Total**
Single				
Homemaker	7%	6%	17%	8%
Clerical	2	2	4	2
Semiprofessional	61	66	45	61
Professional	30	26	35	28
	100%	100%	101%**	99%**
	(791)	(2258)	(674)	(3273)
Married				
Homemaker	13	21	38	23
Clerical	2	1	2	1
Semiprofessional	69	60	45	58
Professional	16	18	16	18
	100%	100%	101%**	100%
	(1230)	(4550)	(1616)	(7396)

*In long-term career aspiration, "professional" contains only male professionals and male managers. It was not possible to code in-between professionals here. The vast majority of women report the desire to be in male professions who are in this male-dominated professional category, not managerial positions.
**Due to rounding.

makers in each strata. When we compare just those women in clerical work across strata, the higher the family of origin income, the greater the likelihood that a low-status clerical worker aspires to be a full-time homemaker. Thus almost four times as many high- as low-income-origin women employed in 1964 in low-status clerical jobs hope to be full-time homemakers in the future.

It is reasonable to conclude that high-income college-educated women who are employed in low-status clerical work tend to be in a "holding pattern." Single women may be employed in such occupations until they are married. Married women may be waiting until their husbands have finished school or are established enough to allow them to enter into full-time homemaking and motherhood careers, which offer possibilities for status and self-fulfillment.

A third possibility is that women in low-status jobs have limited mobility aspirations because of the nature of the work and the difficulty of moving upward in the system (Kanter, 1977). Under these conditions homemaking and motherhood may become more appealing alternatives to employment, especially among women who have greater opportunities to experience satisfaction through their husbands' careers.

A second unexpected finding has to do with the high-status male-dominated occupations in which single women are more likely to be employed. When we control for social strata among single women in these male-dominated occupations (Table 7), we find, as expected, that women in each social stratum are more likely to be employed in the highest-status male professions. But the low- and middle-income-origin single women, not high-income-origin women, are more likely (59 and 58 percent compared to 46 percent) to be in the highest-status male professions. Single women from the most advantaged backgrounds are more likely to be employed in either in-between professions or male managerial positions. The findings for married women in high-status male-dominated occupations (Table 7) likewise show that low- and middle-income women in these occupations are more likely to be in the highest-status male professions, while high-income-origin women are more likely to be employed in male managerial positions.

Hennig (1977) helps to clarify some of our findings, but only for the single woman. Tracing the lives of twenty-five women who were presidents or vice-presidents of large business and financial corporations, she found that they had all excelled academically. "Three years after graduation they were secretaries or administrative assistants either in manufacturing, retailing, banking, public relations or service companies. Most of these positions were created as favors to their fathers. . . . Over the next thirty years, every one of them remained with the same firm until they were rewarded with a top

TABLE 7

EARLY OCCUPATIONAL EXPERIENCES OF SINGLE AND
MARRIED WOMEN EMPLOYED IN HIGH STATUS MALE DOMI-
NATED OCCUPATIONS, BY FAMILY OF ORIGIN INCOME.

High-Status Male-Dominated Occupations	Family of Origin Income			
	Under $5,000	$5,000 to under $15,000	$15,000 or More	Total
Single				
In-Between Professional	24%	20%	30%	23%
Male Manager	17	21	24	21
Male Professional*	59	58	46	56
	100%	99%**	100%	100%
	(146)	(439)	(180)	(765)
Married				
In-Between Professional	33	22	32	26
Male Manager	3	15	28	16
Male Professional	63	63	40	58
	99%**	100%	100%	100%
	(87)	(409)	(149)	(645)

*"Male professional" refers *only* to male-dominated *professions*.
**Due to rounding.

management position" (Sheehy, 1976, pp. 323, 324).[11] This may help to explain why so many more women in my sample from high-income origins are either in low-status clerical jobs or are likely to be in higher-level male managerial positions, on their way up to the few executive positions occupied by women.[12]

All of Hennig's sample had depended on male mentors, who were said to be *in loco pater,* and all were single until their mid-thirties. At this time half of them married within two years, while the others looked for appropriate partners and were unable to find them. A control group of women frozen at middle-management levels were also dedicated to their employers, but all remained single in mid-life. However, this group appears to have been employed as secretaries and managerial assistants in their early careers.

IMPLICATIONS FOR THE FUTURE

While comparable data are not available for female college graduates today, certain general comparisons are possible. First, between 1968 and 1978 female college graduates increased their participation in the labor force from 58 to 66 percent (Brown, 1979). With the increasing demand for women of childbearing age in the labor market in the 1970s, we would expect to find an even larger percentage of such a group of women in the labor force in the 1980s.

In terms of the type of job held by these women, between 1968 and 1978, the percentage of employed female college graduates working in all professional, technical, and managerial jobs (as defined by the Bureau of the Census)[13] *dropped* from 86 to 74 percent (Brown, 1979), with a comparable increase in clerical and sales work and a much smaller increase in low-status service jobs. Between 1940 and 1970 the greatest increase in female employment occurred in jobs that were low in complexity and autonomy, and in educational and training requirements (as demonstrated by the functional nature of the work rather than the educational attainment of the incumbents); they were heavily supervised and, above all, poorly paid (Dubnoff, 1979). Increased educational requirements, or job upgrading, has been shown to exist for men with a tendency toward technicalization of professional jobs (Rodriguez, 1978). Recent estimates are that women will experience a major decline in elementary school teacher openings, the largest source of jobs for college-educated women until today. Instead, the largest proportionate increases in professional and technical women's jobs (the semiprofessions) are predicted to be in the health field, as dental hygienists, medical therapists, and clinical laboratory technologists, with heavy increases in nursing (Rosenbaum, 1979). One out of every four college graduates "will have to enter nontraditional occupations[14] or face unemployment" (Rosenbaum, 1979, p. 8).

What all this implies is that it may be more difficult for women in college today to attain even the levels of occupational achievement that existed in the past. Jaffe and Froomkin (1978) show both male and female college graduates obtaining lower-paying entry jobs and having greater difficulty moving up the job ladder in 1970–1975 than during the previous twenty years. They predict that the continuing decline in teaching opportunities for college-educated women will mean that "increasing proportions of women graduates will start, and probably end, their careers in clerical jobs" (p. 20).

Both cheaper and better-educated labor are increasingly in demand. Thus the vast majority of single women are employed today, and the highest-educated women are the most heavily employed. And increasingly, married women even with very young children are in demand in the marketplace. Any analysis of career and specific occupational experiences of single and married women from different socioeconomic origins must look at the political and sexual economy in which they operate. This must be the task of the future if we truly want to improve home and market experiences and the opportunities of women in our society.

NOTES

1. Information in this section is taken from U.S. Department of Labor, Women's Bureau (1969, 1975), and Hayghe (1978) unless otherwise specified.

2. In 1977 married women (with husbands) made up 57 percent of all women in the labor force, single women only 24 percent.

3. It was felt that since the average family income in the early 1960s was above $5,000, a category of less than $5,000 (the lowest category classified in the NORC analysis) would adequately represent college-educated women from lower socioeconomic strata.

4. All available data indicate that women employed full-time are not necessarily employed both full-time and year-round (U.S. Department of Labor, Employment Standards Administration, 1976). This is likely the case for our respondents too. However, full-time employment rates for professional women are much higher than for other employed women (Patterson and Engelberg, 1978; Deckard, 1979).

5. Almost three-fourths of all women professionals are either teachers or nurses and allied health workers (U.S. Department of Labor, Women's Bureau, 1975). These jobs are typically classified as semiprofessions: bureaucratically organized jobs, whose workers carry out someone else's orders, since they do not have legal monopoly over knowledge and/or delivery of services in their own field (e.g., the medical profession is dominated by doctors rather than nurses). In contrast, traditionally male-dominated professions, such as physicians, lawyers, etc., are only 10 percent female (Theodore, 1971).

6. It is also possible that the experience of being employed may influence a woman to remain single.

7. Both mothers and fathers with graduate educations themselves are more likely than all other parents to have single daughters who are themselves enrolled in graduate school (on a full-time basis, most likely). However, the impact of the mother's education is greater than that of the father's in this case. Moreover, single daughters of *employed*, well-educated mothers are more likely than the daughters of homemaker, well-educated mothers to be in graduate school. This raises the question of the importance of the mother's own educational and occupational experiences as a role model for her daughter.

8. Men are likewise sent to college for the dual purpose of occupational training and "wife hunting." Thus men are sent to college not only to get the necessary training to place them in society's social class system, but also to find the "appropriate" wife who will socialize their children and manage their homes for them.

9. E.g., in low-income-origin families (under $5,000), 72 percent of single women are in the semiprofessions, while 82 percent of married women are so employed. For middle-income-origin women ($5,000 to under $15,000), the figures are 69 percent of the single vs. 76 percent of the married women; and for high-income-origin women ($15,000 or more), they are 51 percent for the single and 63 percent for the married women.

10. Thus, for low-income-origin women, 20 percent of the single and only 12 percent of the married women work in high-status male-dominated occupations. Likewise, in middle-income families, the figures are 21 percent vs. 16 percent; and in high-income families they are 30 percent vs. 20 percent.

11. The importance of mentors in women's careers is substantiated by Epstein (1972) and Poll (1978).

12. Perhaps the classification as secretarial is misleading in the system used by NORC. Or perhaps it simply reflects the kinds of jobs that were made available as favors to the high-achieving daughters of well-to-do men.

13. In this case, professions included both male professions and female semiprofessions.

14. Nontraditional here appears to refer to jobs that do not measure up to the educational qualifications of the college graduate.

REFERENCES

Adams, Margaret. *Single Blessedness: Observations on the Single Status in Married Society.* New York: Basic Books, 1976.

Astin, Helen S. *The Woman Doctorate in America: Origins, Career and Family.* New York: Russell Sage Foundation, 1971.

Bernard, Jesse. *Academic Women.* New York: New American Library Inc., 1964.

————. *Women, Wives, Mothers: Values and Options.* Chicago: Aldine Publ. Co., 1975.

Blaxall, Martha, and Reagan, Barbara B., eds. "Women and the Workplace: The Implications of Occupational Segregation." *Signs,* III (Spring, 1976).

Bowles, Samuel, and Gintis, Herbert. *Schooling in Capitalist America.* New York: Basic Books Inc., 1976.

Brown, Scott Campbell. "Educational Attainment of Workers—Some Trends from 1973 to 1978." Reprinted from *Monthly Labor Review,* February, 1979, with supplementary tables, 54–58 and A–1 to A–22.

Chase, Ivan. "A Comparison of Men's and Women's Intergenerational Mobility in the United States." *American Sociological Review,* XL (August, 1975), 483–505.

Davis, James A. *Great Aspirations.* Chicago: Aldine Publ. Co., 1964.

Deckard, Barbara Sinclair. *The Women's Movement: Political, Socioeconomic, and Psychological Issues,* Second Edition. New York: Harper & Row Pubs. Inc., 1979.

De Jong, Peter Y.; Brawer, Milton J.; and Robin, Stanley S. "Patterns of Female Intergenerational Occupational Mobility: A Comparison with Male Patterns of Intergenerational Occupational Mobility." *American Sociological Review,* XXXVI (December, 1971), 1033–42.

Domhoff, G. William. *The Higher Circles: The Governing Class in America.* New York: Vintage, 1970.

Dubnoff, Steven. "Beyond Sex Typing: Capitalism, Patriarchy and the Growth of Female Employment, 1940–1970." Paper presented at the meetings of the Eastern Sociological Society, New York, March, 1979.

Elder, Glenn. "Appearance and Education in Marriage Mobility." *American Sociological Review,* XLIII (August, 1969), 510–33.

Epstein, Cynthia. *Woman's Place: Options and Limits in Professional Careers.* Berkeley: University of California Press, 1971.

———. "Encountering the Male Establishment: Sex-Status Limits on Women's Careers in the Professions." *Sociological Perspectives on Occupations.* Edited by Ronald Pavalko. Itasca, Ill.: F. E. Peacock Pubs. Inc., 1972.

Featherman, David L., and Hauser, Robert M. "Sexual Inequalities and Socioeconomic Achievement in the U.S., 1962–1973." *American Sociological Review,* XLI (June, 1976), 462–83.

Funk, Nathalie Ostroot. "Social Mobility through Marriage." Unpublished Ph.D. dissertation, University of Chicago, 1969.

Ginzberg, Eli. *Educated American Women: Life Styles and Portraits.* New York: Columbia University Press, 1966.

Glenn, Norval D.; Ross, Adreain, A.; and Tully, Judy Corder. "Patterns of Intergenerational Mobility of Females Through Marriage." *American Sociological Review,* XXXIX (October, 1974), 683–99.

Hayghe, Howard. "Marital and Family Characteristics of Workers, March 1977." *Monthly Labor Review,* CI (February, 1978), 51–54, with supplementary tables.

Hennig, Margaret, with Anne Jardim. *Women & Management.* New York: Doubleday, 1977.

Jaffe, A. J., and Froomkin, Joseph. "Occupational Opportunities for College-Educated Workers, 1950–1975." *Monthly Labor Review,* CI (June, 1978), 15–21.

Jencks, Christopher; with Smith, Marshall; Acland, Henry; Bane, Mary Jo; Cohen, David; Gintis, Herbert; Heyns, Barbara; and Michelson, Stephen. *Inequality: A Reassessment of the Effect of Family and Schooling in America.* New York: Harper & Row Pubs. Inc., 1972.

Kanter, Rosabeth Moss. *Men and Women of the Corporation.* New York: Basic Books Inc., 1977.

Kolko, Gabriel. "Working Wives: Their Effects on the Structure of the Working Class." *Science and Society,* XLII (Fall, 1978), 257–77.

Levine, Adele G. "Marital and Occupational Plans in Professional Schools: Law, Medicine, Nursing and Teaching." Unpublished Ph.D. dissertation, Yale University, 1968.

McClendon, McKee. "The Occupational Status Attainment Process of Males and Females." *American Sociological Review,* XLI (February, 1976), 52–64.

National Opinion Research Center. "Codebook for the June 1961 College Graduate Study." Unpublished manuscript, Chicago: NORC, 1974.

Oppenheimer, Valerie Kincaide. *The Female Labor Force in the United States.* Berkeley: Institute of International Studies, University of California, 1970.

Patterson, Michelle, and Engelberg, Laurie. "Women in Male-Dominated Professions." *Women Working.* Edited by Ann H. Stromberg and Shirley Harkess. Palo Alto: Mayfield Publ. Co., 1978.

Poll, Carol. "No Room At the Top: A Study of the Social Processes that Contribute to the Underrepresentation of Women on the Administrative Levels of the New York City School System." Unpublished Ph.D. dissertation, City University of New York, Graduate Center, 1978.

Poloma, Margaret M., and Garland, T. Neal. "The Myth of the Egalitarian Family: Familial Roles and the Professionally Employed Wife." *The Professional Woman.* Edited by Athena Theodore. Cambridge, Mass.: Schenkman Publ. Co., 1971.

Rodriguez, Orlando. "Occupational Shifts and Educational Upgrading in the American Labor Force Between 1950 and 1970." *Sociology of Education,* LI (January, 1978), 55–67.

Rosenbaum, David E. "Jobs: The Skills, Then The Place." *The New York Times National Recruitment Survey,* October 14, 1979, XII: 1, 8, and 9.

Rubin, Zick. "Do American Women Marry Up?" *American Sociological Review,* XXXIII (October, 1968), 750–60.

Sewell, William H. "Inequality of Opportunity for Higher Education." *American Sociological Review,* XXXVI (October, 1971), 793–809.

Sheehy, Gail. *Passages: Predictable Crises of Adult Life.* New York: Bantam Books and E. P. Dutton & Co., 1976.

Siegal, Karolynn. "Social Class and the Decision to Attend College." Unpublished Ph.D. dissertation, New York University, 1976.

Sokoloff, Natalie J. *Between Money and Love: The Dialectics of Women's Home and Market Work.* New York: Praeger Publ. Co., 1980.

Tavris, Carol. "Women: Work Isn't Always the Answer." *Psychology Today,* X (September, 1976), 78.

Theodore, Athena. "The Professional Women: Trends and Prospects." *The Professional Woman.* Edited by Athena Theodore. Cambridge, Mass.: Schenkman Publ. Co., 1971.

Trieman, Donald J., and Terrell, Kermit. "Sex and the Process of Status Attainment: A Comparison of Working Women and Men." *American Sociological Review,* XL (April, 1975), 174–200.

Trigg, Linda J., and Perlman, Daniel. "Social Influence on Women's Pursuit of a Nontraditional Career." *Psychology of Women Quarterly,* I (Winter, 1976), 138–50.

Tyree, Andrea, and Treas, Judith. "The Occupational and Marital Mobility of Women." *American Sociological Review,* XXIX (June, 1974), 293–302.

U.S. Department of Labor, Employment Standards Administration. "The Earnings Gap between Women and Men." Washington, D.C.: Women's Bureau, 1976.

U.S. Department of Labor, Women's Bureau. *1969 Handbook on Women Workers.* Washington, D.C.: U.S. Government Printing Office, 1969.

———. *1975 Handbook on Women Workers.* Washington, D.C.: U.S. Government Printing Office, 1975.

Vanek, Joanne. "The New Family Equality: Myth or Reality?" Paper presented at the annual meeting of the American Sociological Association, Chicago, September, 1977.

White, Kinnard. "Social Background Variables Related to Career Commitment of Women Teachers." *The Personnel and Guidance Journal*, XLV (March 1967), 648–52.

Women's Bureau. "College Women Seven Years After Graduation: Resurvey of Women Graduates, Class of 1957." *The Professional Woman*. Edited by Athena Theodore. Cambridge, Mass.: Schenkman Publ. Co., 1971.

20/ IS MARRIAGE A PRIORITY? Class Differences in Marital Options of Educated Black Women

Elizabeth Higginbotham

Over the past few decades researchers have found that a high percentage of educated black women are single. This study investigates class and cultural factors leading to that singlehood. Both middle-class and lower-middle-class parents value educational attainment but vary in the degree to which they stress marriage for their daughters. Women from black middle-class homes are expected to integrate careers with family life. Upwardly mobile women from lower-middle-class backgrounds had parents who were not assured of upward mobility solely through marriage and therefore focused on educational success to the exclusion of other goals. The process of being socially mobile necessitates concentrating energy on adjusting to new environments and modes of interaction; consequently it forces many black women from lower-middle-class backgrounds to postpone marriage. It is important to recognize social class origins, along with current social class position, in deciphering the marital patterns of educated black women and other populations.

Every year more adults are remaining single and postponing their first marriage (Glick, 1975). Heretofore most of the research on singlehood has been limited to white, urban, middle-class people (Adams, 1974; Stein, 1976; Etzkowitz and Stein, 1978). There is a need to broaden the study of single people to include all races, ethnic groups, and social classes because the antecedents to and the styles of adapting to singlehood can differ among such groups from those of the dominant culture. In this case, the focus will be on the effect of social mobility on educated single black women.

Early twentieth-century social scientists, such as Charles Johnson, found a high rate of unmarried women as opposed to men among educated black people (Johnson, 1938/1969). Later studies, especially those by black researchers, focused on the problems faced by this population (Cuthbert, 1942; Noble, 1956). While higher education opened up marriage possibilities for black men, these early studies gave an indication that higher education limited marital options for black women. Being black, female, and single in family-oriented white America in the 1930s, 1940s, and 1950s has been described as difficult for black women. Yet during the past two decades an increasing number of men and women of both races are remaining single, and activities and markets are directed toward this growing population. Since singlehood is becoming accepted as a legitimate life style, one cannot examine young, single black women today with the assumptions of isolation and unhappiness that earlier research accepted.

An investigation of current marital trends among the black population still shows higher rates of singlehood among black women than among white women (see Table 1). The percentages of single black women is smaller in the upper age brackets than for the young age groups, which indicates that black women are continuing to marry, but many are doing so later in life. Nevertheless, black people are remaining single at a greater rate than whites. There are relevant demographic factors; for example, there are more black women than black men. Yet this might be balanced by the possibility of interracial marriage, especially for this educated population.

Researchers have often assumed the inevitability of singlehood for black women who pursue higher education, but it is important not to equate getting an education with remaining single. It should be noted that some black women from lower-middle-class and working-class families do marry during and directly after college. Yet the evidence suggests a common mobility pattern which many black women follow in which they postpone marriage.

The data for this study are drawn from a larger study relating social class backgrounds to the mobility strategies of black women who graduated from predominantly white coeducational colleges in a northeastern city in the years 1968 to 1970. There was a total of fifty-six participants, all in their late twenties and early thirties at the time of the study. Of the fifty-six participants, thirty-one were married, five were divorced, and twenty were single. A systematically

TABLE 1

PERCENTAGE OF NEVER MARRIED BLACK AND WHITE
WOMEN BY AGE: MARCH, 1977 (NUMBERS IN THOUSANDS)

| | Black Women | | White Women | |
Age	Total Number	% Single	Total Number	% Single
20–24	1,265	60.5	8,348	42.9
25–29	1,044	26.3	7,623	14.9
30–34	836	14.8	6,538	5.9
35–39	718	13.1	5,368	4.2
40–44	665	5.9	4,931	4.5
45–54	1,211	6.7	10,638	3.9
55–64	945	4.6	9,554	4.7

Source: U.S. Bureau of the Census (1978).

selected group of twenty was chosen from the larger group of fifty six. The twenty women interviewed differed in occupation and marital situation; seven were single, two were divorced, and eleven were currently married.

Although the majority of black students in college in the 1960s and 1970s were among the first generation in their families to attend college, there were also college students from established middle-class families. The social class backgrounds of the participants reflect differences in their parents' economic resources, which influence how the families prepare their daughters for adult roles. Parents' level of education and their occupational positions were used to identify the participants' social class positions.

The two categories used for comparison are "middle class" and "lower middle class." Middle-class families are those in which at least one parent completed college. Most of these parents worked in professional or semiprofessional occupations. For example, three of the participants gave their parents' occupations as: physician and housewife; elementary school principal and teacher; police detective and teacher. These parents had sound economic resources, worked in occupations which were intrinsically rewarding, and had status in both the black and white communities. Because of their positions, they had knowledge of and insights into middle-class institutions that enabled them to help their daughters duplicate their own social class positions.

The participants from lower-middle-class families had parents with some high-school education and often a diploma. These parents worked in a variety of occupations, most of which were stable jobs: fathers were postal clerks, skilled craftsmen, semiskilled factory workers; mothers tended to have clerical or sales positions. The lower-middle-class women were from families often identified as middle class in the black community because of their values and support of community institutions, yet they lacked the economic resources and respected occupations essential for recognition in the wider society. These parents worked diligently to enable their children to advance. Six participants could be identified as coming from homes less financially stable than lower middle class. Parents in this group did not differ significantly in terms of educational attainment from lower-middle-class parents but had been less able to find stable employment. Yet these particular families are unique among poorer black families because of the sacrifices the parents made for their daughters' education. They share with the lower-middle-class families a lack of information available to people more at ease in middle-class institutions, which would shape the type of strategy they develop for their daughters' mobility.

It has been generally accepted in American society that marriage is the ideal state in adulthood. Yet there are distinct differences in the degree to which people are expected and encouraged to marry. Parents of the participants in this study from both social classes communicated high expectations for the educational attainment of their daughters, but they differed in the conscious attempts to socializing their daughters for marriage.

As one can see in Table 2, a higher percentage of unmarried women were from lower-middle-class families, and the fact that the upwardly mobile participants have a higher rate of singlehood than established middle-class black women participants merits close examination.

When participants were asked what expectations their parents had for them with regard to life style, career, and marriage, the women from lower-middle-class backgrounds all answered the question in terms of educational expectations. Karen Johnson (names are pseudonyms to protect the identity of the participants) said, "They wanted me to go to college. When we passed the local university on the bus, my mother would tell me I was going to go there." Asked about marriage, Karen responded that her parents never really talked about marriage.

Neglect of personal life goals was also found in the interviews with married participants from lower-middle-class backgrounds. Educational attainment was stressed in their socialization, and this factor most distinguished their lives from those of their parents. Marriage did not merit special attention from their parents and was not a central focus of adolescence and early adulthood.

In contrast to lower-middle-class participants, women from middle-class backgrounds were expected to marry. Sabrina Powell, a middle-class woman who married after she finished college, remarked that her parents' expectations included both a career and family life. Her

TABLE 2
PERCENTAGE OF RESPONDENTS
MARRIED OR NEVER MARRIED, BY
SOCIAL CLASS BACKGROUND

	Social Class	
Marital Status	Lower Middle	Middle
Married	55	72
Never Married	45	28
Total	100	100

father tended to emphasize preparing oneself for employment and her mother stressed marriage and family. Her parents' commitment to employment for her was shaped by their assumption that her family would have priority over a career.

Participants from both social classes were prepared to overcome racist situations and work hard to attain personal goals, but middle-class parents were more able to provide models of how to integrate a professional career with family life. Most of the middle-class mothers had careers, especially in such traditional female fields as education and social work. Middle-class fathers were also strong role models for professional employment. Middle-class participants also received more guidelines and verbal encouragement to fashion a life style around marriage. Their parents expected them to complete their education, marry, have children, and work. In contrast, lower-middle-class women, the first generation in their families to complete college, were socialized to be upwardly mobile and that was their primary concern.

The respondents were asked to choose the life plan which came closest to the expectation they had during their last year in college. The options ranged from "marriage only" to "career only," and most women selected "marriage, children, and full-time career." This response is similar to other research which has found that college-educated black women expect to integrate careers and family roles (Fichter, 1967; Turner and McCaffrey, 1974). Thirty-two percent of the women from lower-middle-class backgrounds indicated that their expectation at the time was "career only," while only 12 percent of the middle-class women selected this choice.

CONSTRAINTS ON UPWARDLY MOBILE BLACK WOMEN

The experience of being socially mobile has a tremendous impact on the women in the study. An enormous amount of energy is expended in leaving a familiar world and entering another (Strauss, 1971). For many this process means a great deal of loneliness and less emphasis on personal issues. Black parents are instrumental in preparing their children for mobility. The participants vividly described how their parents worked hard to find decent schools, visited the public schools to interrupt racist treatment and to advocate for their children, planned after-school activities, helped with homework, provided a great deal of verbal encouragement, and introduced the goal of college attendance. In addition to the family, other black institutions provided support for mobility. In black churches the participants were rewarded for achievements, assumed leadership roles, and had parental goals and values reinforced. From predominantly white institutions, black women were more likely to encounter barriers to mobility and little support for the emotional aspect of the experience. It was up to the participants themselves to learn about middle-class environments and develop strategies to succeed in those settings. Surviving in school and getting into a good college were primary goals, while other life achievements became secondary.

This study was not a full investigation of the personal difficulties the participants faced. Attention was more specifically directed at the mobility strategies. However, the data revealed that many women did spend a few years coping with personal difficulties in climbing the social class ladder. The trip to college often meant distance from family and supportive black institutions. These women had to develop new support networks, which could take years, and those who remained close to their families had to resolve issues related to their new social status. For example, upwardly mobile women had to seek new models for their work orientation, which included building a career, as well as to help them address more personal aspects of their lives.

Katherine Howell, who is currently single, was from a southern lower-middle-class family and she faced a few difficult years adjusting to her elite, predominantly white northern college. Perplexed by what she interpreted as unfriendly attitudes of other black students, she delayed developing a new support network and found it difficult to confront her parents with her unhappiness. She worked diligently at her courses and made a few friends in her dormitory. A couple of years later, feeling more positive about herself as a student, Katherine again began to reach out to people. Then she dated more and developed closer friendships.

During their college years middle-class respondents gave greater attention to their social lives, while respondents from lower-middle-class backgrounds had some difficulty balancing academic concerns with a social life. Nancy Brooks, a married participant from a lower-middle-class family, said she never thought about marriage while in college. "I did not have good models, in terms of my parents, so I pushed those issues aside. I only thought about a career for myself."

The pattern of attending to social life after one's academic standing is secure appears to be common for many black women (Higginbotham, 1974), especially those from the lower middle class. They tended to get high grades, but many were unhappy. Personal issues were often better resolved once the women had secured their social class positions by completing college and moving into work situations.

LIFE AS A SINGLE BLACK WOMAN

At the time of the study, only seven of the twenty unmarried participants selected "career only" as their current life plan preference. When interviewed, only a few women described themselves as committed to singlehood. Most participants were continuing their lives with work goals in mind but were open to the possibility of marrying. Susan Thomas wrote on her questionnaire, "Career only, but I still would like to be married and have children. Currently I have no marriage prospects and try to accept myself as a single woman." Susan's comments reflect the attitude of many educated black women who are single as they approach their thirties. Such women have an interest in developing a family (Mednick and Puryear, 1975) coupled with the need to be prepared to provide for themselves.

The single women from both social class backgrounds varied in their thoughts about their marital status. On the whole, the women interviewed did not appear unhappy, but they did have to devote energy to developing a social life. A number of women from both middle- and lower-middle-class backgrounds were developing intimate relationships as they became established in their careers, and many would eventually marry. Education has given the upwardly mobile black women leverage which may be converted into personal freedom. The middle-class women often had the economic resources to establish that freedom, but some chose to make establishing a career a priority.

SUMMARY AND CONCLUSIONS

This exploration into the routes to singlehood by educated black women from established middle-class and lower-middle-class families found suggestive differences. First, lower-middle-class parents proposed a mobility channel that precluded early marriage. Second, the experience itself necessitated a heavy commitment which often made personal relationships difficult. Middle-class participants were more likely to be socialized to marry, yet these women also internalized values which encouraged employment and even favored careers.

The parents of lower-middle-class women emphasized higher education to prepare their daughters for social mobility. This strategy is reflective of the fact that even married black women have traditionally been forced to work because racist barriers made it difficult for black men to fully provide for their families (Bernard, 1966: Scanzoni, 1971). Current discussion about the imbalance in the sex ratio and the instability of black male and female relationships may also influence black parents to favor a mobility channel which insures their daughters the essential skills and knowledge to survive. Yet many lower-middle-class parents did not consciously expect their daughters to remain single well into their twenties and thirties.

Even though remaining single can be a successful mobility strategy, it is one with many costs. The postponement of intimate relationships was not easily accepted by the participants. Yet their years of struggling in other educational institutions prepared them to endure the difficult college years and a degree of social isolation during their early adult lives. Even if they were not content with their singlehood, they were by now adept at learning how to cope with it.

To what degree is the priority of marriage at a specific time the outcome of structural constraints (i.e., the experience of being upwardly mobile) and to what degree is it an ideological choice? More research which examines the context of peoples' lives and how various marital situations fit in can expand our knowledge of how people continue to make adjustments to the ever changing postindustrial world around us.

NOTE

This article is a revision of a paper presented at the annual meetings of the Society for the Study of Social Problems in San Francisco on September 4, 1978. The author wishes to thank Lynn Weber Cannon, Bonnie Thornton Dill, Kenneth Wagner, and William J. Wilson for their suggestions and encouragement on this version of the paper.

REFERENCES

Adams, Margaret, 1974. "The Single Woman in Today's Society." In *Intimacy, Family, and Society,* edited by Arlene Skolnick and Jerome Skolnick. Boston, Mass.: Little, Brown.

Bernard, Jessie. 1966. *Marriage and Family Among Negroes.* Englewood Cliffs, N.J.: Prentice-Hall, Inc.

Census, U.S. Bureau of the. 1978. "Marital Status and Living Arrangements: March, 1977." *Current Population Reports,* Series P-20, No. 323. Washington, D.C.: U.S. Government Printing Office.

————. 1977. "Population Profile of the United States: 1976." *Current Population Reports,* Series P-20, No. 307. Washington, D.C.: U.S. Government Printing Office.

Cuthbert, Marion. 1942. *Education and Marginality.* New York: Stratford Press.

Etzkowitz, Henry and Peter Stein. 1978. "The Life Spiral: Human Needs and Adult Roles." *Alternative Life Styles* 1 (November): 434–446.

Fichter, Joseph H. 1967. "Career Expectations of Negro Women Graduates." *Monthly Labor Review* 90 (November):36–42.

Glick, Paul. 1975. "Some Recent Changes in American Families." *Current Population Reports,* Special Studies Series P-23, No. 52, U.S. Department of Commerce, Bureau of the Census. Washington, D.C.: U.S. Government Printing Office.

Higginbotham, Elizabeth. 1980. "Educated Black Women: An Exploration into Life Chances and Choices." Unpublished Ph.D. dissertation, Brandeis University.

————. 1974. "Black College Women: An Exploratory Study." Unpublished paper, Brandeis University.

Johnson, Charles. 1969. *The Negro College Graduate.* College Park: McGrath Publishing Company. (Originally published in 1938.)

Mednick, Martha and Gwendolyn Puryear. 1975. "Motivational and Personality Factors Related to Career Goals of Black Women." *Journal of Social and Behavioral Scientists* 21: 1–30.

Noble, Jeanne. 1956. *The Negro Woman's College Education.* New York: Teachers College Press.

Scanzoni, John H. 1971. *The Black Family in Modern Society.* Boston: Allyn & Bacon.

Stein, Peter J. 1976. *Single.* Englewood Cliffs, N.J.: Prentice-Hall, Inc.

Strauss, Anselm L. 1971. *The Context of Social Mobility.* Chicago: Aldine Publishing Co.

Turner, Barbara and Joanne M. McCaffrey. 1974. "Socialization and Career Orientation among Black and White College Women." *Journal of Vocational Behavior* 5: 307–319.

21/ EMPLOYMENT DISCRIMINATION AGAINST GAY MEN

Martin P. Levine

Contrary to prevailing cultural belief, equal opportunity does not typify American employment practices. Instead, there exists widespread discrimination based upon stereotypical qualities associated with stigmatized statuses. This causes high-status occupations to be restricted for the most part to white, Anglo-Saxon, "moral" men.

Because of sanctions against homosexuality, complete statistics on job discrimination are impossible to obtain. Most gay men avoid sanctions by keeping their sexual orientation hidden, which means that the gay community is largely invisible. This article is therefore based on the scientific and lay literature on male homosexuality and on the author's own research. Public-opinion poll data record a willingness on the part of those questioned to discriminate against gay men, and reports by gay activist organizations also furnish some data. Additional material comes from the author's field work in gay ghettos (Levine, 1979).

WILLINGNESS TO DISCRIMINATE

Public-opinion studies frequently report strong support for barring gays from high-status occupations such as judge, teacher, minister, doctor, and government. For example, a 1977 Gallup Poll reported that a substantial proportion of the public felt strong opposition to the employment of homosexuals as elementary school teachers (65 percent), as clergy (54 percent), as doctors (44 percent), and in the armed forces (33 percent). The polls report little opposition to work in low-status occupations such as beautician or florist, and in such areas as art and music.

Discrimination is usually justified by those polled on the basis of homosexual stereotypes: the hopeless neurotic, the moral degenerate, the nelly queen (cf. Levine, 1979). One poll reports widespread acceptance of these notions among Americans: that for most homosexuals sexual orientation is a curable illness; that homosexuals are dangerous as teachers or youth leaders because they try to get sexually involved with children; that homosexuals corrupt fellow workers sexually; that homosexuals have unusually strong sex drives; and that homosexuals behave like the opposite sex (Levitt and Klassan, 1974, pp. 34–39). Though social science research proves these stereotypes to be totally invalid, they are pervasive.

THE DISCRIMINATORY PROCESS

A professed willingness to discriminate often translates into discriminatory employment practices. Research reveals a pattern of systematic discrimination against gay men in hiring, promotion, and firing. There are two kinds of homosexual stigmas: *discredited* (Goffman, 1963, p. 4), the gay man who is publicly known as homosexual either by his own admission or by official record (labeled by courts, psychiatric institutions, or the armed forces); and *discreditable* (Goffman, 1963, p. 4), those who keep their homosexuality hidden from the nongay world. For each stigma there is a related set of discriminatory employment practices.

HIRING

To secure employment gay men must fill out application forms avoiding mention of sexual orientation. For the discredited gay, information on arrests, hospitalization, and military service often reveals homosexuality.

Arrest questions put gays in a "Catch-22" situation. If they disclose arrests for homosexuality, they will be denied a job. If they do not, they can be fired in the future for lying. "Catch-22" also typifies questions about military service. Employers usually require applicants to sign a release of draft records, which include less than honorable discharges or draft deferments for homosexuality. If the applicant states this, employment is generally refused; if he does not, he is usually discharged when records are checked.

Voluntarily discredited men typically choose to disclose sexual orientation on application forms, for example by listing gay politics as a personal interest. In one study (Adam, in press) résumés identical except for sex and sexual orientation were sent to all Ontario law firms. Adam found that gay-labeled résumés were least likely to obtain interview offers. Another barrier to gays exists in questions on application forms about marital status. Employers use the information as an indicator of emotional stability and sexual preference. A man's single status is usually acceptable up to age thirty, after which he is considered emotionally unstable, alcoholic, or homosexual. Since most gays do not marry, this policy clearly victimizes them. In addition, many employment agencies have special arrangements with employers to code applicants as to suspected sexual orientation. One well-known New York agency places the code H.C.F. (High Class Fairy) on the résumés of suspected homosexu-

als. Such inferences clearly victimize single or effeminate homosexuals and heterosexuals.

Yet many gays avoid disclosing sexual orientation and single status
may be covered over by youth, marriages of convenience, and false
separations or divorces. Official labels are hidden through incorrect
responses or lying. For such gays, discrimination often occurs during
subsequent employment.

AFTER EMPLOYMENT

Discrimination after hiring occurs in lack of promotion. To avoid
being held back, gay men must "pass" by concealing homosexuality
under a heterosexual façade. This may be done through "girl watch-
ing" at lunch, bringing women friends to company social events, or
inventing stories about female dates. A middle-management employee of a New York corporation comments:

> Ken and I have been lovers and living together for two
> years. Since no one in my company knows I am gay—if
> they did, they would fire me—I hide our relationship. . . .
> When talking about what I did over the weekend, I
> change his name to Kate.

Such passing often causes psychological problems: feelings of being
on stage, anxiety over exposure and subsequent sanctions, strain
from artificial behavior and talk (Weinberg and Williams, 1974, pp.
226–228).

Concealing sexual orientation from coworkers and employers is
relatively easy at first but becomes increasingly difficult in long-term
employment, as the exchange of personal information becomes part
of daily conversation: "Are you dating anyone?" "Did you see the
new secretary?" "What did you do over the weekend?" From the
information revealed or not revealed, work associates draw conclusions about sexual preference, and there is some evidence that co-
workers are more likely to know sexual orientation than employers
(Weinberg and Williams, 1974, p. 105).

Nevertheless, employers have developed systematic methods for
discerning sexual orientation, including polygraph tests and private
investigators who question neighbors and follow applicants through
daily activities—actions which clearly violate constitutional rights to
privacy. The founder of a leading industrial intelligence agency
says:

> Establishing someone is a homosexual is often difficult
> but I like to go on the rule of thumb that if one looks like
> a duck, walks like a duck, associates only with ducks and

quacks like a duck, he is probably a duck (Teal, 1971, pp. 231–232).

Obviously such a standard victimizes both gays and nongays.

Many companies have official policies prohibiting the employment of homosexuals and requiring the discharge of any employee who is discovered to be gay. In other cases gays are denied promotions or pay raises:

> Because I'm gay, others on the job discriminate against me. I remain second-best on the job though I'm obviously the best worker. I was given a lower position with less pay than another person on the same job (Bell and Weinberg, 1978, p. 144).

Employers do not always initiate discrimination. Coworkers may make conditions intolerable through abuse, taunts, and even physical violence. They may also use knowledge of concealed homosexuality to advance at the gay's expense:

> I was 40 and had a good position with a bank. A junior employee hired a private investigator who convinced the bank board that I was liable to be blackmailed. I was then asked to resign (Saghir and Robins, 1973, p. 173).

SPECIAL CASES OF DISCRIMINATION

Job discrimination also occurs in regard to occupational licenses, security clearances, and military service (cf. Boggan et al., 1975, pp. 33–73). Over 300 occupations are subject to government restrictions (Boggan et al., 1975, p. 34), and there are more than seven million people in the United States working in licensed fields, including architects, barbers, and teachers. Professional training and experience in the field are the main requisites for licensing, but applicants who have a criminal record or who are not of "good moral character" are denied licenses. Licensing agencies commonly construe homosexuality as evidence of "moral turpitude":

> I finished medical school and had interned before the service. When I came out [of the Air Force with an Undesirable Discharge] ready for residence, the head of the department called me into his office and said he knew about my discharge. When I applied for the final certifying boards he told the board that I was homosexual. I wasn't allowed to take certification (Weinberg and Williams, 1971, p. 119).

The federal government requires holders of jobs that involve access to classified information to possess security clearances. The agencies that confer these clearances consider gays vulnerable to blackmail, and therefore homosexuality is grounds for denying or revoking clearances. Sadly enough, if gays were not in danger of losing jobs upon disclosure of sexual preference, the main reason for blackmail would be gone.

Official military policy calls for the barring or removal of gay men from the armed forces, which leads to later employment discrimination (cf. Humphreys, 1972, pp. 33–36). Military service is a means of upward mobility for countless working-class men. By excluding gays, the armed forces denies them access to an important mobility mechanism and creates severe job discrimination for them in civilian life.

EXTENT OF DISCRIMINATION

How widespread are the discriminatory practices? Four recent studies offer some information (Weinberg and Williams, 1971; Saghir and Robins, 1973; Weinberg and Williams, 1974; Bell and Weinberg, 1978). Each study reports similar aspects of discrimination: homosexuality's adverse effect on career, homosexuality as a cause of non-hiring or of firing. Overall, with a total sample of 1,895 men, 29 percent of the gay male population studied have had their careers negatively influenced by homosexuality and 17 percent have lost or been denied employment because of sexual orientation. We must keep in mind that these estimates are probably extremely conservative, since "many male homosexuals may be discriminated against without their ever having known about it" (Harry and DeVall, 1978, p. 161), and because New York and San Francisco, where most of the respondents lived, are more tolerant of homosexuality than the rest of the country. Even so, these figures indicate systematic, widespread employment discrimination.

The prevalence of discrimination causes many gay men to restrict vocational goals to environments in which their sexuality is accepted. In many cases their occupations are below their educational qualifications or vocational training. Although gays are present throughout the occupational structure, they are disproportionately concentrated in the so-called feminine professions (teacher, librarian), lower white-collar jobs (retail sales, office clerk), and service jobs (waiter, hairdresser), all of which are low paying, somewhat unstable, and accept homosexuality.

CONCLUSION

Job discrimination strikes at the core of the individual's existence. In modern society occupation is the pathway to sustenance, self-realization, income, and self-esteem. By segregating gay men into less desirable and less remunerative positions, employment discrimination seriously reduces gay men's life chances and dissipates their potential contribution to society. To remedy this injustice, we insist that legislation be passed prohibiting employment discrimination against gay people.

REFERENCES

Adam, Barry D. In Press. "Stigma and Employability: Discrimination by Sex and Sexual Orientation in the Ontario Legal Profession." Canadian Review of Sociology and Anthropology.

Bell, Allan P. and Martin S. Weinberg. 1978. Homosexualities: A Study of Diversity Among Men and Women. New York: Simon and Schuster.

Boggan, E. Carrington, Marilyn G. Haft, Charles Lister, and John P. Rupp. 1975. The Rights of Gay People: The Basic ACLU Guide to Gay Persons Rights. New York: Avon Books.

Goffman, Erving. 1963. Stigma: Notes on the Management of Spoiled Identity. Englewood Cliffs, N.J.: Prentice-Hall.

Harry, Joseph and William B. DeVall. 1978. The Social Organization of Gay Males. New York: Praeger.

Hooker, Evelyn. 1965. "Male Homosexuals and Their Worlds." In Judd Marmor (ed.), Sexual Inversion: The Multiple Roots of Homosexuality. New York: Basic Books.

Humphreys, Laud. 1970. Out of the Closets: The Sociology of Homosexual Liberation. Englewood Cliffs, N.J.: Prentice-Hall.

Levine, Martin P. 1979. "Gay Ghetto." Journal of Homosexuality 4, 1 (Summer): 363–377

Levitt, Eugene E. and Albert D. Klassen, Jr. 1974. "Public Attitudes Toward Homosexuality: Part of the 1970 National Survey of the Institute for Sex Research." Journal of Homosexuality 1 (Fall): 131–139.

Saghir, Marcel T. and Eli Robins. 1973. Male and Female Homosexuality. Baltimore: William L. Wilkens.

Teal, Donn. 1971. The Gay Militants. New York: Stein and Day.

Weinberg, Martin S. and Colin Williams. 1971. Homosexuals and the Military. New York: Harper & Row.

———. 1974. Male Homosexuals: Their Problems and Adaptations. New York: Oxford University Press.

PART SEVEN

PARENTING

They may be separated, divorced, or widowed, or may never have been married at all. They are older than most other singles, and their social lives are curbed by the daily responsibilities of child care. They may be independent and self-sufficient, but more likely they are overburdened and financially strained. They are the single parents—and their number is growing all the time.

There were 5.7 million one-parent families in 1978, a jump of 9 percent since 1977. This constitutes 10 percent of the 57.2 million families in the United States and 19 percent of the 30.2 million families with children under eighteen. More than 90 percent of these families are maintained by women; 5 percent are made up of unmarried couples with children present. In 1978, 11 million children were living with their mothers alone, while about 1 million were living with their fathers alone.

The effects of this living situation on children and their parents depend greatly on the resources available. Single parents have three major worries and fears: loneliness, children, and money. Their problems evolve over the course of time. The first months after the breakup are the most traumatic. The newly divorced person must deal with disputes over child support and custody as well as personal problems of depression, self-doubt, desire for revenge, and the need for new involvement. Then come the financial worries. The median income in two-parent families is two to three times that of one-parent families. The economic hardships of single parents reflect the lower wages paid to all women, particularly to minority women, who make up 35 percent of all single mothers. Less than 30 percent of families headed by women reported incomes (in 1974) as high as $10,000, compared with 70 percent of two-parent families. These single parents need skilled child care, part-time jobs with benefits, and easily available health care clinics.

As time goes on, the pressures of single parenthood build. The difficulties of providing for their own and their children's physical, social, and emotional needs result in role overload and fatigue. And what about the single parent's social-sexual life? Nonparents often consider single parents with their attached responsibilities less "marriageable." When, where, and with whom can single parents have intimacy and sex? Many are reluctant to expose their children to dates who spend the night; getting away for weekends or vacations requires child care arrangements. Not surprisingly, single mothers are somewhat less likely to remarry than other single women (Duberman, 1977).

As for the children, those in one-parent homes may be described as "growing up a little faster." Children are resilient and often survive family crisis without permanent damage. They may be given responsibilities that would be considered beyond their capacity in a two-parent home, and be thought of as working in partnership with the parent. Children as "junior partners" receive new rights and authority as well (Weiss, 1979).

The impact of divorce on children is less severe than that of remaining in a troubled two-parent home. Nevertheless, divorce is a crisis for children, with symptoms including separation anxiety, feelings of helplessness and hostility, and loneliness and sadness. Though in most divorce cases today women are still awarded custody, there is a movement by fathers to be granted custody. When fathers are separated from their children they often feel dissatisfied and devalued; they experience role loss and depression and increase in physical problems (Greif, 1979). Some people have found that joint custody, with both parents sharing responsibilities for child care on an equal basis, is beneficial for parents and children. To make joint custody work, both parents must be emotionally mature and willing to communicate and to compromise. Whatever its advantages, current attitudes and institutions seem to indicate that widespread adoption of joint custody will require substantial changes in custody practices and a reexamination of the doctrine "in the best interests of the child" (Roman and Haddad, 1978). Moreover, as Judith Gordon indicates in her article "Single Parents," opposition to joint custody is developing among some feminists.

Judith Gordon uses an award-winning film, *Kramer vs. Kramer,* to point out inconsistencies between popular notions about divorce and the harsher realities. The divorce experience portrayed in this movie, between two affluent professionals, is hardly representative of most marital breakups. Postdivorce households are usually headed by women; and women working full time had median earnings of $8,620 in 1977, compared to $14,630 earned by comparable men. Less than 21 percent of divorced mothers regularly collected child support, and 80 percent of men at all income levels stopped their support payments. What social policies can be developed to decrease the "overload" for single parents that these figures imply? How can the courts and joint-custody arrangements help?

How do the 5.2 million women heading families in this country feel about their situation? "Rarely is the concept put forward that the female-headed family is an acceptable family form or that, once divorced, it is all right for a mother to stay divorced," Janet Kohen,

Carol Brown, and Roslyn Feldberg write in "Divorced Mothers: The Costs and Benefits of Female Family Control." But presumptions in favor of the male-headed family have begun to be questioned as the disadvantages of marriage and the advantages of singlehood emerge. When a couple divorces, the woman loses most of her right to the man's resources, but she also loses her personal dependence and obligations of service. On the other hand, she has exchanged direct dependence on one man for general dependence on male-dominated society. Still, for some women the experiences of heading a family may be more rewarding than their marriages. How can the negative experiences be reduced? Can our society insure women equal access to resources and thereby reduce the costs of divorced motherhood?

Divorced fatherhood is most often a part-time role. For this reason fathers are less popular research subjects and the effects of their participation in children's lives have been little understood. "Child Care Responsibilities of Part-Time and Single Fathers," by Kristine Rosenthal and Harry Keshet, examines the life styles of young divorced fathers. The authors found, for example, that full-time and half-time fathers average considerably less income, the conflicts between work and child care being similar to those of single mothers. At home, men who learned to meet children's practical needs, such as bathing and feeding, began to feel more effective and to feel better about their children. Bringing the criteria of work performance to the parenting role made them more at ease with their new obligations and more open to new relationships with women. The types of socialization these fathers experienced—usually in relation to work—can have positive effects on family life. How might these same patterns, if adopted by women, affect their parental role?

REFERENCES

Duberman, Lucile. *The Reconstituted Family*. Chicago: Nelson-Hall, 1977.

Greif, Judith Brown. "Fathers and Joint Custody," *American Journal of Orthopsychiatry*, 49: 311–319, 1979.

Roman, Mel, and William Haddad. *The Disposable Parent: The Case for Joint Custody*. New York: Holt, Rinehart & Winston, 1978.

Weiss, Robert. *Going It Alone*. New York: Basic Books, 1979.

22/ SINGLE PARENTS: Personal Struggles and Social Issues

Judith Bograd Gordon

> In the beginning they were three. Joanna and Ted Kramer, and four-year-old Billy—his big brown eyes bright with curiosity and wonder. A perfect family. Then one day the mother abandons them. Divorce. And now there are two. Father and son. Caring and cared for, learning what loving and belonging are all about, until there is a bond between them that nothing can break. Nothing and nobody except maybe a mother who almost two years later changes her mind and wants her little boy back. . . . (Corman, 1978, back cover blurb on novel)

So begins the American myth of the "intact" family that is broken apart by a divorce, creating a "single-parent family." *Kramer vs. Kramer* poignantly presents the pain and torment of the dissolution of a marriage and a subsequent struggle for the custody of the child. Reviewers of this film often suggest that it "acknowledges social changes that have come with the women's movement" (Angermann, 1980). Both the film and the novel reinforce the notion that it is aspirations for work and career that lead discontented wives to suddenly leave their children in the care of bewildered husbands. Mrs. Kramer bluntly says as she walks out the door, "Feminists will applaud me" (Corman, 1978, p. 44). This view of the women's movement is often reiterated in current debates concerning changes in divorce procedures, child custody, support, and alimony.

Louis Kiefer, an attorney, sets forth the following argument for joint custody: "Today, as both parents enter the working force each day, many of the traditional assumptions have been challenged . . . it is therefore necessary to consider and perhaps rethink the meaning of custody" (1979, pp. 371–372). Kiefer supports this view by turning to a study by Judith Brown Greif, a psychologist, in which she suggests "we" should do everything possible to maximize contact between the children and both parents through joint custody arrangements. "Families of divorce" should not be approached as "though they truly consist of only one parent, as though the non-custodial parent has ceased to exist" (Greif, 1979, p. 310).

Roman and Haddad (1978) turn to the "feminists" for support, and point out that feminism in itself leads to the inescapable conclusion that women's rights means men's right to children. They conclude that feminists should join in the demands for expanded day care facilities, work patterns that would allow split shifts, economic parity for women, and the recognition that the rights of fathers, expressed through legislation making joint custody the presumption, will in the long run benefit women as well.

Viewing *Kramer vs. Kramer* it is tempting to sigh, "Would that it were true." How simple it might be if the only woes that lead to divorce were the longings of women for freedom, well-paying careers, and new relationships. If that were all there is to it, the remedy would indeed be joint custody and public assistance in the form of baby sitters, day care, and schools. The paramount consideration would be the rights of the children to the same relationship with the father that they had in the intact family (Barbirer, 1979; Kiefer, 1979).

But what was that intact family like? *Kramer vs. Kramer* would lead us to believe that the typical family in America is one in which the husband earns nearly $30,000 a year and supports one child and a wife who dresses like a fashion model and spends her days being a full-time mother. Mrs. Kramer is not touched by inflation and unemployment. After years away from the labor force, she leaves her husband and child and within two years is making more money than the average American professional male, who in 1977 made $18,224 (U.S. Bureau of the Census, 1980).

In truth, the Kramers do not even represent the average American family of four, whose median income ranges between $14,000 and $16,000. Nor does Mr. Kramer represent the majority of the heads of single families—who are not abandoned men but women. As the *Congressional Quarterly* reports, of the 4.9 million single-parent families, 4.4 million were headed by women in 1975.

Mrs. Kramer does not represent the majority of American working women either. Women working full-time year-round had median earnings of $8,620 in 1977, or 59 percent of that of comparable men ($14,630). Although lawyers and psychologists may suggest that strong advocacy can bring about equality, and women continue to call for equal pay for equal work as they have since 1848, we are reminded that change comes slowly if at all. The Census Bureau reports that the substantial earnings differential between women and men remained unchanged between 1970 and 1977, and as the Task Force on Women observed in 1978, even women professionals such as college professors still earn on the average $3,000 less than men professors (President's Commision on Mental Health, 1978). Moreover, the mean family income of female-headed families was less than $6,000, nearly $4,000 less than that of male-headed families. Women maintained 49 percent of families below the poverty level in 1977, and 44 percent of families headed by black women were below poverty. Had Mrs. Kramer gotten custody, she would not have represented the average female single-parent either, for the average single-parent family is not headed by an affluent woman.

Why not? Rubin's study of working-class families reports that many of these women married at very young ages and did not have the kind of education that would permit them to compete for professional positions or well-paying jobs. Others are born poor and remain poor, as do their husbands. But still others become poor via the divorce process. For example, at a 1974 National Organization for Women conference on marriage and divorce, women were encouraged to "speak out" about the socioeconomic realities of their lives after divorce. For the most part these were upper-middle-class and middle-class women. Woman after woman spoke about the hardships they experienced when it was necessary to reenter the job market to support themselves and their children. Most had low child-support payments and no alimony. Overall, only 14 percent of female-headed families are awarded alimony and fewer than half collect it regularly (Wartenberg and Reinhart, 1979, p. 463). Of those women awarded child support, estimates vary as to how many men continue to pay it after the divorce. In one sample, about 20 percent of divorced mothers regularly collected child support, and eight out of ten men in all education, occupation, and income groups had stopped making support payments (Gordon, Johnson, and Held, 1974).

Moreover, as Cassetty reports, child support awards are increasingly low. In her sample, even when gross taxable income exceeded $15,000 per year the proportion of absent fathers who paid support was only two-thirds, and their mean child-support payment was $2,274 per year—only slightly more than half of the poverty level for a family of three. When it was paid at all, child support was regressive; low-income fathers paid a much higher percentage of their income in child support than did high-income fathers (1978). Awards vary from judge to judge and are not revised to keep pace with inflation or the changing needs of children (Wartenberg and Reinhart, 1979, p. 463).

Ironically, these low awards are made to middle- and upper-middle-class women in the name of the women's movement. Judges and lawyers, it appears, react to the rhetoric of the movement and not to the working woman's reality. For example, a superior court judge in California argued that "one of the most significant changes in the law relates to spouse support. . . . Changing social attitudes about divorce and employment of women have, in reality, been reflected increasingly in the court room . . . the increased emphasis on equality for women is incompatible with the idea of lifelong support from a husband" (Goddard, 1972, p. 416).

Reflecting this trend, the women at the NOW conference reported receiving shortened alimony, if any, and low child-support awards. This held true regardless of the women's age, the grounds for divorce, their contributions to property which was in their husband's name, their contributions to the marriage, or their own vocational skills. Young women with children found they had to "go on the State." Upper-middle-class women were awarded $55 in child support a week and required to sell their homes, splitting the money with their husbands. They searched for apartments only to find that the child support did not cover even half a month's rent. As Weiss observes, the ending of a marriage generally results in a decided drop in women's income related to needs, but an increase in men's (Weiss, 1979; Cassetty, 1978).

Among the most bitter are the middle-aged women from middle-class and upper-middle-class backgrounds who gave up their own professional training or career aspirations to do clerical work while helping their husbands establish their own careers. After divorce, they find themselves forced to accept the low-paying jobs their current skills qualify them for, if they can find a job at all after many years out of the job market. As one speaker at the conference reported, a study of divorced women found that a third of the respondents lost savings or pensions, 25 percent lost social security, 50 percent lost furnishings or homes, and 75 percent lost health insurance as a direct result of being divorced. Spokeswomen for the Displaced Homemakers organization note that widows often fare no better, and that the economic ramifications of divorce or widowhood are not ended when children are grown. Women who become poor through divorce may remain poor into old age, for women who have not worked and accrued social security or pension benefits have no resources to fall back on.

Women with young children are particularly at risk. Day care arrangements are inadequate and expensive, and public assistance does not routinely allocate reasonable sums for baby sitters. For example, the current amount given in Connecticut is $25 per week for one child, with a maximum of $30 per week for a family, regardless of size. Who will reliably work ten hours a day for $30 a week? If a woman tries to work part-time, she will find that part-time employment is not only scarce but often does not include fringe benefits such as health insurance or pensions. And even full-time work does not easily pay for good child care, particularly since female workers remain concentrated in low-paying clerical and service jobs.

In addition, the growing unemployment rate has meant that women, regardless of affirmative action, may find themselves the last hired and the first fired. Even well-educated women with professional skills are currently encountering difficulties in finding and retaining positions. Elementary and high-school teachers are not being hired and women who were trained to teach but did not continue to do so during their marriage cannot easily reenter the school system. If they are lucky enough to find a job, they may be fired the following year because of budgetary cutbacks and lack of seniority. Social workers compete for scarce positions as human services are slashed while our defense budget grows. Women college professors who did not publish major books or numerous articles during the period when they were bearing and rearing children may be denied reappointment and tenure as their senior colleagues label them "unproductive." Women of fifty are forced to try to enter the business world at an age when men are being pressured to opt for early retirement at age fifty-five. And single parents do not have the time to engage in the kind of informal social life that so often bears upon career advancement. As MacKinnon points out (1979), the kind of socializing a woman may be asked to do is not always related to economic advancement. No, Mrs. Kramer does not represent even the college-educated women who reenter the job market.

But does Mr. Kramer represent the majority of divorced men? He too, when employed, made far above the average income. Moreover, when unemployed, although middle-aged, he found work immediately, maintaining the stability of his home. In reality many middle-aged men cannot find employment in periods of recession, and several studies show that men who have experienced substantial job instability are more likely to separate from their wives, leaving the children with the mother, than men who do not (Wartenberg and Reinhart 1979, p. 462). Since Mr. & Mrs. Kramer are the exceptions and not the rule, we must seriously question the assumption that marriages dissolve because of the impact of the women's movement.

It is always difficult to assess the real causes for marital dissolution. The grounds for divorce that appear on a court record are not always the reasons for the dissolution of a marriage. Marriages fall apart for a variety of reasons. The following article, "Divorced Mothers," notes that in a sample of thirty women, twenty-four divorces were precipitated by circumstances such as violence, alcoholism, infidelity, and willful nonsupport. In six the spouses felt incompatible. In eight of the thirty the men wanted the breakup more than the women. In a sample of 451 welfare mothers, most important reasons the women gave for the dissolution of the marriage concerned their husbands' physical abuse and their involvement with drugs, alcohol, and other women (Wartenberg and Reinhart 1979, p. 462).

There is one way in which the Kramers are all too representative. Like the majority of divorcing parents, the Kramers did not have a court battle at the time of the uncontested divorce and Mrs. Kramer did not ask for either sole or joint custody. Two years later she changed her mind, and the Kramers returned to court to resolve their postdivorce dispute. As Goldstein, Freud, and Solnit point out, the families of single parents can, at any moment, be intruded upon in the name of justice (1979). On the basis of a quick court appearance, and under the pressures of an adversary proceeding, people find their lives permanently shaped by overworked judges who often have, at best, superficial knowledge of the past history and current situation of the family. Either parent may be denied access to the children; children's lives are disrupted by court decisions. And there is often little opportunity for appeal or redress without great financial and emotional cost.

Such battles are few. More than 80 percent of divorcing couples do not fight in court. Some fight furiously in their lawyers' offices and then resolve their differences in a settlement; others are able to work out an amicable agreement. But even in these cases the legal fees can be so high that even middle-class people cannot afford the bills. A woman who lacks the resources to employ a private attorney is often at a disadvantage in divorce proceedings. And even if she retains an attorney in the hope that the court will order her husband to pay the fee, that hope is not always realized. If she is granted such an award, it often does not cover the full bill and leaves her heavily in debt. If at any time the lawyer believes the fee is becoming so high the client cannot pay it, he or she may withdraw from the case or advise the client to stop the action, no matter how just the complaint.

Happily, custody battles remain few. The reopening of custody is, however, not the only reason for the return to the courts. One segment of the population continually forced back into the legal system is women who need to have child-support orders enforced. The husband may respond by challenging the custody, visitation, and support arrangements, and the battle may be reopened. The resulting lawyers' fees can eat up any child-support arrears which the ex-wife is awarded.

Court action often makes no difference. A recent analysis of a hundred child-support files found that almost half (49 percent) of the absent fathers paid less than 10 percent of their court-ordered child support, and that 19 percent had never paid any. This situation persists in spite of frequent court action against the noncompliant parent (Cassetty, 1978, p. 106).

Rich or employed women can at least choose between supporting their children alone or returning to court. Women who have to resort to public assistance will find that the welfare system in this country not only degrades all who use it, but may force them back into the courts, since federal laws require them to cooperate fully in legal action to collect child support (Cassetty, 1978). Single mothers struggle with their need for such support and their hatred of what it does to them and their families. For the public assistance system opens up the family to constant intrusive scrutiny in return for unrealistic and inadequate allotments. Many women attempt to get off welfare. As Schoer and Moen (1979) point out, of the 7 million mothers who received welfare over a 10-year period, the typical woman was assisted for two years, left welfare, but eventually had to receive it again two years later.

All too often the economic problems of single parents are minimized by those who assume that the single-parent family is temporary. Did not Mrs. Kramer have a boy friend? Yes, but will they marry? Some therapists still suggest that therapy for the divorcing couple ends with "family reconstitution" and "restructuring roles and relationships to include the new spouse" (Goldmeir, 1980, p. 39). But this scheme of things cannot be taken for granted. Some people, particularly women who have custody of young children, never remarry. And there are some single parents who have never been married. The single-parent family must be taken seriously as a family form which may endure through the period in which the child grows up (Solnit, 1980). Thus we cannot base our social policies upon the assumption that the economic travails of the single parent will end with remarriage and that the emotional pain of divorce will be assuaged by a new mate.

SINGLE-PARENT FAMILIES AND SOCIAL POLICY

As single people, single parents share the problems discussed in other selections of this volume, for in a society which values coupledness, the single parent must struggle against prejudice and discrimination. As parents, single parents share the problems discussed by groups interested in parenting. Mediocre teachers, the needs of children, role conflicts, all affect single parents too. But as single parents they encounter troubles which arise out of their situation (Solnit, 1980).

Weiss (1979) observes that the one "fundamental problem in the single parents' situation is the insufficiency of immediate available support." The inadequacy of the resources upon which single parents can draw may, as Weiss puts it, result in "overload." We can therefore link personal troubles to social issues by developing the kinds of policies necessary to work against overloading.

1. *Responsibility overload.* As Weiss (1979) notes, given the reality of child-support awards, the typical single-parent family is headed by a woman who is financially responsible for the household. Proponents of joint custody suggest remedying this situation by splitting the decision-making and child-rearing responsibilities with the ex-spouse. Perhaps. But surely the two-thirds of men who do not pay

their assigned child support cannot be totally unaware of the burden this places on both their ex-spouse and their children. Federal and state governments are aware of that burden and are searching for ways to enforce child-support orders (Cassetty, 1978). This will help those women whose husbands have the resources to support their children, but a poor unemployed man can never contribute enough money to justify the cost of the court case.

2. *Task overload.* As Weiss points out, the average single parent who assumes the responsibility for housekeeping, child rearing, and full-time employment is committed simultaneously to two full-time jobs. Joint custody can mitigate some of these problems but does not necessarily eliminate all the dilemmas of working parents. If a child gets sick when both parents must be at work, it hardly matters if custody is shared, as dual-career families know all too well.

3. *Emotional overload.* According to Weiss, unrelieved responsibility for children is depleting when there is no one to attend to the parent's needs. The loss of intimacy and lack of caring attention for themselves, he argues, can lead single parents to hopelessness and despair (1979). There is, of course, no easy solution to the problem of the emotional pain of widowhood or divorce and the resultant changes in the lives of families.

One solution is a new mate. Another is joint custody (when it works well). Still another is the recognition that the emotional overload of single parents is intensified by a hostile social and economic environment. As Caine notes, widows have a difficult time readjusting their lives after the death of a spouse if their married friends drop them. Such adjustment is even more difficult for the divorced and stigmatized single parent, man or woman, in part because of the very process of divorce itself (1974).

We need to develop social policies and programs to alleviate these pressures on single-parent families. One useful direction is found in the Family Policy Recommendations adopted by the Board of the American Orthopsychiatric Association (1980). These recommendations suggest that the stability and continuity of all American families, including those headed by single parents, would be ensured if we agreed that as a society we wanted to provide for full employment and the allocation of resources to develop preventive services and support systems such as visiting housekeepers, day care centers for the young and the elderly, income support, flexible working hours for working parents, afterschool programs, and neighborhood programs for adolescents and the old.

The emotional overload on single parents is exacerbated in both the pre- and post-divorce by the present adversary system in which parents and lawyers barter time with the children for money. There is shared agreement among many that the current legal procedures by which the family of divorce is created is in desperate need of change. All too often economic considerations are not separated from child custody arrangements. Although related, child custody arrangements depend on more than economics. The attention of divorcing people is best focused not on who pays for what, but on the kind of shared concern that arises out of the need to decide who will in fact care for the children. Who can best meet the child's emotional needs? And under what arrangements?

As Foster and Freed note, no rule of thumb can be used for everyone. "The choice should not be between a preference for sole or a preference for joint custody, without regard to the circumstances of the particular case, but rather the choice should be made without a preference in terms of what best suits the needs of a particular family" (1978, p. 393). But who makes that determination? Matrimonial lawyers who lack knowledge of psychology, sociology, and anthropology but do know how to argue in court? Paraprofessionals with superficial training in behavioral sciences or psychiatry? Teachers who testify about the child as if they knew more than the parents? The judge who, as Sametz notes, probably had no training to equip him to render decisions concerning child custody? Mental health professionals who claim to be able to predict the future on the basis of a set of projective tests and a small number of interviews with the child, the parents, friends, neighbors, and teachers?

Proposals have been made that a combination of these professionals would be best suited to assess the child's environment, and that such assessments should be mandated by the court in all divorce proceedings involving children. But do these observers of the family really know its circumstances better than the family members themselves? Basic sociological research methodology cautions us against applying generalizations to individual cases because of the variation in human relationships. This risk will not be resolved by opening up the family for scrutiny by teachers, lawyers, or neighbors whose own principles of child rearing and family life are not investigated. In the majority of cases, as Goldstein, Freud, and Solnit observe (1973; 1979), the family itself could make a reasonable determination. In some cases, such agreement would be facilitated if the family members entered therapy. Rather than mandate an expensive court investigative procedure, we could follow the recommendations of the President's Commission on Mental Health (1978) and change the financing of mental health care in order to ensure adequate services for all Americans. Reimbursement for all treatment modalities, including family therapy and psychoanalytic treatment, would permit single parents and their children to turn to specialists of their own choice.

The court should be involved only in cases in which people do not wish to use mental health professionals to resolve conflicts, or cannot reach a decision even after they have tried to do so with professional help.

It is, after all, not just task and responsibility overload that lead to emotional overload. It is also the strain of living in a society which contains members who insist upon forcing all people into a mold, while ignoring the consequences of poverty, inequality, and the organization of work. To reduce emotional overload, single parents need, as other people do, a society that uses its resources to shape policies based on the recognition of the diversity of human experiences and the right of all its members, regardless of gender, to have the liberty to pursue happiness in their own way.

REFERENCES

American Orthopsychiatric Association. 1980. Resolutions on Family Policy Accepted at Annual Meeting, Toronto.

Angermann, Chris. 1980. "Kramer *vs.* Kramer: Contemporary Family Fable Soothes Pain with Laughter," *New Haven Advocate,* Jan. 2.

Barbirer, Arthur. 1979. "Rights and Obligations of Custodial and Non-Custodial Parents in Connecticut," *Connecticut Bar Journal,* 53: 356–370.

Caine, Lynne. 1974. *Widow.* New York: William Morrow.

Cassetty, Judith. 1978. *Child Support and Public Policy.* Lexington, Mass.: Lexington Books.

Corman, Avery. 1978. *Kramer vs. Kramer.* New York: Signet Books.

Foster, Henry and Freed, Doris. 1978. "Joint Custody: A Viable Alternative," *New York Law Journal.* Reprint distributed at Conference on Women and the Law, Yale University 1980.

Goddard, W. H. 1972. "A Report on California's New Divorce Law: Progress and Problems," *Family Law Review,* 6:405–421.

Goldmeir, John. 1980. "Intervention in the Continuum from Divorce to Family Reconstruction," *Social Case Work,* 61:39–45.

Goldstein, Joseph, Freud, Anna, and Solnit, Albert. 1973. *Beyond the Best Interests of the Child.* New York: The Free Press.

———. 1979. *Before the Best Interests of the Child.* New York: The Free Press.

Gordon, Judith Bograd, Johnson, Audrey, and Held, Joy. 1974. "How to Legislate Equality: Debates over Family Law." Unpublished paper presented at the Annual Meeting of the Society for the Study of Social Problems, Montreal.

Greif, Judith Brown. 1979. "Fathers and Joint Custody," *American Journal of Orthopsychiatry,* 49:311–319.

Kiefer, Louis. 1979. "Custody Meanings and Considerations," *Connecticut Bar Journal,* 53:370–386.

*Kohen, Janet, Brown, Carol, and Feldberg, Roslyn. 1979. "Divorced Mothers: The Costs and Benefits of Female Family Control," in G. Levinger and A. Moles (eds.), *Divorce and Separation.* New York: Basic Books.

MacKinnon, Catherine. 1979. *Sexual Harrassment of Working Women.* New Haven: Yale University Press.

Roman, Mel, and Haddad, William. 1978. *The Disposable Parent: The Case for Joint Custody.* New York: Holt, Rinehart & Winston.

Rubin, Lillian. 1976. *Worlds of Pain: Life in the Working-Class Family.* New York: Basic Books.

Schoer, Alvin and Moen, Phyllis. 1979. "The Single Parent and Public Policy," *Social Policy,* 9:15–21.

Solnit, Albert. 1980. "Tolerance for Single Parent Families." Unpublished paper presented at the Western New England Psychoanalytic Institute Conference on the Single Parent, Yale University.

U.S. Government Publications:
1976. "Single-Parent Families," prepared by Sandra Stencel. Editorial Research Reports, Washington, D.C., Congressional Quarterly, Inc.
1978. The President's Commission on Mental Health, vols. 1 and 3.
1980. "A Statistical Portrait of Women in the U.S.: 1978." Washington, D.C., Bureau of the Census.

Wartenberg, Esther, and Reinhart, Hazel. "Female-Headed Families: Trends and Policy Implications." *Social Work* 24: 460–472.

Weiss, Robert. 1979. *Going It Alone.* New York: Basic Books.

23/ DIVORCED MOTHERS: The Costs and Benefits of Female Family Control

Janet A. Kohen, Carol A. Brown, and Roslyn Feldberg

Rarely is the concept put forward that the female-headed family is an acceptable family form or that, once divorced, it is all right for a mother to stay divorced. As the position of women relative to men has come under scrutiny, such presumptions in favor of the male-headed family have begun to be questioned (Gillespie, 1971; Bernard, 1972). The myth of the "happy homemaker" has been

*Indicates selection included in this volume.

criticized as analysts have become more aware of both the disadvantages of marriage and the advantages of singlehood (Gove and Tudor, 1973; Rollins and Feldman, 1970). Yet attitudes for or against a woman heading her family tend to be based on opinion rather than on examination of the lives of divorced mothers. Our study provides such an examination by investigating the lives of thirty divorced mothers as they were organized following the first year after divorce. We focus on the issues they must deal with and the costs and benefits that they experience in day-to-day life as family heads.

We expected to find both costs and benefits in being a divorced mother. Motherhood in most Western societies is normatively structured so as to be dependent on wifehood. The social resources made available to men—money, recognition, interpersonal power, social rights—enable them to head families. While lower-class men have fewer resources than upper-class women, each man gets some resources denied to women of his class. Since such resources are not equally and directly available to women, most women must become dependent on husbands for the resources needed to be mothers. In return for a share of these resources, women must provide men with services and satisfactions.

If a couple divorces, the woman loses most of her right to the man's resources, but she also loses her personal dependence and obligations of service. She now stands in direct relationship to society as the head of her family. But male-dominated society neither recognizes a divorced woman's right to head a family nor makes available to her, as a woman, the necessary resources. The divorced mother has exchanged direct dependence on one man for general dependence on a male-dominated society. Employers, welfare officials, lawyers, judges, politicians, school authorities, doctors, even male relatives and neighbors, set the parameters of her ability to take on successfully the role of family head.

Nevertheless, being divorced does make a positive difference. Patriarchal authority is now outside the family, not inside, and the woman can choose to some extent the way in which she will relate to those authorities and the use she will make of whatever formal and informal resources are available.

What has she gained? What are the trade-offs? Are there advantages to divorced motherhood that compensate for the problems? Indeed, does anything change at all?

METHOD OF THE STUDY

From the above perspective and our earlier review of the literature (Brandwein, Brown, and Fox, 1974) we identified a number of dimensions of family life for our research such as economic factors, authority allocation, child care, household management, and social and psychological supports. Since earlier studies were not similarly oriented, we adopted the procedure of interviewing divorced mothers in depth, using general questions that permitted the women to discuss their situation with the broadest possible latitude. In each area of questions we probed for advantages as well as disadvantages of being divorced. For example, we asked, "What are some of the easy things in raising children alone?" "What are some of the problems?" When applicable, we asked interviewees to compare their current situation to their situation when married. We found that the women not only expressed problems we had anticipated, but they also articulated problems and benefits we had not expected.

THE SAMPLE

We interviewed 30 Boston-area mothers who had at least one child under sixteen living with them and who had been divorced or separated from one to five years. This time span eliminated the crisis immediately following separation (e.g., Weiss, 1975) and restricted our sample to women for whom single parenthood had become a stable, but not necessarily permanent, situation. The interviews were conducted in the latter part of 1974.

Potential respondents were located through institutional sources such as youth agencies, health clinics, daycare centers, and organizations of single parents. Several respondents were students at a local college who were found through an author or a colleague; a few were friends of friends of friends; others were friends of previous respondents. To assure their anonymity, no one with whom an author was well acquainted or who was known to more than one of the authors was interviewed. Quotas were imposed to assure that no group was overrepresented in relation to the Boston-area population. Selected background characteristics presented in Table 1 reveal the group's diversity and range.

In each case an institutional representative or individual who knew the woman explained the study and asked if she would agree to be interviewed. If she agreed, her name was then given to us for formal contact. Interviews averaged 3½ hours and were conducted in the respondent's home with no other person present. (Babysitting money was provided to assure privacy and lack of interruption.)

The rapport was excellent, in part because all five interviewers were women in their late twenties and thirties who were familiar with problems of family life, and in part because the respondents had thought a lot about their situations and appreciated an opportunity to discuss them.

Our findings do not always agree with those of other researchers

TABLE 1
BACKGROUND CHARACTERISTICS OF THE RESPONDENTS

Religion		Race/Ethnicity	
Catholic	14	English, Dutch, Swedish	8
Protestant	11	Irish (all or part)	7
Jewish	5	Jewish	5
		Italian (all or part)	4
Age		Black	2
Under 25	2	Foreign-born (Scotch,	
25–29	9	Irish)	2
30–34	7	Greek	1
35–39	6	French-Canadian	1
40–44	4		
45 or over	2	Education	
		Less than H.S.	4
Monthly Cash Income		H.S. diploma	7
$ 0– 499	14	Some college	8
500– 899	8	Nurses' training	3
900–1199	6	College graduate	4
1200 and over	2	Graduate training	4

because we confined our research to the women's lives, and because we used open-ended interviews, always probing for advantages as well as disadvantages of single parenthood as these mothers experienced it. In addition, we eliminated respondents who were still adjusting to the first year of single parenthood. However, in several major areas, such as changes in income, proportion wishing to remarry, and types of problems encountered, our findings are consistent with the patterns reported in earlier studies (Goode, 1956; Kriesberg, 1970; Marsden, 1969).

MARRIAGE: THE WIFE-MOTHER PACKAGE

Most mothers are wife-mothers. Economic and social dependence on a husband is the normal condition of adult womanhood in our society. Most American women marry and 88 percent of married women are dependent on their husbands for at least half of the family's income (U.S. Department of Labor, 1976). All but seven of the mothers in our sample had been similarly economically dependent on their husbands during their motherhood. The exceptions were primarily among women married to low-earning husbands.

Such dependence is not necessarily anticipated by women. Only nine had expected, when they were teenagers, that they would become dependent wife-mothers as adults. Nine others had thought solely of work careers, and eight had expected to combine work and family. Four did not recall specific teenage plans for adulthood.

Whatever the reasons for marriage, husband and children become the package around which the wife/mother makes her life. This combination is seen not simply as a job, but as a way of life.

The distinct activities of the wife/mother (caring for husband and children, washing, cooking, maintaining a household) are transformed from a series of tasks into a personal commitment to her children and husband. No hours mark the boundaries of her involvement—at any time, for as many years as her spouse and children need her, she is expected to respond as wife and mother. Economic and social dependence make it possible for her to fulfill this commitment, but they also are the conditions which enable her husband to exercise the traditional power in the family. As a result, she often chafes at her subordination. One woman now living on child support payments and earnings from part-time domestic service said,

> I think it's strange that men take so much for granted. I don't resent getting meals for kids, but I often resented getting meals for my husband—I couldn't just have a hodge-podge of a meal. My friends did all these things and were happy, but I was going stark raving mad.

The woman's desire for freedom is not necessarily the reason for divorce. As we shall show later, it is often a benefit she realizes only *after* she becomes a single parent. Instead, the precipitating circumstances in 24 of the marital breakups in our survey were traditional—violence, alcoholism, infidelity, and willful non-support; the other 6 were "modern" divorces: the spouses simply felt incompatible. In 8 of the 30 marriages the man had wanted the breakup more than the woman; in 4 the feelings were mutual.

Women may opt out or be pushed out of wifehood, but rarely do they opt out of continuing motherhood. As recently as 1975, in 90 percent of U.S. divorces involving children, the children remain with the mother. Continuing motherhood may be socially prescribed or personally favored. Over 80 percent of the women in our sample said there was "no question" about who would take the children. "It was understood—he got the car, I got the child," said one. For some women, child custody was not voluntary—"I was left with them"—while for others, gaining complete custody of the children was a reason for divorce. Said one mother of five, "I and the kids wanted the breakup—he would have hung right in there. My three teenagers were going to run away—that clinched it. He'll never get the children—I put it in my will."

TRANSITION TO DIVORCED MOTHERHOOD

Women are no more prepared for divorced motherhood than they are for married motherhood. Indeed, they are less so. Cultural models for married motherhood are pervasive, but, as Goode analyzed it in 1956, the divorcée exists in a "social limbo," without an established "place" in the social structure. There are no socially recognized models of successful divorced motherhood to help her know what has to be done and how to do it. The popular wisdom tells her it cannot be done. On an issue so basic as money, 15 of our 30 respondents told us that at the time of their divorces they had no concrete plans for how to support themselves. They knew they must have money, but when they thought about it there were no ready-made answers.

Despite their lack of preparation, the women often felt relieved, if somewhat worried, to be on their own. Twelve reported their feelings about the marital breakup as happy or relieved, another six felt similarly but had some reservations, and 12 were unhappy. Said a mother with five children, "I don't believe in divorce . . . I only did it because I had to . . . it's peace of mind after seven years of hell."

Whether divorce brings relief or unhappiness, it is only the beginning of a new situation that has both problems and rewards. The problems are immediately obvious, for example, lack of money; the rewards may be noticeable only later. This is tied to the nature of change introduced by divorce. The change is not merely a legal or a personal one. It involves a shift from marriage to divorce, from a culturally supported life arrangement to a resource-deprived limbo.

They are non-wives. The lack of a new model to organize their lives around often creates initial problems of self-identity. Our respondents frequently spoke of the initial period as traumatic, frightening, or depressing. "It was like I was asleep for two years," said one. Said another, "Your whole life drops out." Eighteen respondents described such emotional upset during the initial period. Thus, added to the material crisis of breaking up, there is often a psychological crisis (Brown, 1976; Weiss, 1975).

After a while, however, many ex-wives do get back on their feet and the relative merits of the two ways of living can be evaluated. When we talked with them, at least a year after the breakup, we asked if things were easier now or when they were with their husbands. Seventeen women said "easier now," three said "things are harder," and ten said "things are different," with both good and bad aspects. The drawbacks were primarily financial problems and a sense of overwhelming responsibility; the good things were control and emotional growth. In the following sections we will argue that, despite the drawbacks, their experiences of heading a family are often better for these women than were their marriages.

PROBLEMS OF DIVORCE

FINANCES

The resources men bring to families are for the most part withdrawn following the divorce. The fact that female-headed families do not have access to comparable resources is the source of many of the problems divorced mothers face. Such resources include, but are not limited to, money. Only 16 husbands of our respondents provided any financial support to their ex-families and only 9 provided as much as 50 percent of the family's income at any period after the divorce. The woman's own paid work or welfare[1] had to become immediate substitutes. But wages for women workers (full-time, year round) are low: in 1974 they averaged 57 percent of men's wages, due to a combination of job segregation and sex discrimination (Stevenson, 1973; Sawhill, 1975). Welfare is also a minimal form of support, some argue, because of sex discrimination (Komisar, 1973).

From an average pre-divorce family income of $12,500, the women in our sample fell to a post-divorce average of $6,100, a drop of just over half. This overall average obscures an important class difference—the higher they start, the farther they fall. The 8 highest income families dropped 60 percent, the 9 lowest income families dropped only 19 percent. The less the husband had contributed, the less he could take away.

Sixteen of the 30 women turned to AFDC either immediately or within a year. AFDC must be seen as an equivalent of unemployment insurance for mothers.

At the time of the interviews the sample's average income was $8,300,[2] an improvement of one-third over the post-divorce plunge, but still only 66 percent of their average marital income. The improvement had been least among the 8 highest income families and greatest among the 8 poorest. Twenty of the women had part- or full-time jobs; 15 were supported mainly by their jobs, 5 received primary support from their husbands, 2 received primary support from Social Security, and the remainder received the major portion of their family income from welfare.

Economically, a divorced mother may be forced to rely on her ex-husband or on social service agencies for subsidies, whether she is employed or not. The patterns of discrimination in employment and prejudices against the divorced mother can create a "Catch-22" situation. The mother fights for what is usually a low wage job while simultaneously incurring childcare expenses. The problems of one woman typify many:

> I was trying to get into the accounting field. . . . I started
> at the bottom at $90 a week and they promised I would

> move up. I got no promotions, a $2, $3 raise in pay. I couldn't get childcare until I had a job, and people at the job wanted me to have childcare before they would give me the job. They said I had no experience, asked about my marital status, did I have a boyfriend? They were worried about pregnancy. When I was unemployed I couldn't get a job because they said I was "over-experienced"—I had worked three years. At one place I said I'd work for less, but they wouldn't hire me. They had three openings.

If she is not employed, she generally must depend on welfare or on her ex-husband for income. But *help* is never free. These sources of income or service mean more strings, more constraints on her activities and choices. Having her life open to questioning and having rules imposed on her activities limit the woman's ability to determine her life. Said one about her husband, "I have the feeling I'm dependent on him still because of the alimony. He could move away and not send it, and that does affect the way I handle it. If I press too hard, he could take off." Another woman, receiving child support, reported that, "I was doing things to please my husband—he looked around to see if there were any flaws when he visited."

Current social arrangements make it difficult for the divorced mother to be economically responsible for her children, to provide adequate housing for them, to obtain credit or access to other resources necessary for an independent life. These structural arrangements encourage the dependence of women on men.

AUTHORITY OVER FAMILY LIFE

Male-dominated society provides power to men rather than to women. The divorced mother may legally be the head of her family and therefore be legally entitled to make family decisions, to make demands on social institutions, or to protect the family from unwarranted intrusion, but she is not socially legitimated in this role. Time and again the women told us of intrusions that had not happened when their husbands were heads of the family—schools and hospitals ignoring their requests for their children, men attempting to break into the house, landlords refusing to rent to them, their own parents interfering in their lives. "The whole world thinks they can run your life better than you can," said one woman. A common refrain was "they didn't do that when my husband was here." In at least six cases, the ex-husband himself was the biggest offender against the family's privacy and, on occasion, against their safety by barging in, making demands, making sexual passes, or becoming violent.

Whereas a man is accorded the status of head of family automatically, a woman has to "earn" it, through the strength of her personality or her willingness to do battle (Marsden, 1969; Holmstrom, 1973). To constantly validate their claims to authority, women must expend time and energy that are unnecessary for a male head. Belligerence is a frequent tactic. "They wouldn't dare!" said one when questioned about school authorities ignoring what she wanted. Said another about her husband, "He may still have the money, but he knows I won't take it lying down." A third told us that, as a general principle, "It pays to be a bitch, especially when you're on your own."

FAMILY LIFE

The single mother's problems are not merely a function of her female status. She has the same difficulties that any family faces in meeting the day-to-day needs of its members. Despite the industrialization of many areas of family responsibility—such as growing food, making clothes, or educating children—those that are not easily routinized—such as the physical, social, and psychological care of children, housework, emotional support, and the tailoring of market products to meet individual tastes—remain family responsibilities. When marriages break up, these responsibilities are shifted from two parents to one. As one mother put it:

> The hard part is having to make important decisions alone—not having anyone to share with, having the feeling of sole responsibility. There's the constancy of the burden—no one else to take over. A married mother doesn't feel so "on her own."

The personal characteristics of the divorced mother—her ability to manage, her competence, her emotional stability—are not the source of her day-to-day difficulties. As a single parent, she must spread her time to cover all of the family demands. Her personal needs and the individual concerns of family members are squeezed into the interstices of formal schedules. One mother described her day,

> Everything is a trade-off, a continuing conflict. There is no one else to do anything—shopping, dentists, chores, everything has to be done in the evenings and weekends. I need my job, so I can't tell the boss to go to hell and take time off.

Asked the difference between herself and a married mother, another commented, "I have to get up and lose sleep and still go to work the next day and there is no one else to take care of my child. I can't take a breather." Said another, "Life consists mostly of work and child-raising."

The difficulties in family life arise from the structure of our society, but they are viewed as private problems, not public issues (Mills, 1959). Some social policies can and do aid families, i.e., childcare assistance and welfare, but these are often publicly conceptualized as residual services, for people who cannot do what they ought to be doing for themselves.

Finding adequate childcare arrangements is a difficulty for divorced mothers as it is for other mothers. With licensed childcare available for only about 20 percent of the children who need it (Roby, 1973), women who would like to work or go to school may choose to stay at home because facilities are either unavailable or inadequate (Hedges and Barnett, 1972). "It was awful looking for babysitting—they all wanted high pay and no one was good. Having the daycare center has made all the difference—childcare was always a worry."

Housework, repairs, and maintenance must also be sandwiched into the single mother's schedule. Many women do their own repairs, such as fixing appliances or plastering walls, because they cannot afford repair services. Said one mother in our sample, "Who does the fixing? I do. Washing machine, painting, minor repairs, TV—I learned how to do lots of things." More difficult maintenance jobs go unattended—one woman has three broken TV sets because "I can't afford a service person and I can't do it myself." Another cannot get fire insurance on her house—the only item of value the family owns—because the outside staircase is broken and she cannot afford a carpenter. The problems are complex, as one mother explained:

> Someone I wanted to have make repairs on the house, also a washing machine repairman, they won't come because of my being on AFDC. They won't wait to get paid, all they want is money. Same way with the doctor. He was rude to me, said he didn't have time to give my daughter a physical because AFDC takes such a long time to pay. You really do get shoved around, but it's AFDC, not just being divorced. I am ecstatic if anyone will fix anything. I try to fix things myself, if I can't, I call a service person. If someone offers, like this boyfriend . . . but I don't want to get into too much of that unless—you don't ask for favors, "cause then you owe."

STIGMA

In addition to the problems discussed above, the divorced mother finds herself facing stigma as a result of her divorced status and facing discrimination as a female head of household. Treated as irresponsible financially, as "fair game" sexually, often as psychologically disabled, she must repeatedly fight these images in negotiations between herself and those people and bureaucracies around her. Yet she continues to be held primarily responsible for the children and the housework. The divorced father is often seen as doing something special and praiseworthy when he takes care of his children; the divorced mother is seen as just doing her job, even when she is employed full-time (George and Wilding, 1972).

THE BENEFITS OF DIVORCE

Costs are only one dimension of single motherhood. There are also concrete benefits experienced by women who manage their families alone. Married mothers must take their husbands into account in everything they do. Once divorced, mothers no longer have to consult or please them in their daily lives. They have the freedom to please themselves, and this freedom is the basis of definite benefits.

Their freedom is not, however, merely a psychological condition. Gaining control over their lives involves more than changing their own minds; it means a change in the circumstances of their lives. Although their responsibilities may be burdensome, divorced mothers gain control over the money, the children, the standards of housekeeping, and the daily routine which structures family life. Whatever resources they can muster on behalf of the family are under their own control. They may not have much, but whatever they have is theirs to use as they think best.

These benefits are not always apparent to women as they move from marriage to divorce. They have to become independent; they have no choice. But taking over provides an opportunity to learn that they may be better off when they have control, and they may come to enjoy the freedom which is part of independent responsibility.

FINANCES

Even with reduced resources, divorced mothers may feel "better off" and even be "better off" financially. The income a husband contributes to a family is an advantage to his wife only if she has use of it. But a man may consume more than he provides, or he may retain control over the money to the detriment of the needs of the mother and children.

The women with the lowest marital incomes in our sample actually experienced an increase in standard of living after divorce. One mother, employed full-time while her husband "didn't do much," told us what she had expected as a result of divorce: "I knew it would get better—one less to support, plus I'd get help from

AFDC." Said another whose husband gambled, "I knew it would be better—he wouldn't be taking anything out of the till." For these women and several others, divorce meant an end to the husband's power to impoverish the family.

Above the lowest income level the standard of living did drop, but the women's greater control over family income sometimes meant an actual increase in cash at their disposal. Four women said that there would be more money in the family if their husbands were still there, but that they themselves would not be able to control its use. Said one mother of four, whose current income of $9,000 is half of the marital income: "I'd be even worse off because he spends it all. He wanted to go bankrupt. He rents now. He doesn't have a home. I just paid off the mortgage." She added that "It's less worrisome now. Living on AFDC I almost lost my health, but I didn't have to worry about his charge cards, his golf clubs, etcetera."

We do not wish to imply that divorce is financially beneficial for mothers. Most had lower family incomes *and* less cash at their disposal. But sixteen women who now had less income said they *felt* better off because they now decided where the money would go. Said a mother of four who is now on welfare, "I'm better off now. I'm getting less than I had but I'm doing more with it." Said another welfare mother, "I'm worse off now, but I feel better off because I have control of it."

Having control makes the budgeting process easier. "It's much better because I know how much money I have to live on and I just do." Said another about welfare, "It's steady. You know what you've got. You never know what you've got with a husband."

Not every woman felt better off, especially not those who had been married to affluent men. Said one about her reduced income, "I don't worry about what to do with it, just how to get more of it." For these women, problems from loss of income far outweighed the benefits of increased control.

AUTHORITY OVER FAMILY LIFE

Without a husband, the organization of life is often easier and the expenditure of energy less. One woman said about housekeeping: "Lots of women who are married say to me, 'You don't know how well off you are,' because they have to do all the work anyway."

Housework responsibilities were not reduced for all of the mothers. Some found more work as the children got older, or as roommates were added to relieve financial burdens. In other cases, they felt like doing more for their own satisfaction. "I do more housework now," said one woman. "I'm fussier. I don't have to please anyone, so I do it right." Regardless of its amount, almost two-thirds (19) of the women felt happier about doing it: "I had to keep the house spotless or there were arguments. Now I do it when I want to and I don't mind—I even enjoy it."

For these mothers, increased satisfaction followed from the end of supervision by their husbands and the obligation to meet their husbands' standards. The other eleven women either had not changed their attitudes about housework because they "always hated doing it," or they found it worse because they now had to fit it in between their new jobs and their family obligations.

Relationships with their children were another source of increased feelings of mastery. Most of the mothers in our sample felt they were doing a great job of raising their children, an appraisal certainly at variance with the attitudes of the society around them. One comment heard time and again when mothers described their current relationships with their children was "the peace" and the lack of conflict. One of the 18 who mentioned this said: "Easy things? I don't have to cope with or straighten the children out from being with a person with a sick mind." The same change occurred for an older mother who had put up with an alcoholic husband for seven years. "I can spend more time with the children because I don't have *him* to contend with. I don't have to share myself—I'm mother *and* father. There is less problem with discipline, because there's only one authority."

Despite the stereotype that a child will suffer from the absence of a male model, only four mothers actually mentioned this as either an existing problem or a potential problem. There are several reasons for this unexpected finding. In 11 families, the fathers continue to provide a male model through weekly contact with the children. In addition, children in all 30 families have other male models—grandfathers, uncles, neighbors, and mothers' boyfriends. It is commonly assumed that when the father is present he will provide an adequate male model. Several mothers in our sample pointed out that their children were better off *without* the male image that the father had provided.

SOCIAL LIFE

The benefits of independence for the divorced mother in arranging her family life—the finances, the housework, the children—were also evident in her own social life. No longer "half a couple," she can make her own decisions about the friendships she needs or wants. Asked if they had lost any friends because of divorce, several answered as did this woman: "Lose friends? No, because they weren't my friends, they were *his*. Now my friends are different— more intelligent, active people who do things."

"Couple society" did give a predictable structure to social life. Moving away from it was difficult, particularly for women who had been married a long time or who lived in family-oriented neighborhoods. But they did it. They found new friendships with divorced mothers, with married women they saw in the daytime, and with boyfriends or dates they included in their evening hours.

Gaining control over "social time" is like gaining control over money. They may have less, but they can decide how to spend it (Stein, 1976). Having choice over activities is a treasured commodity. "I'm in Parents Without Partners, and in some historian groups about New England history. I wouldn't have done it if I were married. I love to have freedom to do things—I didn't when married."

Control over social life includes control over sex life. They can choose to engage—or not to engage—in sexual relationships. When asked to evaluate their current sex life, 19 women reported that it was better than when married, largely because they had more to say about it. "I have less sex now, and I might add a lot better than before." The other 11 women were less satisfied, either because they had less sex than they wanted, because they found it difficult to have an unmarried sex life while raising children, or because they would have preferred more stable sexual relations with fewer partners.

SELF-CONCEPT

Taking on new responsibilities and doing unfamiliar tasks with little social support are not easy, but the experience of making decisions and mastering tasks forms the basis of a new, more satisfactory self-concept. "I had to work to get back my sense of self-respect," said a mother of four." "On the whole, it is easier now—I can handle things. I don't have a club over my head. I have problems, but at least now I have a fighting chance. I have a mind of my own." Not only in the family but also in relation to outside agencies, women have stronger self-concepts. Says one mother who is doing more with less money, "I'm a fighter now." These changes in self-concept derive from a real increase in their personal power. The women offered a variety of examples of this: "It's easier making all the decisions—decisions are *faster*. All kinds of issues—moral, ethical. Examining values—lifestyle and God. There is no one to answer to but yourself. Your own schedule, own plans." "It's easier now. You can do so much when your mind is free and you don't have any aggravation. Nothing *is* easier, but it *feels* easier. I have to live up to my own expectations, no one else's."

Only seven of the 30 women we interviewed were seriously interested in remarriage. The rest were either ambivalent (10) or disinclined to remarry (13).[3] Opposition to remarriage is often linked to the satisfactions of independence: "I'm not looking for it—not interested. I want to lead my own life. I don't like to report to someone what I'm doing." "There are the horrors of loneliness—but the loneliness with him around was much more acute. I feel pride in making it on my own." "I'm more independent, more demanding than I used to be." "I would have to trust a man a lot to give up my job again—this is my security."

Independence was less clearly indicated by those ambivalent toward remarriage, although it is implied. "I haven't given up the idea, but it's not likely. Maybe someday, to take care of the loneliness in my old age."

Rejection of remarriage did not mean rejection of men or of long-term close relationships. Rather, these women rejected the traditional model of marriage as incompatible with their new identity. They had exchanged domination by, and direct dependence on, a particular man for domination by and dependence on a system. This exchange brought new difficulties into their lives, but it also gave them options that their marriages had precluded. Most were unwilling to give up these options. Their response to this conflict was often to express a desire for alternative male relationships outside of the "marriage model." As one woman commented, "My attitude toward men is—they are nice for friends, they're fine for sex. A good man is a guy who has his own money and enjoys sex. I don't want to take anything from anybody."

National statistics have shown that the majority of divorced mothers have remarried; this indicates that these women's current attitude is not necessarily a predictor of future behavior. Several women in our sample were aware of the disjuncture between desire to remain divorced and objective pressure toward remarriage. One woman now on welfare said:

> I dislike the idea of remarriage. Ninety-seven percent of the time—no way. But an occasional time—mostly when I'm having financial difficulties, when problems are getting me down—I think, "that's what security is going to be."

Another agreed:

> My mother said to me, "The first time marry for love, the second time marry for security." My biggest fear is that I might remarry for security, because with the other pressures I may need that security.

Recent statistics indicate a drop in the remarriage rate (Norton and Glick 1979). Perhaps women today are more willing or more able to act on their expressed desire to remain independent than they were in the past.

POLICY IMPLICATIONS

How can the costs of divorced motherhood be reduced? There is no need for new policy proposals to answer that question. Those policy changes needed to make women autonomous have already been strongly advocated by women's groups and policy makers sympathetic to the situation of women, nonwhites, and the poor. Time and again such individuals and groups have argued that women should have access to the same resources available to men: jobs which pay something approximating a family wage, "automatic" social respect, and the resulting access to housing or credit without harassment. Insuring equal access—or as Rowbotham (1973) has said, "equal exploitation"—means providing equal education, in subject matter as well as in "quality." It means ending job-related discrimination at all levels—in training programs, in hiring, in on-the-job treatment and promotion, and, most essentially, in wages and benefits. It also means equalizing family costs off the job with children's allowances and freely available daycare.

But these or other policies are unlikely to be implemented for a number of reasons. First, government practices and business profits are geared to male-headed families. Keeping women dependent on men provides the conditions for a low-paid labor force as well as making domestic services and childcare a low-cost, wifely proposition. Second, all men have a partial interest in policies that maintain women's dependence. They receive direct personal benefits as the socially approved head of a family: better wages and job opportunities, personal services from women, and rights to make decisions. (We say only *partial* interest, because the high rate of marital dissolution suggests that many men may feel that the services and companionship of a wife and the joys of children are not worth the expense.) Third, these changes are expensive. Opposition to them would come both from business interests, whose profits might be taxed to implement them, and from middle- and lower-income families and individuals who, given the tax structure of the United States, pay a disproportionate share of taxes.

National and local government policy has been addressed more to issues of divorce law than to the needs of families. Some policy changes now under consideration or partially in force, such as no-fault divorce, divorce insurance, displaced homemaker protection, equalizing custody, and the use of HEW to track delinquent child support payments, do address the special situation of divorced mothers. However, they do not attack the underlying causes of their problems—that women get insufficient pay for their work and therefore must rely on husbands to provide the bulk of a family income. Nevertheless, the changes must be welcomed because they provide some immediate improvements, as well as a basis for more holistic changes in the future.

At the local level, divorced mothers themselves, the organized women's movement, and other sympathetic groups and individuals can respond to the needs of divorced mothers by providing services such as crisis intervention or information on locally available services and options. They are doing so in many cities and towns. Policy makers need to recognize that it is better to spend money to support and maintain locally organized services than to encourage expensive professionally organized demonstration projects, which end when the demonstration period ends.

As we said in the beginning of this section, we are not offering new policy proposals. Those that would improve the lives of divorced mothers have been made clearly and consistently in the past. What is needed is political commitment to make women equal members of this society. Ultimately the policy changes divorced mothers need await the time when women, including divorced mothers, have the power to implement the policies they know are needed.

NOTES

The research for this article was partially supported by the Russell Sage Foundation. We would like to thank George Levinger, Marylyn Rands, and Pat Thompson for reading and commenting on an earlier draft. A previous version appeared under a different title in *Journal of Social Issues*, 1976, 32 (1).

1. Welfare for these families is provided through Aid to Families with Dependent Children (AFDC).

2. National statistics (Bane, 1979) show lower average incomes for female-headed families than in our sample. Included in national samples are unwed mothers, teenagers, and aged women, all of whom tend to have very low incomes, as well as female-headed families in low-income rural areas, in states with punitively low welfare payments, and in locations in which there are poor job opportunities.

3. Our finding that 43 percent of our sample opposed remarriage differs little from that of Kriesberg (1970), who found that 52 percent of husbandless mothers in his sample did not want to marry again. Goode combined love and marriage, thus obscuring the difference, yet still found that 30 percent of his sample of divorced mothers felt negatively toward both (1956).

REFERENCES

Bane, M.J. 1979. Marital disruption and the lives of children. In G. Levinger and O.C. Moles (Eds.). *Divorce and separation*. New York: Basic Books, 276–286.

Bernard, J. 1972. *The future of marriage.* New York: World.

Brandwein, R.A., Brown, C.A., and Fox, E.M. 1974. Women and children last: The social situation of divorced mothers and their families. *Journal of Marriage and the Family,* 36, 498–514.

Brown, P. 1976. A study of women coping with divorce. In *New research on women and sex roles.* University of Michigan: Center for Continuing Education.

George, V., and Wilding, P. 1972. *Motherless families.* London: Routledge and Kegan Paul.

Gillespie, D.L. 1971. Who has the power? The marital struggle. *Journal of Marriage and the Family,* 33, 445–458.

Goode, W.J. 1956. *After divorce.* New York and Chicago: Free Press.

Gove, W., and Tudor, J. 1973. Adult sex roles and mental illness. In J. Huber (Ed.). *Changing women in a changing society.* Chicago: University of Chicago Press.

Hedges, J.N., and Barnett, J.K. 1972. Working women and the division of household tasks. *Monthly Labor Review,* 95, 9–14.

Holmstrom, L. 1973. *Two career family.* New York: Schenkman.

Komisar, L. 1973. *Down and out in the U.S.A.: A history of social welfare.* New York: Watts.

Kriesberg, L. 1970. *Mothers in poverty: A study of fatherless families.* Chicago: Aldine.

Levinger, G. 1979. A social and psychological perspective on marital dissolution. In G. Levinger and O.C. Moles (Eds.). *Divorce and separation.* New York: Basic Books, 37–60.

Marsden, D. 1969. *Mothers alone: Poverty and the fatherless family.* London: Allen Lane, the Penguin Press.

Mills, C.W. 1959. *The sociological imagination.* London: The Oxford University Press.

*Norton, A. J., and Glick, P. C., Marital instability in America. 1979. In G. Levinger and O.C. Moles (Eds.). *Divorce and separation.* New York: Basic Books, pp. 6–20.

Roby, P. 1973. *Child care—who cares? Foreign and domestic infant and early childhood development policies.* New York: Basic Books.

Rollins, B., and Feldman, H. 1970. Marital satisfaction over the family life cycle. *Journal of Marriage and the Family,* 32, 20–27.

Rowbotham, S. 1973. *Women's consciousness, man's world.* London: Pelican.

Sawhill, I.V. May 1975. Discrimination and poverty among women who head families. Paper given at Conference on Occupational Segregation, Wellesley College.

Stein, P. 1976. *Single.* Englewood Cliffs, N.J.: Prentice-Hall.

Stevenson, M. 1973. Women's wages and job segregation. *Politics and Society,* 4, 83–96.

U.S. Department of Labor. 1976. *Women workers today.* Washington, D.C.

Weiss, R.S. 1975. *Marital separation.* New York: Basic Books.

*Selection included in this volume.

24/ CHILDCARE RESPONSIBILITIES OF PART-TIME AND SINGLE FATHERS

Kristine M. Rosenthal and Harry F. Keshet

The available literature on divorce, postdivorce family, and adjustments to marital disruption in general focuses on the problems of mother-headed families and fatherless children. The assumption, borne out statistically, is that most children live with their mothers after divorce and that fathers tend to drift gradually away from their ex-spouse and children. Some early studies (Waller, 1938) assumed that after the divorce the father had no role in the children's lives. The generally accepted view that the role of the father is that of economic provider has been supported by the majority of social theorists dealing with the family (Parsons and Bales, 1955; Brenton, 1966). "The traditional male's primary role is in the occupational sector, and it is not altered very much by either marriage or fatherhood" (Duberman, 1977: 148). These attitudes are further reinforced by the complementary view of men as inept at nurturant behavior and thus not suited for childcare (Parsons and Bales, 1955; Henry, 1963; Benson, 1968; Bigner, 1970).

For a long time fathers were little encouraged to participate in the life of their children, and the effects of this participation were little understood. The 1960s produced a great deal of literature focused on the detrimental effects of father absence, but it has been difficult to distinguish these from the effects of the severely reduced economic circumstances of mother-headed families. In several studies which controlled for socioeconomic variables, the absence of the father appeared to have no detrimental effect on the children's development (Nye, 1957; Parry and Phufl, 1963; Crain and Stamn, 1965).

A decade later, the rapidly increasing rate of divorce, the changing ideology about sex-role stereotypes, the new economic and social independence of women, and the attendant pressures for sex-role equality all have contributed to a developing redefinition of the fathering role. There has been new interest in the importance of fathers for children (Biller and Meredith, 1974; Lynn, 1974) and a new consciousness about males participating in the nurturant tasks of family life. "Parenting has become a desirable male role for many, and fathers are accepting major parenting responsibility within the two parent family context and the single parent context" (Warren, 1976).

For many men this new involvement in the fathering role is a direct consequence of marital separation. Faced with the choice of seeing the relationship with their children erased through lack of contact and intimacy, some fathers are opting for the still difficult and strange role of daily caretaker. The number of children who live with a divorced father has tripled in the past ten years, although that still represents only one-tenth of the number of children who live with their divorced mother. Joint custody and informal sharing of childcare are becoming more common among young divorced couples with children. Unlike the once-or-twice-a-month visiting fathers whose parenting role diminishes over time, involved fathers, like single mothers, find themselves with a role overload. They must learn to coordinate work obligations, social life needs, and attempts to create a new family for themselves with the continuing daily responsibilities of childcare (Keshet and Rosenthal, 1978).

The present study was designed to determine the effects of childcare involvement on the lifestyles of young fathers. One hundred and twenty-seven separated or divorced fathers were interviewed about their childcare responsibilities. Each man had at least one child aged three to seven. Twenty-eight of the fathers saw their children at least every other weekend, for a total of six or less days each month—these we have called the "occasional" fathers; 21 of the fathers spent no less then seven days a month, and no more than 13 days with their children—they are the "quartertime" fathers. Twenty-nine of the fathers in the sample spent half of each month with their children, and the remaining 49 are full-time fathers. All respondents live in the Greater Boston Area. They represent a highly educated urban population, close to half of the sample having completed, or about to complete, graduate or professional training. The majority are in professional or semiprofessional occupations (40 percent and 16 percent), another 20 percent are in business, and 16 percent have blue-collar jobs or work in crafts.

The joint-care fathers in the sample had the highest concentration of professional men. This group, as distinct from the full-time fathers, can be assumed to have taken on their childcare voluntarily and to have some flexibility in their work schedules. Eighty-three percent of the fathers worked full-time or more. With increased childcare time the work hours tended to decrease. Income also fluctuated with childcare time. The fact that full-time and half-time fathers average considerably less income gives us some indication of the effect of childcare on the work lives of actively parenting men.

The conflicts between work and childcare experienced by these fathers are similar to those reported frequently by single mothers. Men who during their married lives expected their family to adjust to the demands of their work suddenly find themselves having to coordinate and juggle the schedules of work and childcare. Here accepted standards of nine-to-five duties begin to seem unreasonable. As one father employed by a large engineering firm told us:

> My boss is old-fashioned, he does not care what work I actually do, but he must see me there from nine to five. It is very inconvenient for me, and I knew I could get as much or more work done on a more flexible schedule, but he would not hear of it.

Other fathers who had more work independence found that it was their own expectations they had to overcome:

> I had to give up this image of being a scholar, sitting in the library till all hours of the night. Others in my department did that and they were family men too. But pretty soon I only came in to teach and did some extra work when [son] was not with me. I started to enjoy being at home. After all he would grow up and I might have missed all that, the library would always be there.

The fathers report passing up promotions that might mean a move away from the children, reducing their work hours, and choosing work for its compatibility with the demands of childcare. We must not underestimate the importance of this change for highly achieving professional men. Socialization for career performance is one of the outstanding features of male identity (Pleck, 1975). Much has been written about the general importance of work as a source of well-being for men—work as a source of life purpose (Morse and Weiss, 1955), as a prized self-image (Wilensky, 1966), and as a validating experience (Rainwater, 1974).

The reduction of work involvement has two sources. On one hand, it is a practical response to the overload of demands on the father's time. Even with daycare services, babysitters, and the help of the extended family, although the last is rare for middle-class men, much time and energy are absorbed by the child's needs. On the other hand, as indicated later, eventually childcare becomes defined as another job for which the father has contracted. When this happens the rewards of doing that job well and feeling competent in it begin to compete with work satisfaction, thus reducing the salience of occupational role for the men.

General analyses of work and family in modern America can be summarized as accepting the centrality of work for determining the quality of family life. Dissatisfaction with work is thought to lead to an unsatisfactory family life. This analysis tends to be reversed for women. That is, for women personal satisfactions are seen as dependent on their marital and fertility status, motherhood being the source of major identity. Consequently, the influence of family demands on career decisions has been extensively studied for women but not for men.

To view it in a somewhat different way: women may resist the demands of occupational socialization by the legitimacy of their participation in the family. Men, on the other hand, find little support in rejecting the demands of the work world on behalf of family functions. A woman worker may more easily state that she will not accept overtime because "her children need her" or "her husband does not like it." The same reasons stated by a male worker undermine the expected masculine image of autonomy and independence. Thus, both the desire and the attempt to restructure family participation on the part of a married man may be severely restricted by his own work expectations, the expectations of family members, and inflexible work obligations. Pleck (1975) views the current structure of the male occupational role as a major limitation of the sex-role change in the family.

The divorced father finds himself in a somewhat different situation. His childcare involvement is motivated by the fear of losing a relationship with his children. His newly acquired parenting role— whether as a weekend, half-time, or single father—is a new legal or contractual obligation. Parenting which in a marriage was likely to come second to work obligations is now a legitimate function *on par* with the demands of work. In fact, it acquires many of the characteristics of work, and fathers begin to develop competence, recognize cues for judging themselves as competent, and experience the familiar rewards of a job well done.

Learning to overcome the initial feelings of inadequacy which many fathers experience when doing "women's work" can be more easily overcome when the childcare tasks are seen as a legitimate new assignment to be "worked on." New definitions of fathering have to be developed. "Getting a divorce really made me pause and think what is my role as a father; am I any good at raising the children? I often found myself lacking." But only at first. With additional experience comes competence and self-assurance.

For men, the issue of parenting by themselves is the issue of com-

petence and the ways in which they understand competent performance in caring for and relating to children. Women evaluate parenting more often through their feeling relationship with the child.

The issue of competence and efficacy dominates the self-image of
males. The cultural image of competence is cold and impersonal, but
it also can be a way to think about feelings and to begin to learn how
to function interpersonally. A man who begins to parent and who
can meet the purely practical needs of children—bathing, feeding,
getting them to school on time—begins to feel more effective. This
sense of effectiveness translates into good feelings about the children
and good feelings which he learns that the children have about him.
The crisis often comes when the needs to be satisfied are purely
emotional—the temper tantrum is the most trying event for a newly
independent father.

> It's when she cried and I didn't know what to do for her, I
> didn't understand it. So I would try to figure it out by trial
> and error. Did I do something bad? I go through a series
> of hypotheses. It took a while but I finally learned how to
> figure out what's bothering her. I feel a lot better now. I
> can get an idea what's upsetting her now. I also can get
> her to tell me what's wrong and I can generally do some-
> thing about it.

In describing the same problem, another father contrasted it with
the way he has seen his wife handle it.

> My wife is different. What she does is to just somehow
> intuit what's upsetting our son. Or sometimes she just will
> say you feel sad and not need to know the reason but just
> deal with the sadness. I don't know if you can do that. I
> have to understand what is wrong.

Once the feelings of competence begin to be introduced into the
area of dealing with children's emotions, reinforced by the child's
well-being, the whole area of emotions becomes less threatening for
men. Each father can develop his own criteria for doing a good job
as a father in the way he relates to the children.

For men socialized to believe that feelings must be kept hidden
and are a barrier to effective functioning, experiencing competency
in this area can be a source of positive self-regard.

> Suddenly I found I could really do it. I saw that I could
> take care of the girls and respond to their emotional
> needs as well as run the house.

Bringing the perimeters and criteria of work performance, familiar to men, to the parenting role appears to make men at ease with their new obligations. It also gives the parenting role an external legitimacy and internal satisfaction which undermines the impact of work socialization for men, and frees them to develop a more individually determined balance of work and family commitment.

What remains to be seen is whether these individual adjustments can be maintained over time against the pressures of employees' expectations, especially when new relationships with women may reduce the father's family obligations.

THE CHANGING PATTERNS OF INTIMACY

Freud has been widely quoted as having said the two components of mental health are the ability to work and the ability to love. Both these functions are disrupted by marital breakup. At the time of separation it is difficult for many men to imagine that they could ever again feel closeness with a woman and plan a future with her. Even men who are involved with another sexual partner at the time of separation are wary of commitment. In the case of men who did not desire or initiate the divorce proceedings the process of psychological separation is even slower. These men often have hopes and expectations of reconciliation which to an objective observer appear clearly unrealistic. While the legal separation or divorce decree entitles a man to take up his single life, many are unaware that the psychological divorce may take much longer. Bohannan (1970), in describing the "six stations" of divorce, places psychic divorce at the very last, defining it as a slow process of regaining individual autonomy. Waller (1967) also describes final estrangement between the ex-spouses as complete only some time after the partners have entered new social worlds.

The divorced men themselves describe this time as one of depression or apathy. They may be tired or rushed, transient in their living arrangements, or burdened with childcare. All these become reasons to defend against an immediate involvement with a new partner. Somehow, however, new relationships do get established. We know that approximately 50 percent of the people who get divorced remarry within three years (Glick and Norton, 1977), so that not long after the separation—needing to reassert themselves as attractive males—men begin "dating." The term "dating" is used self-consciously and evokes all the insecurities, hesitations, and posturing that are part of its adolescent origins. It is a time of "trying out" a new self, even though most divorced people do not really enter the world of single people, but that of the formerly married (Hunt, 1966; Cox, 1978).

The relationships retain the status of dating for as long as the dating couple avoids the formation of any mutual ties or obligations, even though at any given moment in time the date might fulfill all the functions of a temporary marriage mate. It is important to the partners that they maintain separate residences and have separate friends and activities. The purpose of the separateness is to underlie the "casual" nature of the relationship. The man is reestablishing his *independence*, which might be easily threatened. It is understood that the relationship could be easily terminated if either party so desired. There should be no mutual property, no need to explain to the children why "he" is not there on Sundays anymore—in other words, as little as possible which might be reminiscent of the marital breakup.

It is difficult if not impossible to adhere to such a definition of dating for a long time with one person. Deliberately or not, communalities develop, friends and children begin to expect the presence of the date, comfortable habits set in. Men who explicitly and determinably wish to prevent such a development, find themselves in the peculiar, and often hard to explain, situation of wanting to break off a relationship precisely because it feels comfortable, and because they are beginning to depend on it for both emotional sustenance and real help around the house. The experience leaves the woman bewildered and bitter. "What went wrong?"

> He wants to break off just when everything is going so well, the children have finally gotten to like me, and we've been so comfortable together, why just last week he said he does not know how he would have managed without me?

It is not often that she can get a satisfactory explanation. "I am just not ready," the man is likely to say obliquely, or else he disagrees over some small matter to create an opportunity to divest himself of the encroaching commitment.

To understand this dynamic, which pervades the patterns of dating and the course of developing and changing relationships, we must remember that issues of power or control, and of dependency, are the major issues roused by the proceedings of marital breakup. Fathers who spend time with their young children after divorce have an opportunity to work out these issues in their parenting relationship, making the parental relationship an important source of personal reconstruction (Keshet and Rosenthal, 1978).

Several authors have discussed the relationship between power and dependency (Blau, 1955, 1964; Thibaut and Kelley, 1959; Emerson, 1962). Emerson (1962) proposes a simple formula in which the power of A over B equals the dependency of B on A. Kemper (1972) views these as central variables in any analyses of adult relationships. As we have stated elsewhere (Keshet and Rosenthal, 1978, p. 1), fathers after divorce often give a great deal of power to their children and become dependent on them emotionally. Following the natural status position of father and child, this situation can be gradually adjusted in accord with the strengthening self-image of the father. The situation is different vis-à-vis an emotional involvement with a new lover. The father's newly emerged independence is threatened because he recognizes aspects of real dependency in his parental responsibilities. Furthermore, to accept and recognize this dependency may undermine his still-vulnerable masculinity. Thus the father who is in fact engaged in the process of personal growth through his childcare adjustments is wary of being interfered with through a new relationship with a woman.

A woman who is socialized to be responsive and helpful, as an important part of her intimate relationship, is most vulnerable to rejection in this situation. She is often surprised to find that the man she was interested in becomes involved in a relationship with another woman who appears to "care" for him much less—that is, offers less housekeeping help. Given this configuration, divorce may, in part, serve the need for autonomy in the area of emotional and parental coping, allowing necessary competence to emerge. Once a man feels good about himself, and secure in his familial capabilities, he may be much more available for a new love relationship.

DATING PATTERNS

Relationships of short duration, or multiple dating, serve to enforce the barriers between new potential partners. All the men interviewed had, shortly after separation, dated more than one woman at a time. The pattern, which appears to repeat, begins with a fairly intense involvement immediately after separation which has the quality of a "port in a storm." The woman in question is often more a confidante than a lover: she listens to complaints against the ex-spouse, the legal system, and whatever other forces seem to conspire against the newly divorced man. She is a witness to his insecurities and a focus in gropings for a new identity. When that first stage is past, however, and some sort of emotional equilibrium is reached, this is rarely the relationship that lasts. For men anxious to try out new powers, the woman who has witnessed his setbacks is not the ideal partner. The time of quiet recuperation with one sympathetic and supportive woman is often followed by frequent and varied dating. After the first year, relationships become more exclusive and of longer duration and may lead to a more serious partnership or cohabitation.

This pattern seems as true for men who have a committed lover waiting for them at the time of the marital breakup as for those whose failed marriages leave them with no one to turn to. It is only after a period of experimentation and heightened dating activity that some men return to their original extramarital lover who may have been the impetus for the divorce. We conclude from our case studies that the patterns of dating following marital separation are not accidental. They appear to be a replay of the unresolved issues of adolescence, such as separation, individualization, differentiation, and finally commitment.

Commitment often becomes defined by sexual exclusivity. The refusal of such exclusivity is another means of delaying such commitment, even when the couple is explicitly or effectively living together. Some couples have an explicit understanding that other sexual partners are permissible for both. Others have not made such an explicit agreement, but neither have they ruled it out. This ambiguity about the permissibility of other sexual encounters reflects, on one hand, the changing attitudes toward fidelity within marriage (Roy and Roy, 1970; O'Neill and O'Neill, 1972), and, on the other, the uses of promiscuity as power; it has been shown that the mate who is less concerned with monogamy and pursues other sexual relationships has power over the partner who desires sexual fidelity and is not promiscuous.

It is also likely that men use their prerogative of seeking out new partners less out of real sexual interest, and more as a reminder to both themselves and their primary partner that they are not in fact married. Such a reminder provides the safety margin that at an earlier stage required the actual breaking off of the dating relationship.

CHARACTERISTICS OF NEW PARTNERS

It was common for the men we interviewed to date women with certain social characteristics. They were frequently considerably younger than the men, of similar social class, and, whether single, divorced, or separated, were unlikely to have children of their own. Only a third of the respondents reported forming "serious relationships" with women who had children. Although such relationships were more common for men in the early stages of separation and seem to represent a desire to reconstruct the marriage configuration, they generally did not last. Whatever the attraction of the ready-made family—the woman whose life is set up for childcare, who can usually include the children of the separated father in the weekly activities, and who has a child-equipped house—it does not last. In the long run, such relationships presented difficulties in coordination and planning for the two partners. A relationship based on the man's needs as a part-time father rarely coincided with what he wanted as a man recovering a sense of his own desirability.

> I dated a woman with children and it was fairly compli-
> cated. She had a time commitment to her own children.
> Her kids entered into our relationship; so did mine. We
> each had to relate to and like each other's kids as well as
> liking and relating to each other.

One father dated a woman because she had a station wagon and on weekends they could all pile into the car and go on picnics which she prepared. Another man dated a woman whose functioning as a mother he admired and realized that he used the time to learn from her how to behave with his own children. In the end, however, the father's own sense of himself as a man apart from his childcare responsibilities tends to assert itself.

Dating women of similar social class characteristics, often of similar work interests or professional concerns, increases the opportunity to separate a sense of oneself as a single adult from that of a part-time parent. This is true both emotionally and in terms of time flexibility. Many of the fathers needed the support of this love relationship immediately after delivering the children to the ex-spouse— a time of more than ordinary stress.

Dating women who did not have children of their own allowed for more time flexibility. Since most fathers take their children on the weekend, dating a woman without children of her own made it easier to plan the time alone on the weekdays when neither had other obligations. It also made it possible for the woman to be of company and assistance to the father when the children were with him and to sleep over on the nights when the children were not there. Divorced women with similar childcare arrangements were likely to resent having to spend time with someone else's children on the weekends when they themselves were free from childcare. One father complained that he had stopped dating a woman with children partly because it was so difficult to have time alone together.

REFAMILYING

Eighty percent of all divorced people eventually remarry. Remarriage often follows a period of cohabitation. By the end of the second year of separation many men are seriously considering living with a woman. Although the stereotype is that it is the woman who pressures for commitment and stability during a dating relationship, we cannot state conclusively from our data that this is so. First of all, we find that the arrangements for time together are often difficult when the man has children who spend some of their time with him. It has been the general pattern in our newly sexually free groups that single people may cohabit with each other on a part-time basis. Gone are the days when there was nowhere to go to spend the night for many sophisticated urban singles. The back of the car, the nervous motel registrations, the phony wedding ring are for the most part just a specter of the 1950s. "Your place or mine" is the current style.

In the general course of events it is usually the man who is likely to stay over at his date's place. There are many reasons for this: women are more likely to care about their environments and have a home which feels and is more comfortable. There will be clean sheets and something for breakfast; this is more than one can expect to find in many a bachelor pad. Many women do not want the experience of having to wash a week of dishes or help put away accumulated papers before they can relax in a romantic atmosphere. Others feel safer and more relaxed in their own house. So her house it is. Pretty soon the man, if he becomes a steady date, finds himself spending more and more time at the house of his lover. He leaves some clothes behind, then some work, and before long he has more or less explicitly moved in. When the decision to live together is made, that is where they stay. Sometimes a stray roommate will move out to allow for additional space, and sometimes the new couple will hunt for a place of their own.

This is much less likely to be the case with the separated fathers. The father feels under some pressure to create a home, at least part-time, for his children. He is therefore more careful about his surroundings and more settled. This is especially true at least in the second year of the separation, when the childcare schedule has become regular and stable. He must spend time at his house, at least when the children are there. He is likely to want to be there at other times as well, first of all because they might want to reach him, but, most important, because he has put an effort into creating a home. His sense of home is already divided between the house that he and his ex-wife had shared and his new domicile, and he may not wish to fraction it further.

The newly separated man, anxious to make his quarters feel like home for himself and his children, is less likely to make himself a part-time inhabitant of his lover's house. It is she, therefore, who must come to his house—a situation that she may be unused to but one that many women do in fact find intriguing or different. She is likely to find there a much more domesticated man, one who is aware of whether or not the dishes are washed, one who does not automatically assume that she will take on the homemaking (in its

true sense) responsibilities, one who may in fact be somewhat possessive of his newly acquired housekeeping skills. Many fathers are still
proving to their ex-spouse and children that they are competent
parents; still proving to themselves that they can maintain control
over their domestic and parental lives; their unwillingness to return
to the division of roles which characterized their marriage may present a very different possibility of coexistence to a new female lover.

A great deal has been written recently on gender roles within a
family. Dual-career families have been of special interest because the
possible conflicts engendered by the interference with the traditional
division of labor between husband and wife "provides us with a
glimpse of emerging family dynamics" (Gordon, 1978). The studies
all emphasize the continuing responsibility of the woman for the
smooth running of the household and the care of the children, even
when the wife's career commitments make sharing of the family
tasks either a reasonable expectation or an explicit decision (Holmstrom, 1972; Rapoport and Rapoport, 1971) Childcare responsibilities are specifically assigned to the wife. In a study of 33 families,
Poloma and Garland (1971) found only one family which they were
willing to describe as egalitarian in that respect. The willing assumption of the childcare, as well as conflict and guilt engendered over
any interference with mothering, has been ascribed to the socialization of women, which emphasizes their family roles (Reiss, 1965;
Rubin, 1976).

The case of men and their children cohabiting with a new sexual
partner provides us with an opportunity to view a family situation
which is almost the reverse of the traditional marriage. The children
are first and foremost the responsibility of the father. The female
partner is usually economically independent, having work of her
own which existed prior to the family situation and which continues
to have priority. Not only are the house and children a major responsibility of the father, but he also views it as his function to
coordinate the members of the household and make sure that they
feel good about each other. This is the "expressive" leadership function described by Parsons and Bales (1955) as the very core of the
wife's role in the family. He retains his dominant status, however,
both in the family as head of the household and in the larger society.
The woman's socialization may lead her to expect to take on the
mother and wife role, but the structural conditions of the particular
circumstance force her to deal with these expectations in a new and
innovative way. We have here, then, within the family a microcosm
of an experimental situation in which the roles are reversed without
a corresponding major change in the wider social structures.

For the woman in that situation the wife and mother roles are an
extension of her love relationship with the man and are mediated by

it. When the direct love relationship with the father is terminated, so is her role vis-à-vis the house and children. This is not unlike the traditional priority of the husband role for men, and the mediation of their fathering through the relationship with the wife (Pleck, 1975).

Younger, childless women, who are more likely to have grown up with expectations of independence and self-assertion, are better equipped emotionally to function within this configuration. It is not unlikely that divorced men who have this mode of coping with their new state gravitate toward this type of women. Men who, on the other hand, are anxious to replicate their previous marital arrangements may be more likely to marry more traditional women or ones who have children of their own from a previous marriage.

ADJUSTMENTS TO COHABITATION

The transition from a dating relationship—in which the woman has her own home to retreat to and functions more like a guest in the father's house—to cohabitation is a major transition because it puts a strain on the equilibrium that has been worked out. Women who have learned to be sensitive to the autonomy needs of the man in and out of the house, and to their own secondary position within the new family, may find that their natural inclination or expectation to take over family responsibilities becomes very strong when the cues for separateness are diminished. In other words, once moved in, can the not-quite stepmother maintain her nontraditional role within the household configuration? And can the man in turn respect her autonomy and maintain his own functioning as the responsible parent despite the clear temptation to increase the reliance on the new partner to a degree which might naturally slip into a relationship reminiscent of the discarded marriage? The couple must evidence a great deal of self-awareness and commitment to the new lifestyle in order to defend themselves against these changes.

The line between commitment to the children expected from a new partner and the participation in childcare responsibility must be most carefully balanced. This is probably one of the most dramatic aspects of the new relationship, and the most frequent source of tension.

There are many aspects of role reversal entailed in sharing parenting with a divorced father. The tone of the relationship is generally set by the fact that the new woman moves into a house already occupied by the father. The house was chosen for its suitability for his childcare obligations, distance from the children's mother or school, and space for their visits, and has been tested by his developing and routinizing his parenting tasks there. If a move is made it is usually for the same reasons as the above; that is, the father's parenting obligations set the perimeters of their decisions.

Since the man's free time is often planned with childcare in mind, the extra energy and attention required by the new arrangement often come in conflict with the established routine. Vacations, weekends, and other times which normally an adult couple would have free for themselves are often the very times when childcare is at its heaviest. The sense that the man is not fully available, practically and emotionally, and that his childcare obligations take priority over his relationship to his lover are the most commonly reported sources of conflict in the first months of cohabitation. Often the separation of time alone and time with the children becomes more difficult than when the couple lived apart. If conflict between the father and the children develops it is more difficult for the new woman to simply absent herself and provide the space for the father to solve it.

Fathers are especially conscious of needing to reassure the children, and perhaps their ex-spouses as well, that the new partner will not usurp the father's time and attention or even the physical space in the house. Many men admitted favoring the children when their lover first moved in. It was difficult to distinguish how much such behavior was meant to reassure the children and how much it was due to their own insecurity in the new situation. The children provided an excuse for creating some real and emotional barriers against the increasing intimacy.

Men who have only recently gained control over their children and a sense of competence in their parenting roles are generally happy to share housekeeping tasks, but are much less eager to relinquish their direct relationship with the children. "I would consult with [her] about helping me with childcare, but basically I was still the parent and they were still my responsibility." There was, in fact, often a special effort on the part of the father to let the children know that he, the father, would continue to be the "real" parent and was not abdicating his rights and responsibilities vis-à-vis the children. At the same time the cohabiting partner had lost the status of a guest in the house which might have given her special privileges and instead had assumed the more modest role of a helper. This is the new family socialization which takes place and further reinforces the role reversal we have described. The new woman is *not*, strictly speaking, a mother substitute, because in most cases the children have a perfectly adequate mother. Instead, she shares the fathering role, emulates his behavior, relies on his approval. As the husband once babysat for his wife, she now "babysits" for him. The traditional fatherly functions of driving children to school or picking them up are often taken over by the new partner.

Most fathers saw such activities as *help for them,* not as direct care-taking of the child.

> It was really nice to have help when I needed it. But I never lost sight of the fact that the children were my responsibility and my enjoyment too.
>
> Sometimes it was really nice not to have anyone else around but me and my children.

Such confessions are painful to hear for the new family member. Fathers were both deliberate and explicit in directing and limiting the amount of interaction between their new partners and the children. Only when a struggle ensued did these situations become more clarified. The demands of the new partner had to be made on emotional grounds, and her bargaining power was perhaps the lowest as compared to the needs of the children and the father.

> Kitty [partner] often resented doing things related to the children. I did not realize what it was I was expecting or how much help I was actually getting until I asked her to pick up the children and she refused.

> Faith accused me of shutting her out when the kids were here. She said I am always limiting what she could do with them. I thought it had to do with not wanting to impose on her, but now I think it had more to do with authority and control. Funny how these old things keep popping up.

In general, the defense presented by the fathers as to why they seemed intent on preserving a distance between their partners and their children had to do with the desire to protect the children from the upheavals of another separation should their new relationship prove to be temporary. In fact, however, it is likely that the fathers were protecting themselves. Having evolved a relationship with the children in which their presence and caring were central and expected, as opposed to the often peripheral relationship which fathers have in intact marriages, these men were unwilling to chance a reversal. The presence of a woman in the household, the memory of a household where the woman was emotionally central in the parenting relationship—threatened with a possibility of such a reversal, many of the men were unsure that in case of real competition for the children's affection their partner might not win because of sex. On the other hand, the temptation to hand over the burdens and trials of childcare responsibility likewise threatened the newly developed parental identity. Thus the somewhat exaggerated effort to assert their authority as a biological parent.

And, finally, we found an unwillingness to share the already seemingly divided affection and loyalty of the children with yet another adult. Many men only too willing to share the drudgery of daily household tasks would have thought twice about sharing the rewards of their parenting.

It was difficult for many of the fathers clearly to define a role for their partner that did not in some way seem to displace either themselves or their ex-spouse. In many cases there was a great fear of engendering even the slightest conflict between the partner and the ex-spouse, and possibly threatening the often informal childcare agreement.

In the majority of the cases, the respondents definitely defined their partners as helpers but not as parents or even parent substitutes, thus explicitly limiting their emotional involvement with the child and reemphasizing their own importance as a biological parent.

> I am not looking for a mother substitute for [daughter]. She already has a mother that she is very close to.

> We are struggling about the extent to which she [partner] wants to be involved [with the children] and can be psychologically involved given her position [here the father emphasized the insecurity and possible transience of the new relationship].

The children themselves participated in many of these struggles. They, too, were wary of forming new dependencies on people whose permanence and status in their lives was not to be trusted. They were often reluctant to allow the partner to care for them even after having known them for years. They competed for the father's attention and protected their special relationship. They often rejected the attempts of the new parent surrogate for emotional closeness, affection, or direction. All respondents reported such experiences of rejection of their partners. Fathers of male children reported this more frequently than fathers of female children.

Despite the resistance, despite the caution and the jealousies, somehow during the first year of living together emotional closeness does become possible between the new woman and the children. Affection becomes openly shared; children freely express their concern for and interest in the newly accepted family member. The relationship appears more mutual and independent of the father and his mediation. The women are able to relate directly to the children and view them as their friends. In many cases, the fathers, having overcome their initial possessiveness, are able to encourage the developing bonds with the children and can now appreciate, unthreatened, the contribution that their partners make to the childcare.

> Jean [daughter] said she loved Wendy [partner]. But she didn't know what to do about it because Wendy was not her mother. She and Wendy were able to talk about it and they both seemed happy. And I was glad that Jean felt that way and glad that they could talk about it.

> The kids like her to kiss them before going to sleep, but they want me to get them ready for bed and put them to sleep. Still they accept her and love her.

The acknowledgment of an independent relationship between the lover and the children indicates a definite shift in the woman's role in the household and indicates the growth of new family-like relationships.

At this point the partner becomes much more active in the parenting. Fathers become freer in discussing problems of childrearing with their partners and consulting them on issues of discipline and authority. Discussion of styles of parenting and standards for children's behavior is also more frequent, indicating the greater participation on the part of the lovers in the direct dealing with the children. The women in turn feel freer to voice their own opinions. As the living situation continues the sharing becomes more total, and the ties of family member to family member become more balanced.

It remains to be seen whether within this reconstituted family the redesigned roles of parental involvement and responsibility, based on the new emotional growth of the fathers and the consciousness of women as independent individuals with their own rights and priorities, can be maintained even when they run counter to the expected family functioning. It may be that the drastic reduction of the responsibilities on the part of the woman for the maintenance of the family unit and the increased involvement of the father are necessary preconditions for the development of a truly egalitarian or symmetrical marriage. It will also be interesting to see whether these innovative roles are maintained when the couple begins to have children of their own, in addition to the father's previous offspring.

Our original interest in separated fathers was based on the hypothesis that the structural demands of childcare would force changes in the lives of men, with the result that their behavioral and personality profiles might look more like those of women. We had not anticipated the extension of that change to a new family configuration. It may be that the emphasis on boundaries and control, which is the result of male socialization in relation to work, when carried to the area of the family has positive consequences. The same patterns, assimilated by women, may provide them with a basis for freeing themselves from some of the negative aspects of the mothering function and female socialization for family membership.

REFERENCES

Bensen, L. (1968) Fathering, A Sociological Perspective. New York: Random House.

Bigner, J. J. (1970) "Fathering: research and practical implications." Family Coordinator (October): 357–362.

Biller, H., and D. Meredith (1974) Father Power. New York: David McKay.

Blau, M (1964) Exchange and Power in Social Life. New York: John Wiley.

——— (1955) The Dynamics of Bureaucracy. Chicago: Univ. of Chicago Press.

Bohannan, P. (1970) Divorce and After. Garden City, NY: Doubleday.

Brenton, M. (1966) The American Male. New York: Free Press.

Cox, F. D. (1978) Human Intimacy: Marriage, the Family and its Meaning. St. Paul, MN: West.

Crain, A. J., and C. S. Stamn (1965) "Intermittent absence of fathers and children's perceptions of parents." J. of Marriage and the Family 27: 344–347.

David, D. S., and R. Brannon [eds.] (1976) The Forty-Nine Percent Majority: The Male Sex Role. Reading, MA: Addison-Wesley.

Duberman, L. (1977) Marriage and Other Alternatives. New York: Praeger.

Emerson, R. M. (1962) "Power dependence relations." Amer. Soc. Rev. 27: 31–41.

Glick, P.C., and A. Norton (1977) "Marrying, divorcing and living together in the U.S. today." Population Bull. 32 (October).

Gordon, M. (1978) The American Family. New York: Random House.

Holmstrom, L. L. (1972) The Two Career Marriage. Cambridge, MA: Schenkman.

Henry, J. (1963) Culture Against Man. New York: Random House.

Hunt, M. (1966) The World of the Formerly Married. New York: McGraw-Hill.

Kanter, R. M. (1977) Work and Family in the United States: A Critical Review. New York: Russell Sage Foundation.

Kemper, T. D. (1972) "Power, status, and love," in D. R. Heise (ed.) Personality and Socialization. Chicago: Rand McNally.

Keshet, H., and K. Rosenthal (1978) "Fathering after marital separation." Social Work 23 (January): 11–18.

Komarovsky, M. (1976) Dilemmas of Masculinity. New York: W. W. Norton.

Levine, J. (1976) Who Will Raise the Children? Philadelphia: Lippincott.

Lynn, D. (1974) The Father: His Role in Child Development. Monterey, CA: Brooks-Cole.

Morse, N. C., and R. S. Weiss (1955) "The function and meaning of work and the job." Amer. Soc. Rev. 20: 191–198.

Nye, F. I. (1957) "Child adjustment in broken and in unhappy broken homes." Marriage and Family Living 19: 356–361.

O'Neill, N., and G. O'Neill (1972) Open Marriage. New York: Avon.

Parry, J. B., and E. M. Phufl (1963) "Adjustment of children in 'sole' and 'remarriage' homes." Marriage and Family Living 25: 221–223.

Parsons T., and R. Bales (1955) Family, Socialization and Interaction Process. New York: Free Press.

Pleck, J. (1975) "Work and family roles: from sex-patterned segregation to integration." Paper presented at the annual American Sociological Association meetings. San Francisco, August.

Poloma, M. M., and T. N. Garland (1971) "The married professional woman: a study in the tolerance of domestication." J. of Marriage and the Family 33: 531–540.

Rainwater, L. (1974) "Work, well-being and family life," in J. O'Toole (ed.) Work and the Quality of Life. Cambridge, MA: MIT Press.

Rapoport, R., and R. Rapoport (1971) Dual Career Families. London: Penguin.

Reiss, I. L. (1965) "The universality of the family: a conceptual analysis." J. of Marriage and the Family 27 (November): 443–456.

Roy, R., and D. Roy (1970) Honest Sex. New York: New American Library.

Rubin, L. B. (1976) Worlds of Pain: Life in the Working Class Family. New York: Basic Books.

Thibaut, J. W., and H. A. Kelley (1959) The Social Psychology of Power. New York: John Wiley.

Waller, W. (1967) The Old Love and the New. Carbondale, IL: Southern Illinois Press.

——— (1938) The Family. New York: Dryden.

Warren, R. L. (1976) Family Maintenance in Father Only Families. Study Project, Brandeis University.

Wilensky, H. L. (1966) "Work as a social problem," in H. S. Becker (ed.) Social Problems and Modern Approach. New York: John Wiley.

PART EIGHT

AGING

What do we know about singles and aging? One of the few analyses done on the elderly never-married tells us that they tend to be lifelong isolates who are not especially lonely in old age. They are like the married elderly in the sense that both are more positive than divorced or widowed aged persons. Being single in old age avoids the desolation of bereavement following the death of a spouse (Gubrium, 1975). A study of older women points out that the never-married had the best physical and psychological health and were the best able to cope by facing up to problems and taking action. Experience with living alone appears to increase independence and autonomy and to have some beneficial effects for coping effectively (Wood, 1979).

Only 12 percent of the 11 million single people over the age of sixty-five are never-married; 3 percent are separated, 77 percent widowed, and 7 percent divorced. There are dramatic differences in the statistics for men and women. Most notably, 75 percent of men over the age of sixty-five are married and 14 percent are widowed, while only 37 percent of the women in this age group are married and 52 percent are widowed. The number of older never-married people is significant and their characteristics are varied, yet they have most often been considered worthy of study only in comparison to "normal" married subjects. The authors of the articles in this part focus on different aspects of aging singles' experience. All agree that the existing body of research is incomplete and that their studies point the way for much future investigation.

The never-married differ significantly from other elderly. Rita Braito and Donna Anderson, in their study "Singles and Aging: Implications for Needed Research" explore mental health, happiness, social relationships, and job commitment among the never-married. Because this group may not have children to live with when they become unable to live alone, the plans never-married elderly people make for aging and retirement may not include some of the alternatives available to others. And the increasing number of highly successful college-educated women who are less likely to marry, combined with the increasingly popular view of singleness as an acceptable style of life, keeps the number of never-marrieds increasing.

Braito and Anderson find most current data contradictory. For example, the mental health of the unmarried is poorer in general than the mental health of the married. Though as a group women have poorer mental health than men, the reverse is true of single women and men. In other areas studied, the authors believe that inappropriate questions were asked of subjects, enabling conclusions to be drawn only about the quantity and not the quality of their friendships. They also note a lack of control for factors such as income, occupational status, and support networks in evaluating the happiness of the elderly.

The authors ask, "Will the single life continue to impact on men more negatively than on women? Will the growth of the single population lead to increased social support and development of living arrangements? How do racial and ethnic differences affect the life styles of older never-married singles?" Additional research is needed to answer these questions and to develop supportive social policy for the older single population.

What does growing old mean for the gay person? "Elderly Homosexual Women and Men" looks into the adaptation of homosexual women and men over fifty. Fred Minnigerode and Marcy Adelman point out that this group has rarely been studied, partly because they are difficult to survey, and principally because of societal attitudes toward both aging and homosexuality. The authors interviewed women and men from middle- and upper-middle-class backgrounds, almost all of whom reported having good to excellent health. They also investigated the effects of the physical changes of age on self-concept; attitudes toward retirement; problems of loneliness; and the lifelong struggle to gain self-acceptance and self-esteem.

What are the causes of lifelong singlehood? Russell Ward explores this question in his article "The Never-Married in Later Life." He suggests that lifelong singles may come from relatively impoverished family backgrounds or have low educational and occupational attainment which would make it difficult to take on the responsibilities of marriage. Alternatively, they may have higher educational and occupational attainment, be more career-oriented, and have less time for dating and mating. Does their singlehood make them less happy, or do they compensate through other social involvements and thereby avoid the problems associated with marriage or its dissolution?

REFERENCES

Gubrium, Jaber. "Being Single in Old Age," *Aging and Human Development* (1975) 6, 29–41.

Wood, Vivian. "Singles and Aging." Paper delivered at the annual meeting of the National Council on Family Relations, Boston, August 1979.

25/ SINGLES AND AGING: Implications for Needed Research

Rita Braito and Donna Anderson

"**B**achelors and spinsters are a topic of much common sense speculation but of remarkably little social scientific research" (Spretzer and Riley, 1974, p. 533). This is true for both the young and the old. It is only recently that such people as Adams (1976), Gilder (1974), Stein (1976), and Libby (1977) have focused on singles as manifesting a life style that warrants investigation. We therefore have little information upon which to build an understanding of the life styles and problems of the never-married elderly. Although much of the data related to singles has used the term single to include the never-marrieds, divorced, widowed, and sometimes separated, we focus here on what is known about the never-marrieds for several reasons. The first is, the plans the never-married make for aging and retirement may not include some of the alternatives such as moving in with their children available to those who have married and had children. The second reason is that we have a larger population of women going to college, which appears to be related to maintaining the never-married state (Bernard, 1972). Third, as singleness is viewed as a healthy alternative to marriage, and childlessness is not stigmatized, more men and women will choose to remain single. Thus the number and proportion of the never-marrieds will probably continue to increase.

Given the fact that of the over-sixty-five population 8 percent are never-married, it is important to understand this population when establishing social policy. The never-married population is diverse, and it is important to determine what their current life styles, mental health, happiness, concerns, and problems are.

MENTAL HEALTH AND OVERALL HAPPINESS

A problem in trying to portray an accurate picture of the mental health of single persons is the lack of uniformity of existing studies. Studies have been conducted across a wide range of mental illnesses ranging from depression and mild disorders to psychoses, and recent analyses suggest that we must carefully consider the type of mental illness when trying to draw demographic conclusions (Dohrenwend and Dohrenwend, 1969; Lemkau, 1974; Overall, 1971). Also problematic is the fact that some studies have been community oriented while others have concentrated on the currently institutionalized and/or those seeking psychiatric counseling. Instrument reliability and adequate definitions of mental health are also problems.

However, one fairly consistent finding stands out: statistically the mental health of the unmarried is poorer than that of the married. They are diagnosed as mentally ill more often and generally spend more time in the hospital, which indicates poorer recovery rates (Turner and Gartell, 1978). On the other hand, never-marrieds generally fare better than the divorced, separated, widowed (Gilder, 1974; Radloff, 1975; Pearlin and Johnson, 1977; Stein and Susser, 1969, indicate some inconsistencies).

Another finding is that, as a group, single men appear to have a greater tendency to become mentally ill than single women (Gove, 1972, p. 38). Glenn (1975) reports that single women are consistently happier than single men and that married persons report greater overall happiness than single persons.

Very few studies of marital status and mental health have been concerned with the aged. Among those that have, the findings are contradictory. Bellin and Hardt (1958, p. 158), using a community sample of persons sixty-five and over, reported that the never-married had lower mental health rates than the widowed, divorced, and separated but higher rates than the currently married; and that the rates were slightly higher for single men than for single women. Stein and Susser (1969, p. 108), using a British population of people who had sought psychiatric help, found that for the age groups forty to fifty-nine and sixty-plus the never-marrieds had the poorest rates. Comparisons by sex indicate that single men had poorer rates than all men except the widowed in the younger age group and the divorced in the older group. Single women had the highest rates of all women for the younger age group and were surpassed only by the divorced in age group sixty and over. Single men had higher rates than single women in both groups. There were also differences by sex and marital status in terms of type of diagnosis. Cooper (1966, p. 9), looking at identified psychiatric cases in general practice in Great Britain, found that single men had higher rates than married men in all categories except sixty-five and over, although none were statistically significant. Single women had lower rates than married women in all categories. Comparing single men to single women, each had virtually the same rates for ages forty-five to sixty-four, but at sixty-five and over, single men had a lower rate than single women.

In 1960 Gurin found that single women were less depressed than single men and suggested that a clue to the reason lay in men's inability to form and maintain meaningful personal attachments. The much quoted 1966 Knupfer, Clark, and Room article, "The Mental Health of the Unmarried," concludes that "single men are in fact more socially isolated and more antisocial than single women." However, when we look at the tables we find that the differences between single males and single females are not great and depend upon the questions asked. Gove (1972) cited Knupfer et al.'s conclusion that there is a tendency for single women to form and maintain close interpersonal ties, while single men are apt to be independent and isolated, which was based upon data that showed more men than women living alone. But single men may live alone for reasons quite aside from personality defects. For example, it has traditionally been more socially acceptable for women to live together, and since single men are often more economically secure, they may better afford to have separate households.

In considering the data on aging, it is important to note that having a close friend, a confidant, rather than a large number of friends, is one of the most important factors in social adjustment. What is needed is to identify quality as well as quantity of friendships. Perhaps we should ask single, never-married respondents whether they feel isolated, or if they have a low quality of friendships. We could try to determine if those living alone experience different levels of well-being than those living with siblings, dependents, or lovers. Most of the data reporting positive social support do not include simultaneous control for the never-married status, for social class, and for age. Therefore we cannot identify the different types of social relationships and the implications of the living arrangements as they relate to these factors. Investigations of such social relations have ignored changes that occur as people age beyond sixty, and we have not inquired into the alternative life styles available to the never-married elderly because of our beliefs about the aged and about human sexuality. Nor have we looked at differences between rural and urban populations, where density of elderly populations may affect the size and strength of the social network.

Glenn (1975) reports that single women are happier than single men, but the pattern of reported happiness is much different for the two sexes. Men report being happiest during ages forty to fifty-nine (30 percent) and less so at sixty and over. Women, however, remain the same in both age groups. Bernard (1972, p. 34) reports that "at ages 45 to 54 the gap between single men and women is a veritable chasm" because of differences in education, income, and status of occupation between men and women. But it is possible that single men have to adjust to aging and closed opportunities at the same time, while women have adjusted earlier. It may mean they have had different support networks which have hindered or facilitated the adjustment. Research is needed to ascertain whether support groups exist and, if so, who they are and how they affect adjustment. Answers to these basic question can provide a better understanding of the elderly who have remained single.

LIVING ARRANGEMENTS

Although we have mentioned living arrangements in discussing social relationships, it is important to note again the differences between single men and single women. The following table is based on a study by Bernard (1975), using data from the Bureau of the Census. As this table shows, the percentage differences between single men and women in living arrangements are not great. Further research is needed to determine the way different life styles relate to mental health status, and what factors influence living arrangements. Under what conditions do singles become heads of households, live alone, or live with relatives or nonrelatives? How are the obligations within a particular living arrangement perceived and are they shared?

JOB COMMITMENT

According to Glick (1975), older singles are more concerned with career expansion and less preoccupied with getting along well with others in their work. They have money to spend on leisure activities and advanced education. Yet Glick also reports that singles are often left out of informal networks of an organization and hence out of spheres of decision making. Reporting on some research by Jacoby (1974), Stein (1976) suggests that corporation executives perceive singles as being less emotionally stable and more apt to make snap judgments. Of the 200 men and women Stein (1976, p. 10) interviewed, 40 percent reported discrimination in finding a job or being promoted. This was true even though a study by the Institute of Life Insurance states that for single adults, work and a fulfilling career are the most important life goals. Kanter (1977) has suggested that women are excluded from executive positions because management prefers people like themselves in positions of trust. Perhaps single men too are perceived as less trustworthy because they are not like management in their marital status. Both Stein (1976) and Jacoby (1974) report such feelings.

Atchley (1976) is one of the few people who has reported on work orientations of retired women. When income was introduced as a control variable, the never-married showed a more positive work orientation. Braito (1970) reported that single nurses were more apt to experience relative deprivation (a comparison of the salary made

TABLE 1

LIVING ARRANGEMENTS OF

SINGLE MEN AND WOMEN OF DIFFERENT AGES*

Living Arrangement	Single Women	Single Men	Summary	
1. Head of Family				
35–44	16.6%	6.6%	women exceed men	10.0%
45–54	19.4	16.8	women exceed men	2.6
55–64	18.3	13.7	women exceed men	4.6
65–74	12.1	16.1	men exceed women	4.0
2. Living Alone				
35–44	26.7	25.8	women exceed men	0.9
45–54	29.7	34.4	men exceed women	4.7
55–64	37.9	35.9	women exceed men	2.0
65–74	48.8	50.2	men exceed women	1.4
3. Living with Relatives				
35–44	45.0	51.8	men exceed women	6.8
45–54	37.8	35.8	women exceed men	2.0
55–64	32.3	40.1	men exceed women	7.8
65–74	25.9	16.8	women exceed men	9.1
4. Living with Nonrelatives				
35–44	11.6	15.8	men exceed women	4.2
45–54	13.1	12.0	women exceed men	1.1
55–64	11.5	10.2	women exceed men	1.3
65–74	12.1	8.0	women exceed men	4.1

*This is a combination of portions of Bernard's (1975) tables 7 and 8 with comments added.

with the salary they felt they should make). She also found that single people who were highly satisfied with their jobs were more apt to make higher salary demands. Braito and Powers (1977), utilizing the same nursing population, have also suggested that singles may make demands for increased salaries because they would not be as concerned with maintaining current salary distribution within the family.

Single women (Bernard, 1972) have been identified as better educated, having higher IQs, being more upwardly mobile, and having a higher occupational status than single men. Gilder (1974) similarly suggests that where men and women work at the same job, women are socially superior.

Extensive research is needed on work commitment of the never-married. What are the implications of job commitment for retirement? If singles are very committed, and have focused on their work to the exclusion of other activities, retirement could be more difficult for them. On the other hand, it is possible that they have adapted to discrimination by expanding alternative social networks and thus might adjust more easily. Since job opportunities and self-enhancement vary by occupation, it is important to determine the impact of social class and marital status simultaneously as it relates to all aspects of work. Are singles more discriminated against in managerial or in working-class jobs or does it make no difference? What are the retirement concerns of singles? Is job commitment easier or more difficult for them? How is it related to support activities after retirement?

CONCLUSION

In most studies singles have been used as a comparative group, rather than as an independent target of legitimate research. Here we have explored directly their mental health and happiness, social relationships, and job commitment.

Singlehood is expected to increase because of demographic factors, more education for women, and perhaps increasing attractiveness of the never-married status. Will it continue to affect men more negatively than women? Will increasing social support in terms of numbers provide for the development of more satisfactory living arrangements? Racial and ethnic data on never-married singles are notably absent from the literature, and future research should certainly include these variables.

The never-married should be focused upon as a legitimate research concern. Their mental health, happiness, job commitment, social relationships, and living arrangements need to be understood if adequate policy is to be developed and implemented for this growing population.

REFERENCES

*Adams, Margaret. 1976. Single Blessedness. New York: Basic Books.

Atchley, R. C. 1976. "Orientation Toward the Job and Retirement Adjustment Among Women," in Time, Roles and Self in Old Age, Jaber F. Gubrium (ed.), New York: Human Sciences Press, pp. 199–208.

Bellin, S., and R. Hardt. 1958. "Marital Status and Mental Disorders Among the Aged," American Sociological Review 23 (April): 155–162.

Bernard, Jessie. 1975. "Note on Changing Life Styles: 1970–1974," Journal of Marriage and the Family 37 (3):582–593.

*Indicates selection included in this volume.

Bernard, Jessie. 1972. The Future of Marriage. New York: World Publishing Company.

Braito, Rita. 1970. Conflict Legitimation and Forms of Protest. A dissertation submitted to the University of Minnesota, August, 1970.

Braito, Rita, and Edward Powers. 1977. "What the Other Half Thinks: Implications of Female Perceptions for Work Demands," Sociological Inquiry, 47:59–64.

Cooper, Brian. 1966. "Psychiatric Disorder in Hospital and General Practice," Social Psychiatry 1(1):7–10.

Dohrenwend, Bruce P., and Barbara S. Dohrenwend. 1969. Social Status and Psychological Disorder: A Causal Inquiry. New York: Wiley. (Reported in Lenore Radloff, Sex Roles, 1:249–265.)

Gilder, George. 1974. Naked Nomads. New York: Quadrangle.

Glenn, Norval D. 1975. "The Contribution of Marriage to the Psychological Well-Being of Males and Females," Journal of Marriage and the Family 37 (August):594–601.

Glick, Paul C. 1975. "A Demographer Looks at American Families," Journal of Marriage and the Family 37 (February):15–26.

Glick, Paul C. 1975. "Some Recent Changes in American Families," Current Population Reports, 52:23.

Gove, Walter R. 1972. "The Relationship Between Sex Roles, Marital Status, and Mental Illness," Social Forces 51 (September):34–44.

Gurin, G., J. Veroff, and S. Feld. 1960. Americans View Their Mental Health. New York: Basic Books, Inc.

Jacoby, Susan. 1974. "49 Million Singles Can't All Be Right," New Times Magazine, February 17:41–49. Reported in Peter J. Stein, "Being Single: Bucking the Cultural Imperative." A paper prepared for presentation at the American Sociological Annual Meetings, New York City, New York, 1976.

Kanter, Rosabeth Moss. 1977. Men and Women of the Corporation. New York: Basic Books, Inc.

Knupfer, Genevieve, Walter Clark, and Robin Room. 1966. "The Mental Health of the Unmarried," The American Journal of Psychiatry 122 (February):841–850.

Lemkau, P. V. 1974. "Epidemiologic Contributions to Psychiatric Classification." Paper presented at meeting of American Public Health Association, New Orleans, October. (Cited in Lenore Radloff, Sex Roles 1:249–265.)

Libby, Roger W. 1977. "Creative Singlehood as a Sexual Life-Style," in Marriage and Alternatives: Exploring Intimate Relationships, Roger W. Libby and Robert N. Whitehurst (eds.), Glenview, Ill.: Scott, Foresman and Company.

Overall, John E. 1971. "Associations Between Marital History and the Nature of Manifest Psychopathology," Journal of Abnormal Psychology 78 (2):213–221.

*Pearlin, Leonard I., and Joyce S. Johnson. 1977. "Marital Status, Life-Strains and Depressions," American Sociological Review 42 (October): 704–715.

Radloff, Lenore. 1975. "Sex Differences in Depression—The Effects of Occupation and Marital Status," Sex Roles 1:249–265.

Spreitzer, Elmer, and Lawrence Riley. 1974. "Factors Associated With Singlehood," Journal of Marriage and the Family 36 (August):533–542.

Stein, Peter J. 1976. "Being Single: Bucking the Cultural Imperative." A paper prepared for presentation at the American Sociological Association Annual Meetings, New York City, New York.

Stein, Peter J. 1976. Single. Englewood Cliffs, N.J.: Prentice-Hall, Inc.

Stein, Zena, and Mervyn Susser. 1969. "Widowhood and Mental Illness," British Journal of Preventive Social Medicine 23:106–110.

Turner, R. Jay, and John W. Gartell. 1978. "Social Factors in Psychiatric Outcome: Toward the Resolution of Interpretive Controversies," American Sociological Review 43 (June): 368–382.

26/ ELDERLY HOMOSEXUAL WOMEN AND MEN

Fred A. Minnigerode and Marcy R. Adelman

While the field of gerontology has grown rapidly in the past few decades, little attention has been given to the lives of homosexual women and men during their later years (e.g., Binstock & Shanas, 1977; Birren & Schaie, 1977). A few recent studies, however, have begun to examine adaptations of aging homosexual women and men (Kelly, 1977; Kimmel & Ralph, Note 1; Minnigerode & Adelman, Note 2). On the other hand, while the study of homosexuality has had a long history in the field of psychology, seldom has research attention focused on the problems and adaptations of homosexual women and men over sixty years of age (e.g., see bibliographies by Morin, 1976; Weinberg & Bell, 1972). Probably this particular subgroup has been excluded from empirical research not only because of sampling difficulties but also because of some combination of societal attitudes toward aging and toward homosexuality (Bennet & Eckman, 1973; Churchill, 1967; Minnigerode, 1976; Weinberg, 1972).

. . . .

. . . The present article summarizes relevant findings obtained in a small-scale pilot study conducted in 1975–1976 (Minnigerode &

Adelman, Note 2). These preliminary findings sharpened our focus on certain important variables presently being examined. . . .

METHOD

The pilot study involved four- to five-hour tape-recorded interviews with structured and open-ended questions. Six homosexual men and five homosexual women, sixty to seventy-seven years of age, participated in the pilot study. With respect to age, the sample of homosexual men was not only older but more heterogeneous than the sample of homosexual women. The men ranged from sixty-one to seventy-seven ($\bar{X}$ = 68.0 years); the women ranged from sixty to sixty-nine years of age ($\bar{X}$ = 63.6 years). Five out of six men lived alone; one lived with his former lover, with whom he had been living for the past fifteen years. Four out of five women lived alone; one had been living with her lover for the past twenty-seven years. Respondents were contacted through friendship networks and through homosexual organizations such as G40+, a social organization in San Francisco for homosexual people forty years of age and older.

It is not assumed that these respondents are representative of older adults, heterosexual or homosexual, living in the San Francisco Bay area. Regarding their socioeconomic and physical health status, the pilot sample of men and women compare favorably with others in their age group. Educational and occupational levels achieved by respondents indicate middle- to upper-middle-class backgrounds. Most respondents had had at least some college education and many of them had been employed in professional and managerial positions. At the time of the interview, most respondents had retired from full-time employment. When asked, "Do you consider your own health to be excellent, good, fair or poor?" almost all respondents reported their health to be "good" or "excellent."

RESULTS AND DISCUSSION

PHYSICAL CHANGES

Age-related change in physical appearance is often thought to have greater negative effect on self-concepts of women than those of men (Sontag, 1972). How homosexual respondents perceived these changes in physical appearance were examined in the pilot study. Men more often than women seemed to evaluate these changes negatively. . . .

A man commented, "When you're young, you don't appreciate how great it is to be young and attractive." Comments such as these were not made by the women, who seemed to show less concern about age-related physical change on self-concepts (i.e., body image). . . .

WORK AND RETIREMENT

The relative importance of work was examined throughout the work histories of respondents. Men tended to assign higher priority to work than did women. When asked what he considered the most important accomplishment in his life, a homosexual man answered, "I was successful in my field as a social worker; I was very much respected in my field."

We also wanted to find out if respondents had ever experienced discrimination in employment because of sexual preference. Three out of six homosexual men reported that they had lost a job, or jobs, when their homosexuality was found out. . . . None of the women reported having felt discriminated against because of sexual preference; however, two of the women did mention having felt constraints on their occupational careers because they were women.

Attitudes toward retirement were generally positive and were frequently accompanied by a sense of relief, as demonstrated in the following comment by one of the men:

> Well, I was eager to have it [retirement] come along as much out of curiosity as anything else. And it was a turning point, because then I didn't have work interfering with me and I could start doing the things I really wanted to do. That's when I no longer had to hide my homosexuality and I went out and celebrated by getting into the [gay] parade and all manner of things that I considered *quite* bold and so refreshing.

SOCIAL BEHAVIOR

Closest friends of the respondents were generally members of the same sex. Similar friendship patterns have been reported in previous studies of sixty-year-old, presumably heterosexual, men and women (Lowenthal, Thurnher, Chiriboga et al., 1975). Most respondents indicated they maintained contact with family members who weren't necessarily aware of the respondent's homosexuality. Interestingly, a few respondents mentioned maintaining close contact with family members who were also homosexual. Respondents interviewed in the pilot study generally did not seem estranged from either family members or friends. One woman who had previously been married reported a continuing close relationship with her children:

> Having my children has been the most satisfying thing [in life] because they've turned out well and it gives me . . .

even though at the time I was so afraid that I was making horrible mistakes and everything. . . . But, anyway, they are both honest and productive and trying to lead interesting lives and do interesting things. And so, I guess, they are really the most satisfying thing in my life. . . .

All respondents mentioned that they had been reared with religious backgrounds. Only two respondents indicated current religious affiliation. One woman reported herself to be Zen Buddhist; one man a Unitarian. Respondents, by and large, had little to do with mainstream religious organizations during their later years.

Most respondents reported participation in social, political, and service organizations. They were involved in such diverse organizations as the Sierra Club, Common Cause, G40+, Society for Individual Rights, and a women's credit union. None of the respondents reported interest in or attendance at senior citizen centers.

We are currently examining lover/spouse relationships, friendships, and kinship networks as support systems in later life. Family and friends might play different roles in the lives of homosexual and heterosexual men and women during old age. Membership and participation in voluntary associations, including religious organizations, are also being examined.

PSYCHOLOGICAL FUNCTIONING

Aspects of psychological functioning investigated in the pilot study include: (a) dimensions of self-concept; and (b) feelings of loneliness and morale.

1. *Dimensions of self-concept.* Dimensions of self-concept were: age-status identification; salience of homosexuality; and self-acceptance and self-esteem.

Age-status identification has been shown to correlate with other measures of physical and psychological well-being in later life (Bennet & Eckman, 1973). Previous research suggests that the age-status system in life cycles of homosexual men may not differ from those of the general population (Minnigerode, 1976). Respondents were asked, "Do you consider yourself to be young, middle-aged, or old?" Homosexual men generally viewed themselves as middle-aged; women showed greater variability of response. One sixty-nine-year-old woman considered herself "old," but had never considered herself "middle-aged." Another woman, sixty years old, considered herself "young." She added, "Once I caught myself acting old. . . . I was so surprised . . . but I won't be old till after I die."

Salience of homosexuality in self-concepts was investigated by asking respondents, "Has your homosexuality become more or less important over the past few decades?" Whether their homosexuality became more or less important varied among respondents, but no systematic difference obtained between the sexes. Sex differences seemed to emerge, however, in terms of what being homosexual meant. The men frequently viewed their homosexuality in terms of sexual activity. The women generally viewed their homosexuality in terms of personal identity and/or interpersonal relationships.

Gaining self-acceptance of self-esteem was mentioned by almost every respondent as being a long, sometimes lifelong, struggle. As one seventy-seven-year-old man said, "Oh, I think the greatest accomplishment [in life] is to learn to live at peace with oneself . . . and if there is any disturbing factor, which homosexuality certainly is, to have come to terms with it. And I think that can well occupy most of your life."

These three dimensions of self-concept (age-status identification; salience of homosexuality; and self-acceptance and self-esteem) as well as other indices of self-concept (Block, 1961) are presently being examined. We are presently looking for answers to questions such as the following: (a) What factors determine perception of oneself as "old"? (b) What consequences follow from an "old" self-concept? (c) What does being homosexual mean to men and women during their later years?

2. *Feelings of loneliness and morale.* In order to identify possible psychological problems, self-reported morale and feelings of loneliness were examined. A six-item morale scale was employed (Thompson, 1973), but sample size was too small to make meaningful comparisons, Loneliness, however, seemed to be a problem for many respondents. When asked, "How often do you feel lonely: Very often, often, seldom, or never?," most respondents reported feeling "very often" or "often" lonely. Although loneliness is not uncommon in old age (Atchley, 1972), it may occur frequently among aging homosexual men and women. Although there has been some speculation that problems of loneliness are characteristic of aging homosexuals (Allen, 1961; Stern, 1961), it is probably rather more characteristic of all the elderly, and some studies have suggested that among homosexuals increasing adjustment comes with age (Weinberg, 1972).

We are currently taking an in-depth look at psychological well-being (Bradburn, 1969), sources of life satisfaction (Neugarten, Havighurst & Tobin, 1961), and how emotional difficulties, such as loneliness, are managed.

SEXUAL BEHAVIOR

The relative importance of sexual activity and the relationship between sexual and affectional needs were examined in the pilot study. Retrospective data suggested that throughout their lives men assigned higher priority to sex than did women. One sixty-nine-year-old man indicated the high priority given to sex: "Sex was so much uppermost in my mind—about getting it, and how to get it, and where to get it."

While all respondents reported that frequency of sexual activity had decreased over their lives, men generally reported higher rates of current sexual activity than did women. While all the men remained interested in sex and sexually active, women varied from total lack of sexual interest to fully active sex lives.

With regard to the relationship between sexual and affectional needs, the women generally satisfied their sexual needs within the context of affectional relationships; this pattern was not always descriptive of the men. All the women and two of the men reported an integration of these needs.

A man told us:

> [Sex] is now a much more considered thing, and I don't care for spur-of-the-moment intimacy. I feel that it must grow out of love, be a complement to love rather than a result of physical arousal, physical excitement. As a younger man, there were then more sex experiences arising out of casual contact.

PERSONAL PERSPECTIVES ON THE LIFE COURSE

First homosexual experiences generally occurred earlier in men's lives than in women's. The men frequently identified themselves as homosexual before this first experience, which usually occurred during adolescence. One man said:

> I suffered as a teen-ager under the knowledge, secret knowledge, that I was drawn to men and not to women. I was very disturbed thinking about it because in my day, you know, being known as a homosexual.... [After the first experience] I became reconciled to the fact that I liked to be gay and did not consider myself a freak or an outcast.

The women, on the other hand, generally identified themselves as homosexual (or lesbian) after their first homosexual experience, which generally occurred in their twenties. Every woman also mentioned that homosexuality was not considered an appropriate topic for discussion with either homosexual or heterosexual friends. As one woman said:

> When I was about twenty, I would go skiing with a group
> of ten women friends. Everybody was gay but we just

didn't even speak about it, talk about it, or discuss it in any way. We had this little chalet that we rented. We just went up and stayed all night and went to bed [laughs] and got up in the morning and cooked and went skiing and went home at night. And there was never any mention of lesbianism or what it meant.

We asked respondents how homosexuality influenced their lives. Responses varied considerably. One of the men said:

This is like asking what would it be like . . . would your life have been any different if your eyesight was slightly defective, or if you had one lame leg. The answer is that it's in the background of everything you do. I feel that it has created a narrower horizon than life would otherwise have had for me. I feel also that because of it, I have used in my life less initiative than I would otherwise have. I have been, in a sense, not crippled, but cramped because of it.

A sixty-nine-year-old woman agreed that homosexuality had influenced her life. She saw its influence as enriching rather than as "cramping":

I lived in a little suburb for a while outside of Buffalo. It was kind of a snobbish little place where people played bridge and golf and got married in their twenties. I might even have gotten married and had a family, when I think of it now. And in a way, I'm glad I didn't get stuck in that conventional community and turn into a bridge person, playing golf or going to the country club and those things. I am glad in a way. If I had been "normal" . . . Am I saying "normal"? . . . a heterosexual, in those days, I might have fallen into that scheme of life, and not known any of the diversity that I have had.

The present paper has outlined some of the variables currently being investigated. We hope soon to understand more clearly the adaptations that homosexual men and women make to growing old. The study of elderly homosexuals can serve to increase our understanding and appreciation of the diversity of life styles adopted by the aged to preserve their uniqueness and individuality. Our further research, comparing elderly homosexual and heterosexual life experience, will provide further information about the effect of sexual orientation on adjustment to later life in America.

NOTES

1. Kimmel, D. C., & Ralph, W. M. Gay people grow old too: Life-history interviews of aging gay men. Paper presented at the convention of the Gerontological Society, New York City, 14 October 1976.

2. Minnigerode, F. A., & Adelman, M. R. *Adaptations of aging homosexual men and women.* Paper presented at the convention of the Gerontological Society, New York City, 14 October 1976.

REFERENCES

Allen, C. The aging homosexual. In I. Rubin (Ed.), *The third sex.* New York: Basic, 1961.

Atchley, R. C. *The social forces in later life.* Belmont, California: Wadsworth, 1972.

Bennet, R., & Eckman, J. Atttiudes toward aging: A critical examination of recent literature and implications for future research. In C. Eisdorfer & M. P. Lawton (Eds.), *The psychology of adult development and aging.* Washington, D.C.: American Psychological Association, 1973.

Binstock, R. H., & Shanas, E. *Handbook of aging and the social sciences.* New York: Van Nostrand Reinhold, 1977.

Birren, J. E., & Schaie, K. W. *Handbook of the psychology of aging.* New York: Van Nostrand Reinhold, 1977.

Block, J. *The Q-sort method in personality assessment and psychiatric research.* Springfield, Illinois: Thomas, 1961.

Bradburn, N. M. *The structure of psychological well-being.* Chicago: Aldine, 1969.

Churchill, W. Homosexual behavior among males. Englewood Cliffs, New Jersey: Prentice-Hall, 1967.

Kelly, J. The aging male homosexual: Myth and reality? *Gerontologist,* 1977, **17,** 328–332.

Lowenthal, M. F., Thurnher, M., Chiriboga, D., et al. *Four stages of life.* San Francisco: Jossey-Bass, 1975.

Minnigerode, F. A. Age-status labeling in homosexual men. *Journal of Homosexuality,* 1976, **1,** 273–276.

Minnigerode, F. A. Attitudes toward homosexuality: Feminist attitudes and sexual conservatism. *Sex Roles,* 1976, **2,** 347–352.

Morin, S. F. An annotated bibliography of research on lesbianism and male homosexuality (1967–1974). (Ms. No. 1191) *JSAS Catalog of Selected Documents in Psychology,* 1976, **6,** 15.

Neugarten, B. L., Havighurst, R., & Tobin, S. Measurement of life satisfaction. *Journal of Gerontology,* 1961, **16,** 134–143.

Sontag, S. The double standard of aging. *Saturday Review of the Society,* 23 September 1972, 29–38.

Stern, J. *The sixth man.* Garden City, New York: Doubleday, 1961.

Thompson, G. B. Work versus leisure roles: An investigation of morale among employed and retired men. *Journal of Gerontology,* 1973, **28,** 339–334.

Weinberg, G. *Society and the healthy homosexual.* New York: St. Martin's, 1972.

Weinberg, M. S., & Bell, A. P. *Homosexuality: An annotated bibliography.* New York: Harper & Row, 1972.

27/ THE NEVER-MARRIED IN LATER LIFE

Russell A. Ward

The marriage relationship supports a wide range of social, emotional, and sustenance needs. These supports may be particularly important for older people, who face social losses through retirement or poor health. Numerous studies indicate that widowhood creates severe social, psychological, and financial problems (e.g., Larson, 1978; Lopata, 1973). But what of the 5 percent of persons sixty and over who have never married (U.S. Bureau of the Census, 1975)? Are they thereby "sentenced" to loneliness and unhappiness in their later years?

Only very sparse information is available about older people who have never married. A few British studies indicate that single older persons are more isolated than those who are married (Townsend, 1957; Tunstall, 1966; Willmott and Young, 1960) but are not necessarily more lonely. Larson (1978) notes that studies differentiating unmarried statuses indicate "that the well-being of single people tends to be roughly equivalent to that of married persons, while widowed, divorced, and separated persons tend to have lower reported well-being" (p. 114), but this conclusion is based on only two cited studies (Kutner et al., 1956; Pihlblad and Adams, 1972), and the latter compares only married and widowed persons.

Gubrium's (1974, 1975) research on twenty-two never-married older people in Detroit appears to be the only work focusing to any extent on singlehood. While the never-married were more isolated, they were similar to the married with regard to loneliness, life satisfaction, and anomie. They had a "single" style of living, preferring more solitary pursuits and greater independence, and perceived no stigma associated with it. Gubrium also points out that the never-married do not experience the "desolation" of widowhood or divorce.

The generalizability of the few available studies of singlehood in later life is extremely limited, since they are all characterized by geographical restriction and small numbers. This is not surprising, given the rarity of singlehood throughout the life cycle. But understanding the lives of single elderly people has an important function. The experiences of aging are affected by the system of age stratification in any society (Riley et al., 1972), but they vary with other social positions (sex and race, for example). Investigation of the various social locations of older people can clarify which aspects of aging are universal and which are particular to social position. Since almost all arguments and studies about the social aspects of aging focus on the married or previously married, it is not clear whether their conclusions are about the process of growing old as such or about changes in marital status in later life. A more explicit examination of singles in old age would help sort this out

NEVER MARRYING: CAUSES AND CONSEQUENCES

Stein (1976) notes that those who never marry are often stereotyped as "swingers" or "lonely losers" who are in some way inadequate. Available data, however, indicate that this image is inaccurate. Single women tend to have greater education, occupational status, and intelligence than married women (Glick, 1975; Spreitzer and Riley, 1974), suggesting that career orientation makes marriage less attractive for women. Spreitzer and Riley (1974) also found single women to be disproportionately firstborns, which they suggest leads to a less romantic view of marriage because of early roles as surrogate parents. Single men do not display the heightened educational and occupational attainment found in single women (Bernard, 1972; Spreitzer and Riley, 1974), but they are more likely to be only children compared with their married counterparts, suggesting greater achievement socialization. Spreitzer and Riley (1974) found that single men and women both came from more "pathological" families (instability, low-quality family relationships).

Stein has conceptualized the choice of being single or married as a balance between pushes and pulls toward being married and pushes and pulls toward being single. The few in-depth studies of singles and their life styles indicate that the primary "pull" for remaining single is a desire to preserve psychological and social autonomy (Adams, 1976; Edwards and Hoover, 1974; Stein, 1976). Adams argues that psychological integrity and social independence are cardinal features of single personality, and that those who do not marry are intent on maintaining a "territorial integrity of the spirit" (p. 199).

Many never-married persons appear to achieve this (Adams, 1976; Edwards and Hoover, 1974; Stein, 1976). They view fluidity and variety in social relationsips, rather than the exclusivity of marriage, as an advantage that promotes opportunities for personal growth while still protecting autonomy. Life styles are geared to preserving personal independence and development of one's own faculties—privacy, self-expression through work, freedom of movement, and preoccupation with expanding experiences, philosophical insights, and imaginative conceptions of life (Adams, 1976).

The successful singles in these small-scale studies do not appear to be representative of the never-married, however, since national surveys of representative samples indicate that married persons are happier than all types of unmarried persons, including the never-married (Campbell, 1975; Glenn, 1975). Single women tend to be happier and better adjusted than single men (Campbell, 1975; Knupfer et al., 1966), and it has been suggested that marital roles are less beneficial and more stressful for women than for men (Bernard, 1972; Gove, 1972). But although single women are happier than single men, single women are nevertheless less happy than married women.

What accounts for the lower happinesss of those who never marry? Since empirical research does not substantiate the "loser" stereotype of singles, their lower happiness is most likely attributable either to the lack of gratifications associated with marriage or to the difficulties of living in a marriage-oriented world.

Berger and Kellner (1975) note that "marriage occupies a privileged status among the significant validating relationships for adults in our society." It is a primary arena of identity and self-realization, providing "backstage" areas for personal control and intimacy (Laslett, 1978). To the extent that marriage is successful in fulfilling these needs, the never-married may be less happy precisely because they lack this "significant validating relationship."

Apart from the actual gratifications of marriage, the never-married may also be less happy because of the "considerable difficulties of being single in a society where being paired is widely regarded as the only natural, sane, healthy, and proper way to be" (Edwards and Hoover, 1974, p. 1). The lack of institutional definition and support for single life styles undercuts the personal and social identity of the never-married, contributing to feelings of guilt and embarrassment, fear of loneliness, and psychological weariness from initiating and sustaining a life style which lacks a supportive ideology in the larger culture (Adams, 1976; Edwards and Hoover, 1974; Stein, 1976).

It is not entirely clear, however, how age affects the viability of a single life style. On the one hand, the happiness of those who never marry may rise with age, as they come to terms socially and psychologically with singlehood. It is more likely, however, that being single becomes less viable in later life. Adams (1976) and Stein (1976) note that the autonomy of successful single living requires economic independence, which may decline in old age. Psychological and social autonomy may also create problems as retirement, poor health, and other age-related changes reduce social life space and mobility. Fluidity and independence become disadvantages when one lacks the resources (health, money, social roles) to take advantage of them. The extended family plays an important supportive function in this regard, but the never-married possess smaller family networks. Finally, Adams (1976) has suggested that psychological latitude for the change and personal growth characteristic of single life styles may decline with age, making single living more problematic.

DATA AND METHOD

The General Social Surveys, conducted annually since 1972 by the National Opinion Research Center, contain data on representative samples of the noninstitutionalized population of the continental United States aged eighteen and older. The six years through 1977 yielded 9,120 interviews, including 3,557 with persons aged fifty and over (1,461 with those aged sixty-five and over). These include 162 persons aged fifty and over who have never married (sixty-eight aged sixty-five and over). This sample of never-married older persons is larger and more representative than any used in previous research. From 4 to 6 percent of those in every age group over fifty had never married.

The General Social Surveys include a wide range of questions about the demographic, social, and psychological characteristics of respondents. Variables measuring family background, socioeconomic status, subjective well-being, relationships with family and friends, and other social involvements are used in this study. While some questions were asked during all six years of the surveys, others were asked less frequently; unless otherwise noted, data analyzed below are from all six years.

In analyzing sources of singlehood, comparisons are drawn between the never-married and the ever-married (married, widowed, divorced, and separated). In analyzing consequences, four categories of marital status are used: married, widowed, divorced or separated, and never-married. Analysis of contingency tables is utilized to test differences among the categories. Analyses are for persons aged fifty and over. Analyses were also carried out separately for those aged fifty to sixty-four and sixty-five and over, but the patterns reported here did not vary by age.

Multiple classification analysis (MCA), a form of analysis of variance, is used at the end of the analysis. Analysis of variance, and the F-test, can test whether marital statuses differ in mean happiness sufficiently to reject a hypothesis of equal means in the population. MCA determines the extent of change in these simple means when controls (covariates) are introduced into the analysis. F-tests measure the significance of the differences in the net means, controlling for covariates.

Since the total number of respondents analyzed here (3,557) is quite large, small differences can be statistically significant. Some findings are reported as "no difference" because, although statistically significant, they are trivial (on the order of five percentage points). In addition, the number of single persons is not large (though it is much larger than in previous research), especially when broken down by age or sex. Thus these findings should be viewed as exploratory, rather than conclusive.

FINDINGS

ANTECEDENTS OF SINGLEHOOD

There were no sex differences in the likelihood of remaining single into later life. Similarly, family background variables (father's occupation, father's and mother's education, whether the mother worked) did not differentiate the never-married from the ever-married for either sex. Respondent's education was a predictor of singlehood, but only for women. Women who continued their education beyond high school were significantly more likely to remain single (16.4 percent) than those who did not (4.2 percent for those completing high school, 2.6 percent for those with less; $X^2 = 61.6$, p = .0001).

CONSEQUENCES OF SINGLEHOOD

Well-being. Table 1 indicates the association between marital status and two indicators of subjective well-being—global happiness and perception of life as exciting—for persons twenty-five to forty-nine and those fifty and over.

Looking first at happiness, the never-married are disadvantaged relative to the married in both age groups. This disadvantage moderates somewhat for older respondents, since the never-married rank a bit higher than the widowed and divorced, but they are still less happy than the married. The patterns are identical for both men and women, though both single and married women are happier than their male counterparts.

Excitement shows a different pattern. Among younger respondents, the never-married apparently lead the most exciting lives, with both single and married males rating their lives as slightly more

TABLE 1

RATINGS OF GLOBAL HAPPINESS[a] AND EXCITEMENT[b] BY
MARITAL STATUS, FOR YOUNGER (25–49) AND OLDER (50+)
RESPONDENTS[c]

	Married	Widowed	Divorced/ Separated	Never Married
Happiness				
Age 25–49				
% "very happy"	39.4%	20.5%	16.5%	15.5%
N	3,368	73	461	393
		$X^2 = 248.8$, p = .0001		
Age 50+				
% "very happy"	43.2%	23.8%	20.3%	26.1%
N	2,379	781	256	161
		$X^2 = 196.1$, p = .0001		
Excitement				
Age 25–49				
% "exciting"	47.9%	39.5%	40.2%	54.4%
N	2,147	43	316	261
		$X^2 = 31.6$, p = .0001		
Age 50+				
% "exciting"	41.3%	30.1%	33.7%	33.0%
N	1,536	519	178	94
		$X^2 = 23.3$, p = .0001		

[a]"Taken all together, how would you say things are these days—would you say that you are very happy, pretty happy, or not too happy?" (This question was asked in 1972–1977.)
[b]"In general, do you find life exciting, pretty routine, or dull?" (This question was asked in 1973, 1974, 1976, 1977.)
[c]Tests of significance (X^2) are based on complete tables, using all three categories of the dependent variables. In the 6 tables in this article, p refers to the probability that results reported occur by chance. For example, p = .01 indicates that the probability that these results occurred by chance is less than 1 in 100; p = .001 indicates that the probability that these results occurred by chance is less than 1 in 1,000; etc.

exciting than those of their female counterparts. This advantage reverses to a disadvantage for older respondents, however, as all unmarried categories rank below the married in excitement (men again indicated slightly more excitement than women). Thus on both counts—happiness and excitement—the never-married are disadvantaged relative to the married in later life, and differ little from the widowed or divorced.

Health and income. Married persons were only slightly more likely to rate their health as good or excellent than the never-married (62 to 55 percent, with 52 percent for divorced and 49 percent for widowed; $X^2 = 43.8$, p = .0001). Not surprisingly, the *family* income of never-married persons was significantly lower than for married for both sexes, but the relationship between marital status and *respondent's* earned income varied for men and women. Married males earned significantly more than those who were single (83 percent of married males who earned any income in the previous year earned at least $6,000, compared with 59 to 67 percent for the other categories of marital status; $X^2 = 21.7$, $p = .0001$). Single women, however, had the highest income of any marital status category (although differences were not statistically significant). There appears to be no clear pattern for health or income which can explain the lower happiness of single persons, especially females.

Living arrangements. Of course the never-married are much more likely to live alone than the married. Compared with widowed and divorced persons, however, the single are slightly less likely to live alone (60, 73, and 64 percent, respectively) and much more likely to live with someone who is not related to them (40 percent of the single, 17 percent divorced, 12 percent widowed, and 1 percent married; $X^2 = 398.2$, $p = .0001$).

Social contacts. Relative isolation in living arrangements for the never-married could be counteracted by increased community involvement. This is not apparently the case, however, for either men or women. Compared with the married, the never-married were not more likely to belong to voluntary associations (three-quarters of

TABLE 2

FREQUENCY OF CONTACT WITH NEIGHBORS[a]
AND FRIENDS[b] BY MARITAL STATUS (AGED 50+)

	Married	Widowed	Divorced/ Separated	Never Married
Neighbors:				
Daily or weekly	23.7%	31.9%	32.9%	31.5%
Monthly	26.6%	27.3%	21.2%	28.8%
Less than monthly	49.7%	40.8%	45.9%	39.7%
N	1,148	385	146	73
		$X^2 = 18.2$, $p = .006$		
Other Friends:				
Daily or weekly	11.9%	17.7%	18.5%	17.8%
Monthly	39.5%	28.6%	32.2%	30.1%
Less than monthly	48.6%	53.8%	49.3%	52.1%
N	1,147	385	146	73
		$X^2 = 22.7$, $p = .001$		

[a]"How often do you spend a social evening with someone who lives in your neighborhood?"
[b]"How often do you spend a social evening with friends who live outside the neighborhood?" (These questions were asked in 1974, 1975, and 1977.)

TABLE 3
HAPPINESS AND EXCITEMENT BY
WORK STATUS, FOR THE MARRIED
AND NEVER MARRIED (AGED 50+)

	Working	Retired
Married		
% "very happy"	40.9%	47.5%
N	1,000	569
	$X^2 = 7.3$, p = .03	
%"exciting"	46.0%	42.8%
N	628	390
	$X^2 = 13.8$, p = .001	
Never-married		
% "very happy"	32.4%	21.0%
N	68	62
	$X^2 = 4.4$, p = .11	
% "exciting"	44.7%	24.3%
N	38	37
	$X^2 = 3.5$, p = .18	

both belonged to at least one) or to attend church (approximately one-half of both attended weekly). The widowed and divorced were least likely to belong to a voluntary association (66 percent), and the divorced were least likely to attend church weekly (35 percent). Married persons see neighbors and other friends least frequently, but the differences are small (Table 2). When asked how much satisfaction they derived from friendships, married persons were *most* likely to indicate "a very great deal" or "a great deal" (76 percent), followed by widowed (72 percent), never-married (68 percent), and divorced (60 percent); ($X^2 = 27.6$, p = 0001).

Work. Work represents an additional community involvement which may compensate for lack of marital gratifications. Those who had never married, however, were not more likely to say they would continue to work if they "were to get enough money to live as comfortably as you would like for the rest of your life," nor were there any marital-status differences in the ranking of various aspects of work: high income, no danger of being fired, short working hours, chances for advancement, and feelings of accomplishment.

While these results suggest that the never-married are not more "attached" to work, retirement does appear to create more problems for them (Table 3). Retirement had a more negative effect on both happiness and excitement for the never-married than for the married. While the differences for the never-married are not statistically significant because of their small numbers, these findings suggest that loss of the work role creates more difficulties for those who have never married. Indeed, the never-married who are still working are roughly equivalent in excitement to their married counterparts (44.7 and 46.0 percent), though they are less happy.

Family ties. Never-married persons do appear to be disadvantaged in the frequency and quality of family ties. The never-married were least likely to see relatives on a daily or weekly basis (24 percent for single, 35 percent divorced, 37 percent married, and 42 percent widowed), though the differences were not statistically significant (this was measured in only three of the six years). They were also substantially (and statistically significantly) less satisfied than married persons with their family lives, though other patterns varied by sex (Table 4). Divorced men were less satisfied than never-married or widowed men, while the differences among these were small for women (though the single were least satisfied). Apart from those who were married, women were more satisfied with their family lives than men. Lack or dissolution of marriage, especially divorce, apparently affects the quality of family life more for men than for women.

TABLE 4
SATISFACTION WITH FAMILY LIFE[a] BY MARITAL STATUS, FOR MALES AND FEMALES

	Married	Widowed	Divorced/ Separated	Never Married
Males				
Family satisfaction:				
High	84.3%	47.7%	33.0%	49.2%
Low	15.7%	52.3%	67.0%	50.8%
N	1,050	128	94	63
		$X^2 = 212.9$, p = .0001		
Females				
Family satisfaction:				
High	83.2%	63.3%	59.5%	53.4%
Low	16.8%	36.7%	40.5%	46.6%
N	876	520	131	58
		$X^2 = 95.8$, p = .0001		

[a]"For each area of life I am going to name, tell me how much satisfaction you get from that area.... Your family life." Coded: High = "a very great deal" or "a great deal"; Low = "quite a bit," "a fair amount," "some," "a little," or "none." (This question was asked in 1973, 1974, 1975, 1976, and 1977.)

TABLE 5
CORRELATIONS BETWEEN GLOBAL HAPPINESS AND EX-
CITEMENT AND OTHER FACTORS, FOR THE MARRIED
AND NEVER MARRIED (AGED 50+)

	Happiness		Excitement	
	Married	Never Married	Married	Never Married
Health	.27*	.40*	.27*	.27*
Income	.12*	.21*	.20*	.16*
Education	.08*	.16*	.23*	.40*
Frequency of contact with:				
Relatives	.06*	.04	.01	.03
Neighbors	.06*	.10	.10*	.11
Friends	.11*	.29*	.12*	.19
Satisfaction with:				
Family life	.31*	.27*	.26*	.03
Friendships	.25*	.22*	.22*	.30*
Number of groups belonged to	.08*	.26*	.22*	.32*

*Statistically significant at p = .05.

SOURCES OF WELL-BEING

The foregoing analyses indicate that never-married older people are less happy than those who are married, and find their lives less exciting. What accounts for these differences? The differential impact of retirement is one possibility, as indicated in Table 3. This suggests that different factors contribute to the subjective well-being of the married and never-married. Table 5 presents correlations of happiness and excitement with various factors for both groups.

Health, income, education, contact with friends, and voluntary association participation are better predictors of happiness for the never-married than for the married. This suggests that: 1) the fluidity of single life styles is more affected by factors that affect mobility (health and income), 2) education is more critical to the achievement of a successful single life style, and 3) nonfamily relationships (friends and clubs) are more important in the lives of the never-married. It is noteworthy, however, that satisfaction with family life is equally important to the happiness of the married and the never-married.

Education, contact with friends, and group participation are better predictors of excitement for the never-married than for the married. Thus education and nonfamily relationships are again more critical to successful single living. It appears, however, that "family life" affects the happiness of the never-married, but not the extent to which their lives are exciting.

Earlier results indicate that, apart from living alone, the never-married differ most from the married in having lower incomes and less satisfying friendships and family life. Table 6 reports multiple classification analyses of happiness utilizing these variables as controls, both separately and in combination. The first column again indicates that without these controls the never-married are less happy than the married, and only slightly happier than the widowed or divorced. Controlling for family income and for satisfaction with friendships did not alter this pattern. Controlling for family satisfaction, however, results in the single being more similar to the married (though still slightly less happy) than to the widowed or divorced. This finding was not replicated for respondents aged twenty-five to forty-nine, indicating that family satisfaction assumes greater importance for the older never-married than for their younger counterparts.

The meaning of satisfaction with "family life" is ambiguous in this context, of course. In one sense, those who are not married do not have a family life, so the meaning of their response is unclear. The fact that this variable is so important in Table 6, however, and becomes more important with age, suggests something other than a measurement artifact. Marriage is an aspect of family life, so the single may be less happy simply because they are not married. Alternatively, their dissatisfaction may stem from less involvement in extended family networks. In any case, dissatisfaction with family life appears to be a major reason for the lower happiness of never-married older persons relative to married persons.

SUMMARY AND CONCLUSIONS

These data shed relatively little light on the causes of lifelong singlehood. Of course numerous possibly relevant individual characteristics are not measured—family socialization patterns, personality, personal preferences and values, physical attractiveness, etc. The only difference found was for females—education beyond high school was associated with singlehood (though the never-married were a small minority even for this group)—which may be attributable to sexual discrimination in the occupational marketplace. Career-oriented women must focus their resources and energies to a greater extent than career-oriented men to overcome financial, social, and psychological obstacles to careers for women. This heightened commitment deflects them socially and psychologically from marriage. Career-oriented women may face additional stigma which affect their relationships with men. Since educational and occupational attainment is becoming less unusual and more favored among women, and to the extent that sexism is declining in the marketplace, this

TABLE 6
MULTIPLE CLASSIFICATION ANALYSES OF GLOBAL HAPPI-NESS[a] BY MARITAL STATUS, CONTROLLING FOR FAMILY IN-COME, SATISFACTION WITH FRIENDS, AND SATISFACTION WITH FAMILY LIFE

| | Mean Happiness | | | | |
	No Controls	Controlling Family Income	Controlling Satisfaction with Friends	Controlling Family Satisfaction	Controlling All Three
Married	1.67	1.68	1.64	1.67	1.68
Widowed	1.99	1.94	1.97	1.91	1.91
Divorced or separated	2.07	2.06	2.01	1.92	1.93
Never-married	1.89	1.84	1.86	1.76	1.75
Significance of F-test	.001	.001	.001	.001	.001

[a]Happiness coded: 1 = very happy, 2 = pretty happy, 3 = not too happy (asked all six years).

educational difference in singlehood may lessen or vanish for future cohorts of older women.

The viability of a single life style does appear to vary with age. Among younger respondents, the never-married were less happy than the married, but they also considered their lives more "exciting" (interesting?). Since a desire for personal growth and autonomy is a major motivation for remaining single, this excitement is evidence of success. The unhappiness may simply be attributable to the difficulties of being single in a marriage-oriented culture. Single living becomes less successful in later life, however, particularly with regard to excitement.

Single life styles have a very fluid, autonomous quality, and single living has little institutional or ideological support. Success requires personal resources to maintain this fluidity and autonomy. Such accompaniments of aging as poor health and lower income lessen the viability of this life style. Loss of the work role is more consequential for the never-married, who lack structured family roles to fall back on. The heightened importance of education to the happiness and excitement of the never-married also indicates that the poorly educated have greater difficulty acquiring and sustaining satisfying single life styles. This suggests that the findings reported here may be at least partly cohort-specific, since only 36 of these 162 never-married older persons had more than a high school education. Future cohorts of better-educated singles may prove more successful in later life.

The relative unhappiness of the never-married can perhaps also be attributed to the simple fact that they lack those social and psychological gratifications which flow from the marital relationship—affection, intimacy, shared activities, esteem, etc. Gubrium (1975) has suggested that single older people may have difficulty "locating" their social personalities, since they lack the interpersonal expectations and routines, and associated self-evaluation and self-validation, which arise in a relationship as involved and intimate as marriage. Compared with married older persons, the never-married do not belong to more clubs, do not see friends and neighbors much more often, and in fact express less satisfaction with their friendships, perhaps because they expect more from them. While the never-married may have a variety of confidants, they lack the regular, ready-made confidant represented by a spouse. A shrinking life space in old age makes this a critical deficit.

The marriage relationship also provides greater access to the extended family, a supportive institution which becomes increasingly important in later life as role loss and poor health reduce social contacts. The extended family represents a fluid social network to compensate for and replace ties which are lacking or lost. The never-married see their relatives less, and are less satisfied with their family lives. One could expect never-married persons to require greater institutional assistance in old age, including nursing homes, because of less access to family assistance.

In some respects, the never-married appear to be better off than the widowed or divorced. Their global happiness is higher, especially when the figures are controlled for family satisfaction. They do not encounter the "desolation" of widowhood and divorce, and this desolation (recent isolation) affects loneliness more than isolation (Townsend, 1957; Tunstall, 1966). But the gist of these findings is that the never-married are a vulnerable segment of the older population, which contradicts Larson's (1978) conclusion that they are equivalent to the married. The divorced and separated, however, appear to be even more vulnerable, ranking lowest of any marital-status group in global happiness. The results in Table 3 suggest that divorced older males are particularly vulnerable. The family seems to coalesce around divorced women, since their family satisfaction is roughly equivalent to that of the single and the widowed. Divorced men, however, display substantially less family satisfaction than people in any other marital status, male or female.

The disadvantages apparent for older never-married persons relative to their younger counterparts may be attributable to cohort differences, rather than to any "natural" decline with age in the viability of singlehood. Any viable life style requires support—legal, economic, social, and psychological. Current older cohorts of the never-married have lacked this, but future cohorts may encounter a more favorable social climate. Stein (1976) points to attitudinal studies showing declining attractiveness of marriage. A wider range of alternatives is becoming acceptable; and ideologies and opportunities which promote and support single life styles are increasing (Adams, 1976; Bernard, 1972). The never-married may find later life less problematic in the future.

The findings reported here by no means exhaust the need for knowledge about the never-married in later life, and the ways in which the nature of aging varies by marital status. The implications and viability of singlehood are likely to vary at different stages of the life course. We need to know more about the sources of satisfaction and dissatisfaction for the never-married, how these change with age, and the extent to which the never-married confront different personal issues and tasks (both social and psychological) as they age. There is evidence here that the family is an important supportive institution in the lives of older people, helping counteract the shrinkage in social networks which may accompany aging. Rather than being less dependent upon this, the never-married may be more so because of the fluidity and tenuousness of their life styles. Retirement appears to be more consequential for those who lack other well-defined institutional roles, such as marriage. Thus investigations of older people in relatively rare social locations help inform us about universalistic and particularistic aspects of the aging experience. Such research also addresses the impact of aging on the consequences of other social locations.

NOTE

The data used in this study were made available by the Inter-University Consortium for Political and Social Research. The data were originally collected by James A. Davis of the National Opinion Research Center, University of Chicago, and were distributed by Roper Public Opinion Research Center, Williams College. Neither the original collector of the data nor the Consortium bear any responsibility for the analyses or interpretations presented here. This article originally appeared in *Journal of Gerontology* 34(1979):861–869.

REFERENCES

Adams, M. *Single blessedness: Observations on the single status in married society.* Basic Books, New York, 1976.

Berger, P., & Kellner, H. Marriage and the construction of reality. In D. Brissett & C. Edgley (Eds.), *Life as theatre*. Aldine, Chicago, 1975.

Bernard, J. *The future of marriage*. Bantam Books, New York, 1972.

Campbell, A. The American way of mating: Marriage si, children only maybe. *Psychology Today*, 1975, *8* (May), 37–43.

Edwards, M., & Hoover, E. The challenge of being single. J. P. Tarcher, Los Angeles, 1974.

Glenn, N. The contribution of marriage to the psychological well-being of males and females. *Journal of Marriage and the Family*, 1975, *37*, 594–600.

Glick, P. Some recent changes in American families. *Current Population Reports*, 1975, P-23, No. 52.

Gove, W. The relationship between sex roles, marital status, and mental illness. *Social Forces*, 1972, *51*, 34–44.

Gubrium, J. Marital desolation and the evaluation of everyday life in old age. *Journal of Marriage and the Family*, 1974, *36*, 107–113.

Gubrium, J. Being single in old age. *Aging and Human Development*, 1975, *6*, 29–41.

Knupfer, G., Clark, W., & Room, R. The mental health of the unmarried. *American Journal of Psychiatry*, 1966, *122*, 841–51.

Kutner, B., Fanshel, D., Togo, A., & Langner, T. *Five hundred over sixty*. Russell Sage Foundation, New York, 1956.

Larson, R. Thirty years of research on the subjective well-being of older Americans. *Journal of Gerontology*, 1978, *33*, 109–125.

Laslett, B. Family membership, past and present. *Social Problems*, 1978, *25*, 476–90.

Lopata, H. *Widowhood in an American city*. Schenkman, Cambridge, Mass., 1973.

Pihlblad, C., & Adams, D. Widowhood, social participation and life satisfaction. *Aging and Human Development*, 1972, *3*, 323–30.

Riley, M., Foner, A., & Johnson, M. *Aging and society. Volume 3: A sociology of age stratification*. Russell Sage Foundation, New York, 1972.

Spreitzer, E., & Riley, L. Factors associated with singlehood. *Journal of Marriage and the Family*, 1974, *36*, 533–42.

Stein, P. *Single*. Prentice-Hall, Englewood Cliffs, N.J., 1976.

Townsend, P. *The family life of old people*. Routledge and Kegan Paul, London, 1957.

Tunstall, J. Old and alone: A sociological study of old people. Routledge and Kegan Paul, London, 1966.

U.S. Bureau of the Census. Social and economic characteristics of the older population: 1974. *Current Population Reports*, Series P-23, No. 57. U.S. Government Printing Office, Washington, D.C., 1975.

Willmott, P., & Young, M. *Family and class in a London suburb*. Routledge and Kegan Paul, London, 1960.

THE MARITAL STATUS
OF THE
U.S. POPULATION, 1979

TABLE 1

MARITAL STATUS OF THE U.S. POPULATION (AGE 18 AND OVER) BY SEX AND AGE, 1979

Marital Status	Total Population (18 and over)	Percentage of Total Population	18–19	20–24	25–29	30–34	35–39	40–44	45–54	55–64	65–74	75 and Over
Men												
Single	16,970,000	23.3%	94.9%	67.4%	30.2%	14.9%	8.2%	8.4%	6.9%	5.2%	5.6%	4.9%
Separated	1,513,000	2.1	0.2	1.2	2.0	3.1	2.6	2.8	2.4	2.2	2.1	1.2
Divorced	3,471,000	4.8	0.1	1.7	5.5	7.3	6.9	7.1	5.7	4.7	3.9	2.2
Widowed	1,945,000	2.7	0.0	0.0	0.2	0.2	0.2	0.6	1.8	3.4	9.3	24.0
Married	48,816,000	67.1	4.8	29.7	62.1	74.6	82.2	81.2	83.2	84.4	79.2	67.7
Total	72,715,000	100.0%										
Women												
Single	13,644,000	16.9%	83.1%	49.4%	19.6%	9.5%	6.6%	5.1%	4.4%	4.6%	6.0%	6.2%
Separated	2,409,000	3.0	1.2	3.1	4.3	4.3	4.1	4.6	3.3	2.0	1.4	0.4
Divorced	5,355,000	6.6	0.9	3.2	7.8	10.2	9.8	11.1	8.2	6.5	4.0	2.2
Widowed	10,449,000	13.0	0.0	0.1	0.5	0.8	1.6	2.8	7.6	18.8	41.2	69.7
Married	48,771,000	60.5	14.8	44.2	67.7	75.2	78.0	76.5	76.3	68.1	47.5	21.5
Total	80,628,000	100.0%										

Source: U.S. Bureau of the Census, Current Population Reports, Series P-20, No. 349, "Marital Status and Living Arrangements: March 1979," U.S. Government Printing Office, Washington, D.C., 1980.

TABLE 2
THE NEVER-MARRIED SINGLES, 1979

Age	Men	Women	Total	% Difference
18 & 19	3,813,000	3,475,000	7,288,000	4.6% more men
20–24	6,545,000	5,003,000	11,548,000	13.4% more men
25–29	2,661,000	1,789,000	4,450,000	19.6% more men
30–34	1,180,000	777,000	1,957,000	20.6% more men
35–39	528,000	448,000	976,000	8.2% more men
40–44	460,000	299,000	759,000	21.2% more men
45–54	761,000	520,000	1,281,000	18.8% more men
55–64	510,000	504,000	1,014,000	.6% more men
65–74	358,000	504,000	862,000	17.0% more women
75 and over	154,000	324,000	478,000	35.6% more women

Source: U.S. Bureau of the Census, Current Population Reports, Series P-20, No. 349, "Marital Status and Living Arrangements: March 1979," U.S. Government Printing Office, Washington, D.C., 1980.

TABLE 3
THE SINGLES POPULATION (NEVER-MARRIED, DIVORCED, WIDOWED), 1979

Age	Men	Women	Total	% Difference
18 & 19	3,818,000	3,511,000	7,329,000	4.2% more men
20–24	6,711,000	5,344,000	12,055,000	11.4% more men
25–29	3,162,000	2,545,000	5,707,000	10.8% more men
30–34	1,771,000	1,678,000	3,449,000	2.6% more men
35–39	981,000	1,224,000	2,205,000	11.0% more women
40–44	878,000	1,112,000	1,990,000	11.8% more women
45–54	1,588,000	2,387,000	3,975,000	20.2% more women
55–64	1,296,000	3,258,000	4,554,000	43.0% more women
65–74	1,197,000	4,293,000	5,490,000	56.4% more women
75 and over	984,000	4,093,000	5,077,000	61.2% more women

Source: U.S. Bureau of the Census, Current Population Reports, Series P-20, No. 349, "Marital Status and Living Arrangements: March, 1979," U.S. Government Printing Office, Washington, D.C., 1980.

Acknowledgments continued.

Leonard I. Pearlin and Joyce S. Johnson, "Marital Status, Life-Strains, and Depression." Reprinted by permission of the authors and the American Sociological Association from *ASR,* vol. 42, October, 1977, pp. 704–715.

Anne R. Somers, "Marital Status, Health, and the Use of Health Services: An Old Relationship Revisited." Reprinted by permission from *JAMA,* vol. 241, No. 17, 4/27/79, pp. 1818–1822, copyright 1979, American Medical Association.

Paul C. Glick and Graham B. Spanier, "Cohabitation in the United States." From the *Journal of Marriage and the Family,* February, 1980, pp. 19–30. Copyrighted 1980 by the National Council on Family Relations. Reprinted by permission.

Eleanor D. Macklin, "Cohabiting College Students." From *The Family Coordinator,* October, 1972, pp. 463–471. Copyrighted 1972 by the National Council on Family Relations. Reprinted by permission.

Margaret Adams, "Living Singly." Reprinted by permission from *Single Blessedness* by Margaret Adams © 1976 by Margaret Adams, Basic Books, Inc., Publishers, New York.

Natalie J. Sokoloff, "Early Work Patterns of Single and Married Women." Reprinted by permission.

Elizabeth Higginbotham, "Is Marriage a Priority? Class Differences in Marital Options of Educated Black Women." Reprinted by permission.

Martin P. Levine, "Employment Discrimination Against Gay Men." Reprinted by permission. A different version of this article appeared in the *International Journal of Sociology,* vol. 9, December, 1979.

Judith Bograd Gordon, "Single Parents: Personal Struggles and Social Issues." Reprinted by permission.

Janet A. Kohen, Carol A. Brown, and Roslyn Feldberg, "Divorced Mothers: The Costs and Benefits of Female Family Control." Reprinted by permission from *Divorce and Separation: Causes, Contexts, and Consequences,* ed. by George Levinger and Oliver C. Moles, © 1979 by The Society for the Psychological Study of Social Issues, Basic Books, Inc., Publishers, New York.

Kristine M. Rosenthal and Harry F. Keshet, "Childcare Responsibilities of Part-Time and Single Fathers." From *Alternative Lifestyles,* Vol. 1, No. 4 (November, 1978), pp. 465–491, reprinted by permission of the publisher, Sage Publications, Inc.

Rita Braito and Donna Anderson, "Singles and Aging: Implications for Needed Research." Reprinted by permission.

Fred A. Minnigerode and Marcy R. Adelman, "Elderly Homosexual Women and Men." From *The Family Coordinator,* October 1978, pp. 451–456. Copyrighted 1978 by The National Council on Family Relations. Reprinted by permission.

Russell A. Ward, "The Never-Married in Later Life." Reprinted by permission of *The Gerontologist* from *The Journal of Gerontology* 34 (1979): 861–869.

DATE		